LONDON FOG

LONDON
FOG

The Biography

CHRISTINE L. CORTON

The Belknap Press of Harvard University Press
Cambridge, Massachusetts · London, England
2015

Second Printing

Library of Congress Cataloging-in-Publication Data

Corton, Christine L., 1958–
London fog : the biography / Christine L. Corton.
pages cm
Includes bibliographical references and index.
ISBN 978-0-674-08835-1 (hardcover : alk. paper)
1. Fog—England—London.   2. London (England)—Climate.   3. London
(England)—History.   4. London (England)—Description and travel.
5. Cultural property—England—London.   I. Title.
QC929.F7C57 2015
551.57'509421—dc23
2015011953

Book design by Dean Bornstein

To Richard, Matthew, Nicholas, and Tuppence

Contents

LONDON FOG

The Birth of London Fog

I

London has always been susceptible to mist and murk. True London fog, thick, yellow, and all-encompassing, was born in the 1840s, when the city's rapid expansion multiplied the number of domestic coal fires and mingled their smoke as it poured out into the atmosphere with the noxious emissions of factory chimneys and workshops in the early stages of the industrial revolution in the capital. It reached maturity in the 1880s, when its repeated visitations during the winter months caused widespread social anxiety and nervous concern about crime and disorder and inspired many writers to treat it as a looming presence, alive and malignant. And it began a long decline already before the First World War, diminishing in frequency and density until legislators could no longer tolerate the dangers it posed to health and began to take decisive measures to control it. In 1962 it finally died, killed off by the Clean Air Act passed by Parliament a few years before.

In most parts of the world fog has always been a natural phenomenon, clouding the air with tiny water particles when the climatic conditions are right. The same has been true for centuries of Britain's capital city. London has never enjoyed a particularly clear atmosphere. The Thames basin, hemmed in by low hills, has always been prone to lingering dampness and mist, and as the city grew slowly during medieval and Tudor times, complaints were voiced with increasing frequency about the pollution of the air by the smoke coming from wood fires, notably those used for the extraction of lime, and by the burning of "sea-coal" brought to London by boat from Newcastle and used for domestic and commercial fires alike. "Sea-coal" was originally a term for coal that could be found washed up on the beach from seams open beneath the sea. This could be collected easily from the seashore, but later the term seems to have been used for any coal brought to London by sea. Peter Brimblecombe notes that there was a street in London called Sacoles Lane as early as 1228, writing that "it does signify a very early beginning to the importation of coal into London."[1] No less a personage than Queen Elizabeth I confessed "herself greatly grieved and annoyed with the taste and smoke of sea-coales."[2] The problem grew more serious and led to attempts to legislate against the smoky atmosphere in the reign of her successor, James I. An Act to forbid the use of sea-coal in London breweries was passed by the House of Lords in 1623; but it was unenforceable, so in practice nothing happened.

The complaints continued. In 1676 the scientist Robert Hooke, approaching the city on horseback, estimated the cloud of smoke over London to be half a mile high and twenty miles long, while, earlier, in 1652, the Dutchman Lodewijk Huygens, looking over the capital from a similar vantage point (possibly Hampstead Heath or Highgate Hill), found the medieval cathedral of St. Paul's "too much obscured by smoke" to see clearly. It was recognized instinctively that an atmosphere of this kind could not be good for the health of the city's inhabitants. John Graunt, who analysed London's Bills of Mortality in 1676, thought that "the smoak of London" was dangerous "for the suffocations which it causes," while the merchant Thomas Tryon, whose book *The Way to Health* turned Benjamin Franklin into a vegetarian, wrote in 1700 that the "unwholesome airs" of London created "stinking, gross sulphurous Smoaks" that were "Pernicious to Mankind."[3]

The most famous denunciation of London's smoky atmosphere in the seventeenth century and indeed for a long time afterwards, however, was penned by the diarist John Evelyn (1620–1706). Entitled *Fumifugium; or, The Inconvenience of the Aer and Smoake of London Dissipated*, it was published in 1661. Already ten years earlier, in 1651, Evelyn had complained that London was obscured by "such a cloud of sea-coal, as if there be a resemblance of hell upon earth, it is in this volcano in a foggy day: This pestilent smoak."[4] In 1661 he was even more vociferous, denouncing the "Clowds of Smoake and Sulphur, so full of Stink and Darknesse" that enveloped the "Glorious and Antient City."[5] Evelyn followed the science of Kenelm Digby (1603–1665), who applied an atomic theory to air pollution in which the atoms of coal smoke were perceived as sharp and pointed:[6] "This is that pernicious Smoake which sullyes all her [London's] Glory, super-inducing a sooty Crust or Fur upon all that it lights, spoyling the moveables, tarnishing the Plate, Gildings and Furniture, and corroding the very Iron-bars and hardest Stones with these piercing and acrimonious Spirits which accompany its Sulphure; and executing more in one year, than exposed to the pure *Aer* of the Country it could effect in some hundreds."[7]

Evelyn proposed to alleviate the evil of smoke by relocating smoke-producing industries outside London and providing a circle around London of sweet-smelling plants and hedges so that their delicious scents could waft into the city and dispel the fumes. According to Evelyn's own diary he presented his tract to King Charles II: "[the King] was pleased I should publish it by his special Command; being much pleas'd with it."[8] Later in his diary Evelyn mentioned the drafting of a Bill by Sir Peter Ball against the smoke nuisance, though nothing more was heard of it.[9] While some people, like Evelyn, were aware of the problem, nobody was seriously prepared to do anything about it.

Evelyn did not accept that the geographical situation of London was particularly unhealthy. It was, he claimed, "built upon a sweet and most agreeable Eminency of Ground." He exonerated "the *Fumes* which exhale from the Waters and lower Grounds lying Southwards, by which means they are perpetually attracted, carried off or dissipated by the Sun, as soon as they are born, and ascend."[10] Evelyn thought smoke most unhealthy, declaring that it "causeth *Consumptions, Phthisicks,* and the Indisposition of the *Lungs,* not only by the suffocating aboundance of *Smoake,* but also by its *Virulency;* For all *subterrany* Fuell hath a kind of *Virulent* or *Arsenical* vapour rising from it."[11] Indeed, he charged, London's "*Inhabitants* breathe nothing but an impure and thick Mist, accompanied with a fuliginous and filthy vapour."[12] Evelyn put the blame for the smoke problem firmly on industry. The objectionable smoke was emitted, he wrote, "not from the *Culinary* fires, which for being weak, and lesse often fed below, is with such ease dispelled and scattered above, as it is hardly at all discernible."[13] Lime kilns were worst of all, poisoning "the *Aer* with so dark and thick a Fog."[14]

Fumifugium was reprinted in 1772, when the editor, Samuel Pegge the elder (1704–1796), reported on how conditions had worsened in his own time. He noted the increase of "glass-houses, foundries, and sugar-bakers, to add to the black catalogue" and singled out specific sources of pollution such as "the fire-engines of the water-works at London Bridge and York Buildings."[15] He conceded the impossibility of moving all smoke-producing works outside the city, as Evelyn had suggested, but he wondered if the law should forbid major polluters such as brewers and manufacturers of glass and sugar from building works in town. Their buildings, he recommended, should only be set up at a certain distance from the town. Pegge's recommendations were not followed. His perception of worsening atmospheric conditions in the city was shared by many of the foreign visitors who came to London during the eighteenth century. Already in 1748 a Swedish traveller, Pehr Kalm (1716–1779), reported of the view from St. Paul's that "the thick coal smoke, which on all sides hung over the town, cut off the view in several places."[16] In the 1760s the French visitor Pierre-Jean Grosley (1718–1785), a travel writer and man of letters, noted that "smoke . . . forms a cloud which envelops London like a mantle, . . . the smoke, which, being mixed with a constant fog, covers London, and wraps it up entirely." A year's sojourn in the city convinced him that the situation was getting worse: "the smoke," he warned, "gains ground every day: if the increase of London proceeds as far as it may, the inhabitants must at last bid adieu to all hopes of ever seeing the sun." Grosley tempered his criticism of the London atmosphere by his admiration of the English love of walking, even on foggy days, specifically April 26 in St. James's Park, when objects could barely be distinguished at a distance of four steps but when the park was nonetheless filled with walkers who were, Grosley admits, "an object of musing and admiration to me during the whole day."[17] Grosley, it seems, was an early French admirer of British energy and pluck.

The German scientist Georg Christoph Lichtenberg, visiting the city in the 1770s, was so oppressed by a foggy day that he found himself "writing by the light of a candle (at half-past ten in the morning)." The Prussian pastor Karl Philipp Moritz, writing in 1782, reported that "everything in the streets . . . seemed dark even to blackness," while the composer Joseph Haydn, living in Great Pulteney Street during his first triumphant musical visit to England, wrote on November 5, 1791: "There was a fog so thick that one might have spread it on bread. In order to write I had to light a candle as early as eleven o'clock."[18] The fog was responsible according to the fifty-nine-year-old Haydn for a severe attack of rheumatism that he described grumpily as "English."[19]

A few years later, in 1809, Eric Gustaf Geijer (1783–1847), a Swedish historian and later Rector of Uppsala University, came to England as tutor to the son of a wealthy Stockholm merchant. He complained of "London's miasma, a premonitory *Deus Terminus* of a world's capital. . . . One penetrates ever deeper into an atmosphere of coal smoke in whose twilight moves an unending multitude of people."[20] London's sky was, he claimed, "made of coal smoke": "London is a foggy, smoky hole."[21] The following year Louis Simond (1767–1831), a Frenchman who had emigrated to America before the Revolution and who toured Great Britain in 1810–1811, complained, "It is difficult to form an idea of the kind of winter days in London; the smoke of fossil coals forms an atmosphere perceivable for many miles."[22]

How could London's air be improved from this desperate condition? Suggestions made by Pegge in his reissue of Evelyn's *Fumifugium* included the charring of sea-coal, so it would yield less smoke, and the building of chimneys "much higher into the air . . . to convey the smoke away above the buildings, and in a great measure disperse it into distant parts, without its falling on the houses below."[23] This idea of high chimneys was taken up by William Frend (1757–1841) in the early nineteenth century in a pamphlet with the unwieldy title *Is It Impossible to Free the Atmosphere of London in a Very Considerable Degree, from the Smoke and Deleterious Vapours with Which It Is Hourly Impregnated?* (1819). It does not seem to have had much impact, however. Meanwhile, Evelyn's influence continued into the early nineteenth century, inspiring in 1822 an article in the *Quarterly Journal of Science, Literature, and the Arts* on *Fumifugium*. The article linked Evelyn's proposals to the establishment of a House of Commons select committee aiming "to inquire how far it may be practicable to compel persons using Steam-Engines to erect them in a Manner less prejudicial to public health and public comfort."[24] The article compared "the grievances occasioned by the smoake of London 160 years ago, when the metropolis was not one-sixth its present extent, with those which are now matter of complaint" and proposed to enquire "how far the evil was then, and is now, susceptible of diminution, or removal."[25] The writer questioned the efficacy of Parliament in such matters, for "as soon as Parliament is prorogued, and the smoke-burners out of town, we relapse into our pristine fuliginosity, and the pretty-behaved chimneys upon the river-side, which awhile seemed to have forgotten their office, again evolve their wonted columns of sable smoke."[26] The smoke of London, the writer concluded pessimistically, "always grievous, is now scarcely tolerable."[27] In fact, as the writer had forecast, very little resulted from the 1819 select committee apart from a minor strengthening of the law on nuisances: "To get redress it was still necessary for the plaintiff to prove nuisance, not for the defendant to be restrained from committing the nuisance in the first place."[28]

As this suggests, even as late as the 1820s the problem was described as one of smoke rather than of fog. London, indeed, had long since been known colloquially as the "smoke" or the "great" or "big" smoke, especially by country people. Although the first reference to this usage is from a revised edition of a *Slang Dictionary* published posthumously by the London bookseller and bibliophile John Hotten (1832–1873) a year after his death, and earlier editions of the dictionary do not include a reference to the "smoke," his text indicates earlier, and frequent, usage: "Country-people, when going to London, frequently say they are on their way to the SMOKE, and LONDONERS, when leaving for the country, say they are going out of the smoke."[29] John Evelyn too was concerned mainly with smoke and its effects on London's atmosphere. Nowhere does his *Fumifugium* mention yellow as a characteristic colour of polluted air in the capital. What he was describing, then, was not true London fog as it came into being in the early Victorian era. Nonetheless, his document laid the foundations for much of the debate on the smoke problem in the following centuries.[30] There were two sides to the argument, vigorously disputing where the blame should be laid. Evelyn's claim that industry was to blame was forcibly contested by the author of the 1822 analysis, who claimed that it was "folly to ascribe any sensible influence upon the great mass of London smoke to some few steam-engine chimneys, while every house is busy in the work of contamination."[31] This debate continued throughout the nineteenth century. It was one of many reasons that action to combat air pollution was stalled, since no one could agree on whether the greater proportion of blame should be attached to the industrial or the domestic user, and both sides resisted legislation to effect change, preferring to invoke the sanctions of the legislature on the other.

The idea of forbidding the use of coal as a fuel, as had been attempted in earlier times, was obviously impractical, given the lack of any alternative sources of heat and energy once England's forests had been felled to provide timber for the navy and fuel for fires. Initial attempts to intro-

Figure 1.1 "Window Studies: A Harmony in London Smut" directly represents the connection between coal and London's air. The illustrator is George Du Maurier, who later wrote *Trilby*. (*Punch*, 16 February 1889, p. 78). Courtesy of the President and Fellows of Wolfson College, Cambridge.

duce legislation were directed against factories and steamships that gen-erated energy through the burning of coal. Michael Angelo Taylor (1757–1834), Member of Parliament (MP) for Durham, managed to achieve the passing of a Bill which required the furnaces of steam engines to consume their own smoke in the early 1820s.[32] This Bill was based on new designs of furnaces which were being introduced to show that it was possible to reduce smoke. But there was no real force behind the Act in terms of pu-nitive or financial penalties to make any difference. Industrialists were understandably reluctant to take the blame for smoke pollution. They pointed the finger at the domestic chimney as a source of smoke pollu-tion, but it was difficult to interfere with the right of the householder to use coal for heating and cooking, and there were no satisfactory alterna-tive sources of energy. The campaign, such as it was, fizzled out.

The reissue of Evelyn's *Fumifugium* and the writings of men such as William Frend and Michael Angelo Taylor all reflected the fact that smoke was beginning to be compounded as a nuisance in London by a new kind of phenomenon: London fog. Of course, some authors pointed to the fact

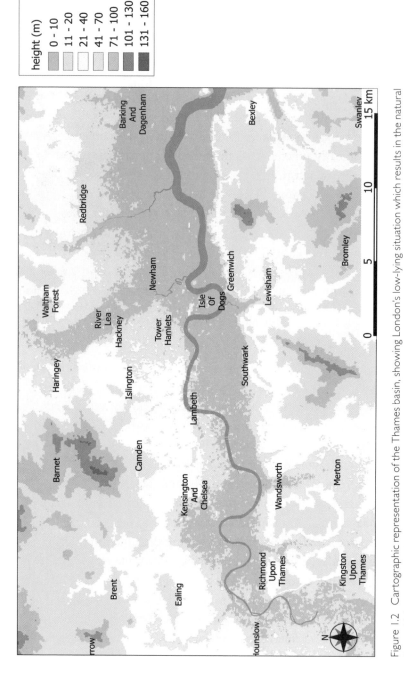

Figure 1.2 Cartographic representation of the Thames basin, showing London's low-lying situation which results in the natural fogs which were exacerbated by industrial and domestic pollution. Contains public sector information licensed under the Open Government Licence v3.0.

that London, surrounded by the hills that enclose the Thames basin, from Hampstead Heath, Highgate, and the gravel outcrops of Epping Forest in the north and east to the Downs in the south and the Chilterns in the west, was peculiarly susceptible in winter to mists caused by the well-known meteorological phenomenon of temperature inversion, when warm air coming over with a weather front traps cold air beneath it, stopping pollutants from being raised from the ground or even from chimneys into the upper atmosphere for hours or even days on end.[33] A few authors in the early nineteenth century indeed persisted in viewing air pollution as natural in origin, a view that led to a pessimistic conclusion: "there might be some amelioration of the atmosphere, although our locality and climate always render it turbid and misty, independent of adventitious effluvia."[34] By the beginning of the nineteenth century, however, this view was becoming increasingly difficult to sustain.

There had been occasional "Great Stinking Fogs" in the capital as early as the seventeenth century, but by the early 1800s London fogs were increasing in frequency and taking on a new character, thick, widespread, and prolonged. An "extraordinary fog" was reported on November 5, 1805, and another on the same day the following year.[35] During a fog that occurred on January 10, 1812, *The Times* reported: "For the greater part of the day it was impossible to read or write at a window without artificial light."[36] The meteorologist Luke Howard (1772–1864), best known for devising the system of naming different types of clouds, noted that London was plunged into darkness in the middle of the day, with lamps being lit in the shops, and concluded, "were it not for the extreme mobility of our atmosphere, this volcano of a hundred thousand mouths would in winter, be scarcely habitable."[37] Fogs were lasting longer, too: in 1813 one was reported to have begun on December 27 or 28 and lasted until January 3, 1814.[38] The prolonged gloom, extending more than ten miles to the east of the city boundaries, offered enterprising thieves plenty of opportunities to boost their income, as a report on the Foreign Secretary's attempt to leave London by coach attested: "Lord and Lady CASTLEREAGH and their Suite, when they reached Whitechapel, on Monday evening, were forced to procure men to sit upon the trunks and boxes fixed to the carriages, different attempts having been made by some villains to cut them off. They had intended to sleep at Chelmsford, but owing to the fog it was

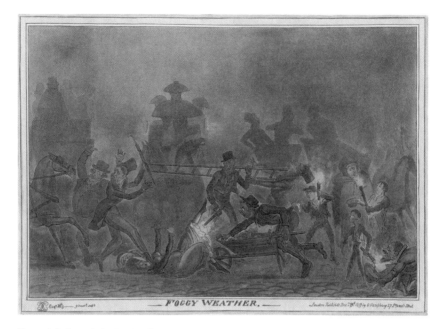

FOGGY WEATHER.

Figure 1.3 *Foggy Weather* by George Cruikshank. This hand-coloured etching was published on December 29, 1819, at the height of the foggy season. A woman is in danger of having her neck severed by a man's foot, while her skirts look as if they might be set alight by a torch. A ladder also poses a threat in the centre, while oncoming horses and carriages are a menace to everyone. The linklighters (see p. 86) are taking the opportunity to pick pockets. © The Trustees of the British Museum.

with the greatest difficulty that they reached Rumford, by the aid of flambeaux."[39]

As the German lawyer and traveller Johann Georg Kohl (1808–1878) commented, "it must be fine weather for pickpockets and other scamps, who can be out of sight in a moment."[40] London fog created confusion and fear. The British caricaturist George Cruikshank (1792–1878) reveals this aspect in an 1819 print (Figure 1.3). Confusion reigns as coaches and horses collide with people in the foggy streets. The linklighters, who were employed to light people through the streets, appear to add to the mayhem by waving their lit torches in people's faces and bodies; one, at the centre, is taking advantage of the situation and picking the pocket of the trader whose cart has been the cause of a woman tumbling down. A dandy steps on to the fallen woman's neck. Linklighters were often associated with crime, a theme that extended even to the twentieth century. A man, presumably trying to carry on his trade, creates mayhem with a ladder. Cruikshank's print is a comic interpretation of the impact of fog on London's streets, but as fogs grew thicker and more frequent, people began to view the confusion they created more with trepidation and horror than humour. Some people at least were aware of the dangers to health, too. A tombstone in Kensal Green Cemetery testified to the recognition by some that fog could cause serious damage to people's health. It commemorates "L. R. / Who died of suffocation in the great fog of London / 1814."[41]

Another prolonged visitation occurred in 1817, lasting from December 22 to January 2, 1818, when the fog was so thick that *The Times* reported that within doors "it was impossible to read without a candle."[42] Fogs became even more frequent during the 1820s, when occurrences were reported in 1820, 1821, 1822, 1826, 1828, and 1829, though none of them seems to have lasted more than a couple of days.[43] Literary men started to take notice of the phenomenon. In 1822 a London fog attracted the attention of the poet Lord Byron (1788–1824), who wrote in *Don Juan* (1822) of "a wilderness of steeples peeping / On tiptoe through their sea coal canopy, / A huge, dun cupola, like a foolscap crown / On a fool's head—and there is London town!"[44] Here is an image of polluted nature: the black smoky atmosphere of London is like the level top of a forest, the steeples the higher trees breaking through; but the forest colour is dirty brown rather than a natural green. It is "sea-coal" that has wrought the change. And the atmosphere also seems like a rounded vault or dome, as often found supported on columns over a tomb.[45] Londoners were being buried underneath the fog. Some saw it as black, the colour of death. When Thomas Carlyle came to London from Scotland in 1824, he wrote to his brother: "O that our father sey [could see] Holborn in a fog! With the black vapour brooding over it, absolutely like fluid ink. . . . The thick smoke of it beclouds a space of thirty square miles."[46]

Luke Howard was one of many who noted the increasing occurrence of fogs in the 1820s, reporting on the gloom cast by thick fog in January 1826: "Lamps and candles were lighted in all the shops and offices."[47] In the revised edition of his book, *The Climate of London,* published in 1833, Howard reported a fog which occurred on November 11 and 12, 1828: "The effect was most distressing, making the eyes smart and almost suffocating those who were in the street, particularly asthmatic persons."[48] The frequency of fogs at the end of the 1820s seems to have been unprecedented. In November 1829 *The Times* commented that at midday "the neighbourhood of the Royal Exchange was nearly in midnight gloom," although some people, who did not have to go out, could accept the loss of the day by pretending that it was really the evening.[49] Less than a month later the newspaper reported another London fog, during which "the shops were lighted the same as at night."[50]

In the 1830s fogs continued to increase in frequency. In December 1830 alone there were reports of dense fogs on the eighth, fifteenth, and twenty-fifth to twenty-sixth, with further reports in every successive year apart from 1831–1832 and 1836 (and the list may be incomplete). William Cary, an instrument maker in London, provided weather tables for the *Gentleman's Magazine* that recorded a steady increase in foggy days in the early decades of the nineteenth century.[51] The American writer Nathaniel Parker Willis (1806–1867), visiting London in 1834, described St. Paul's seen from the top of Shooter's Hill as "half enveloped in a dim and lurid smoke."[52] Charles-François Daubigny's (1817–1878) painting *St. Paul's from the Surrey Side* (1873) depicted St. Paul's as Willis described, although at a later date (see Figure 1.4). The idea that St. Paul's should be smothered by smoke was another repeated image both in art and writings of the time. It supported the idea that London, through its fog, had become godless and irreligious. Daubigny visited England during the Franco-Prussian War, when he met Claude Monet. His attitude to the atmosphere of London certainly reflected that of many Londoners. He wrote in October 1870, "It's eleven o'clock in the morning. So much for the climate. Fog! Visibility less than two paces."[53] His picture provides a reason for London's atmospheric problems with its clutter of coal barges at its foot and the smoking chimneys on the left. The smoke from the chimneys rises up into the sky, discolouring it to a yellowy grey. St. Paul's is beginning to recede visually because of the smokiness of the atmosphere, and the clouds in the sky look yellow and heavy. Other markers of modernity, such as the steamboats, the steam train travelling across the bridge, and the smoking chimney in the foreground, also provide evidence of the causes of the London fog. The yellow-green colour of the atmosphere on the left makes us feel that it is the beginnings of a pea-souper fog. The decaying wharves on the right of the painting provide a darker frame to

Figure 1.4 *St. Paul's from the Surrey Side*, by Charles-François Daubigny. Daubigny first visited London in 1866 and returned in 1870–1871 to escape the Franco-Prussian War. The painting is dated 1873 and so was completed from initial sketches and finished in a studio after he returned to France. © The National Gallery, London; presented by friends of Mr. J. C. J. Drucker, 1912.

the murky picture of Blackfriars Bridge. Long before this, by the 1840s at the latest, the association of London with fog rather than simply with smoke had become inescapable and was attracting widespread comment.

The Times reported "dense fog" at the end of November 1840; in 1841 it began providing lists of accidents on the river as boats bumped into each other in the murk; in 1842 there were four separate visitations of fog at the beginning and end of the year; in 1843 there were two more, described as "darkness visible," bringing traffic to a complete standstill; there were three more in November and December the following year, when "a sort of 'Egyptian darkness' seemed to overshadow the city and west-end."[54] Newspaper journalists and reporters were beginning to grope for metaphors to vary their descriptions of the phenomenon, whether from John Milton's *Paradise Lost* with its "darkness visible" specifically to describe hell or from the biblical account of the plagues of Egypt. In 1840 the versifier Peter Styles branded it unnatural. Country fogs, he wrote, were "gentle things." But "London fogs are all made up / Of strange and monstrous things, / Which nature, scorning to receive, / Back on the city flings."[55] Mixing coal fumes with water vapour, fogs continued to occur several times a year for the rest of the decade and beyond. They had become a permanent feature of the city's winter months.

The reason for the increase in the number of foggy days in London town was not some change in the climate but a rapid increase in the quantity of pollutants, above all from coal fires, that mixed with naturally occurring water vapour at times of temperature inversion to create a London fog, coloured yellow from the sulphurous emissions trapped beneath the cold air above the city. The more smoke and soot in the atmosphere, the more likely a fog was to form and the longer it was likely to last. And in the 1820s and 1830s smoke and soot from coal fires were spreading through the air in ever-increasing quantities as the city began to grow apace with the impact of the industrial revolution. London's population, around a million in 1800, had grown to one and a half million twenty years later and passed the two million mark in the 1830s.[56] Helped by the growth of communications—canals, metalled roads, and by the 1830s railways as well—London was becoming an economic hub, with industries typical of a major city, such as paper, printing and publishing, instrument engineering, gas and power, chemicals, leather and luxury goods, and, even more important in terms of population growth, public administration, the law, and professions and services of many kinds.[57] As hundreds of thousands of people flocked to the capital to find work or make their fortune, new suburbs emerged, extending the city's housing in all directions; and every house had its coal fire, belching quantities of sulphur-laden smoke into the air during the winter months.[58]

Other parts of the country were growing fast during these decades too, and other centres of industry also suffered from polluted air: the "Black Country" in the West Midlands got its name around this time from the soot and smoke that covered it; Edinburgh had for many years been known by its soubriquet "Auld Reekie." But there was nothing quite like London fog. True London fog was thick, persistent, and above all basically, though not exclusively, yellow in colour. In a genuine London fog, as the writer Edward Frederic Benson (1867–1940) noted in his novel *Image in the Sand* (1905), "swirls of orange-coloured vapour were momentarily mixed with the black," and "all shades from deepest orange to the pale gray of dawn succeeded one another."[59] Later scientists studied the colours of the fogs in order to work out what caused them. Soot particles

Figure 1.5 "Well, If Ever I See Sich a Fog as This in All My Born Days" shows a figure resembling Charles Dickens's character Mrs. Gamp, with her trademark umbrella, as she peers into the gloom. A policeman and a lamp merge into one item in the background. (*Punch*, 8 November 1856, p. 189). Courtesy of the President and Fellows of Wolfson College, Cambridge.

could change the colour from yellow to brown in patches. In 1853 a fog was described as "grey-yellow, of a deep orange, and even black."[60] What would be a white mist in the country, one newspaper commented in 1901, "becomes a brown, sometimes almost black, one in the metropolis": "Our myriad chimneys pour forth smoke—or innumerable particles of unconsumed carbon—producing the effect of mud in water."[61] Joseph Ashby-Sterry (1838–1917), in his poem *November*, wrote succinctly. "'Tis sometimes yellow, sometimes brown. A London Fog!"[62]

The yellow colour was caused by the fog's high sulphur content. A scientific study of urban fog published in 1896 noted: "Town fog is mist made white by Nature and painted any tint from yellow to black by her children; born of the air of particles of pure and transparent water, it is contaminated by man with every imaginable abomination. That is town fog."[63] For Londoners a typical November fog was predominantly yellow, coloured by the greater proportion of home fires in the capital: "When the Major returned to London, which he did in time for the fogs of November, . . . the valet was arranging his toilette in the deep yellow London fog," as William Makepeace Thackeray (1811–1863) put it in his novel *Pendennis,* published in 1850.[64] Black it may have been in parts, especially when the soot content was high, but overall true London fog was mainly coloured yellow, as one observer after another noted from the 1840s onwards. One writer recorded a conversation on the topic in 1853:

> "What a dreadful fog there is to-day!"
> "Nothing of the kind, Madam. Cloudy and wet, perhaps, and a little misty; but a fog—no Madam, that haze is not a fog. Fogs are yellow and black; in a fog, the carriages and foot-passengers run against one another. It hurts your eyes, and takes away your breath; it keeps one in doors. But this is not what a Londoner would call a fog."[65]

London fog had been born; now it had to be given a name.

II

Finding a term to describe what Taylor called "November's mantle" was a far from simple task. In the seventeenth and eighteenth centuries Londoners and visitors to the capital city had complained above all about smoke rather than fog. Before the nineteenth century "fog" was often synonymous with "mist." John Kersey's *English Dictionary* of 1702 disappointingly substituted tautology for definition by describing fog as "a fog or mist" and mist as "a mist or fog." In the same dictionary smoke was detached from both fog and mist, being defined purely as "smoke, and to smoke," underlining the fact that Londoners at this time did not as a rule conflate the two.[66] Fog was natural, smoke unnatural. Still, in the 1785 *Dictionary of the Vulgar Tongue,* Francis Grose (1731?–1791) did equate fog with smoke, although under "smoke" he did not include any mention of "fog."[67] Slightly later, in *A New Dictionary of All the Cant* (1795) by Humphrey Potter (1747–1790), "fog" is also defined as "smoke."[68]

Perhaps these two dictionaries of slang and underworld argot were recording a special usage of the terms. Yet in 1819 William Frend treated "smoke" and "fog" as synonyms in his treatise on "deleterious vapours" in London: "I believe, that, if the smoky atmosphere of this great city was exchanged for a purer air, none of the inhabitants, or the occasional visitors of the metropolis, would lament the loss of their black fog."[69] At the same time some observers recognized early that London fog was neither simply mist nor smoke but a combination of the two. George Leman Tuthill, a medical doctor from Soho Square, told the Select Committee of the House of Commons on Steam Engines and Furnaces in 1819 that he "conceived that the fog peculiar to London, so different in its sensible properties from any fog in the country, depended upon the smoke of the metropolis, and was prejudicial in many diseased states of the lungs."[70] Yet if London fog was not like other fogs and was peculiar to the metropolis, then what should it be called?

Already at the end of the 1840s what was to become perhaps the most popular of all the names given to London fog was already in use: the "pea-souper." It is not included in any of the major dictionaries of the late eighteenth and early nineteenth centuries, signifying the fact that the true, deep-yellow London fog had not yet become noticeable or frequent enough to impinge on the popular consciousness. The first use that the modern *Oxford English Dictionary* quotes of the expression comes from 1849, in a citation from the American writer Herman Melville (1819–1891), famous for his vast, baggy, and iconic novel *Moby-Dick* (1851).[71] Melville wrote in his *Journal of a Visit to London and the Continent*, "Upon sallying out this morning encountered the oldfashioned pea soup London fog—of a gamboge color. It was lifted, however, from the ground & floated in mid air. When lower, it is worse."[72] The American novelist Henry James, on his first visit to London, was tempted to take to his bed during the day because of "the pea-soup atmosphere of Piccadilly."[73] Another reference to the phrase appeared in 1871 in the *New York Times:* "In London, particularly, where the population are periodically submerged in a fog of the consistency of pea-soup."[74] In 1889 the newspaper repeated the metaphor, headlining a story, "Pea-Soup Fog in London" and adding: "New-York's Worst Fog Does Not Approach It."[75]

"Pea soup" has indeed become a popular metaphorical representation of fog, and its use extended well into the late twentieth century. An earlier edition of the *Oxford English Dictionary* cites an example from *Good Words* in 1883, referring to the "'pea-soupy' character so distinctive of those whose advent we in cities so dread."[76] In 1887 the *South Australian Advertiser* referred to "a succession of 'pea-soup fog' days" experienced by London a month or two previously.[77] Both America and Australia, of course, had direct ties to England and a large migrant population from the mother country, so that the use of the term may have derived from visitors to or from London. "Pea-souper" has proved a durable euphemism. Thomas Cook, the travel company, used the term to promote winter cruises abroad as late as 1937. The advertisement urges people to go abroad "when London is groping its way home through a typical 'pea-souper.'"[78] References to "pea-soupers" in *The Times* mostly date from the mid-twentieth century. In 1950 a story noted the twenty-first anniversary of the National Smoke Abatement Society and the reduction of the "real old-style peasouper,"[79] a rather optimistic proclamation since London was visited by its most deadly fog only two years later. Although the article did acknowledge that there was more to be done, it also represented the "pea-souper" as a thing of the past.

Melville's description of the colour of the fog as "gamboge" highlights its yellowness (gamboge is a deep yellow pigment derived from the resin of the gamboge tree and commonly used to dye the robes of Buddhist monks, especially in Cambodia—the two names are related). *The Oxford English Dictionary* also refers to pea soup "chiefly in reference to its usual dull yellow colour and thick consistency."[80] Yet we usually think of pea soup as green rather than yellow; indeed, today it usually is, like the green peas of which it is made. Even in the 1820s a cookery book indicated that pea soup should be green, but warned that the soup should not be allowed to boil, "or the green colour will deaden and become a tawny yellow."[81] But pea soup was more traditionally yellow as it was made of dried yellow split peas, a staple food of the urban poor in an age when refrigeration had not yet arrived and fresh vegetables were hard to obtain in the middle of a vast conurbation such as London and were expensive to buy. Pea soup was a simple dish, high in protein but inexpensive to purchase. It was closely associated with poverty. A pamphlet titled *Means of Providing Cheap Food* and published in Dublin during the potato blight of 1845–1846 printed a number of recipes giving variations of pea soup for the impoverished and starving Irish.[82] The association even made its way into literature, when Thomas Hardy underlined the combination of aristocratic lineage and present poverty in *Tess of the d'Urbervilles* (1891) by having Tess refer to an old silver spoon, marked with the family's heraldic symbol, which was "so worn that mother uses it to stir the pea-soup."[83]

Thick, viscous, opaque, and impenetrable, only the very densest London fogs deserved to be called pea-soupers in the eyes of some people. As James Payn (1830–1898), an Old Etonian novelist and versifier and regular contributor to Charles Dickens's periodical *Household Words,* noted in 1890: "The fogs we have had this year have been made too much of—perhaps because they were our first fogs; but, like the efforts of a certain famous yet obscure poet, you could see something in them if you looked long enough, which is not the case of a genuine Peasouper."[84] The densest London fogs were often described, like pea soup, as a form of sustenance avoided by anyone who had the means to do so. In 1833 Thomas Carlyle (1795–1881), who had moved to London two years before, complained bitterly about "that horrid flood of Spartan black-broth one has to inhale in London."[85] Perhaps it reminded him of the frugal sustenance he had endured at the grim school he went to in Annan, near his home village of Ecclefechan, in the Scottish lowlands. The humorous Victorian magazine *Punch* used a more conventional image in 1850: "March," it observed, "is said to come in like a lion, and go out like a lamb; but of November, on account of its fogs, it may generally be said, that it comes in like a basin of pea soup, and goes out like a plate of peas pudding."[86] This too was a dish made of yellow split peas and served mainly to the poor, known as "pease-pottage" when it was given to convicts on their way through southern England to be transported to prison settlements in Australia.

A couple of years later Thomas Miller (1807–1874), an often impoverished writer himself, also decided to opt for the thicker version: "It is something like being imbedded in a dilution of yellow peas-pudding, just thick enough to get through it without being wholly choked or completely suffocated. You can see through the yard of it which, at the next stride, you are doomed to swallow, and that is all."[87] Its thickness, substance, and carbon smell gave it the tangible quality of food—but always food associated with poverty—pea soup, pease pudding, or black broth. And fog was indeed more likely to be experienced in the poorer districts of the capital. The prevailing wind direction in London from west to east meant that the poorer areas in the east were directly affected by the smoke generated in the wealthier areas in the west of London; as early as 1662 the economist Sir William Petty (1623–1687) noted that the better-off citizens of the capital moved to the western parts of the city to escape "the fumes, steams and stinks of the whole Easterly Pyle, which where sea-coal is burnt is a great matter." Some decades later the magistrate and novelist Henry Fielding praised the western suburb of Ealing, which was "guarded from the smells and smoak of London by its distance."[88] By the nineteenth century much of the smoke and pollution was also generated within the industrial eastern part of London itself. The East End had the highest density of factory chimneys, as well as houses packed tightly next to each other, all with their own domestic chimney pots puffing out smoke. In addition, its low-lying position, especially near the river, meant that the smoke was not as easily dissipated there as it was on higher ground. But fog could affect other parts of London as well. There was no way to guarantee immunity from it, and many newspaper reports commented on how it would settle in one small area although other parts of London could be clear. By contrast, the greatest fogs could spread across the whole city, covering an area of two hundred square miles or more.

Fog could thus appear as a kind of food ingested or inhaled, not only by the poor. Early and mid-Victorian concepts of illness and infection tended to attribute disease to the influence of miasmas. After the first major outbreak in Britain of the hitherto unknown and extremely dangerous epidemic disease of cholera in 1832, which seemed to undermine the idea that infections were spread from person to person, fevers and epidemics were ascribed by medical authorities to poisoned air created by decaying matter and rising from the ground. Cholera arrived in London at a time when fogs were becoming more frequent and more dense; both seemed to be related to dirt and pollution; both affected mainly the poor, even if cholera flourished in the summer months and fog in the winter.[89] Fog was a kind of miasma made visible, and it seemed obvious that, like

Employer. "Where have you been all this time ?"
Office-Boy. "I went out for my lunch, Sir, and got lost in the fog."
Employer. "Fog! It's a perfectly fine day."
Office-Boy. "The fogs this year are very local, Sir."

Figure 1.6 A more modern view of London fog in which it is used as an excuse for lateness after the lunch break, showing how a fog could be concentrated in a single street or area. The illustrator was George Belcher, a regular contributor to *Punch* who became a Royal Academician in 1946. (*Punch*, 14 January 1931, p. 37). Reproduced by kind permission of *Punch* © Punch Limited.

the smoky atmosphere of earlier periods, it must pose a danger to health and in particular to the lungs, especially of those who were already vulnerable, such as the very young or very old, asthmatics, or bronchitics.

Towards the end of the century observers began to note a link between a sudden increase of deaths and the occurrence of foggy weather, just as writers such as John Graunt and Thomas Tryon had linked smoke

pollution with health problems in an earlier era. Yet many writers surprisingly commented not on the danger of fog but on its reassuringly nu-
tritional quality. The Canadian writer Sara Jeannette Duncan (1861–1922)
emphasised these aspects in her novel *An American Girl in London* (1891): "It
was no special odour or collection of odours that could be distinguished—
it was rather an abstract smell—and yet it gave a kind of solidity and nutri-
ment to the air, and made you feel as if your lungs digested it. There was
comfort and support and satisfaction in that smell."[90] Other writers from
across the Atlantic were scornful of its qualities: the American feminist
and war correspondent Inez Haynes Irwin (1873–1970), a friend to many of
the French Impressionist painters, lauded in her 1919 essay "The Californiacs" the superior quality of California fog, which she claimed was "not
distilled from pea soup like the London fogs; moist air-gauzes rather,
pearl-touched and glimmering."[91] Bob Hope, the famous London-born
American comedian, on the other hand, claimed that California smog was
"fog with the vitamins removed."[92] Whether nourishing or debilitating,
fog appeared to many people, therefore, as a thickening of the air so intense as almost to turn it into a liquid so viscous as to be almost a solid.

III

"Pea-souper" might have been the commonest name given to classical
London fog, but it was by no means the only one. The novelist Charles
Dickens, indeed, popularised the term "London ivy" in *Bleak House*,
written in 1852–1853, to describe the sooty particles left clinging to the
nameplate outside the firm of Peffer and Snagsby, law stationers. Peffer,
the firm's founder, had died, leaving Snagsby the sole proprietor: "For
smoke, which is the London ivy, had so wreathed itself round Peffer's
name, and clung to his dwelling-place, that the affectionate parasite quite
overpowered the parent tree."[93] Dickens's metaphor is characteristically
complex and ambiguous. "Affectionate" the smoke may have been, but
in Dickens's sentence it becomes a metaphor of clinging, suffocating death.
The verb "wreathed" encourages the reader to think of a funeral wreath,
often made of ivy. But Dickens was far from being the only writer to use
the term. Whether or not he had actually coined it himself, it had become
a common term by the 1880s. "London ivy" was used by other writers to

denote smoke and fog as threat. In 1889 *Sporting Life* referred for example to "a very severe cold caught by nine hours contact with London ivy."[94] Here we seem to have a cold fog, rather than smoke as originally suggested by Dickens's use of the metaphor. According to *The Routledge Dictionary of Historical Slang* "London ivy" was also associated with dust, especially by cockneys, emphasising its origins in particles deposited by smoke or fog.[95]

Far more common, however, was the description of fog as "London particular." Dickens first employed the term in an article which appeared in his periodical *Household Words*. The article, co-written with W. H. Wills, describes conditions in Spitalfields, an area of East London known for its clothing industry. One weaver the authors interviewed in 1851 complained of the effect the fog and the particles it deposited had on his products: "The blacks (London genuine particular) got into the white satins, despite the best precautions of the workpeople, and put them into an ugly, foxy, un-saleable half-mourning, sir."[96] A few months later Dickens used it again in *Bleak House,* one of whose central characters, Esther Summerson, the new arrival to London, refers to such "a dense brown smoke that scarcely anything was to be seen," as if "there was a great fire." Guppy, the cockney swell, replies that it is only a "London particular." Esther views the phenomenon as smoke, but Guppy describes it as a fog; even in the early 1850s there could still be confusion between the two.[97]

The term "London particular" was pregnant with meaning. It conveyed a familiar intimacy. John S. Farmer and W. E. Henley, who produced the first systematic dictionary of what they called *Slang and Its Analogues,* published in seven volumes between 1890 and 1904, cited "London Particular (or London Ivy)" as commonly used terms meaning "a thick yellow or black fog, the product of certain atmospheric conditions and carbon: formerly peculiar to London."[98] Farmer and Henley noted that a "particular" was another name for a mistress, perhaps hinting that Londoners felt as ambivalent about fog as some married men may have felt about their extramarital affairs. More importantly, however, a "London particular" was a special quality of brown Madeira wine imported solely for the London market. References to "London particular" wine are found at least as early as the 1790s, and the term became extended to yellow-brown London fogs by analogy.[99] "London particular" specifically implied uniqueness, an enviable exclusivity to the capital city, but could also be

Figure 1.7 *A Thoroughbred November & London Particular* by Michael Egerton, engraved by George Hunt, published by Thomas Mclean, London, 1827 (colour litho), English School (nineteenth century). The term "London particular" appears to have become an accepted term for fog by 1827, the date of this engraving. Private Collection / The Stapleton Collection / Bridgeman Images.

seen in ironic terms. Fogs of this colouring and density were not to be found elsewhere, not even in the most polluted cities of the Midlands and the industrial North.

Next to "pea-souper," "London particular" was by far the most commonly used term for London fog. It appears for example in the caption to an 1827 cartoon by the amateur artist and social satirist Michael Egerton. The background shows a mêlée of people who are being led through the fog by various linklighters, boys or men who carried lighted torches with them and would offer to light the way through the fog for a charge. One of them is pointing his torch to the ground, to allow the people who have engaged him to avoid treading in puddles. The yellow handkerchief that the gentleman in the foreground is holding to his mouth indicates his concern to protect himself from the diseased and polluting miasmatic atmosphere. His clothes are those of a Regency-style dandy, but he is paying no attention to the oncoming horses and carriage and is obviously in danger of being run over; perhaps he cannot see them through the fog. The print gains its satirical edge from the contrast between the world of fashion and the grubbiness of a grimy, foggy, and dirty city.

"London particular" was widely used as a term for the combination of fog and smoke, but as in the case of pea soup, it came during the second half of the century to be employed with a degree of nostalgia. As early as 1855 the *New York Times,* describing a homegrown American fog, wrote that it had "nothing of the characteristics of our 'old London particular' except density."[100] The possessive suggests that the writer was a homesick ex-Londoner. In 1884, in a lecture on storm clouds and plague winds, the leading Victorian art critic and historian John Ruskin told his audience, "You are all familiar with one extremely cognizable variety of that sort of vapour—London particular; but that especial blessing of metropolitan society is only a strongly-developed and highly-seasoned condition of a form of watery vapour which exists just as generally and widely at the bottom of the air, as the clouds do."[101] "London particular" and "pea-souper" were brought together in the twentieth century by a recipe called "London particular," which is in fact, not surprisingly, a traditional pea soup. The recipe is accompanied by a picture of an open book, which is, appropriately enough, *Bleak House.*[102] The page opened is the illustration of Guppy and Jobling discovering the smouldering remains of Krook's body after the episode of spontaneous combustion, in which the eccentric rag and bottle merchant vanishes into thin air, leaving an oily puddle behind him.[103]

As scientific investigations of the constituents of London fog and its causes got under way, however, a fresh linguistic term came into use. It

A CLASSIC CALENDAR; OR, MYTHS FOR THE MONTHS.

Figure 1.8 "December" shows Science, in the guise of a short-sighted man, confronting the figure of Fog rather feebly with his umbrella. Fog is represented as the cyclops Polyphemus, who is thumbing his nose at Science. (*Punch's Almanack for 1889*, 6 December 1888). Courtesy of the President and Fellows of Wolfson College, Cambridge.

was devised by the scientist Henry Antoine Des Voeux, the honorary treasurer of the Coal Smoke Abatement League, who concisely defined a "London particular" in 1904: "I think that it is essential to recognize that we are discussing two things which are in their essence entirely different. The essence of one is moisture, the essence of the other smoke, . . . and to-day the true 'fog' has shifted away from London, and we are suffering especially to-day, from what is known as the 'London particular,' which I should like to name 'smog,' to show that it consists much more of smoke than of true fog."[104]

"Smog" in due course came to be used, however, to refer to photo-chemical air pollution from motor-car exhaust emissions, rather than to sulphurous mixtures of coal smoke and mist. The term became particularly widely used in the United States, where the problem was worst. In Alison Lurie's *Nowhere City* (1965) the smog of Los Angeles provides the main character with a reason for being unable to settle down to life in LA, and the novel explores the relationship between the smog and a general social disorientation and lack of boundaries.[105] More recently the term "smog" has denoted air pollution through forest fires, above all in Indonesia, resulting from vast clearances of woodland to make way for agricultural development. Whatever the term's connotations, it never really took off as a way of referring to London fog. A series of letters in *The Times* in 1953 indicated that the linguistic issue remained a continuing topic of debate, even though the word "smog"—a blend of "smoke" and "fog"—was meant to put an end to this. "Limerick" wrote to the editor to demand, "Why 'smog' the urban atmospheric issue? Mist consists of droplets of water. Fog is the addition of coal smoke to that. So why add verbal redundancy to physical discomfort?"[106] The General Secretary of the National Smoke Abatement Society, Arnold Marsh, however, argued that "the words 'mist' and 'fog' usually suggested two different degrees of visible water vapour or droplets in the air, but, as any mariner will confirm, neither word implies the presence of smoke."[107] J. B. Sanderson wrote that it was significant that the use of the word "smog" seemed to have increased greatly during 1953. "For smoke abaters, this word was a valuable addition to the political vocabulary; 'fog' is almost a natural phenomenon, 'smog' is an evil to be eliminated."[108] But he was writing towards the end of London fog's life span, and the term was little used to refer to it, except in retrospect.

IV

"Pea-souper," "London ivy," "London particular," "fog," or "smog": all denoted the same problem. Almost as soon as Queen Victoria came to the throne, in 1837, the capital city became the victim of repeated visitations of a thick, yellow, sulphurous vapour that plunged the streets into darkness, choked the lungs, and turned day into night. Contemporaries began to think of ways of combatting the evil. It was not going to be straightforward, as the industrial age relied heavily on coal as its main source of heat and energy and, through gas, lighting as well. Legislation now focussed on demanding cleaner smoke by ensuring that as high a proportion of the fuel was burned as possible so that less was wasted in the smoke escaping from the chimneys, thereby promoting an argument that would be seen as economically favourable to the factory owner by using fuel more efficiently. It was recognised early on that a purely ecological argument based on cleaner, healthier air would not be conducive to change. In Elizabeth Gaskell's *North and South* (1854–1855) the first sight of the industrial town, Milton, where most of the narrative takes place is of the factories "puffing out black 'unparliamentary' smoke."[109] This reflects the passing of the 1844 Act for the good government of Manchester, in which it was demanded that "every Furnace in any Mill shall be constructed so as to consume the Smoke arising from such Furnace."[110] The novel's industrialist and hero, Mr. Thornton, explains that he has converted his chimneys to make their use of fuel more economical and not because he is being forced to by Parliament. Unfortunately, his example was not followed by many others. Factory owners, especially, proved resistant to supporting any legislation since they were concerned to avoid the expense of updating existing furnaces or installing new ones or providing better training for stokers. Tougher action would be required to make any significant change.

Londoners did their best to cope with the nuisance. It was important to insist that it was business as usual during a fog, and not only in shops. The growing use of gas lamps and lanterns made it easier for institutions to carry on their daily work as efficiently as possible and to control their own environment through the use of artificial light, from "the city offices and warehouses" which in 1842 were "enveloped in a dense fog, rendering

Figure 1.9 "A London Fog." The man in a top hat on the right is distracted by a linklighter, enabling an urchin to pick his pocket. The article accompanying the picture refers to fogs "of the colour of pea-soup." (*Illustrated London News*, 2 January 1847, p. 8). Reproduced by kind permission of the Syndics of Cambridge University Library.

it necessary to use artificial light," to "churches and chapels" where, again in 1844, "it was necessary to have the lamps lighted to enable the cler-gymen to proceed with the service."[111] It was fortunate indeed that gas lighting had been set up in most of London's main streets during the previous decades, starting with Pall Mall in 1807.[112]

But as the gloom deepened, voices were raised to demand that steps be taken to lighten up the city by pushing back the ever-increasing presence of smoke and fog. The political constellation that had so frustrated reformers such as Taylor, Pegge, and Frend began to change in the 1830s and 1840s. Reform was on the agenda. During the early Victorian period, not least as a consequence of the cholera epidemic of 1832 and even more of a second epidemic in 1849, a "sanitary revolution" got under way, with social reformers and medical men arguing with ever-greater insistence that Britain's industrial towns and cities urgently required a massive cleanup. Just as the sanitary revolution cleaned up houses and streets, with sewage disposal systems, clean water supplies, street-sweeping services, waste-disposal regulations, washbasins and water closets, so too the Victorians sought an atmospheric revolution, making the urban air clean and safe for all to breathe.[113]

Leading figures in the hygienic reform movement turned their attention to the atmospheric problems of London and other great cities of the industrial age. Sir Edwin Chadwick (1800–1890), perhaps the leading figure in the movement, called in 1842 for the use of anthracite (a very-high-carbon form of coal) instead of the impure, smoke-producing soft coal in common use at the time.[114] Sanitary and hygienic reformers were concerned about atmospheric pollution not least because evidence was accumulating to suggest its negative effects on people's health. Fog, as Charles Manby Smith pointed out in 1853, created "a misty atmosphere fraught with catarrh and influenza."[115] Miasmatic theories of disease, at their height in the 1850s, contributed further to associations such as these. People tried to protect themselves from inhaling the fog by covering their mouths with a handkerchief, as shown in numerous contemporary illustrations.

Not only people's noses and mouths but also their eyes suffered, and enterprising manufacturers devised fog glasses to be worn as protection. In 1849 the satirical magazine *Punch* made fun of this practice by advising people "to test the alleged power of these glasses, by putting them on, and plunging our head into a tureen of cold pea-soup."[116] Perhaps, *Punch* continued, the glasses should be sent to France, where politics had been plunged into a fog of revolution and political upheaval, or even to politicians in Britain, whose rhetoric, presumably, was equally impenetrable. The same article even illustrates horses wearing fog glasses (see Figure 1.10). Their appeal continued, however, as shown in Figures 1.10 and 3.5, a sketch from 1872, in which an elderly lady wears fog glasses and covers her mouth with a handkerchief. But these were mere palliatives, comical not just for their appearance but also because they were so obviously ineffective.[117] Pressure was growing for legislative action.

In 1843 William Mackinnon (1789–1870), a Scotsman who sat in the House of Commons as a Tory member of Parliament for a series of decaying coastal towns in the Southeast, launched an eight-year campaign to introduce laws to reduce smoke pollution. The time appeared ripe for

Figure 1.10 Examples of fog glasses. *Punch* takes a satirical look at these glasses designed for people by showing them on horses as well. Left: from *Graphic*, 9 November 1872, p. 437; reproduced by kind permission of the Syndics of Cambridge University Library. Right: from *Punch*, 17 November 1849, p. 194; reproduced by kind permission of the President and Fellows of Wolfson College, Cambridge.

action. The Lord Mayor and others had presented a petition to Parliament on February 24, 1842, complaining of smoke from factories. Another petition had been presented on July 18 of the same year by the Earl of Glengall from the Corporation of London for means to remedy the smoke nuisance, and a third was presented on June 13, 1843, by the vicar of Rochdale, a northern industrial town. The vicar, John Molesworth, happened to be Mackinnon's brother-in-law, so it was no coincidence that in 1843 Mackinnon moved successfully to set up a committee to investigate the "means and expediency of preventing the nuisance of smoke arising from fires or furnaces."[118] Mackinnon's committee met sixteen times and interviewed a wide variety of witnesses about the problem, including the scientist Michael Faraday. After its report, delivered on August 17, had been challenged, Mackinnon convened another committee that carried out further interviews and reported in 1845.

Among the witnesses, Abraham Booth, a chemical engineer as well as a professor, teacher, and reporter for the daily press in London, described an area known as the Belvedere Road or Narrow Wall in Lambeth: "In a district of about two acres there are about 25 chimneys attached to different furnaces. . . . There are two breweries, two shot manufactories, six saw-mills, one black-lead factory, one engineering establishment, two connected with the Lambeth Waterworks, two boiler mills, one emery manufactory, one India rubber manufactory, two glass manufactories, two coke ovens, one lime-kiln, and one hat manufactory." The only industry that had attempted to prevent the expulsion of smoke had been the sawmill. It had fitted a Chanter smoke-burning furnace, which Booth said, "answers the purpose well." But in New Street Square "there are no less than seven chimneys attached to furnaces belonging to printing-houses"; in the district of Regent's Canal "there are now a great many saw-mills and large manufactories have recently been established from which a great deal of smoke is given off," and "one of the most noxious nuisances towards the eastern part of the town is that of Whitbread's brewery, in Chiswell-street," in which "the poor people said it was useless to clean their windows, because they would soon be dirty again."[119] Nothing was being done to mitigate the nuisance. Smoke producers did not necessarily need to be large manufacturers. The witness cited the example of Bucklersbury, a main street in the City where "there are nine cooks' shops, and from half-past 9 to half-past 10 o'clock you can scarcely see your way from one end of the street to the other; and at the counting-houses opposite the clerks are fined 6d. each if they leave their books open, so great is the quantity of carbon deposited, and if they try to rub it out with India-rubber it leaves a black mark."[120]

All of this contributed in Booth's view to the generation of dangerous London fogs in which sooty particles were ingested by people, with deleterious effects on their health: "Their inhalation is shown by the black mucus expectorated from the lungs during a November fog so peculiar to London."[121] Yet nobody could produce any concrete evidence of the health dangers posed by smoke. The paramount consideration was the nuisance it caused. Mackinnon's committee investigated whether smoke could be prevented by mechanical means, through the use of specially designed furnaces such as those designed by Josiah Parkes, Charles Wye Williams, and John Juckes. Other options reviewed were the use of high-grade coal from Wales or, bizarrely, the introduction of fresh air into London from the country through pipes, although this was quickly dismissed as impractical. One brewery in Tottenham Court Road used anthracite, but this was because, the owner confessed, "the gentlefolks in the squares compelled us to do it": regular coal "made so much smoke in the drawing-rooms and injured the furniture."[122] The committee recognized the role of domestic coal fires in generating smoke and fog but did not think there was any practical way of regulating it. So it focused on industrial emissions. This was its undoing. Its reports led to no fewer than six attempts to introduce some kind of Bill, in 1844, 1845, 1846, 1848, 1849, and 1850, but they were all successfully defeated by those who represented industrial interests. Some industrialists defended the dirty atmosphere by suggesting that this meant a healthy economy. One writer exclaimed, "Thank God, smoke is rising from the lofty chimneys of most of them! For I have not travelled thus far without learning, by many a painful illustration, that the absence of smoke from the factory-chimney indicates the quenching of the fires on many a domestic hearth, want of employment to many a willing labourer."[123]

Powerful voices were raised in the House of Commons against the proposed legislation, including that of John Bright (1811–1889), the celebrated champion of free trade and free enterprise. "The House," he declared, "might employ itself much better than in this peddling legislation, which never could be attended with useful and permanent results."[124] Government interference of the kind Mackinnon proposed was, thundered another opponent, an ironmaster from Staffordshire, when interviewed by the committee, "worse than one of the plagues of Egypt."[125] Since Mackinnon was supported by *The Times*, the political elite's leading newspaper, the government thought it expedient to commission an expert report from a chemist and a geologist, who opined that reducing soot and smoke was perfectly feasible if good-quality coal was burned; the key lay in the introduction of effective enforcement of whatever legislative provisions were introduced. The publicity given to the issue prompted further anti-smoke measures in the late 1840s, included for example in the Public Health Act of 1848, but they were all shot down by Bright, who boasted that he had opposed every smoke Bill that had come before

Parliament. The 1848 Bill, he declared, "contained all the absurdities of all the former measures put together."[126] It was not necessary to introduce legislation; if smoke abatement saved money, then factory owners would introduce it themselves. Bright did not see that the real question was the damage inflicted by factory emissions on the community at large. Frustrated by the obduracy of the factory owners and their sympathisers in the Commons, Mackinnon remarked testily that there was a good deal of truth in the remark of the eighteenth-century Prime Minister Sir Robert Walpole "that the country gentlemen will, like their own sheep, lie down to be fleeced, but if you touch the manufacturing interests they will yield nothing but grunts."[127]

A couple of years later a leading sanitary reformer, Sir John Simon (1816–1904), the Medical Officer of Health for the City of London, managed to achieve the insertion of a smoke clause into the City of London Sewers Bill, which became law in July 1851. There was some provision for effective enforcement, and in the first year of its operation 115 notices were served on offenders. But the Act only covered the "square mile" of the old City of London, and it was not adopted by the rest of the metropolis.[128] More successful were the efforts of Lord Palmerston (1784–1865), in his role as Home Secretary. In 1853 he introduced a Bill into the House of Commons promising to curb smoke emissions in London. *The Times* viewed the measure as part of the general cleanup of the capital in the sanitary revolution, seeing it as a consequence of the fact that "the old English gentleman of the modern time is a very clean animal, rejoicing in ablutions of all sorts."[129] The measure, it thought, in one of the lengthiest and most impassioned denunciations of atmospheric pollution in the capital to date, was long overdue: "Is it possible that we can ever get out of this thick canopy of smoke, that grows like a huge atmospheric fungus over the metropolis, that mingles with the fog below and the clouds above, and that only waves this way or that way as the wind may blow, but never wholly leaves us? Let any one go to Hampstead or Blackheath, or even to Hyde Park, and see what a solid formation it is that hangs over our heads; how impenetrable, how ferruginous, and say whether it will ever disappear. It seems hoping against hope to dream of it."[130]

Smoke and fog, the paper lamented, destroyed nature—"whole tribes of plants disappear from cultivation at the approach of chimneys"—and blackened the surface of buildings: "We white-wash, and distemper, and paper, and paint, and gild, and clean, . . . doing the work over and over again, but all to no avail." Yet, the writer warned, industrialists had "a vested interest in compelling us to consume their smoke." Living in the clean air of the suburbs, they come into town once a week by rail "to see how the chimney draws and how the till fills," then go back home, leaving the inhabitants of "modern Babylon" to suffer as "smoke penetrates the pores of our skin and the air vessels of our lungs, converting the human larynx into an ill-swept chimney." The paper feared that industrialists would bring about the defeat of the Bill in the House of Lords.[131]

The Bill was indeed vigorously opposed by members who feared that it would cause "great expense to the manufacturers of London."[132] But Palmerston, an energetic proponent of social and sanitary reform, denounced them in no uncertain terms as "a few, perhaps a 100 gentlemen, connected with these different furnaces in London, who wished to make 2 000 000 of their fellow inhabitants swallow the smoke which they could not themselves consume, and who thereby helped to deface all our architectural monuments, and to impose the greatest inconvenience and injury upon the lower class. Here were the prejudices and ignorance, the affected ignorance, of a small combination of men, set up against the material interest, the physical enjoyment, the health and the comfort of upwards of 2 000 000 of their fellow-men."[133]

The Bill passed both Houses of Parliament and duly passed into law as the Smoke Nuisance Abatement (Metropolis) Act, which was amended three years later, after Palmerston had asked for progress reports on implementation and realized that more needed to be done ("One or Two Convictions," he minuted, "would soon set the Rest on the alert").[134] An Inspector of Nuisances was appointed to check smoke emissions from factories; by 1887 there were ten full-time and forty part-time policemen working for Palmerston. In eight months from August 1854 to March 1855 there were 124 convictions and fines totalling more than £500, a not inconsiderable sum at the time. Smoke-consuming devices such as the Juke's furnace did exist and had proved successful, and no fewer than 7,875 of them were in use in London by 1861.

Yet, impressive though this number seems, it represented only a small proportion of the industrial chimneys in use in the capital. And the 1853

Act failed altogether to deal with domestic fires.[135] Inspection was far from
easy, nor did anyone take up the suggestion made by the General Board
of Health in 1854 that a special constable be installed at the top of the Monument, the column in the City of London erected as a memorial to the
Great Fire of 1666, to spy on smoking industrial chimneys.[136] It was not
until 1914 that air-monitoring systems were introduced which worked on
a standard basis. London fog, smoke, soot, and dirt were thus increasingly
recognised as problems and repeatedly debated during the nineteenth
century; yet no practical solutions were found, and the problem grew
worse with the continued expansion of the capital, with home fires,
factories, and machines producing ever-greater quantities of pollution into
the atmosphere. Far from being banished by mid-century as the legislators
and sanitary reformers hoped, London fog had become so dense and
so frequent that it was becoming ever more closely identified with the
London scene. No winter was complete without at least one lengthy fog,
and often there were more. As the great age of the realist novel began,
Victorian writers of fiction took note of the fog and thought of ways of
using it in their work. The scene was set for fog's entry into the world of
the imagination. Fog's formlessness lent itself to a wide variety of representations and metaphorical usages, perhaps even more so than other,
comparable phenomena such as mud or dust. Fog's obvious origins not
just in nature on the one hand or human agency on the other but in a
synthesis of the two encouraged representations that pitted nature
against culture or exploited fog as a metaphor for the dissolution of contour and form in human society, the moral order, and the urban world.
The first novelist to deploy fog's ambiguity for literary purposes and the
writer whose use of it had a greater impact than that of any other was, as
we shall now see, Charles Dickens.

CHAPTER TWO

Dickensian Gloom

I

Charles Dickens (1812–1870) was the most successful and most popular novelist of his day. Born in Portsmouth, he lived for most of his life in or near London and used the capital city as the setting for the great majority of his works. So powerful was the impact of his vivid depiction of London, its streets, its buildings, and its inhabitants, especially of the poor, the marginal, the eccentric, and the criminal, that "Dickensian" has become a generally accepted term to describe the squalor and gloom of the poorer parts of the city in the Victorian era.[1] For a novelist like Dickens, London fog lay close to hand as a metaphorical tool in the depiction of character and its relationship to its environment. Later writers, indeed, saw Dickens, in a sense, as the creator of London fog in the popular consciousness. "The very atmosphere declared him: if I gasped in a fog, was it not Mr Guppy's 'London particular'?" wrote another novelist, George Gissing (1857–1903) later in the century.[2] In *The London Life of Yesterday* (1909), Arthur Compton-Rickett (1869–1937), author of a widely read history of English literature, noted that there was fog in Roman times, but "from the account of the Roman Historian we should adjudge it less obnoxious than the 'London particular' so feelingly described by Dickens."[3] The journalist and best-selling travel writer Henry Vollam Morton (1892–1979) wrote in his *In Search of London,* "Charles Dickens has done more than any writer to create and perpetuate a picture of early Victorian London, with its fogs, its filth and squalor."[4]

Dickens knew his London well. He had spent much of his childhood there and had walked the streets, rather than take horse-drawn cabs, because of the economic hardships his family experienced. He was a part of London, and London was a part of him. London had a mythic aura for the young Charles Dickens before he even began writing. The solid reality of London streets and buildings was as familiar to him as the dark cloud of smoke that perpetually lay over the city. In *Barnaby Rudge* (1841) London is "a mere dark mist—a giant phantom in the air."[5] In *Martin Chuzzlewit* (1843–1844) London on first viewing is "a city in the clouds."[6] In *David Copperfield* (1849–1850) London appears as a vapour: "I saw all London lying in the distance like a great vapour, with here and there some lights twinkling through it."[7] Yet in his earliest novels, *The Pickwick Papers* (1836) and *Oliver Twist* (1838), he makes no real mention of London's thick, yellow, viscous, and persistent fogs. Almost as soon as they became an inescapable and constantly recurring feature of the capital's everyday life in the winter months, however, he began to use them in his writing.

The Old Curiosity Shop, published in 1841, showed Dickens displaying for the first time his mastery in the use of London fog as an extended metaphor. The novel's central character, "Little Nell," a virtuous thirteen-year-old orphan whose parents have died in poverty, is looked after by her grandfather, a shopkeeper who tries to secure her financially by gambling. Predictably, he loses, borrows money to try to make good his losses, and soon finds himself deeply in debt to the moneylender Daniel Quilp, a deformed, hunchbacked dwarf who is the very embodiment of evil. Quilp forecloses on the debt and takes possession of the shop, forcing Nell and her grandfather to leave London and live from hand to mouth. Nell's friend Kit, who worked in the shop, tries to track them down, as does Quilp, who is convinced that the grandfather has concealed a fortune somewhere and is only pretending to be poor. Taking a dislike to Kit, Quilp frames him as a thief and has him arrested. Kit is found guilty and is due to be sentenced to possible transportation to Australia before his innocence is revealed. Another character, the initially weak-willed Dick Swiveller, who works for Quilp's lawyer, the corrupt attorney Sampson Brass, and his sister Sally, is also looking for Nell in the company of her ne'er-do-well brother. After an illness, the reformed Swiveller proves that Quilp's charges against Kit are false and obtains his freedom. Exposed as a perjurer and damned by Brass's confession of the plot to condemn Kit, Quilp flees and is drowned in the Thames. But there is no happy ending: Kit and his friends finally discover Nell's whereabouts, but it is too late; she dies of exhaustion brought on by her sufferings, and her grandfather is left with his grief, although partly consoled by his brother, who had been lost to him and is now discovered.

A summary of the plot can do no justice to the novel's richness of language and imagery. Fundamental to the depiction of character is the contrast between nature and virtue on the one hand and industry and vice on the other. Fog and smoke play a central part in the characterization of its central villain, Quilp, who is associated with all types of man-made smoke— cigar smoke, pipe smoke, chimney smoke. He shares the characteristics of the polluting industrial town. Chimney smoke does not cause him the discomfort that people usually experience; in fact he appears to enjoy it:

> Mr Quilp once more crossed the Thames, and shut himself up in his Bachelor's Hall, which, by reason of its newly-erected chimney depositing the smoke inside the room and carrying none of it off, was not quite so agreeable as more fastidious people might have desired. Such inconveniences, however, instead of disgusting the dwarf with his new abode, rather suited his humour; so, after dining luxuriously from the public-house, he lighted his pipe, and smoked against the chimney until nothing of him was visible through the mist but a pair of red and highly inflamed eyes, with sometimes a dim vision of his head and face, as, in a violent fit of coughing, he slightly stirred the smoke and scattered the heavy wreaths.[8]

Quilp is constantly trying to impede vision through his smoke and through his tricks. Here he uses the smoke to make himself virtually invisible. Quilp even pits one form of smoke (the coal smoke) against another (his self-produced cigar smoke), creating an "atmosphere, which must infallibly have smothered any other man." Quilp's association with smoke emphasises his devilish, almost supernatural qualities. Later in the book the night fog has the same effect on the light from Quilp's counting-house as the smoke had on Quilp's eyes; it makes the house seem "inflamed and red . . . as though it suffered from it like an eye."[9]

Quilp uses smoke in a diabolical way to discomfit other people— especially Sampson Brass, of whom we are told "that tobacco-smoke always caused him great internal discomposure and annoyance."[10] This fact has obviously not escaped Quilp's attention: "Quilp looked at his legal adviser, and seeing that he was winking very much in the anguish of his pipe, that he sometimes shuddered when he happened to inhale its full flavour, and that he constantly fanned the smoke from him, was quite overjoyed and rubbed his hands with glee," an episode illustrated in Figure 2.1.[11] In Dickens's novels there is a recurrent theme of evil characters

Figure 2.1 An illustration from *The Old Curiosity Shop* (1841), by Charles Dickens, showing Quilp and Tom, Quilp's employee, smoking, with the lawyer Sampson Brass trying to compete. Quilp, the villain of the novel, knows that Brass does not smoke, but he has insisted he join them, thereby making him feel very ill. Illustration by Hablot Knight Browne, known as "Phiz." (1815–1882). Courtesy of the President and Fellows of Wolfson College, Cambridge.

being linked to atmospheric pollution. Quilp sleeps "amidst the congenial accompaniments of rain, mud, dirt, damp, *fog,* and rats."[12]

If Quilp represents the unacceptable face of the new industrial city, then it is only right that he should be destroyed by forces unleashed by nature, as indeed he eventually is. After many cruelties and crimes Quilp is finally brought to justice, not from the legal proceedings of the state whose agents are pursuing him but from two great, natural, elemental forces—the water of the River Thames and the fog of London. Retribution is made complete through fire, another natural element. Natural justice is personified in the dramatic scenes of Quilp's last hours by fog, mist, and clouds: "The day, in the highest and brightest quarters of the town, was damp, dark, cold and gloomy. In that low and marshy spot, the fog filled every nook and corner with a thick dense cloud."[13] Curiously,

Figure 2.2 *The Thames above Waterloo Bridge,* by Joseph Mallord William Turner. Painted in 1835, this wonderful painting is one of the earliest to depict London in the fog. A buyer could not be found, and the painting remained unfinished. Accepted by the nation as part of the Turner Bequest 1856. © Trustees of the Tate Gallery, London.

although fog was seldom reported in the press as affecting high ground, Dickens insists in *The Old Curiosity Shop* that it covers both the highest and the lowest areas of London: no one could escape retribution for his sins. Dickens builds up the atmosphere of an extremely foggy day around the river: "Every object was obscured at one or two yards' distance. The warning lights and fires upon the river were powerless beneath this pall and but for a raw and piercing chillness in the air, and now and then the cry of some bewildered boatman as he rested on his oars and tried to make out where he was, the river itself might have been miles away."[14] Up to this point both fog and cloud are viewed interchangeably. In the next paragraph the fog changes to mist, as it takes on a personal, supernatural character: "The mist, though sluggish and slow to move, was of a keenly searching kind. No muffling up in furs and broad-cloth kept it out. It seemed to penetrate into the very bones of the shrinking wayfarers, and to rack them with cold and pains."[15]

As the narrative proceeds, the "dense mist" is seen "to thicken every moment," "the fog had so much increased."[16] The imagery gives the reader a sense of Quilp being resolutely hounded down before the authorities actually arrive on the scene. "It was about eight o'clock; but the dead of the darkest night would have been as noon-day, in comparison with the thick cloud which then rested upon the earth and shrouded everything from view." The passage has a biblical feel of retribution, reminiscent of the darkness that descended over the Egyptians in the book of Exodus.[17] Yet Quilp misinterprets the fog as an ally, remarking, "It will be a good night for travelling anonymously. . . . A good, black, devil's night this."[18] Quilp moves outside and darts forward towards the river "as if into the mouth of some dim, yawning cavern."[19] He locks a gate behind him to forestall his pursuers. But he misses his footing and falls into the river. At the point of death Quilp achieves a clear awareness and understanding of what is happening. He has enjoyed being the master of manipulation; he now understands that his actions are leading to his own death, for by locking the gate he has prevented anyone from coming to help him. The fog, for which he had been so grateful earlier as a means of escape, will prevent him from being seen and rescued.

This realisation is made more terrifying by the repetition and rhythm of the passage: "He could hear the knocking at the gate again—could hear a shout that followed it—could recognise the voice. For all his struggling and splashing, he could understand that they had lost their way, and had wandered back to the point from which they started; that they were all but looking on while he was drowned; that they were close at hand, but could not make an effort to save him; that he himself had shut and barred them out."[20] Retribution is heightened further by the elements, whose punishments parallel Quilp's own cruelty in life. The statement that "the strong tide filled his throat" recalls his own lusty drinking habits and his repeated attempts to cause pain to people by making them drink spirits hot enough to scald.[21] His "yell" and his "wild and glaring eyes" all emphasise his grotesque animal character in life as well as in death.[22] Even when the river has given up toying with its catch, as depicted in Figure 2.3, the notion of games, so enjoyed by Quilp in his life, is reinforced as his "hair, stirred by the damp breeze, played in a kind of mockery of death—

Figure 2.3 An illustration from the 1841 novel *The Old Curiosity Shop* by Charles Dickens, in which Quilp lies dead, a victim of the fog, the river, and his own villainy. Illustration by Hablot Knight Browne. Courtesy of the President and Fellows of Wolfson College, Cambridge.

such a mockery as the dead man himself would have revelled in when alive."[23]

Another element, that of fire, destroys Quilp's dwelling. Again it is Quilp who had caused this when he left his favoured haunt and clumsily knocked over the stove. The final few lines complete Quilp's punishment. The fog seems to have disappeared. It is as though the whole of nature has been revolted by his crimes: "The sky was red with flame, and the water that bore it there had been tinged with the sullen light as it flowed along."[24] It is a hell-like picture suggesting that Quilp is destined for the inferno. The scene recalls the "lurid glare hanging in the dark sky; the dull reflection of some distant fire" in an earlier scene set in a factory.[25] The savage nature of Quilp's death is in direct contrast to the peaceful rest into which Nell falls three chapters later and which is narrated, not directly, but as already having happened, in the past perfect tense. Quilp's death is reported as if it is happening in real time, emphasising the horror of it. Nell's body is left as if she were still alive; Quilp's is a "deserted carcase."[26] The death of Quilp in a natural fog shows nature reasserting itself by ridding the world of a particular pollutant.

Dickens's narrative, in which Quilp, the unacceptable face of the city, is destroyed by the forces of nature, involves a depiction of London fog as natural rather than artificial. It is not yellow or brown but misty, cloudlike. It may be that Dickens set the novel in the mid-1820s partly in order to make this more plausible, as well as to allow Quilp to be buried at a crossroads as a suicide, a practice banned in 1826. Dickens was always concerned to provide his novels with verisimilitude. Accidental drownings in fog, such as Quilp's, for example were not uncommon at the time. A report in *The Times,* dated December 18, 1835, describes six drownings during a fog. Of the three where an inquest had been held, the verdict was, in all cases, that the people had "accidentally drowned" with a strong recommendation that the dock areas where they had been drowned should be better protected against such incidents. Another report made it clear that there could be no question of suicide:

> FATAL ACCIDENTS DURING THE FOG—On Saturday night five young men, tanners, . . . amused themselves by playing leap-frog, and while doing so found their way to a narrow passage leading direct to the river, a few yards below Cherry-garden Stairs. While amusing themselves here, three of the young men, unconscious of being so near the water, owing to the dense fog which prevailed, walked into the Thames. Their companions, who were close behind, on hearing the splash, turned back and called out loudly for assistance. Their cries were heard by the Thames-police, named White and Bennett, who were passing by the stairs in one of the police gallies at the time. They instantly rowed to the spot . . . and in about 20 minutes afterwards found the bodies and conveyed them ashore to a public-house. The unfortunate young men have all left wives and families. They had been so long in the water when found by the Thames police, that there appeared no chance of restoring animation.[27]

A recurring factor in the press reports of these drownings is the incidence of drinking and illegal activities undertaken by those victims before they drowned. The five young leap-frogging tanners in the preceding report from *The Times* were said to have been "out on a 'spree'" after "receiving their wages"; it is emphasised twice that they were "amusing themselves" and had earlier caused a disturbance which had led to their imprisonment for a short time before they drowned.[28] The tone of the report is one of disapproval, even of rebuke: how could young men with wives and families behave in this way?

Drink and crime, as well as irresponsibility, played a role in contemporary discourses on accidental drownings. Nearly two years later *The Times* wrote of a surveyor called Fox, who found

> the body of a man lying on his back in the mud, adjoining the Orchard-house-wharf, from which it is supposed he had walked during the fog into the water, which on the tide receding left him in the mud, . . . and recognized it to be that of a man named John Higgins, *alias* Elliott, whom he had met coming out of the Orchard-public-house in Poplar, on Wednesday night. Higgins resided for many years in Essex-street, Whitechapel, and has left a wife and seven children. He was known to be connected with some persons carrying on illicit distillation, and Fox discovered on his person two skins which had recently contained whisky, the produce of a private still, a pot and a measure.[29]

Quilp, we are told in *The Old Curiosity Shop,* has just brewed himself "a great bowl of hot punch" from which he drinks "a long deep draught, as if it were fair water and cooling to his parched mouth." He takes "another draught from the bowl" before he is forced to leave his bachelor residence.[30] No wonder he loses his way and falls into the river. Like Quilp, too, victims of accidental drowning seem not to have been able to swim; but even had they possessed this skill, they would have found it difficult to survive in the Thames because of the density of the river traffic. The 1834 report in *The Times* notes that the police "who instantly rowed to the spot . . . cleared away the barges near the stairs."[31] This level of overcrowding along the Thames was commonplace and would have meant that a drowning man could have easily been pulled under the water, not only by the boats anchored in the docks but also by the frequent traffic along the river. Thus Quilp is killed when he bumps against the hull of a ship. Endeavouring to make "one loud cry," he is denied even this as the "resistless water bore him down before he could give it utterance, and, driving him under it, carried away a corpse."[32]

A QUALIFIED GUIDE.

Befogged Pedestrian. "Could you direct me to the river, please?"
Hatless and dripping Stranger. "Straight ahead. I've just come from it!"

Figure 2.4 "A Qualified Guide." *Punch* as usual shows the lighter side of the perils of London fog. This illustration concerns the constant danger of falling into the river during foggy weather. (*Punch*, 25 January 1905, p. 55). Courtesy of the President and Fellows of Wolfson College, Cambridge.

||

The fog represented in *The Old Curiosity Shop* is part of the natural world in London; it reveals that Dickens still has hope for the urban environment to share its space with nature, even allowing nature to wreak vengeance on that emblem of industrial pollution, Quilp. When Dickens came to write *Martin Chuzzlewit* two years later, the fog had changed; it was a fog that no longer dispensed natural justice but one that imposed confusion on the city and its inhabitants. The novel opens with a facetious genealogy of the Chuzzlewit family, who then meet to greedily fight over the fortune of Old Martin Chuzzlewit (who is not even dead). The old man has tried to secure his future by engaging an orphan girl, Mary Graham, as his companion and carer, but his grandson, young Martin Chuzzlewit, falls in love with her, thus threatening to ruin his plans. The grandfather not only disinherits him but also secures his dismissal from his pupillage at the architectural practice of the morally bankrupt and hypocritical Seth Pecksniff, who has taken him on in the hope of being looked on favourably in the old man's will. Young Martin leaves with a jolly companion, Mark Tapley, to try to make his fortune in America. While there, young Martin catches a fever and almost dies. The experience makes him a better man.

Pecksniff has another pupil, Tom Pinch, but he leaves Pecksniff when he realizes that his master, instead of training them, is paying them nothing more than a pittance while claiming their work as his own. Pinch departs to London, where he rescues his sister Ruth from servitude as a governess. Meanwhile, Old Martin's brother Anthony Chuzzlewit, a wealthy miser, dies mysteriously, leaving his wealth to his son Jonas Chuzzlewit. Jonas is courting Charity Pecksniff, Seth's daughter. However, he then turns his attentions to her sister, Mercy, whom he later marries and begins to treat badly. He also falls in with the petty thief and conman Montague Tigg, who blackmails him when he discovers that Jonas had planned to kill his father for his money and at the very least had hastened his death. Jonas proceeds to murder Montague Tigg, but he is discovered and commits suicide. Old Martin, who had been secretly supporting Tom Pinch by arranging a congenial job for him, now reveals himself as a hero rather than a villain. He had only disapproved of his grandson's marriage out of vanity, having wanted to arrange it himself. He exposes Pecksniff for the fraud that he is, and he gives his blessing to Mary's marriage to Martin, who has returned a better and poorer man from America.

The narrative begins in Salisbury, but from very early on in the novel the characters begin to look towards London. Even before young Martin and Tom Pinch leave, both are likened to "a pair of Whittingtons . . . without the cat," reinforcing the idea of London as a place to make a fortune.[33] The action moves to London when Seth Pecksniff and his daughters, Charity and Mercy, go there in Chapter 8. The reader follows an uncomfortable journey undertaken by Mr. Pecksniff and his daughters to the capital, by coach. When they arrive, it is very dark—"it might have been midnight"—and the fact that it is morning is only indicated by the "bustle" of the street in which they are dropped.[34] The height of the buildings shuts out the light from the street, and "there was a dense fog too."[35] London is enveloped in a double darkness, making it appear unreal, demarcated from the rest of the country by its cloudy, foggy atmosphere, "as if it were a city in the clouds, which they had been travelling to all night up a magic beanstalk."[36] They have moved from one fairy tale, "Dick Whittington," into another, "Jack and the Beanstalk." And just as Jack eventually climbed the beanstalk to gain a fortune, so too Whittington was made Lord Mayor of London and discovered that its streets were metaphorically paved with gold. Yet both Jack and Dick Whittington were forced to meet and overcome severe challenges before making good. London presents particular challenges to the entire Pecksniff family. Mercy enters an unhappy marriage with Jonas Chuzzlewit, Charity tries to find a husband but is jilted at the altar, and Seth Pecksniff is bankrupted through his dealings with the fraudulent Anglo-Bengalee company. For this family, at least, the promise of fortune turns out to be illusory as the events of the novel unfold, whereas the other characters who turn to London do, at least, find happiness, if not fortune, in their own way.

Fog is not just a setting for fairy-tale elements in the story, as "a city in the clouds." The reality of a foggy day is introduced by the statement that "there was a thick crust upon the pavement like oil-cake."[37] The kind of polluted fog which Londoners endured often left greasy, oily deposits on surfaces such as windows and pavements, adding to the general amount of filth left on the streets (fog and frost came together to make things worse, as reported in *The Times* in 1840: "On Saturday the metropolis was visited with a dense fog accompanied by a frost, which rendered the streets exceedingly slippery and travelling dangerous.")[38] Dickens describes this condition in his novella *A Christmas Carol* (1843), written at the same time as *Martin Chuzzlewit:* "The city clocks had only just gone three, but it was quite dark already: it had not been light all day: and candles were flaring in the windows of the neighbouring offices, like ruddy smears upon the palpable brown air."[39] The writing admirably describes the tangible quality of the dirty air, suggesting the smears a London fog was wont to leave on the pavement and surrounding buildings.

After arriving in this atmosphere, Pecksniff navigates himself and his daughters through the fog to Todger's Boarding House, where the family will stay. The journey is portrayed in a way that echoes the great haste in which Pecksniff undertakes it. He "dived across the street," indicating his speed of departure but also adding to a sense of the watery nature of the foggy atmosphere. The whole description of London adds to the confusion and alienation in its use of the superlative—the "courts" are the "queerest" and the alleys are of "the strangest." The "archways" are the "blindest"—blind because the fog does not allow one to see beyond them to the other side, giving the impression that they lead nowhere, surely another hint that the earlier notion of London as a place to make a fortune is mistaken. In addition, through the personification of the "archways," London becomes not only a setting but a character in this mad dash of Pecksniff's. And all of this is undertaken "in a kind of frenzy: now skipping over a kennel, now running for his life from a coach and horses."[40] Here, too, Dickens was taking his cue from the real dangers posed by London fogs. Contemporary newspaper reports recorded many accidents, sometimes fatal, of pedestrians being run over by traffic in just such circumstances: "Two young females, while crossing from Coventry-street to Sydney's-alley," as *The Times* reported during a major fog of 1829, "were knocked down by the leader of a stage coach and were much injured."[41]

As for Pecksniff and his party, blundering about in the fog in their search for Todger's Boarding House, they seem to be completely lost. When they appear to reach their destination, the density of the fog means that they have to trust Mr. Pecksniff's judgement that it is the Monument, since "for as to anything they could see of the Monument, or anything

Figure 2.5 "A Fog in the Streets of London." The accompanying article concludes with a pastiche of Milton's *Paradise Lost*: "No light, but rather darkness visible.... Regions of bother, doleful shades, where cabs / And 'busses can't drive on in peace at all / Nor people walking tread the pavement safe." (*Illustrated London News*, 12 January 1867, p. 48). Reproduced by kind permission of the Syndics of Cambridge University Library.

else but the buildings close at hand, they might as well have been playing blindman's buff at Salisbury."[42] A few chapters later when Martin Chuzzlewit says goodbye to Mary Graham, on his way to find his fortune in America, fog again descends, this time to illustrate Martin's blindness to Mary's feelings. Mary has been forbidden to see young Martin by his grandfather. They meet on a "morning, which was clad in the least engaging of the three hundred and sixty-five dresses in the wardrobe of the year. It was raw, damp, dark and dismal; the clouds were as muddy as the ground; and the short perspective of every street and avenue was closed up by the mist as by a filthy curtain."[43] Fog, mist, and clouds are used interchangeably throughout the novel, as in *The Old Curiosity Shop*.

The preceding passages display Dickens's creativity in abundance, not least as he uses the fog to highlight the different personalities of the characters. Martin's bitter despair at the weather only accentuates his own selfish thoughtlessness: "He might perhaps have gone on to reflect that of all mornings in the year, it was not the best calculated for a young lady's coming forth on such an errand, either."[44] Mark Tapley, in his usual fashion of trying to make the best out of any situation, uses the fog in order to avoid being seen to stare at the young sweethearts; in order to give them the appearance of privacy, he "surveyed the fog above him with an appearance of attentive interest."[45] When Martin places his arm around Mary's waist, he beholds "Mr. Tapley more intent than ever on the fog."[46] When it is necessary, Mark is able to see beyond the fog, as when Mary thanks him for his support of Martin with a kind glance which "he brought his eyes down from the fog to encounter, and received with immense satisfaction."[47]

Fog has become London from this point, yet it robs London of shape and form and renders it indeterminate, mysterious, and confusing. In *Martin Chuzzlewit* the city attempts to thwart the traveller by hiding itself beneath the fog, creating confusion and panic. The natural and man-made worlds have become indistinguishable, with snow confused with the sooty deposits which are part of the fog. Reality appears to have dissolved under the weight of the fog and is turned into a fairy tale or a child's game. The passage describing the Pecksniffs' arrival in foggy London is short, barely covering a page of text, but the power of the description fully conveys the sense of London threatening to dissolve into confusion, even madness. By this stage London fog has turned in Dickens's imagination from a natural force, as portrayed in the mid-1820s setting of *The Old Curiosity Shop*, into a brown, filthy curtain concealing the dangers that life in the city held. Yet as the happy fate of most of the characters in *Chuzzlewit* suggests, London could still be seen beneath its veil as an organized community with its own moral rules, rules that could triumph in the end. In later novels, however, Dickens began to use fog as a metaphorical expression of a much darker view.

III

LONDON. Michaelmas term lately over, and the Lord Chancellor sitting in Lincoln's Inn Hall. Implacable November weather. As much mud in the streets, as if the waters had but newly retired from the face of the earth, and it would not be wonderful to meet a Megalosaurus, forty feet long or so, waddling like an elephantine lizard up Holborn Hill. Smoke lowering down from chimney-pots, making a soft black drizzle with flakes of soot in it as big as full-grown snowflakes—gone into mourning, one might imagine, for the death of the sun.

Fog everywhere. Fog up the river, where it flows among green aits and meadows; fog down the river, where it rolls defiled among the tiers of shipping, and the waterside pollutions of a great (and dirty) city. Fog on the Essex Marshes . . . Fog in the eyes and throats of ancient Greenwich pensioners, wheezing by the firesides of their wards; fog in the stem and bowl of the afternoon pipe of the wrathful skipper, down in his close cabin; fog cruelly pinching the toes and fingers of his shivering little 'prentice boy on deck. Chance people on the bridges peeping over the parapets into a nether sky of fog, with fog all round them, as if they were up in a balloon, and hanging in the misty clouds.[48]

So begins what is perhaps the most famous passage on London fog to be found in all literature: the opening passage of Dickens's novel *Bleak House,* which appeared as a book in 1853, the same year as Palmerston's Smoke Abatement Act, though the novel was published in weekly magazine instalments begun the previous year. For many people it is this opening passage that instantly comes to mind when thinking about London fog.

In these pages the smoke lowers down, rather than circling upwards, preparing us for the idea that this is not a world in which the normal prevails. Nature has been perverted. Instead of soft white snow, there is a "soft black drizzle"; and just in case we need further reinforcement of the metaphor, the simile follows of the "flakes of soot in it as big as full-grown snowflakes." Unnervingly, the soot flakes, because of their blackness, metaphorically appear to have "gone into mourning, one might imagine, for the death of the sun."[49] In the space of a few lines we have moved from the beginning of time, with "a Megalosaurus, forty feet long or so, waddling like an elephantine lizard up Holborn Hill," to the end of time, with the death of the sun.[50] Upriver, in the countryside, fog "flows" in a natural setting, but in the "dirty" city it "rolls defiled" by black soot, polluted and unhealthy.

Dickens's symbolic purpose in describing this foggy, raw, and dirty day is soon made clear: "The raw afternoon is rawest, and the dense fog is densest, and the muddy streets are muddiest, near that leaden-headed old obstruction, appropriate ornament for the threshold of a leaden-headed

A SCENE NEAR TEMPLE-BAR, DURING THE FOG.

Figure 2.6 "A Scene near Temple-Bar, during the Fog." Temple-Bar was originally designed to regulate trade into the City and became well known as a traffic bottleneck, made worse in the fog. The structure is now situated to the north of St. Paul's Cathedral, at the entrance of Paternoster Square. (*Illustrated London News*, 23 November 1844, p. 336). Reproduced by kind permission of the Syndics of Cambridge University Library.

old corporation: Temple Bar."[51] At the heart of the fog "sits the Lord High Chancellor in his High Court of Chancery."[52] "Never can there come fog too thick, never can there come mud and mire too deep, to assort with the groping and floundering condition which this High Court of Chancery, most pestilent of hoary sinners, holds, this day, in the sight of heaven and earth."[53] Chancery represents all the political and social institutions which, like the tangle of shipping on the river, are static and incapable of motion: "For it is government inaction that allows the immense sanitary problem to remain unsolved. It is government inaction that leaves raw sewage uncollected . . . and that thereby is to blame for the deadly effluvia of this fog that poisons the city's air."[54]

Dickens then pursues the image with the Lord High Chancellor sitting "with a foggy glory round his head"; a brief "can see nothing but fog."[55] In the same way the Lord High Chancellor looks in vain for illumination, both light and knowledge, from "the lantern in the roof, where he can see nothing but fog."[56] The whole court is dim in all senses. Members of the High Court are "mistily engaged" in a case and, very much like the foot pedestrians in the opening of the novel, are "tripping one another up on slippery precedents, groping knee-deep in technicalities, running . . . against walls of word."[57] "Well may the court be dim, with wasting candles here and there; well may the fog hang heavy in it, as if it would never get out; well may the stained-glass windows lose their colour, and admit no light of day into the place."[58] Like the sun of the opening page, the candles give out little light, and they are wasting away. The fog has intruded into the internal space of the court from the outside, and there is a sense that the fog is imprisoning the court and its proceedings. As "the Lord High Chancellor looks into the lantern that has no light in it, and where the attendant wigs are all stuck in a fogbank!" we recall again the ships of the opening scene which are also seemingly prevented from moving forward by the fog.[59]

Bleak House is a novel centred on the Court of Chancery, an institution which had become notorious for delays, vested interests, and huge costs. In developing its immensely complex and multilayered plot, Dickens uses a double narrative technique. Half of the story is narrated by an omniscient, third-person narrator, but the other half is told by the story's heroine, Esther Summerson; the narrative control switches back and forth. Esther is a sensible, practical character who is brought up by her aunt, as her mother is unknown until her identity is revealed at the end. Her aunt cruelly refers to her as her mother's "disgrace," and the truth behind her birth is one of the novel's many secrets.[60] Esther is befriended and helped by John Jarndyce, who has inherited the Chancery case of

Figure 2.7 This photograph was taken on January 24, 1934, by Fred Morley. It shows an eerie scene in Lincoln's Inn Fields, the setting for Charles Dickens's novel *Bleak House* (1853). The feeble lamp and the figure in silhouette convey the isolation that could be felt in a thick London fog. Fred Morley / Getty Images.

Jarndyce and Jarndyce. The case has existed so long in Chancery that it has become a standing joke, but the consequences of it are very serious: John Jarndyce's uncle, indeed, has shot himself in frustration and madness at never seeing the case come close to any resolution. Nearly all the individuals in the huge cast of characters are directly or indirectly affected by Chancery. Even John Jarndyce, who refuses to become involved in the case, takes on the role of guardian to Ada Clare and Richard Carstone, who are wards of Chancery and potential heirs to one of the wills contested in the case, until they are of legal age and able to control their own affairs. Esther is invited to be Ada's companion, and all three go to live in Jarndyce's home, Bleak House.

Part of the corrupting influence of the Jarndyce case is that it has allowed the ruin of an area of London known as Tom-all-Alone's. It is falling to pieces, and only those who are the poorest and most helpless in society live there. One of these is the waif Jo, who is illiterate and ignorant. He earns a pittance by sweeping the streets at crossings and begging money for his services from passersby. Part of the biting social criticism of the novel is directed towards the lack of Christian responsibility which allows Jo to exist without its intervention. Jo is befriended by "Nemo," an impoverished and anonymous legal copywriter. Nemo rents a dismal room in a house owned by the rag-and-bottle merchant Krook, who collects old legal documents, seeing himself as another version of the Lord Chancellor. The miserable copyist Nemo dies early on in the novel, from an opium overdose, but not before his writing has been recognised by Lady Dedlock, who, we discover, was his lover before she married the aristocrat Sir Leicester Dedlock. Before Nemo had fallen into destitution and anonymity, he had fathered an illegitimate child on Lady Dedlock, who turns out to be Esther. This is the "shame" of which Esther's aunt constantly spoke before her death. Lady Dedlock betrays herself by fainting with surprise at seeing Nemo's familiar hand in front of the family's lawyer, Tulkinghorn, who sets out to discover Lady Dedlock's secret in order to obtain a hold over her.

This is only a partial retelling of an enormously complex plot which hinges on secrets, lost wills, and unscrupulous lawyers. The numerous subplots make the novel for some readers as confusing as the lawsuit that

forms its core. Nevertheless there are many connections between characters that only gradually become clear as the narrative progresses. Even
the unhappy Jo, the crossing sweeper, proves to be the link between the
aristocratic Dedlocks and the poor copyist Nemo. When Lady Dedlock,
poorly disguised as a servant, is led by Jo to the unhealthy cemetery near
Tom-all-Alone's where he knows her former lover Nemo to have been
interred, she shrinks both from Jo and from the hideous environment
"into a corner of that hideous archway, with its deadly stains contami-
nating her dress."[61] When she goes to pay Jo, she is reluctant to touch
him: "She drops a piece of money in his hand, without touching it, and
shuddering as their hands approach."[62] She fears catching a fever through
physical contact with Jo. But the stains are not only physical; they are also
moral: her visit to the graveyard leads to the revelation of her former lover
and the existence of their illegitimate child, Esther Summerson. For her, as
an aristocratic married woman, it is social death. For Jo the graveyard may
be where he picks up smallpox, which he passes on to both Esther and
her maid, Charley. Jo dies from the disease, but both Charley and Esther
survive after a long illness, although Esther is not left unscarred.[63]

In *Bleak House* fog mingles with smoke and noxious vapours to pose a
real threat to life and health, hastening the death of Richard Carstone
from tuberculosis. Similarly the physical body of the landlord Krook, who
dies from the improbable cause of spontaneous combustion brought on
by excessive consumption of alcohol, is reduced to nothing more than a
thick yellow liquor, like a mixture of fog and mud. His death might well
have been caused by a miasma, for he bursts into flame on "a fine steaming
night to turn the slaughter-houses, the unwholesome trades, the sew-
erage, bad water, and burial-grounds to account, and give the Registrar
of Deaths some extra business. It may be something in the air—there is
plenty in it."[64] On the night of Krook's death both Snagsby, the owner of
a law stationery shop, and Jobling, a minor character and friend of Guppy's,
agree: "It's a tainting sort of weather."[65] As Guppy arrives to discuss a
business matter with Krook later in the evening, he is discomfited by
the amount of soot falling: "See how the soot's falling. See here, on my
arm! See again, on the table here! Confound the stuff, it won't blow off—
smears, like black fat!"[66] When both Jobling and Guppy go to Krook's

room to find the source of the soot and yellow liquid, they find nothing there but his smouldering body. Krook has almost literally turned into pea soup. Disease, pathological, psychological, moral, is carried through the atmosphere.

Mr. Jarndyce's imaginary East Wind is also linked to the theme of miasma. As guardian of Ada and Richard, the two wards of Chancery, as well as benefactor to Esther, he has inherited the Chancery case, but he refuses to have anything to do with it. Whenever he feels disturbed by unpleasant events or opinions, he blames the "East Wind," instead of, as Ada and Esther discover, wanting to "blame the real cause of it, or disparage or depreciate any one."[67] The East Wind was proverbially the icy wind that irritated the spleen, leading to grumpiness; when it is metaphorically blowing, Jarndyce retreats to the Growlery, as he calls his study. But it was not merely metaphorical. In London, where industrial emissions were concentrated in the East End, the prevailing wind was in the west, but, the antiquary John Timbs (1801–1875), writing in 1855, noted, "Suppose the wind to change suddenly to the east, the great body of smoke will be brought back in an accumulated mass; and as this repasses the town, augmented by the clouds of smoke from every fire therein, it causes the murky darkness."[68] Timbs had no problem seeing the connection between fog and the East Wind: "Sometimes the fog is caused by a very ordinary accident,—a change of wind, thus accounted for."[69]

The East Wind also carried infection. In 1851 Dickens made this point at an anniversary banquet of the Metropolitan Sanitary Association. When asked to propose a toast to the Board of Health, he suggested "that no one can estimate the amount of mischief which is grown in dirt; that no one can say, here it stops or there it stops, either in its physical or its moral results . . . is now as certain as it is that the air from Gin Lane will be carried, when the wind is Easterly, into May Fair, and that if you once have a vigorous pestilence raging furiously in Saint Giles's, no mortal list of Lady Patronesses can keep it out of Almack's."[70] *The Times* reported in a similar vein on December 1, 1840: "The fog on Saturday night was particularly dense westward of the metropolis. From 3 o'clock in the afternoon in the neighbourhood of Kensington, Hammersmith, and more eastward, a thick darkness overspread the atmosphere by which persons compelled to be out were quite unable to see one inch before them. From that hour links and candles, with and without candlesticks, were used by persons of all classes, male and female, the proprietors of the omnibuses not suffering their vehicles to run after dark in consequence of the fog."[71] In the same way the slum quarter of Tom-all-Alone's is the subject of a heartfelt cry by Dickens: "Even the winds are his messengers, and they serve him in these hours of darkness. There is not a drop of Tom's corrupted blood but propagates infection and contagion somewhere. It shall pollute, this very night, the choice stream (in which chemists on analysis would find the genuine nobility) of a Norman house, and his Grace shall not be able to say Nay to the infamous alliance. . . . Verily, what with tainting, plundering, and spoiling, Tom has his revenge."[72] It is the road-sweeping urchin, Jo, a ghastly representation of what Tom-all-Alone's can produce, who passes his infection on to Esther Summerson. Disease and corruption are carried through miasmatic forces that bring the sufferings of the exploited poor home to roost with the uncaring rich.

The fog also impairs and degrades the senses: "Fog gets in the eyes and throats of ancient Greenwich pensioners. . . . Chance people on the bridges peeping over the parapets into a nether sky of fog, with fog all round them, as if they were up on a balloon, and hanging in the misty clouds."[73] The novel is pervaded by images of blindness. Krook's shop is described as "blinded besides by the wall of Lincoln's Inn, intercepting the light."[74] Even Mrs. Snagsby, wrongly convinced that her husband is Jo's father, announces, "you can't blind ME!"[75] Esther's knowledge of having herself contracted Jo's disease is confirmed when she tells her maid that the disease had made her go blind.[76] The Jarndyce case, in which Richard Carstone becomes involved, damages vision. Thus John Jarndyce sorrowfully notes of his ward, "Jarndyce and Jarndyce has warped him out of himself, and perverted me in his eyes."[77] And, worse still, "it is in the subtle poison of such abuses to breed such diseases. His blood is infected, and objects lose their natural aspects in his sight. It is not *his* fault."[78] Just as fog distorts objects and renders them formless, so too does the metaphorical infection of the blood by the moral miasma of the Chancery proceedings. When the Jarndyce lawsuit is finally resolved with all monies lost in the cost of conducting the case, John Jarndyce, in a true spirit of friendship and forgiveness, visits Richard Carstone, who is now dying, and he notes: "The clouds have cleared away, and it is bright now. We can see

Figure 2.8 *A London Fog,* by Charles Albert Ludovici (1820–1894). Ludovici's son described it as "representing a group of ragged crossing-sweepers in a thick London fog tossing an old black top-hat in the air with their birch brooms." The picture was rejected at the Paris Salon of 1863 but was then hung at the Salon des Refusés, where it was "bought by the Emperor Napoleon III, whom it no doubt reminded of the days when he lived in London as an exile" according to his son, Albert Ludovici, in *An Artist's Life in London and Paris 1870–1925* (1926), p. 57. Reproduced by kind permission of Amgueddfa Cenedlaethol Cymru—National Museum of Wales.

now."[79] Richard vows to "begin the world" and says this with "a light in his eyes."[80] When he looks back, it is, he says, to "where I shall be able to recall my many faults and blindnesses."[81]

The world described in the opening of the novel was dominated by the darkness of the fog, but darkness pervades throughout: "DARKNESS rests upon Tom-all-Alone's. Dilating and dilating since the sun went down last night, it has gradually swelled until it fills every void in the place."[82] The darkness is not simply a feature of nighttime. When Allan Wood-court, the doctor, takes Jo away to provide care, they emerge as from a dungeon and "come up out of Tom-all-Alone's into the broad rays of the sunlight and the purer air."[83] The characters' attempts to gain a clearer vision are not only restricted by the fog but are also offset by the emphasis on blindness, darkness, and a bewildering of the senses throughout the text. Even the inability to read, to make sense of letters as a whole, a re-curring theme in the novel, is likened in Jo's case to being blind.[84] Jo is described as being "in a state of darkness" by Chadband, a hypocritical preacher, who says that he cannot see Jo clearly "because you are in a state of obscurity."[85] But Dickens makes the point that he is still God's child and describes him as "looking up at the great Cross on the summit of St. Paul's Cathedral, glittering above a red and violet-tinted cloud of smoke."[86] God, it almost seems, is looking back from the cloud in anger at the world's mistreatment of the orphan boy. Even though Jo has just been recently spoken to by a member of the church, religious comfort is as far away as the cross on St. Paul's Cathedral—"so golden, so high up, so far out of his reach."[87] Just before his death Jo slips into the "obscurity" identified by Chadband: "It's turned wery dark, sir. Is there any light a-comin? . . . I hear you, sir, in the dark, but I'm a-groping."[88] The light, which has been denied to Jo in life, appears, we are told, in death: "The light is come upon the dark benighted way. Dead!"[89]

Dickens's point in opening the novel in a foggy scene of obscurity and darkness is to create not only a powerful metaphor for the world of Chancery but, as the subsequent metaphorical chiaroscuro of *Bleak House* suggests, a more general metaphor for the state of London. It is a place where light is largely denied to individuals—whether this is the light of religious comfort to individuals like Jo or the light generated by educa-tion or just a physical light which is denied by the smoke and fog. The smoke creates a world in mourning for the sun in the beginning of the book; the smoke around St. Paul's Cathedral, as Jo rests, reveals angry tints of colour at society's treatment of the boy. The character who seems most successfully able to piece the obscure connections together is Mr. Bucket, the detective. When he attempts to find Lady Dedlock in London, we are told: "Sometimes he would get down by an archway, or at a street corner, and mysteriously show the light of his little lantern. This would attract similar lights from various dark quarters, like so many insects."[90] He can make connections within the city by showing his light, but in the end it is not good enough. He finds Lady Dedlock only after she has died. Like his name, Bucket's claim to piece together the puzzle presented to the reader by the opening pages is empty.

The only baby born within London in the novel is that of Caddy Jellyby, and she is born deaf and dumb—another allusion to deprivation of the senses. Is Dickens commenting on the unsustainability of life bred within the unhealthy, dark, and polluted air of the city?[91] He certainly sees the blight of the city spreading outwards. A letter that Dickens sent to the philanthropist Angela Burdett-Coutts at about this time shows that the problem was very much at the forefront of his mind: "Go into any common outskirts of the town, now, and see the advancing army of brick and mortar laying waste the country fields and shutting out the air."[92] Already in 1829 George Cruikshank commented on the expansion of the city in his cartoon "London Going out of Town: The March of Bricks and Mortar" (Figure 2.9). In this picture the clouds of smoke from domestic and industrial chimneys are polluting the countryside before the army of building equipment, represented by chimney pots, moves in to the countryside. The haystacks and farm animals can only flee in terror. Again the dome of St. Paul's disappears behind the billowing black smoke. Yet in Dickens's novel London's "lurid glare" hangs over St. Albans and even over Bleak House itself. The house is thus unable to provide a suitable retreat to warrant, if not a happy ending, at least an ending that promises peace to the major surviving characters, for it is still too close to London.

In *Bleak House* the fog has become a signifier of London, its institutions, and its social constitution to a far more powerful degree than in Dick-

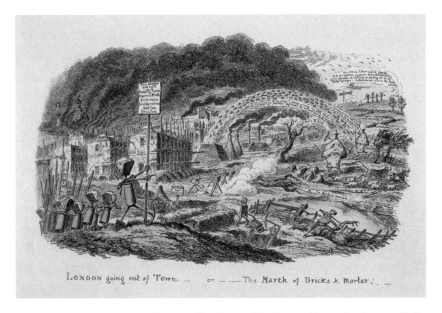

LONDON going out of Town. — or ——The March of Bricks & Morter. —

Figure 2.9 *London Going out of Town—The March of Bricks and Mortar,* by George Cruikshank, showing the rapid growth of London as early as 1829, which in this vision meant increased pollution, as shown here by the amount of smoke coming from the chimneys. Cruikshank was willing to show the householder as more responsible for the smoke than the industrialist. © The Trustees of the British Museum.

ens's previous work. The first word may declare that it is "London," but the need to establish this simply highlights that the city is dissolving beneath its fog and mud.[93] When Esther Summerson arrives in the city, the first thing she notes is the confusion, "when every conveyance seemed to be running into us, and we seemed to be running into every other conveyance"; the second thing is the fog.[94] Fog is triumphant; it plunges the city and the novel's characters into a world of darkness, madness, and despair from which it is only possible to emerge by leaving the city altogether. This is in fact the conclusion to the novel. Esther marries her true love, the doctor Allan Woodcourt, Jarndyce buys them a version of his own home, Bleak House, in Yorkshire, and they are visited regularly by Jarndyce, Ada, and her child, as well as Caddy and other characters: far away enough from London to be safe.

IV

"London is a vile place," Dickens wrote in a letter in 1851: "Whenever I come back from the Country, now, and see that great heavy canopy lowering over the house tops, I wonder what on earth I do there, except on obligation."[95] As Dickens grew older, his view of London became more pessimistic. This change became apparent above all in his last completed novel, *Our Mutual Friend,* written in 1864–1865. It opens memorably with Gaffer Hexam, assisted by his daughter Lizzie, salvaging a corpse from the river, an activity which brings him a regular source of income. The body appears to be that of John Harmon, the heir to a fortune made by his father, a misanthrope and miser, through the accumulation of dust piles. With John Harmon dead, the fortune reverts to Noddy Boffin, a servant to the late dustman. The kind-hearted Boffin and his wife invite Bella Wilfer to live with them—she has been betrothed to John Harmon since childhood, even though she has never met him. She is beautiful but seemingly heartless, desiring only money. Boffin employs a secretary, Rokesmith, to deal with his affairs, and he begins to suspect him of admiring Bella. She is, initially, scornful of the secretary's advances, but when Boffin begins to display miserly tendencies and is unpleasant to Rokesmith, she leaves the Boffin household and marries the secretary in spite of his poverty. It transpires, however, that Rokesmith is really John Harmon. It was not Harmon's body found in the river but that of a man who had attacked him. Harmon has decided to remain "dead" to see whether he wished to take up his inheritance and marry Bella. Mr. Boffin had only acted the part of a miser in order for Bella to discover that she loved Rokesmith/Harmon for himself and not for his fortune.

Meanwhile, Lizzie Hexam's father, falsely accused of murdering Harmon by another riverside scavenger, the villainous Rogue Riderhood, is drowned. Lizzie is desperate for her brother, Charley, to better himself, and she sends him away to get an education. Charley's schoolteacher, Bradley Headstone, meets Lizzie and falls desperately in love with her, so much so that he becomes mad with jealousy when she rejects him. He realises that she has fallen in love with Eugene Wrayburn, a solicitor who had met Lizzie in the wake of Harmon's apparent death and has been wooing her since. But she is too poor to be accepted by his family, on whom he relies for money. Wrayburn, realising that the schoolmaster also loves Lizzie, deliberately taunts him into madness. Headstone attacks Wrayburn, leaving him for dead. It is only Lizzie's rowing skills which save him from drowning as she takes him swiftly to receive medical care. Riderhood then tries to blackmail the schoolmaster, having realised his crime; but they grapple together, and Headstone ensures that they both fall into a dangerous weir and are drowned. The plot is resolved when Wrayburn finally accepts that Lizzie is good enough to be his wife, even though poor; and John Harmon comes into his fortune to share with his wife, Bella, who, it turns out, is not heartless at all. It is a novel of class and money and of their superficial attractions, represented most clearly perhaps in the character of "Fascination" Fledgeby, a sinister and hypocritical moneylender.

London fog plays a major role in metaphorical terms. It first emerges in the opening chapter of the third book of *Our Mutual Friend*. Indeed its very employment at the beginning of a new section strikes a keynote. Dickens is making a point about the state of society. He describes a city defined by fog. The surrounding countryside is foggy too, but there it is "grey, whereas in London it was, at about the boundary line, dark yellow, and a little within it brown, and then browner, and then browner, until at the heart of the City—which call Saint Mary Axe—it was rusty-black."[96] Dickens's employment of colours transforms observation into metaphor to symbolise the crisis of the city, a crisis that he seems to have envisaged as ultimately leading to the destruction of London and its people. His geography of fog is almost purely metaphorical. The boundary line to the city is "dark yellow." The boundary is both substantial, in the sense that the change of colour creates a physical marker of the city, and insubstantial, in that it is made of fog, which can easily be passed through. London is separated from the rest of the country by this barrier, but it does not stop people from entering it. The yellow colour of the boundary line indicates the sulphurous nature of the fog, but the colour also acts as a warning; at sea the yellow flag denoted fever, not just yellow fever but any dangerous contamination.[97] As the description moves closer to the city's centre, the colour moves from a "dark yellow" to brown, and then the brown becomes darker until it becomes a "rusty-black." On one level this only confirms the opening line of the chapter, that "the fog was heavy and dark." But the gradual darkening colour of the city fog achieves so much more. It supplies a sense of tension as Saint Mary Axe becomes a Dickensian heart of darkness. But there is a casualness on the part of the writer as to where the heart of the city is—"which call Saint Mary Axe"—indicating that he could just as easily have lighted on other areas within the city instead; the deliberate arbitrariness points the reader to the fact that this is a metaphorical geography. Saint Mary Axe is not unique. The description of the gradual darkening of the city as we move towards its centre is both dramatic and frightening. Saint Mary Axe is the home of Riah, the gentle Jew, the unwilling employee and shield of the mon-eylender Fledgeby. And it is in the context of this area as the place of business of Pubsey & Co., a cover for Fledgeby's nefarious monetary activities, that the reader has to situate the metaphorical significance of the fog's description.

The "heart of the City" is "rusty-black," not just black, as the foul air causes "animate London" to suffer from "smarting eyes and irritated lungs."[98] "Rust" was a common slang term in Victorian London for money, which is so much a part of this novel—especially money which is allowed to "rust," because it is not put to good use.[99] Part of John Harmon's reluc-tance to appear in public and confess that he is not dead is because the Boffins have inherited his father's money: "Because he sees them happy with it, making a good use of it, effacing the old rust and tarnish on the money."[100] Old Harmon's money is no longer allowed to corrode and rust in the darkness of the fog. We are told that "inanimate London was a sooty spectre, divided in purpose between being visible and invisible, and so being wholly neither."[101] This indeterminacy highlights the patchy nature of some London fogs; it also makes the environment formless and cre-ates spectres or ghosts out of the usually solid urban backdrop. The passage appears to reveal a world of nightmarish fantasy. The Podsnaps, representatives of the new in society, are described in ponderously solid and heavy terms; yet they are often only seen in reflections. Miss Podsnap's view of her father, a pompous and opinionated man, is significantly gained from "the reflections of it in her father's boots, and in the walnut and rose-wood tables of the dim drawing-rooms, and in their swarthy giants of looking-glasses."[102] People have placed too much faith in the value of money and live in an environmental nowhere. Appearances are deceptive, and what appears as solid may not be so at all, because it is based merely on money or even just the appearance of having it.

When suddenly the perspective is moved to a vantage point above the city, similar to that of people in a balloon looking down on it, as in the opening of *Bleak House,* the threat of the fog becomes extreme, even apocalyptic: "From any point of the high ridge of land northward, it might have been discerned that the loftiest buildings made an occasional struggle to get their heads above the foggy sea."[103] In a novel centred on the River Thames and its activities, including drownings, it is appropriate that the buildings are described as if they are struggling to keep their heads above water. Of course it was not unusual to see the fog as a sea when looking down on it. Ever since the late eighteenth century, when balloon flight had made it possible to rise above the clouds and mists, this image had become standard. The idea of the sea also ties in with the two most potent images in the novel, water and dust; fog is a combination of both. Water imagery, in all its forms, was an important poetic symbol in many of Dickens's novels.[104] In this novel the Thames is a force that connects all levels of society. Characters are drawn to the river; Lizzie Hexam and her father, Gaffer, make their living from the river, as indeed does Rogue Riderhood, and of course on a larger scale the river is key to the city's commercial success. The river and money are very much connected.

Just as important, the river is a possible means of transformation, of rebirth through baptism in its waters. John Harmon and Eugene Wrayburn almost lose their lives in the river but emerge from the experience changed men. Harmon comes to terms with his past, and Wrayburn survives to accept his love for Lizzie in spite of the difference in their rank in society. The river is not a force for good or evil but is seen as neutral; redemption is dependent on the protagonists' willingness to change. The villain Rogue Riderhood is run down by a steamer on the foggy Thames, as fog and water join together to test his potential for redemption. Riderhood's immersion in the water leads his daughter to hope that a changed man might emerge from this near-death experience: "If he should happily come back to resume his occupation of the empty form that lies upon the bed, his spirit will be altered."[105] But when he revives, he is shown to be "unimproved," and later he is drowned again—this time without a reprieve.[106] Just as there is hope for individual regeneration in the novel, we can also see hope for the city's redemption through immersion in the foggy sea, in a similar way to the new world created by the righteous Noah after the biblical flood. Riah is described as "ever wading through the fog," and he "waded to the doorstep of the dolls' dressmaker."[107] He will not be drowned by the fog; he does not need redemption because he embodies true moral values in his person.

London invests all its energies into money, the making of money, or the pretence of possessing money. It is in danger of destroying itself through its loss of spiritual awareness and common humanity. It will be destroyed not only by water but also by the dust which is part of fog's composition. Indeed the connection between dust and money or gold is made implicit in a number of ways in *Our Mutual Friend*. Boffin is the "golden dustman," and the Harmon fortune is based on the dustheaps which are integral to the novel's landscape. From about the sixteenth century "dust" was also a colloquial word for money. The happy resolution of the novel is indicated by the removal of the dustheaps to realise their monetary value so that John and Bella Harmon can circulate the money within society in a positive way. Fog is the product of an accumulation of dust and waste in the air; it reveals what happens when nothing is done about the root causes of pollution.

On a metaphorical level the novel shows the city being suffocated because of its emphasis on commerce, rather than on Christian values of charity and neighbourliness. The buildings try to keep their heads above the "foggy sea," above which "the great dome of Saint Paul's seemed to die hard."[108] Many Victorians saw St. Paul's Cathedral and especially the dome as a comforting and continuing symbol of the nation's religious and moral state. Its presence was a visual signifier of London, a symbol of continuity with the city's past and of an enduring religious presence. Fog was its enemy in a metaphorical as well as a literal sense, not only blackening, pitting, and scarring its external surfaces but frequently obscuring it from view. The fact that St. Paul's was often viewed through a haze of smoke or fog revealed to many people the lack of religious feeling amongst the populace. It seemed to symbolise a growing disregard for religion, especially a religion that appeared hazy or meaningless in their everyday lives. For example the American writer Nathaniel Hawthorne observed St. Paul's disappearing behind the smoke in 1857, re-

Figure 2.10 George Vicat Cole exhibited *The Pool of London* in 1888. Prime Minister William Ewart Gladstone wrote on 25 January 1894 to Robert Chignell that he remembered: "The picture seemed to speak and to say: 'You see here the summit of the commerce of all the world.'" This painting separates smoke from fog: the failure to make a connection between the two suggests why measures to clean up London's air came to nothing. Presented by the Trustees of the Chantrey Bequest 1888. © Trustees of the Tate Gallery, London 2015.

flecting that the dome might have been made of that very vapour which hid it from view:

> When I reached Saint Paul's, the sunny intermixture . . . was at its minimum, so that the smoke-cloud really grew black about the dome and pinnacles, and the statues of Saints looked down dimly from their standpoints on high, faintest, as spiritual consolations are apt to be, when the world was darkest. . . . The whole vast Cathedral had utterly vanished, leaving "not a wrack behind";—unless those thick, dark vapours were the elements of which it had been composed, and into which it had again dissolved. It is good to think, nevertheless (and I gladly accept the analogy and the moral) that the Cathedral was really there, and as substantial as ever, though these earthly mists had hidden it from mortal eyes.[109]

Dickens's earlier novel *The Old Curiosity Shop* (1841) describes a similar sight: Nell and her grandfather, escaping from London, reach a hill on the outskirts of the city: "On top of that the traveller might stop, and—looking back at old Saint Paul's looming through the smoke, [see] its cross peeping above the cloud (if the day were clear) and glittering in the sun."[110] Here the cross is a sign of hope, although hope is not given to Nell and her grandfather in this context: it is an anonymous "traveller" who might look back and not the "escapees."

However, in *Our Mutual Friend* the spiritually corrupt city threatens the death of its most potent religious symbol, which "seemed to die hard." St. Paul's is drowning, experiencing the fate of many of the characters in this novel. Yet Dickens does leave some room for hope for the city, for regeneration by improved relationships among individuals.[111] In *Our Mutual Friend* the scene which takes place on the roof of Pubsey & Co. fulfils this function. Pubsey & Co. is owned by Fledgeby, one of the villains of the novel. Riah, who works for him, allows Lizzie Hexam and her friend Jenny Wren, a disabled girl who works as a dolls' dressmaker, to rest in the roof garden he has created. Lizzie is trying to improve her reading with Jenny's help. The absence of anything grand is emphasised by the description of the "common basket of common fruit" that rests near the women. In addition "a few boxes of humble flowers and evergreens completed the garden." Yet, although it is apparently a humble and simple scene of slight interest, the description that follows illustrates the tension between this almost pastoral scene and the city: "the encompassing wilderness of dowager old chimneys twirled their cowls and fluttered their smoke, rather as if they were bridling, and fanning themselves, and looking on in a state of airy surprise."[112] The ordered nature of the roof garden turns the surrounding chimneys into a "wilderness." The term "wilderness," usually associated with the natural world, here becomes associated with the unnatural smoke-producing chimneys, which are likened to emblems of a decaying class—"dowagers." This is a haven that appears to be secure from the smoke of the city, even from the interruption by Fledgeby, who cannot appreciate its quiet and air when Jenny points it out. "'The quiet!' repeated Fledgeby, with a contemptuous turn of his head towards the City's roar. 'And the air!' with a 'Poof!' at the smoke." Jenny continues: "But it's so high. And you see the clouds rushing on above the narrow streets, not minding them, and you see the golden arrows pointing at the mountains in the sky from which the wind comes, and you feel as if you were dead."[113]

NOBODY THAT KNOWS THEM COULD DOUBT THE RESPECTABILITY OF THESE TWO GENTLEMEN, YET YOU WOULD HARDLY CREDIT THE UNNECESSARY PANIC THEIR IMAGINATIONS CAUSED THEM THE OTHER NIGHT IN THE FOG !

Figure 2.11 "Nobody That Knows Them Could Doubt the Respectability." This *Punch* cartoon shows the extent to which London fog could transform any innocent image, even of two respectable gentlemen, into something much more terrifying. (*Punch,* 19 February 1870, p. 72). Courtesy of the President and Fellows of Wolfson College, Cambridge.

Reading this scene in conjunction with a later foggy scene, also centred on Saint Mary Axe, illustrates how tightly knit the novel is. In the former scene the smoke is denied access to the humble paradise created above street level; in the latter Riah comes out of the door of the same building but this time at street level, goes "into the fog, and was lost to the eyes of Saint Mary Axe. . . . Thither he went at his grave and measured pace, staff in hand, skirt at heel; and more than one head, turning to look back at his venerable figure already lost in the mist, supposed it to be some ordinary figure indistinctly seen, which fancy and the fog had worked into that passing likeness."[114] Riah is worthy to enter heaven because of his goodness, but the fog, a polluting by-product of the city that represents London in all its negative aspects, confuses passersby into believing that Riah is an ordinary citizen. Dickens here uses the fact that fog was often infamous for changing the appearance of reality, not only dissolving it into seemingly formless states but also playing visual tricks. Appearances deceive. Fledgeby is using the venerable Jew as a front for his business, so that he avoids being seen as avaricious and inhuman. This is easier because people's "fancy" presumes that Riah, because he is Jewish, will display these negative qualities himself. Later Fledgeby himself departs into the fog, but first he changes from his "Turkish garments" to "invest himself with Christian attire."[115] The seeming Christian does, in reality, act the pagan. And just in case we have missed the point, "The murky fog closed about him and shut him up in his sooty embrace. If it had never let him out any more, the world would have had no irreparable loss, but could have easily replaced him from its stock on hand."[116] Whereas Jenny, Lizzie, and Riah seem protected from the smoke on the pastoral island of the rooftop, Fledgeby is seized by the fog, a symbol of the city, and embraced as if they are one. How different this fog is from the one described in *The Old Curiosity Shop!* In the earlier novel the natural fog envelops and helps destroy the evil Quilp. Here the polluted fog of the city embraces the villainous Fledgeby as one of its own.

V

Many critics have discussed Dickens's increasingly pessimistic view of London in relationship with his use of fog as a metaphor: "The barrier of pollution that insulates the metropolis from nature is dense with the ominous idea [of] an irreversible catastrophe for human existence."[117] In fact even in the later novels signs of hope can still be glimpsed through the fog, reflecting the ambivalence that Dickens, like other Londoners, felt towards the fog in everyday life. In *Our Mutual Friend* the same fog described at the beginning of the third book continues to affect London later that day. We have been told that the fog is thicker down towards the river, not an uncommon situation.[118] The running down of Rogue Riderhood by a steamer in the fog, at this point, provides an obvious comparison to the description of Quilp's death in *The Old Curiosity Shop*. In the later novel the events are narrated from the point of view of the onlookers through the fog and not from the victim's point of view. This creates a mystery as to who has been run over. Riderhood, as is obvious from his first name, is a villain and rogue, and his near-dead body is also referred to as "it," objectified in the same way as Quilp's body.[119] The fog impedes vision: "for every boat that put off sculled into the fog and was lost to view at a boat's length."[120]

Fog is obviously ultimately to blame for the accident. Fog could be seen as a murderer, even a moral executioner, acting in the cause of justice as in *The Old Curiosity Shop*. Yet the scene does not contain the horror conveyed in Quilp's death; in fact there is a good deal of humour in it: "Some man fell in with a splash, and was pulled out again with a roar of laughter."[121] A general tolerance is shown to London fog represented by the onlookers blaming not the fog but the steamer: "She was the Murderer, bound for Gallows Bay; she was the Manslaughterer, bound for Penal Settlement."[122] Even the fog seems to join the chorus of condemnation of the boat: "The whole bulk of the fog teemed with such taunts, uttered in tones of universal hoarseness."[123] The ship's lights are described in human terms by their blinking, and the steam is almost as if the ship is having to blow her nose: "Them's her lights, Miss Abbey, wot you see a-blinking yonder," and "She's a-blowing off her steam, Miss Abbey, and that's what makes the fog and the noise worse."[124]

This scene describes the feelings of confusion, indeterminacy, and tension so often brought about by London fog. Figures are "blurred," and "lights moved spectrally." Yet there is a sense of comradeship and a desire to help on the part of the Londoners down by the river. Confusion is stopped by Miss Abbey, the owner of the public house to which Riderhood is ferried, taking control of the situation and ensuring that everything is done to help the injured man. The local London community shares a collective purpose through the fog to help save Riderhood, even though, as he revives, there is a feeling that he is not worth saving. In this late novel there is still a sense of what one commentator has referred to as "a small sustaining community of the kindhearted within the urban wasteland."[125] London fog, together with one of its constituents, smoke, in Dickens's novels is often seen in opposition to nature.[126] Yet there are many instances where nature survives. *The Old Curiosity Shop* depicts a natural fog wreaking justice on the villain Quilp, that odious representative of industrialisation. The flower garden on Riah's rooftop in *Our Mutual Friend* survives in spite of the smoke and noise about it. Even in the London of *Edwin Drood*, Dickens's final, unfinished novel, there is "one of those nooks where a few smoky sparrows twitter in smoky trees, as though they called to one another, 'Let us play at country.'"[127]

For the most part Dickens uses fog as a metaphorical representation of the troubling meanings of the new urban reality of London. Its rapid growth had led to anxieties of loss of control and potential chaos. Despite the persistence of small enclaves of community spirit, offering a continuing glimmer of hope for the future, London's fog harks back to the beginning of time, with its misty swamps, as well as referring to the present confusion and disorder. The Megalosaurus is involved immediately following the mention of smoke in the opening page of *Bleak House*. A connection between the two is inevitable. Fog and smoke had become consistent and identifying elements in London life. Fog becomes an agent of confusion, as well as a symbol for it, dissolving familiar patterns of nature. By turning daytime into night, it even confuses the natural order of the day. In *Bleak House* Esther Summerson finds London strange, "the stranger from its being night in the day-time," a phenomenon which was often commented on in newspaper reports: "From an early hour of the morning and during the day the fog in the city and many other parts of London was so dense, that the gas in the various shops was kept burning, and in many private houses candles were lighted."[128] Because of this strange reversal, gaslights, in Dickens's words, are turned into strange "night creatures that had no business abroad under the sun."[129]

Often fog is seen in direct competition with the light. In *Our Mutual Friend* this competition is seen by Dickens in dramatic terms as a murderous struggle "with a sobbing gaslight in the counting-house window, and a burglarious stream of fog creeping in to strangle it through the keyhole of the main door."[130] The gaslight, a symbol of Victorian modernity, is portrayed in *Our Mutual Friend* not only as the weaker of the two but as submitting without a fight to the fog as it menacingly invades the space of the counting-house.[131] "Fascination" Fledgeby, the shadowy owner of the counting-house, squeezes as much monetary interest out of his clients as he can, in the same way that the fog is attempting to strangle the life out of the gaslight. Fledgeby is part of the novel's criticism of those elements of society who do not make good use of their money. This extends from individuals like Fledgeby and the miserly Harmon senior, whose spirit pervades the novel, up to the government, which does not do enough to alleviate the misery of the poor. The end is marked by the

TERRIFIC APPARITION

Seen during the Recent Fog at Westminster.

Figure 2.12 "Terrific Apparition." A *Punch* cartoon showing London fog's transformative potential. Even a light could create more fear than reassurance. (*Punch,* 20 March 1869, p. 109). Courtesy of the President and Fellows of Wolfson College, Cambridge.

appearance of sunlight, a reversal of the miserliness of old Harmon, as Mrs. Boffin so accurately asks: "And as if his money had turned bright again, after a long long rust in the dark, and was at last a beginning to sparkle in the sunlight?"[132] The idea of fog is deployed by Dickens increasingly over time as a vehicle of a negative view of London, yet he never entirely lets the prospect of redemption disappear from sight.

Dickens saw that just as much as fog was a part of London life, it was also a metaphor for London itself. In its indeterminacy it could be classed as fog, cloud, or mist; and this allowed him to use the image in many ways. In *The Old Curiosity Shop* the fog becomes a vehicle for revenge on the part of the natural world against the evil symbol of industry, Quilp; it is not the same oily and greasy fog of the later books but one which is natural and therefore provides an apt source of retribution. The fog described in his later novels reflects a darkening of his view of London. In *Bleak House* the fog causes the dissolution of the individual in the same way the law seeks dissolution of the individual. It is a world where all suffer from the fog but none seems connected, a world in which confusion and madness take a part and in which enlightenment is denied to those who need it. Dickens's final completed novel, *Our Mutual Friend,* reveals a city defined by its fog, but it also suggests indeterminacy in the way it divides the city between visible and invisible. Its formless nature is still one that can transform Fledgeby, the villain of the novel, into the righteous Christian, whereas Riah, the Jew, is seen only as the heathen. In *Our Mutual Friend* both animate and inanimate objects are drowning beneath the fog.

By the time Dickens came to write *Our Mutual Friend,* in the mid-1860s, London fogs were recurring at frequent intervals during the winter months, each one lasting for days or even weeks at a time. As the city continued to grow, its population to multiply, its industries to expand, and its social differentiation to grow more obvious and more extreme, fog came to stand even more starkly than in Dickens's later novels for the moral turpitude that observers began to fear was overwhelming the capital city. Many critics have noted a gradual change in Dickens's view of London as he grew older. They distinguish between the optimism of the earlier works and the pessimism of the later ones.[133] His pessimism was far from unique among contemporaries. Not long after his death, in the 1880s, public fears and anxieties about London fog's ability to heighten social tension and encourage social deviance and rebellion reached their height, as we shall now see.

CHAPTER THREE

King Fog

I

For many hundreds of years Smithfield Market, in the City of London, had served as the main centre of distribution for cattle, sheep, pigs, chickens, and other animals destined for the slaughterhouses, butchers' shops, and dinner tables of the capital. By the middle of the nineteenth century 220,000 head of cattle, one and a half million sheep, and uncounted numbers of other animals were being driven through the streets of London every year to be sold at Smithfield. Complaints about the noise, the filth, the stench, and above all the terrible cruelty with which the drovers forced the animals to stand tightly packed in the auction rings eventually led to wholesale reform. In 1868 Smithfield was reconstructed as a dead-meat distribution centre served by underground railway lines, and the livestock market was moved to the Royal Agricultural Hall in Islington, to the north of the City, constructed for this purpose earlier in the decade. At that time it was the largest exhibition hall in the world. Since livestock was now banned from the City, the Royal Smithfield Club, a society formed at the very end of the eighteenth century for the improvement of breeding in cattle, sheep, and pigs, moved its annual show to Islington as well.[1]

If the organizers thought that by doing so they would be able to escape not only the teeming humanity of the City but also its periodically awful climatic conditions, they were gravely mistaken. The annual Smithfield Club cattle show coincided in December 1873 with one of the worst fogs in living memory. A contemporary described it as "one of the thickest and most persistent of this century" so far.[2] Another tract described the city as being "enveloped in a misty shroud of almost unprecedented density."[3] Whether it began, as the commentator Georg Hartwig claimed in his book *The Aerial World: A Popular Account of the Phenomena and Life of the Atmosphere,* on December 8, 1873, or a day later, as most other commentators thought, all sources agree that this "dense black fog" continued for a week or more, until December 14.[4] "The unpleasant thickness and pungency of the fog-laden atmosphere," reported the *Daily News,* "bore heavily on the fat cattle which stood openly panting and coughing in a very distressing way."[5] Animals began to be distressed as early as the first day of the fog "and exhibited symptoms as if they had been inhaling a noxious gas."[6] By the time the show closed that evening, efforts had been made to introduce more air into the building by opening doors and ventilators. But this had no effect. It may have slightly cooled down the hall, but this would not have helped to introduce purer air, since the fog had not abated and the lack of wind would have meant that the stagnant air in the hall would not be forced out. In order to cool down the overheated hall and reduce the competition for any oxygen that still remained, the gas lamps were extinguished. Other measures included trying to damp down the dust created by the numerous visitors during the day by sprinkling water over the floor. The American writer Mark Twain (pseudonym for Samuel L. Clemens; 1835–1910), who was in England doing a reading tour, commented on the situation: "The cattle are choking & dying in the great annual Cattle Show, & today they had to take some of the poor things out & haul them around on trucks to let them breathe the outside air & save their lives. I do wish it would let up."[7] The organisers of the cattle show employed extra watchmen to keep an eye on the cattle, in conjunction with veterinary surgeons, who remained in the hall overnight to assess the situation.

Despite all this, according to the *Daily News,* the distress of the animals increased hourly: "By daybreak two had died where they lay in the Hall, and by nine o'clock the reception yard was full of the great suffering animals, panting piteously in a state closely akin to suffocation; while in the interior of the hall sobbed and panted others nearly, if not quite in as bad a state."[8] During the course of Wednesday it was reported that another animal had died in the reception yard. Several had been slaughtered before they could be removed. Two had died in the vans after permission to remove them had been granted. Others had had to be slaughtered after they had been removed elsewhere. By Thursday morning, according to the Smithfield Club's own records, ninety-one cattle had been removed at the request of their owners or agents, and, "of these, 50 were slaughtered, some died in the vans in which they were taken away, and some recovered."[9] The losses were devastating. Contemporaries coined the phrase "fog fever" to describe the epidemic of respiratory ailments and deaths among the cattle.[10] The *Daily News* had no doubt as to the cause: "That the sole ailment is suffocation is proved by an examination of the animals that have died or been slaughtered, their lungs being found gorged with black blood. No case of disease has occurred; indeed, the veterinary surgeons would much prefer an outbreak of contagious disease to the present visitation, as they would know how to cope with that, while now they are powerless."[11] Sheep and pigs did not suffer to a great extent under these conditions—possibly, as the *History of the Smithfield Club* suggests, because they "kept their heads comparatively covered in the straw, thus, as it were, filtrating the fog during respiration."[12] The saga of the 1873 Smithfield cattle show was widely reported and was one of the most sensational demonstrations of just how deadly London fog could be.

The fog took its toll on the human population as well; one commentator described how many people reported that "in the evening a choking sensation was felt in breathing."[13] The potential of the fog's deadly impact on human beings was discussed in the medical press shortly afterwards. The *Medical Times and Gazette* of that week raised the issue under the title "Killed by the Fog." The title distinguished between those people who were killed in accidents due to the lack of visibility in the fog and those who were killed because of the fog's direct impact on their health and above all on their respiratory system. The article acknowledged that spells of very cold weather were already accepted as increasing the death rates of the elderly and vulnerable. It considered that "the influence of a fog is not so apparent to those of the outer world," the general public, as it was from the statistics of the Registrar-General.[14] It cautioned people against following the age-old advice of ensuring good ventilation even in cold weather: "The extreme discomfort we have seen in some cases during the last few days has been distressing to witness, and has in some instances ended in death; but an easy death is almost preferable to the sufferings of some who yet remain, but whose condition is hopeless."[15] Other medical journals also highlighted the dangers of the foggy atmosphere. It could cause extreme discomfort to people with lung complaints or to the elderly. The *Medical Times* sympathised because to "an irritated lung the combination of cold and smoky air is particularly unbearable. Violent coughing ensues; and whilst the patient coughs he cannot breathe, and cough materially interferes, moreover, with circulation."[16] In 1886 deaths from bronchitis in London were estimated at 11,000; a week's fog such as that of December 1891 was said to have killed about 700.[17]

The *British Medical Journal* ran a series of reports from different London hospitals to assess the impact of the fog, including the usual list of accidents that had occurred because of the poor visibility. Charing Cross Hospital stated: "Persons in good health who were living in the fog suffered much bodily discomfort, and smarting of the conjunctivae was frequently accompanied by severe frontal headache. To invalids, however, and especially to those suffering from disease of the lung, the atmosphere was most distressing. . . . The death-rate amongst the in-patients suffering from heart and lung-diseases was greatly increased."[18] The publication of the Registrar-General's weekly statistics on deaths quantified in human terms the deadly impact of the fog and sparked an ironic discussion in *The Times:* "We are very glad indeed to hear that 780 Londoners above the average died the week before last of the fog. We do not want them to die, of course, but if they were to die, it is better that they should die of the fog, and so get rid at once of the superstition that the most disagreeable, inconvenient, dangerous, and spirit-depressing visitation which falls on Londoners is somehow 'good for us.' It is not good for us, any more than for cattle, but bad, as the Registrar's return shows."[19] Early in the new year, 1874, *The Times* decided to run another article on the subject (which had first appeared in *The Lancet*) to give maximum coverage to the mortality statistics published a couple of weeks previously: "The Registrar-General's weekly returns show that whereas the death-rate in London for the week ending December 6 was 23 per 1,000, in the following week, when the fog was prevailing, the rate rose to 27, and in the week afterwards the full effect of the fog is shown by the remarkable death-rate of 38 per 1,000. The deaths returned from phthisis and disease in the respiratory organs in the same weeks were 520, 764, 1,112."[20] Not surprisingly, the 1873 fog mortality gave rise to widespread concern. In particular it had a powerful impact on the young meteorologist Rollo Russell (1849–1914), third son of the former Prime Minister Lord John (later Earl) Russell and briefly, in the 1870s, guardian to the later philosopher Bertrand Russell.

A shy and retiring man, Rollo Russell, who lived on the outskirts of London, near Richmond Park, was shocked by the recurring fogs of the 1870s and set out to document their adverse effects on the lives of the city's inhabitants.[21] Published in 1880, his pamphlet London Fogs became a bestseller and acted as a powerful influence on stimulating debate. The pamphlet highlighted the higher death rates during a fog that lasted off and on for eight days in late January to early February of that year. He noted the higher-than-average number of deaths from respiratory diseases but also a sharp increase in deaths from whooping cough: "The excess of deaths in London during the three weeks was 2,994, and of these probably at least 2,000 may be ascribed to the character of the fog alone, and not to the cold."[22] Russell listed the dangers of the polluted air on the urban population and emphasized the greater threat to the population to the east of the city:

> Owing to the prevalence of westerly winds the eastern portion of the town suffers more from smoke and fog than the western, and from this and other reasons its inhabitants present an unhealthy appearance altogether unlike that of the country population. The evil effects of smoke upon health may be roughly classed as follows: Actual suffocation of healthy persons; aggravation of lung diseases, bronchitis, and nervous disorders; prostration of convalescents and others from want of fresh air; effects similar to those produced more conspicuously by dust in grinding mills, factories of textile fabrics, etc., by the constant presence of small solid particles in the air, weakening the system and shortening life; effects upon the mind and spirits, resulting frequently in a resort to alcoholic drinks, producing disease; damage to eyesight by want of light and use of gas; accidents by railway, road, and river.[23]

The "resort to alcoholic drinks" was taken up in a literary context in the 1888 novel Will It Lift? The Story of a London Fog. The novel opens in a fog so thick that the driver of the horse-drawn cab, Jarvis, is confused but not as much by the fog as "by certain inward applications that he had swallowed to 'keep the fog out.'"[24] When the hero of the novel, Gilbert Craske, calls aloud for his cab in the same thick fog, he is only greeted by a voice "that in the thick of a London fog must have been patronizing some liquid anti-fog protector to a large extent."[25] And when Gilbert, now completely lost and disoriented, bumps into a policeman, the gentleman of the law

THE FOG.

" LAUKS, MUM, IT WAS THAT THICK, SAIRY AN' I COULDN'T FIND THE WAY
TO THE PUBLIC-'OUSE ! "

Figure 3.1 "The Fog" shows the connection between drinking and London fog in a humorous way typical of *Punch*. Again a figure reminiscent of Dickens's Mrs. Gamp, as indicated by her umbrella and name, is used to make the point: Sairy Gamp was very fond of a drink herself. (*Punch*, 27 February 1869, p. 84). Courtesy of the President and Fellows of Wolfson College, Cambridge.

accuses him of "taking a drop o' something to keep the fog out."[26] The humorous tone of these descriptions is surprising since the novel was written by the Reverend J. Jackson Wray (1832–1892), who ran the Whitefield's Chapel in Tottenham Court Road. Wray was a prolific writer of novels, and all have an overt religious tone; but he appears to have accepted realistically the need to imbibe a certain amount of alcohol to keep the fog out.

Wray describes a typical London fog: "The all-pervading fog peculiar to that month of gloom . . . had settled thick and dark and heavy upon street and square . . . wrapping all things in its chill moist garments, hiding all things beneath its dense grey pall."[27] This is followed by an ironic jibe at a great city that can still produce such fogs. "It is well known that the metropolis of Great Britain is not to be equalled, much less is it to be surpassed, in the manufacture of a real downright, thorough-going article of this kind. . . . The sombre shades of night were rendered still more sombre by the dense amalgam of smoke and vapour which made of the mighty city nothing more than a huge brown blotch beneath the leaden sky."[28] Later the criticism is more overt, with "the dense amalgam of carbon, dust, and vapour which the Londoners prefer to breathe and to be half choked with, rather than to be compelled to consume their own smoke."[29]

The opening pages are set in Tottenham Court Road, an area that Wray would have known well from his work as a minister. The action begins as a woman tries to cross over the road, described as an "adventurous plunge into the deep fog-ocean." But she is knocked over by a four-wheeled cab. The cab driver is convinced that it is a young rascal playing tricks in the fog, and it is only his fare, Gilbert Craske, who insists on looking properly and finds the woman, fallen faint near to the horse. A few drops of the cabbie's liquid refreshment revive the woman. Gilbert, a bluff, cheery, middle-aged man, evidently just over from Australia, where, he informs the woman, "you never have to swim in greasy pea-soup or live in a smoky kitchen with an eternal washin' going" on."[30] He insists on taking her to her home in his cab, which is but a short journey geographically, but the fog of course ensures that it takes much longer. The reader anticipates a romance between the victim of the fog and her saviour, but when her front door is opened, it is by a "comely lady" with "silver hair" and wearing a widow's cap whom Gilbert immediately recognises as his sweetheart many years ago before he was forced through poverty to leave England and make his fortune in Australia. The widow, with her two grown-up daughters, has only recently come to London and lives in straitened circumstances. She had been forced to leave her own home in the country upon her husband's death, as their farm had been poorly managed by him when alive.

Gilbert has of course made a huge fortune in Australia, and the rest of the novel is largely concerned with him trying to rediscover the widow in London. The fog metaphor is repeatedly used throughout the book as the mystery continues of the widow's whereabouts. Her daughter, the victim in the fog, is suspicious of the man's attempts to locate her and unwittingly makes it more difficult for Gilbert to find her: "Little did the maiden know of the brighter day that would have dawned on her and those she loved if only the fog would lift."[31] The idea of the fog lifting as a metaphor for the mystery being cleared up is repeated several times. When Gilbert's own son decides to join his father in England from Australia, it is primarily because he thinks his father is too open hearted and will be duped: "I'm afraid that London fog he wrote about has fogged him in another fashion."[32] Later the idea is repeated as the son worries that "the girl he found in the fog, and all that happened after it, has befogged him to such an extent that he's lost his general bearings."[33]

Through many twists and turns all is resolved when Gilbert discovers the widow and her two daughters back in the village where they all grew up. He marries the widow, after having bought the farm that she had had to give up, and the two daughters are also married, one to Gilbert's own son. The other daughter has been made ill by the fog, and her health is only saved when she is able to return to the country, "drawing in a good long breath, as though she was determined to force out the last atomic particle of London smoke, and make the most of her time and opportunity—fresh air."[34] Wray's story is essentially a simple love story of two people who have lost each other over time and circumstance and who may lose each other again through the fog. It is, of course, the London fog that brings Craske to his long-lost love through her daughter's accident. Wray takes the opportunity to use the image of the fog in simple metaphorical terms but also to illustrate the tendency to drink alcohol in the fog and its impact on general health.

The fog of December 1879, it was reported, was the densest yet; and the Registrar-General of Births, Deaths and Marriages recorded a 200 percent increase in mortality during the foggy period. The *New York Times* reported that London had suffered "a week of night" as the fog "has poisoned some of our citizens to death," adding that the fog had "set pedestrians crying aloud in the streets lest they should be run over, and they have not always cried successfully."[35] Russell's warnings of 1880 reflected among other things the increase in the incidence of fog that had continued through the 1860s and 1870s. Searching old records and compiling new ones, meteorologists were able to document the increase of foggy days from the 1870s onwards. One investigation of 1892 concluded that the number of foggy days per year in London had increased from an average of thirty-six in 1871–1875 to forty-three in 1876–1880 and from fifty-five in the period 1881–1885 to sixty-three in 1886–1890.[36] Another noted that the average number of days in the year during which London had suffered from "dense fogs" (not further defined) rose from 2.4 in the decade 1811–1820 to 9.3 in the decade 1881–1890, while days of "ordinary fog" a year rose from 18.7 days in 1811–1820 to 54.8 in 1881–1890.[37] According to some estimates, fog covered the metropolis on almost one day in four in the late 1880s, meaning that most days in winter were foggy days. Smoke-polluted cloud added to the murk, and even on relatively clear days visibility was limited.[38]

But it was the 1873 fog that led to the hope that something would be done to improve the quality of the capital's atmosphere.[39] The issue had already been placed on the agenda by William Mackinnon in the 1840s, and the Smoke Nuisance Abatement Act of 1853 had introduced some important new sanctions, underlined by the incorporation of smoke-control clauses in sanitary legislation in 1858 and 1866 and the Public Health Act of 1875. These made control measures mandatory rather than permissive and had some effect on smoke produced by factories and industrial enterprises. But they in no way kept pace with the headlong expansion of the city or with the growth in emissions from domestic coal fires. By 1880, it was calculated, there were more than three and a half million fireplaces in the London conurbation. Imports of coal to the capital had increased from just under five million tons in 1862 to nearly eleven million tons twenty years later. Palmerston's legislation had been swallowed up in the huge increase of the capital's population.[40]

The last two decades of the century saw the expansion of London continue apace, particularly in the suburbs; the population of Greater London increased from just over two million in the 1830s to three million in the 1860s, four million in the 1870s, six and a half million at the turn of the century, and well over seven million by the outbreak of the First World War.[41] New suburban and underground railways were built to link the newly inhabited areas on the outskirts of the city with the centre; new industries came to the capital; the Port of London and the newly constructed docks created the largest seaport in the world. All this brought a vast increase in atmospheric pollution, as ever more factory chimneys and home fires, steam engines, merchant ships, and steam cranes belched their smoke-laden fumes into the air. London fog reached the height of its historical career in these decades, just as social commentators began to express growing anxiety about the unbridled expansion of the city, its uncontrollable growth, and the increasing social threat that, as they saw it, emanated from the conurbation's poorer districts, around the docklands and in the East End, where the poorly paid, the casually employed, and the jobless congregated in cheap tenement buildings or loitered on dingy street corners. Theft, prostitution, violence, drunkenness, and even riot and rebellion loomed over the imagination of the respectable Victorian citizen.

Fog became a symbol for the threat to the clear outlines of a hierarchical social order as it dissolved moral boundaries and replaced reassuring certainties with obscurity and doubt. The threat posed was not just a social threat, however, but also an individual one. It allowed the criminal, the deviant, and the transgressive to roam the streets unhindered and unobserved. And it placed them in a position to impose their authority on the respectable. This was particularly the case with linklighters, who proved to be the most durable visible theme of this perceived threat. Before gas lighting, linklighters, or links, would be paid to provide light through the dark streets and so avoid thieves and other criminals. These boys, or occasionally men, would carry a stick, with a rag

dipped in tar attached to the top, which could be easily lighted. It was suspected that links were often criminals themselves and would lure unsus-
pecting people into alleys, where other criminals would lie in wait. With
the coming of gas lighting to the main streets of London, there was no
more need to hire linkboys except during a London fog, when the
usual street lighting was next to useless. The anxiety concerning the position of linkboys is evident from a picture in *Punch* in 1865 (Figure 3.2).
The sketch shows two boys who feel that they are "Masters of the Situation" enough to make them behave like highwaymen, commanding the
bewhiskered gentleman to stand and deliver or suffer the consequences.
Whether they were actually of any real use was sometimes a matter for
doubt, as a sketch from an earlier issue of *Punch* illustrates (Figure 3.3).
The linkboys who appeared on the streets every time there was a fog were
generally portrayed in *Punch* and other journals as dark and smutty urchins, wielding torches that gave out as much smoke as light (Figure 3.4).

It was not only people and animals that suffered from the fog; plants
were also affected. An article that appeared in the *Gardener's Magazine* a
month after the events of December 1873 reviewed its impact. The plants
most immediately affected were orchids, which had been in healthy
bloom before but were now left "flowerless, flabby, and deficient of healthy
greenness in their leaves." The flowers that had fallen to the floor of the
greenhouse were so "mildewed and soiled as not to be worth picking up."
Camellias also suffered, but this was only evident a few days after the fog,
when their buds fell off "like a shower of green hailstones." Holly bushes
appeared unaffected by the weather. The glass covering of the green-
houses showed visible traces of the fog's impact. Inside "the light was
perceptibly dimmed by a greasy deposit" which was difficult to remove.[42]
After the 1952 smog the journal *Smokeless Air* similarly investigated the
impact on plants and argued that often the damage might not be evident
until months later. During the winter months, when fogs were most
common, the magazine pointed out that plants growing outdoors were
usually in a dormant phase: "Evergreens were, however, coated with a
thick greasy deposit of soot . . . not likely to be washed off very readily with
rain."[43] The plant's stomata were likely to be clogged with soot, and the intensity of light reaching the chlorophyll was also likely to be reduced. This
would materially affect the healthy growth of the plant in later months.

THE FOG, JANUARY 21ST., 1865.

Link-boys (Masters of the Situation). "IF YER DON'T GIVE US A SHILLIN' WE'LL SINGE YER WHISKERS!"

Figure 3.2 "The Fog, January 21st., 1865" shows the power that linklighters could wield over the most surprising people. Here they threaten a tall, powerfully built gentleman. (*Punch*, 18 February 1865, p. 72). Courtesy of the President and Fellows of Wolfson College, Cambridge.

" I'm Monarch of all I Survey!"

Figure 3.3 "I'm Monarch of All I Survey!" *Punch* again reveals the power of the linklighter. Ironically his monarchy only extends as far as the light shows through the London fog. (*Punch,* 8 November 1856, p. 182). Courtesy of the President and Fellows of Wolfson College, Cambridge.

Gardeners sought solutions to the problem of the unhealthy atmosphere by planting fog-resistant varieties, the most successful of which was the London plane tree, first recorded at the turn of the seventeenth century. The specimen that is probably the oldest in London is located at the southwest corner of Berkeley Square. The London poet Amy Levy (1861–1889) dedicated a poem to its smoke-resistant qualities:

Figure 3.4 "By Torchlight." This illustration from *Living London*, a three-volume work written by George R. Sims in 1902–1903, depicts a cocky linklighter, cigarette in mouth and hand resting in his pocket. The worried-looking woman leads her elderly husband by his scarf. He looks uncomfortable, as he is in danger of being either strangled by the scarf or suffocated by the fog. Behind are shadows of the chaos caused by the foggy conditions. © Science Museum / Science & Society Picture Library.

> Green is the plane-tree in the square,
>   The other trees are brown;
> Among her branches, in and out,
>   The city breezes play;
> The dun fog wraps her round about;
>   Above, the smoke curls gray.[44]

As this suggests, the London plane very quickly became the most popular tree in London. Its leaves are shiny, which means that any soot from the air can be easily washed off, while its bark very picturesquely peels off almost continuously, thus cleaning itself.[45] It also can withstand drought, grow in poor-quality soil, and provide good shade in the summer. The tallest London plane in London has reached 30–35 metres.

The effects of fog on nature were not lost to Rollo Russell, the first writer on London fog to combine physical with moral anxiety in its depiction. For him fog posed a spiritual threat, and he listed "moral evils" produced by these clouds of smoke-filled water vapour; the loss of sunshine caused "an increase in the use of spirituous liquors, which again lead to disease, misery, and death. The winter gloom of London is very unfavourable to sobriety."[46] The loss of the natural world, whose view was blotted out by the haze of pollution, meant to Russell the loss of "sermons from nature which humanity has need of."[47] God's influence, he thought, could be seen in the natural world and moral lessons gained from its observation, but all this was lost to those who most needed it in the man-made city of London. Drink, crime, disorder were the consequences. More generally, after the turn of Continental powers to economic protectionism in 1879 and with the growing economic competition to British industry from Germany and the United States, Britain was increasingly felt to be in a state of decline. To economic concerns were added military ones. It was not merely with respect to the huge fogs of the year that one contemporary described 1879 as "a year of continuous gloom. Cheerless weather, bad trade, unforeseen political disasters," he went on, "have made up the staple of experience in the United Kingdom, with only here and there a bright interval to relieve it."[48] Theories of hereditary degeneracy began to make their influence felt, linking urban gloom with physical and moral enfeeblement, above all of the lower classes.[49] In 1896 Laurence Binyon (1869–1943), a poet and art historian best known to posterity for his poem "For the Fallen," customarily recited on Remembrance Sunday in memory of the Allied dead of the First World War, put the association of the moral and physical degeneracy of the urban poor with London fog clearly in his verses on Deptford, just south of the river Thames in the dockland area:

> Alas! I welcome this dull mist, that drapes
> The path of the heavy sky above the street,
> Casting a phantom dimness on these shapes
> That pass, by toil disfeatured, with slow feet
> And sad mistrustful eyes; while in the mire
> Children a mockery of play repeat,
> Drearly to satisfy their starved desire.[50]

The fog has overcome natural appearances, instincts, and desires, leaving even to children the possibility of enacting only a "mockery of play."

These themes were to be repeated and enlarged upon in many different ways in the fiction of the 1880s and 1890s. Social peril, immorality, crime, and disorder were all represented in depictions of fogs which dissolved moral as well as physical boundaries. Clear contours of behavioural convention as well as the sharp lines of urban architecture were obscured. All threatened the end of a society that depended on its citizens being clear about the differences between right and wrong, order and chaos, civilization and barbarism, just as Dickens's fog caused society to regress to the primeval swamp inhabited by the Megalosaurus. As the art critic and historian John Ruskin put it in 1884, what he called "plague-winds" might express modern society's lack of honesty and moral decency, but a London particular, indeed, was a punishment from God, for in "London fog the air itself is pure, though you choose to mix up dirt with it, and choke yourself with your own nastiness."[51]

II

In the last quarter of the nineteenth century unease about the atmosphere of London and the medical consequences of these urban fogs took on a figurative form in a series of popular novellas and short stories. Their literary quality could not hope to match that of Dickens's work: this was a form of pulp fiction, only marginally better in quality than the Victorian "penny-dreadfuls" so popular at the time. But the fact that depictions of fog were now entering the realm of popular fiction shows how pervasive its influence had become. The first of these novellas appeared in 1880 and was written by William Delisle Hay, a popular writer and sometime Fellow of the Royal Geographical Society. Little is known about Hay; he was born in the early 1850s (sources differ as to exactly when), but his date of death is unknown. He was a pioneer of science fiction and novels of the future, of which his best known, or most notorious, was *Three Hundred Years Hence* (1881), a racist fantasy in which the white race saves the earth by killing off all the other races on it. *The Doom of the Great City; Being the Narrative of a Survivor, Written A.D. 1942* (1880), purports to recall events which the author imagines taking place in February 1882, two years after the actual publication of the novella, from the perspective of sixty years after the narrator's involvement.

The Doom of the Great City tells of a major black smoke-fog that had lasted since Christmas and destroyed all life in the capital on the fateful day of the narrator's birthday. By setting the disaster shortly after the date of writing, the author gave his story a contemporary resonance and lent it a prophetic quality. It was written as a warning of a possible impending ecological disaster brought about by the dirty atmosphere and constituted a hyperbolically imaginative response to the medical and scientific literature of the time which warned of the dangers of the smoky atmosphere. Hay's story took much further Dickens's increasing pessimism about the urban environment, especially of London, and reflected a widespread feeling that such cities were growing too rapidly at the expense of a supposedly more idyllic rural lifestyle. City dwellers were not only physically unable to compete with their country counterparts; they were becoming morally incapable as well.

The survivor in Hay's story recounts his narrative from his exile in New Zealand, having fled from the horrors of the events he is about to recount. He describes his own rural idyll, as a loving grandfather celebrating his birthday, surrounded by his numerous family, "turning the assemblage to a profit" by picking peaches and oranges to send to the market. This is in contrast to the London of his youth, where "the monotonous drudgery of . . . City life" is likened "to the 'hard labour' of a prison."[52] In his youth, he says, he was compelled to leave university and move to London in order to earn a living after his father's death. Supporting his mother and sister, who had also been forced out of his father's country rectory, the narrator has an intense loathing of London and chafes under the newly imposed hardships of city life. This reflects the author's own experience. In his autobiographical book on New Zealand, published in 1882, Hay narrates how he had gone there as an immigrant but had been forced to return to London: "Not until a few days before I left its shores had I any other idea but that the rest of my life was destined to be that of a colonist. . . . Circumstances, which have nothing to do with this chronicle, caused me to lay down axe and spade, and eventually to become a spoiler of paper instead of a bushman."[53] Hay's evident hatred of London and obvious hankering after country life may well have been the products of this disappointment. New Zealand, as the title of his book suggested, was for him a "Brighter Britain," with British civilization rebuilt in a natural world far removed from the foggy atmosphere of the mother country's capital city.

In *The Doom of the Great City* the narrator's highly critical description of London centres on its "murky atmosphere, the dingy gloom."[54] Over the previous weeks before the disaster "London had been stifled in a fog of varying density."[55] The writer wonders whether "anyone ever attempted to write a history of London fogs, their gradual rise and progress, or gradual increase in duration and density up to their terrific culmination." He proffers the standard historical and scientific description of the fog used by many writers and journalists of this time. Mist is a natural weather condition of London "especially in those districts lying near to the river, or to localities that had originally been marshes." But the natural mists have been corrupted, "supercharged with coal smoke, with minute carbonaceous particles, 'grits' and 'smuts' with certain heavy gases, and with a vast number of other impurities."[56]

The dirty atmosphere, as well as being uncomfortable and dangerous to health, is not merely a physical phenomenon. It also provides a veil through which the narrator sees "the odious colours of the evil that lies hidden behind the awful pall": "Sadly, solemnly, grievingly, I must repeat—the old metropolis of England harboured Vice and Sin as its dearest, most cherished inhabitants. Evil!"[57] This evil extends to all walks of life, from corruption in the law and business to sexual promiscuity and the increase of prostitution: "Among the higher ranks of society immorality was so common as to excite but small attention. . . . Down through the middle class filtered every evil of aristocratic birth, losing nothing in the process . . . while up from the lowest depths there constantly arose a stream of grosser, fouler moral putrescence, which it would be a libel on the brutes to term merely bestiality."[58] The immoral and depraved deeds of Londoners are enacted under the darkness of the foggy day in which "garotters, burglars, and all the guilds of open crime revelled in contented impurity."[59] The narrator, newly arrived from the country, a first-generation Londoner and an unwilling city dweller, is appalled by the low standard of London's morals and the high level of corruption in all sections of London life. Here fog is a metaphor for lack of moral clarity, the inability to draw visible boundaries between good and evil, honesty and corruption, chastity and vice.

The fog brings moral retribution, like a biblical plague. When the narrator leaves London for Dulwich to stay with friends on his birthday, their discussion is centred on an as-yet-unconfirmed story that people have been "choked with the fog; regularly strangled and killed outright" in Bermondsey.[60] The story provokes a debate between the narrator and his host, Mr. Forrester, and his host's physician son, Wilton. The narrator, invigorated by the cleaner air of Dulwich, becomes more optimistic:

> It began by my observing that I could not understand how the fog—however bad it might be—could become sufficiently thick or poisonous as to destroy life. Moreover, we had been accustomed, more or less, to London fogs ever since London existed, and I had never heard that people had been killed by them in that way before. . . . My argument therefore was, that as the fogs had not before been found directly hostile to life, it was to be presumed they were not so now, since no distinctly new element had been imported into them. . . . I was inclined to take the usual Londoner's view, and to scoff at the idea of a time-honoured nuisance turning out an actual danger.[61]

The elder Forrester points out the "clear evidence that the fog injured health, even to the point of proving very quickly fatal to old people, and to those who were suffering from chest complaints or pulmonary weakness of any kind. . . . The statistics of the death-rate showed this to be so

Figure 3.5 "London Sketches—A November Fog," illustrating the role of the linklighters and the way in which criminals made use of the fog (see specifically the pickpocket on the right-hand side of the picture). Chaos abounds as people and carriages threaten to crash into each other and objects like an umbrella are dropped on the ground. The article accompanying this rejects November as the month of fogs as "we have seen denser specimens in December, January, and even in February." (*Graphic*, 9 November 1872, p. 437, p. 431). Reproduced by kind permission of the Syndics of Cambridge University Library.

beyond dispute." Even though the narrator's host accepts these statistics, along with the possibility that an "intensification of the fog would tend to the detriment of human life," he cannot believe that the fog has caused the deaths rumoured in Bermondsey.[62]

It is left to the physician and scientist, Wilton Forrester, to explain scientifically how death might occur. He remembers a case, two years previously, of a cabman who had mysteriously died. The cause was felt to be too much drink, leading him to fall off his cab. In fact a postmortem examination showed that "the cause of death was evident from the state of the lungs and air-passages, which were highly congested. The bronchi and tubes ramifying from them were clogged with black, grimy mucus, and death had evidently resulted from a sudden spasm, which would produce

suffocation, as the lungs would not have the power in their clogged condition of making a sufficiently forcible expiratory effort to get rid of the
accumulated filth that was the instrument of death."[63] People could choke
to death because of the amount of detritus inhaled through breathing in
the dirty fog. The postmortem results echoed those found in the exami-
nations of the dead cattle after the Smithfield cattle show of 1873. But the
black mucus is also a sign of the internal corruption at the heart of man.
Just as the fog provides a veil for society's immorality, so it begins to in-
fect people both morally and physically.

The men's fear of the fog becomes reality the following morning when
they set out to discover why the postman has not arrived. When they
reach the main street in Dulwich, they are greeted by the sights and
sounds of a panic-stricken crowd. London has been cut off "by an impenetrable wall of fog," and the borders between the healthier suburban districts and the deadly "Great City" take on the physical dimensions of an
actual wall.[64] It is almost as if the city has placed itself in quarantine. This
is similar to the way Dickens describes the fog as a series of differently
coloured borders as it gets closer to London in *Our Mutual Friend*. The city
has in fact become a real as well as a metaphorical prison.[65] There is a
sense that life is being destroyed in London as an act of purification. This
outcome has indeed been foreseen by "men who dared to think for themselves, who looked for the coming of some social cataclysm, and who
were heard to compare the 'Great City' to those Cities of the Plain that
the old Biblical legend tells of as being destroyed by fire from heaven."[66]
It is of course not fire that destroys London, as it had Sodom and Go-
morrah, but its opposite elements—water trapped in air—in other words
fog. People and classes could behave corruptly and wickedly because they
were hidden from view by the darkness of the atmosphere. Hay's fictional
fog has turned from a means of concealment into an instrument of retribution. Attempts "to penetrate the vaporous veil" and enter the city fail,
with men being forced to return, "scared and choking to speak of dead
men lying in the street whose bodies they had stumbled over, to tell of
the suffocating intensity of the dreadful fog."[67]

With all communication to the centre of London cut off and no way
of knowing the extent of the disaster or whether its contamination might
begin to move further outwards, many people panic and travel further

into the country. The narrator, fearing for his mother and sister, who have remained in London, knows that he has to find them. He begins to make his way alone towards the city. His journey takes him from Dulwich to Camberwell, over Vauxhall Bridge, via the Strand to the City. London has become a heart of darkness, "a black obscurity," and the Strand is now "the very heart and home of Horror itself."[68] The dead are everywhere. Death appears to have been instantaneous. A sentry on guard outside Buckingham Palace still stands upright, seemingly still on guard duty, even though he has died at his post. The fog has affected all: rich and poor, high and low, the actors on stage in a theatre and the audience which had been enjoying the show. There are poignant contrasts—a wealthy mother and her two daughters in a splendid carriage, on their way home from a grand entertainment, have become "victims of that clammy, relentless fog" and lie not far from "two miserable little bodies in the gutter, two poor little ragged urchins, barefooted, filthy, half-naked outcasts of the stony streets, their meagre limbs cuddled round each other in a last embrace, their poor pinched faces pressed together and upturned to heaven."[69]

When the narrator finally reaches his home, a picture of domestic normality greets him—the cat on a chair, his mother and sister sitting next to each other—but they are all dead. They are not part of the corruption of the city, but they have been contaminated by the fate of all who are bound within it: "One common doom, one common sepulchre of gloomy fog, there was for the richest and the poorest, the best and the worst alike."[70] Just as Dickens makes the point that the corruption which spreads through Tom-all-Alone's in *Bleak House* affects all levels of society by showing the spread of smallpox, so Hay shows that nobody will be spared the fatal impact of the corruption of the city through fog. Corruption is a deadly force that will spread to destroy all that is good in society as well as all that is evil. The final fate of London after "the GREAT EVENT" is not detailed, and the only hint of reform is the bland statement that "the tendency of modern times has been to curtail the inordinate increase of large cities."[71] For Hay's narrator, sickened by the horror of his experience, however, living in a smaller city is not an option. He goes to New Zealand, we are informed, because it was "a virgin wilderness," although ominously he also comments that it is "now one of our most populous rural districts."[72]

The Doom of the Great City is part of an emerging late-Victorian literature condemning the unregulated growth of towns, especially that of London. It is an example of a "tale of the future," a genre which was becoming increasingly popular and included among other works of fiction Edward Bulwer-Lytton's *The Coming Race* (1871) and Richard Jefferies's *After London* (1885) and a later story that had a striking resemblance to Hay's.

III

"The Doom of London," by Robert Barr (1850–1912), published in 1892, twelve years after *The Doom of the Great City,* resembles Hay's book in more than just its title. Barr was originally born in Scotland but moved with his family to Canada when he was only four years old. Encountering London fog for the first time as an adult, he quickly felt the need to write about it, publishing "The Doom of London" in 1892. It appeared in the *Idler* magazine, of which, with Jerome K. Jerome, he was co-founder as well as contributor. A friend of Arthur Conan Doyle, Barr was described by the creator of Sherlock Holmes in 1924 as "a volcanic Anglo- or rather Scot-American, with a violent manner, a wealth of strong adjectives, and one of the kindest natures underneath it all."[73] In the March 1905 issue of the *Idler,* Barr reprinted his story, as he said, "on account of recent fogs."[74] He had overheard people talking about his "Doom of London" during one of these fogs, and this had inspired him to resurrect it. In an editorial in the same issue Barr recalled how after the original publication of his story, he had been sent the pamphlet of Hay's earlier narrative by an artist, living in Paris. In an accompanying note the artist had accused him of plagiarism. Barr admitted, "the evidence [was] so conclusive that no sane man would have taken my word against it."[75] Yet, he went on, "I had never seen the pamphlet before, nor heard of it."[76] Even if we treat this denial with the scepticism it deserves, Barr's publication and republication of "The Doom of London" still indicates that he was exploiting what was obviously a major anxiety of the day. The reception of the story also benefited from the accumulated information which was appearing in newspapers and other nonfiction sources on the subject of fog. With every new week-long pea-souper, the column inches devoted to London fog in the press grew, and the debate about its causes intensified.

Barr's short story depicted, from the vantage of the distant future, events which purportedly occurred in the last year of the nineteenth century or in other words not long after the time of writing.[77] The narrator, a survivor of a disaster which has killed millions of people in London, is encouraged to tell his story because he wishes to defend the inhabitants from twentieth-century criticism by men like Professor Mowberry of Oxford University, who "endeavours to show that . . . Londoners were so dull-witted and stupid, so incapable of improvement, so sodden in the vice of mere money-gathering, that nothing but their total extinction would have sufficed, and that, instead of being an appalling catastrophe, the doom of London was an unmixed blessing."[78] This story, like Hay's, thus has a moral dimension. But whereas Hay concedes that there are some good people in London (all of whom, however, meet a terrible end), Barr makes no exceptions. Darwinian theories of evolution had shown that in order to survive a race must continually adapt and improve. By refusing to clean up the environment, Londoners were unwilling or unable to adapt and were destined to become extinct.

Like Hay, Barr describes the origins of the fog. However, writing from an imagined, distant future, Barr finds it necessary to describe these for his readers because "fog has now been abolished both on sea and land."[79] Fog is "simply watery vapour rising from the marshy surface of the land, or from the sea, or condensed into a cloud from the saturated atmosphere."[80] This natural phenomenon is then corrupted: "London at the end of the 19th century consumed vast quantities of a soft bituminous coal for the purpose of heating rooms and of preparing food. In the morning and during the day, clouds of black smoke were poured forth from thousands of chimneys. When a mass of white vapour arose in the night these clouds of smoke fell upon the fog, pressing it down, filtering slowly through it, and adding to its density. The sun would have absorbed the fog but for the layer of smoke that lay thick above the vapour and prevented its rays reaching it."[81] The problem of atmospheric pollution is here firmly laid at the door of the householder. There is no role for industry as a polluter, reflecting a widespread belief in the 1890s that it was not responsible. Earlier in the century parliamentary legislation had emphasised the need for industry to consume its own smoke. Industrialists tried to point the finger at the domestic fire as the main polluter, but there was a continued general reluctance on the part of legislators to see household smoke as part of the problem. In 1880 another doctor opined in *The Times* that the fogs were of two descriptions, those which arose in "the atmosphere and those which came from the earth or river-generated mists. The mists were not peculiar to London; but the peculiar noxious character of London fogs was owing to the atmosphere being charged with particles of carbon which escaped combustion in domestic and other fires."[82] Yet in a meeting of the Kensington Vestry, reported in the same article, Major-General Boileau "doubted whether a London fog was smoke."[83] Until such dilemmas could be resolved, the problem would appear insoluble. Moreover, if it was thought that domestic fires were a contributory factor, it would be necessary to interfere with the family home, which was felt to be politically unacceptable.

Londoners therefore either ignored fogs or tried to put up with them in various ways. In the latter part of the nineteenth century, designers even came up with ingenious decorative windows which could fake sunlight on a foggy day using electric light. As the advertisement stated, "a powerful electric lamp is hung outside in the balcony, with a dark side to the street, and painted white inside."[84] In this way people could imagine the world was bright outside at noon, even though the fog was ensuring that it was not. Such expediencies can be found in the imaginative literature of the day as well. In George Gissing's novel *Isabel Clarendon,* published in 1886, one of the characters, Vincent Lacour, has the financial means to accept the loss of the day through the fog and notes that "with a blazing fire and drawn curtains, it was just possible to counterfeit the cheerful end of day." But even Gissing's character realises that imagining that morning was evening was not a reasonable solution for most people, and he wonders how others "go to business even such mornings as this."[85] Gissing's character shows blissful ignorance of the contribution made by his blazing fire to the fog whose effects he was attempting to mitigate; and indeed even at the time Gissing was writing, there was still public uncertainty about the main causes of London's fogs.

But a gradual change in attitudes was beginning to admit that the domestic fire might be the main polluter. An article in *The Lancet* in 1880 reflected this change of direction and viewed the problems as getting worse because of the increasing population: "There is little doubt that the nuisance is extending. As the population increases chimneys increase also, and there are now, at least, as many chimneys as persons in this over-grown town. As the smut-producing area is being increased, it is obvious that the central parts of that area are certain to be overcast whenever the wind is much short of half a gale, no matter what may be its direction."[86]

It was in this atmosphere of growing concern about air pollution that Hay and Barr wrote their stories. Barr's narrator saw the failure of people to undertake their own measures to reduce smoke emissions as evidence of a complacency so irresponsible as to be almost criminal: "In the first place, fogs were so common in London, especially in winter, that no particular attention was paid to them. They were merely looked upon as inconvenient annoyances, interrupting traffic and prejudicial to health, but I doubt if anyone thought it possible for a fog to become one vast smothering mattress pressed down upon a whole metropolis."[87] Barr's narrator was initially no more responsible than anyone else in this respect. He mocks an American who has invented a portable, personal oxygen-producing machine to promote well-being and good health. The machine is reputedly even effective on a foggy day. The inventor tries underhand methods to introduce his machine to the head of the narrator's firm, which leads to him being dismissed. Discouraged, the inventor departs, leaving his device on the narrator's desk. And the narrator describes the arrival of the fog on a Friday in November in the usual calm and accepting terms as a fog might be described in a newspaper: "The fog did not seem to have anything unusual about it. I have seen many worse fogs than that appeared to be. As day followed day, however, the atmosphere became denser and darker, caused, I suppose by the increasing volume of coal-smoke poured out upon it. The peculiarity about those seven days was the intense stillness of the air. We were, although we did not know it, under an air-proof canopy, and were slowly but surely exhausting the life-giving oxygen around us, and replacing it by poisonous carbonic acid gas."[88] In Hay's work people die by breathing polluted air. Barr ignores the science and kills them by depriving them of air of any kind.

Barr was fully aware of the lack of scientific foundation to his story; in fact it almost caused him not to publish it. He felt that for "a story of this kind, to be successful, [it] must either be built on a foundation of probability, or it must be so skilfully written that the reader forgets or ignores its lack of probability." He determined to obtain support for his thesis before publication by requesting the opinion of two eminent scientists. One of them, John Tyndall (1820–1893), wrote a letter that seemed to imply support: "As far as he could judge, such a catastrophe might happen, although the fog would need to be very dense and the weather very calm if sufficient air to keep the Londoners alive did not percolate under the edges of the coverlet, as it were." But perhaps the letter should not be taken at face value. Tyndall refused to allow Barr to publish his letter at the same time as the story was published, suggesting he had some serious anxieties about its possible reception in scientific circles. If he did, then they were certainly justified. A short time later Barr received the very opposite response from Professor Thomas H. Huxley (1825–1895), by this time a famous scientist who had made his name as a vigorous, even aggressive advocate of Darwin's theory of evolution. Barr described it as a "crusher." "It was a four-page letter, and began by saying he had read my story with much amusement. (I thought I had written a tragedy.) The great man went on to say that I would need to nail the edges of my fog down all round London and then cement it to the earth. Even if I did this he was not sure that my projected homicide would be successful. He suggested a rubber blanket instead of a fog."[89] Huxley, it may be relevant to note, had close family connections with industrialists and was a strong believer in the merits of technocracy. For him overpopulation was the chief cause of human misery. He was not inclined to give much credence to stories that portrayed industry as a cause of mass death.[90] Intimidated by these comments, Barr had resolved not to publish his story; but his co-editor, Jerome K. Jerome, had insisted that it should be printed, arguing that they "were not issuing a scientific review, but a popular monthly of fiction."[91]

The idea of London possessing distinct borders is carried further in Barr's story, making it appear as if it is now a self-contained, but airless, box. The disaster takes seven days to unfold. As with the creation of the world, the seventh day is a day of rest; in this story it reveals people who look as if they are resting but who are in fact dead from suffocation. When the narrator realises that all of the people in his firm, including his employer, are dead, it still takes him time to realise the extent of the catastrophe. Initially he thinks that the noxious vapours are local to his company, some carboys having perhaps been broken in the cellar. Only when he opens a window with the idea of getting help does the narrator realise that the pollution of the air goes further than his own office building: "The street was silent and dark in the ominously still fog, and what now froze me with horror was meeting the same deadly, stifling atmosphere that was in the rooms."[92] In desperation he picks up the American inventor's oxygen device and puts it on. It works. The portability of the oxygen machine allows the clerk mobility, and his first instinct is to follow his usual route home and go down to the Cannon Street underground station. He realises the foolishness of this action in retrospect: "He would have known that there could be no trains at Cannon Street station, for if there was not enough oxygen in the air to keep a man alive, or a gas-jet alight, there would certainly not be enough to enable an engine fire to burn, even if the engineer retained sufficient energy to attend to his task."[93]

In fact the underground tunnel provides a safe passageway into the enclosed environment of the city, and enough pure air is able to get through from its opening in Ealing to maintain some human life. The sight which greets the narrator is one of panic and confusion. The scene is set in semi-darkness: "The electric lights burned fitfully. The platform was crowded with men, who fought each other like demons, apparently for no reason, because the train was already packed as full as it could hold."[94] The Londoners' reliance on machines leads them to forget that the train needs a human being in order to work it. When a driver is found, he fights the narrator for the oxygen machine, but as he grabs it, he falls off the moving train. Fortunately the narrator no longer needs the machine to survive. The train is heading outwards from London. "A western gale had sprung up," and the forceful wind, supplied by nature, is able to disperse the fog. The narrator goes on to relate that "one hundred and sixty-seven persons were rescued from that fearful heap of dead" at Cannon Street Station; but many of them died within a couple of days of being rescued, while "others never recovered their reason."[95]

Of the people on the train most were dead, but of the two rescued alive "one, . . . his clothes torn from his back in the struggle, was sent to an asylum, where he was never able to tell who he was."[96] In Hay's story the people died off-stage; Barr shows the deadly struggle for life in the railway station directly and describes vividly the horrific way in which many people die. Londoners left alive become madmen. The narrator is the only seemingly rational person left to tell the tale. In both stories the inhabitants of London are described as degenerate. In Hay's story the degeneracy is mainly moral. In Barr's story people are generally "so dull-witted and stupid, so incapable of improvement, so sodden in the vice of mere money-gathering," that they have lost all human feeling; they have reverted to the status of animals.[97] Both authors think the only possible outcome of such moral decline is catastrophe.[98] Fog becomes a metaphor for the sickness of urban society; at its extreme it is used to portray the death of London in its entirety. Barr's character Professor Mowberry, with many others, drew comparisons between the stupidity of Londoners and the thoughtlessness of the inhabitants of Pompeii, who had been "making merry at the foot of a volcano."[99] But the eruption of a volcano is a natural phenomenon; the smoke-fog that kills so many in Barr's story is a natural phenomenon corrupted by the acts of man.

IV

The apocalyptic moral pessimism of Hay and Barr paralleled a rapidly growing discourse of social conflict and tension in the 1880s and early 1890s. These years saw repeated attacks by Irish Fenians and Continental anarchists on the capital city, with the offices of the Local Government Board blown up in 1883, part of Victoria station destroyed in 1884, and attempts made to dynamite the police headquarters at Scotland Yard, again in 1884, as well as the offices of *The Times*. Books, articles, and pamphlets poured off the presses reporting on the East End as a "dark continent" and advocating wholesale clearance of its slums.[100] The anxiety reached a climax in the disturbances of February 1886, when the threat of "outcast London," the casually employed and disorderly poor who lived and worked in the London docks, took on a very real physical form. A protest meeting of the unemployed in Trafalgar Square on February 8 turned into a riot, with "roughs" overturning carriages, throwing stones through the windows of gentlemen's clubs in Pall Mall, and looting shops in South Audley Street. The next day, as a dense fog descended upon London, "roughs" gathered in Trafalgar Square again, and shops were boarded up. The housewife, Marion Sambourne, in her diary reveals the fear felt by the middle classes: "Did not go out on account of fog & afraid of riots."[101] The double danger of the fog and riots seemed to link up in people's minds. The fog thickened on February 10, and "the disorderly classes" gathered in Trafalgar Square again. A mass panic descended on the West End, with rumours flying around that 10,000 dockers were marching in, destroying property as they came. Mobs were said to be converging on the centre of the capital from Kentish Town and Whitechapel. The police forcibly dispersed crowds in Deptford and the Elephant and Castle. In Cumberland Market 2,000 people gathered in thick fog to hear a speaker who did not turn up: "Many rough-looking characters were revealed by the light of the lamps" as the police moved in to break up the crowd. Similar though less severe scares in the next two or three years contributed to a reorientation of charity and social reform efforts among the middle classes, which tried to separate the deserving poor from a "degenerate" residuum by providing them with regular employment.[102]

On January 29, 1885, a young Scottish doctor, James Cantlie, gave a widely discussed address on "degeneration amongst Londoners" at Parkes Museum of Hygiene. For him the casually employed "residue" of labour in London showed typical signs of moral degeneration amongst the city's inhabitants. The novelist Henry James also commented on the physical condition of town dwellers, especially those in London. Yet he saw "the people who bear the distinctive stamp of that physical, and mental degradation, . . . the pallid, stunted, misbegotten," as exceptions: "when such exceptions are taken the observer still notes the quantity and degree of facial finish, the firmness of type, if not always its fineness, the clearnesses and symmetries, the modelled brows and cheeks and chins, the immense contribution made to his impression, above all, by the elements of complexion and stature."[103] Much of the medical discussion centred on the impact of the foggy air on the stature and health of the Londoner. For many commentators the fog was one of numerous aspects of London life that shortened the lives of inhabitants, causing "phthisis" (tuberculosis) and other respiratory diseases and blocking natural daylight, which contributed to "the enfeebled vitality" and "pale faces" of the city's inhabitants.[104] In 1891 the novelist George Gissing also noted the effect of fog on mental well-being, referring to a "thick black fog [which] penetrated every corner of the house. It could be smelt and tasted. Such an atmosphere produces low-spirited languor even in the vigorous and hopeful; to those wasted by suffering it is the very reek of the bottomless pit, poisoning the soul."[105]

A year before the 1886 riots medical opinion proposed clean and fresh air as the cure for London's social ills. "He who would find the centres of decay in a nation, still on the whole robust and active, must seek for them at the points of social tension," argued an article in *The Lancet* in February 1885: "The proofs of pressure, starvation, and atrophy, of vice and of brutal reversion, and of their results are all to be found here."[106] The "means of cure" for such degeneracy were "fresh air and exercise." The writer was optimistic: "We have good hope that the national mind, recognising that there is degeneration and that it is curable, will continue to treat it with sympathy, as it has begun to do, and will direct upon it the fresh air of public discussion and the healthy exercise of a wisely corrective legislation."[107] Writers such as Hay and Barr translated into metaphor the debates about social tension characteristic of the 1880s and early 1890s; for them too clean air in a metaphorical as well as a literal sense was the solution to social conflict, just as fog brought it to a head.

For a number of other journalists and writers in the late 1880s and early 1890s too, fog appeared as a metaphorical expression for a huge social threat looming over the metropolis. The opening passage of *The Big Bow Mystery* (1891) by Israel Zangwill (1864–1926), a Jewish playwright and novelist known popularly as "the Dickens of the Ghetto," expressed this clearly: "On a memorable morning of early December, London opened its eyes on a frigid grey mist. There are mornings when King Fog masses his molecules of carbon in serried squadrons in the city, while he scatters them tenuously in the suburbs; so that your morning train may bear you from twilight to darkness. But today the enemy's maneuvering was more monotonous. From Bow even unto Hammersmith there draggled a dull, wretched vapor, like the wraith of an impecunious suicide come into a fortune immediately after the fatal deed."[108] Notable among the many military metaphors of fog as the invading king is the reference to "his molecules of carbon"; although sometimes it was the coal that took on a regal role, as in "Old King Coal," and fog was simply his imp, commonly known as "the Fog Demon." *Punch* highlighted this connection as early as 1880 with the poem " 'Old King Coal' and the Fog Demon." It begins

Figure 3.6 "'Old King Coal' and the Fog Demon." King Coal has a cup of carbonic acid by his side; the fog is detailed with the illnesses it causes, including asthma, bronchitis, phthisis, pleurisy, and catarrh. The artist is Sir John Tenniel (1820–1914), the illustrator of *Alice's Adventures in Wonderland*. Preceding the illustration is a parody of the nursery rhyme "Old King Coal was a merry old soul" demanding legislation: "Well, yes, Old King Coal *is* a jolly old soul, / And 'twill be a long time 'ere the world wags without him; / But he needs constitutional check and control." (*Punch,* 13 November 1880, pp. 222–223). Courtesy of the President and Fellows of Wolfson College, Cambridge.

with "Well, yes, Old King Coal *is* a jolly old soul" but goes on to say that "The Smoke Fiend, his comrade, 's a murderous ghoul, / With long patient London is playing Old Gooseberry."[109] An illustration accompanied the poem (Figure 3.6). Both the scientific community and the literary community were at last beginning to agree on what the populace had long known: that there was a connection between the fogs of London and the carbon emitted from its chimneys.

By this time the term "King Fog" had joined the more affectionate Dickensian terms "London particular" or "pea-souper" as a more aggressive, more masculine designation. Fog was now so frequent and so intense that it virtually ruled the city. When in 1883 George Augustus Sala (1828–1895) noted "Queen's weather!" as he went out one morning, it was purely a coinage of his own. Sala, an English journalist of Italian parentage and author, among other things, of sadomasochistic pornography (published under a pseudonym), continued with his description of the weather but seemed unclear whether "the Winter King or the Fog Fiend would be the predominate potentate."[110] "King Fog" was, however, a far more commonly used expression. In 1888 *Punch* heralded the arrival of "KING FOG, who paid his first state visit of the season to his own capital": "The royal progress was celebrated by grand fantasias on A Thousand Respiratory Organs, Baron BRONCHITIS was out with his Bandannas borne by four hoarse-men . . . and in the train of KING FOG followed the celebrated General DEPRESSION, with deputations from the various states of Ill-health and Indi-gestion. The rear was brought up by bands of Roughs, Burglars, and Policemen at a respectful distance."[111] An illustration on the following page echoes again the nursery rhyme theme of "Old King Coal is a merry old soul" but this time it is to do with the possibility of finding coal under London. Science is warned of making this discovery as "if they find him [Old King Coal] under London" it will lead to "the plague and the pother, Oh! The shindy and the smother."[112]

Another article in *Punch* the same year was headed, "In the Days of King Fog." It referred to a foggy spell that lasted from January 9 to 13 of 1888 and was accompanied by an illustration (Figure 3.7). People, it noted, were coughing and spluttering; the dangers to health were palpable, not only to those suffering from bronchitis; and the fog also brought out "roughs," as it had done two years before.[113] The dangers to individual health and collective social order were now foremost in people's minds. King Fog's rule over London in the 1880s and 1890s prompted others to regard it in apocalyptic terms too. Nineteen years after Rollo Russell's first essay on London fog, the meteorologist was now striking a far more dramatic tone. In a lecture delivered to the Building Trades Exhibition in 1899, he claimed that the factory system, symbolised by the fog and smoke, had spread out and taken over the city, destroying the natural world and diminishing the influence of God in people's lives. The constant gloom and pollution were producing a race of people who were regressing, both physically and mentally. He highlighted instances in which London's gloom was actually seen in terms of the end of the world: "Occasionally we see paragraphs in the country papers portraying the alarm caused by the occurrence of intense gloom about midday at long distances from London. This happened at Farnham, for instance, two or three years ago, and it was said that several people, scared by the phenomenon, took it for

Figure 3.7 "In the Days of King Fog." Science lies powerless, cowering beneath the fog on the bottom left. Imps issue from the chimneys. This illustration is accompanied by a poem, in which King Fog boasts that he rules the land: "Give Science my defiance! there is not the least rel- / iance on one plan or one appliance she suggests. / Smoke-prevention? That's her joke, for her schemes all end / in smoke." (*Punch*, 21 January 1888, pp. 26–27). Courtesy of the President and Fellows of Wolfson College, Cambridge.

the end of the world."[114] Yet a number of writers took these themes, so crudely expressed in the sensational fiction of Hay and Barr, and turned them to more sophisticated metaphorical uses. Foremost among these was Robert Louis Stevenson (1850–1894), author of a range of enduringly popular novels including the perennial favourite children's story *Treasure Island* (1883). Stevenson knew all about respiratory problems; he suffered from them all his life. Born and educated in Scotland, he arrived in London at the end of October 1873, on his way to overwinter in the south of France, where he recuperated before returning to London the following spring. He was thus fortunate to miss the great fog of December 1873 by a few weeks. Constantly travelling in search of a healthy climate, he ended his days in the South Pacific, dying in Samoa in 1894. Despite the fact that he spent relatively little time in London, however, Stevenson's contribution to the literature of London fog fitted in well to the discourse of the 1880s.

V

Peter Ackroyd has described Stevenson's short novel *The Strange Case of Dr. Jekyll and Mr. Hyde* (1886) as "the greatest novel of London fog," yet on close inspection there is in fact very little fog in it, nor is fog used as a practical part of the plot, for example by concealing the murderer's actions.[115] Perhaps what makes the novel appear foggy in the reader's memory is its obsession with secrecy and concealment. The greatest secret in the novel is of course that the evil Mr. Hyde is in fact the kindly and decent medical scientist Dr. Jekyll, who has discovered how to use chemical powders to bring out a side of his personality that will be free of moral restraint and convention. Jekyll is unable to control Hyde, who becomes increasingly evil and begins to dominate his more moral side and progressively escapes Jekyll's control. The novel gains its iconic power from its depiction of the evil that is supposedly within all human beings and its constant war with humankind's better impulses.

The single significant fog in the novel does, however, play an important figurative and literary role. It follows Hyde's murder of the Member of Parliament Danvers Carew. The fog lasts from the early hours of the morning through to the evening and provides the background to a cab journey taken by the lawyer Mr. Utterson, who has been asked to

Figure 3.8 *Big Ben* (1894), by the Irish painter Rose Maynard Barton. In this aestheticizing representation the colours are softened and the world is orderly. This idea is reinforced by the seat of government, the Palace of Westminster, in the background. Private Collection / Photo © Chris Beetles Ltd, London / Bridgeman Images.

identify the body of his murdered client. The gloom which the fog creates becomes a mirror of Utterson's feelings of confusion. His thoughts are of "the gloomiest dye" as he journeys through the fog with Police Inspector Newcomen to the house that Dr. Jekyll has rented for his other persona, Mr. Hyde, who is suspected of having committed the murder.[116] Utterson suspects some strong bond between his friend Dr. Jekyll and Mr. Hyde, a bond which extends to Jekyll's having made a will in Hyde's favour. As Jekyll's lawyer, Utterson is aware of the will, but its terms seem strange to him, since it leaves the doctor's assets to Hyde in the event not only of his death but also of his disappearance. Why, Utterson wonders, should the respectable Dr. Jekyll anticipate his own disappearance? What dangerous game has he become involved in?

Nor does Utterson understand the generosity Jekyll has shown to Hyde, who is surely of recent acquaintance and whom Utterson has never met. He thinks that Hyde must be blackmailing Jekyll. He is worried that Hyde's relationship to Jekyll will be revealed, to the detriment of his friend, when Hyde is arrested for having killed Danvers Carew; this will undoubtedly have a very damaging effect on Jekyll's reputation. Utterson's concerns are such that even he feels soiled by a general sense of guilt: "when he glanced at the companion of his drive, he was conscious of some touch of that terror of the law and the law's officers which may at times assail the most honest."[117] Once the police are involved, there is no way any wrongdoing can be entirely kept quiet. The fog, in its capacity to absorb light and make one feel walled in, provides a signifier of the law closing in around Utterson and Jekyll.

Fear of disclosure is a major theme of the story. Eventually the truth is revealed in a series of letters, written by various people, which are stored in Utterson's safe, away from prying eyes. Utterson has been specifically directed not to open them until after Jekyll's death or his disappearance. This stipulation is adhered to even though Utterson at one point is desperate to "disregard the prohibition and dive at once to the bottom of these mysteries."[118] Throughout the novella a code of silence ties the professional men together. Their adherence to conventions of confidentiality is based not only on professionalism but also on a masculine belief in the virtues of keeping quiet that is practised by all the men in this very male novel. Utterson, his friend Enfield, and even Poole, the servant, all refuse to take on the role of the detective. The Police Inspector is not accepted as part of the established professional circles in which the lawyer and doctor move. His name alone, Newcomen, signifies his parvenu status. Personal and professional secrets cannot be divulged to him. For this reason Utterson will not disclose Hyde's relationship to Jekyll to the police, even though a Member of Parliament, a friend of Utterson's, has been murdered.

As Utterson and Newcomen drive along, they pass through "the first fog of the season" at "nine in the morning" in October.[119] More fogs are clearly expected. "A great chocolate-coloured pall," writes Stevenson, "lowered over heaven." This funereal image had by the 1880s become a commonplace.[120] The social investigator Henry Mayhew (1812–1887), founder and sometime editor of *Punch* and author of *London Labour and the London Poor* (1851), noted for example that London fogs "are often so dense as to require the gas to be lighted in midday, and they cover the town with a most dingy depressing pall."[121] A pall, the cloth used to cover the whole of a coffin, with a body inside, became a cliché denoting the suffocating and concealing properties of a fog.[122] Looking back on-turn-of-the century London from 1927, the author Shaw Desmond (1877–1960) similarly described "smoke-palled London," its inhabitants "pale ghosts surprised by the dawn."[123] Writers reached unthinkingly for the word "pall" as soon as they started to describe a London fog.

Stevenson's use of the word, however, is more reflective. In the context of *Dr. Jekyll and Mr. Hyde* likening the fog to a pall is singularly appropriate, since there really is a dead body, this being the morning after Carew's horrific murder. But why should the "great chocolate-coloured pall" lower *over* heaven? "Lower" does not only refer to a descent downwards but also has a secondary meaning of threatening. In Stevenson's novella heaven itself is concealed by the fog, so terrible is the crime that has been committed. In Christian terms Dr. Jekyll has interfered with the order of God's creation, and this has resulted in murder. Just as the fog transforms London, so have the chemical powders transformed Hyde. The world of *Dr. Jekyll and Mr. Hyde* is one of inversion. Daylight consists of "a marvellous number of degrees and hues of twilight; for here it would be dark like the back-end of evening; and there would be a glow of a rich, lurid brown, like the light of some strange conflagration."[124] The fog reveals to Utterson a variety of colours but also lends a sense of confusion.

Figure 3.9 *Study of Westminster Bridge* (1878), by Giuseppe De Nittis (1846–1884). De Nittis uses Westminster Bridge to divide the river Thames from the sky above it. Smoke billows out from the traffic on the bridge and the sky hangs heavy with black clouds. Two days before his death he recollected his time in London, with "those half-days spent [...] painting in the midst of the fog," in which De Nittis allegedly said cost him his health according to Edmond de Goncourt, *Diario. Memorie di vita letteraria 1851–96,* 19 August 1884, p. 323. Trans. by Dr. Bianca Gaudenzi. Mondadori Portfolio / Bridgeman Images.

The wreaths of fog are "swirling." Occasionally "the fog would be quite broken up."[125] The passage gives the reader a sense of the confusion and gloominess which Utterson is experiencing.

Occasionally the fog breaks up, as the elements war with each other: "the wind was continually charging and routing these embattled vapours."[126] It is a battle between light and dark, as the "lamps . . . had been kindled afresh to combat this mournful reinvasion of darkness."[127] In an interval of visibility Utterson sees "a dingy street, a gin palace, a low French eating-house, a shop for the retail of penny numbers and two-penny salads, many ragged children huddled in the doorways, and many women of many different nationalities passing out, key in hand, to have a morning glass."[128] In the persona of Hyde, Jekyll has allowed himself to fall very far indeed.

The prominent place of women in this low environment reflects a recurring anxiety about the nature of social decay. Patriarchal society produces its Hydes, but there is a matriarchal world too of horror and chaos. The juxtaposition of women leaving to have a drink with the ragged children abandoned huddled in doorways emphasises their dereliction of the maternal responsibility on which the Victorians were so insistent. Worse than this, they take their house keys, denying the children access to their homes and a warm refuge from the cold, wet fog. The fact that they are forsaking their responsibilities for drink makes it even more obscene. The need to pay for alcohol often meant that women resorted to prostitution. The connection between drink and streetwalking would not have been lost on the contemporary reader; nor would the meaning of Soho, where Hyde lives and which was very much associated with French prostitution.[129]

But the fog only allows a brief glimpse of this scene: "the next moment the fog settled down again upon that part, as brown as umber, and cut him off from his blackguardly surroundings."[130] It is all a stark contrast with the street in which the rear entrance to Jekyll's house is situated: "The inhabitants were all doing well, it seemed, and all emulously hoping to do better still, and laying out the surplus of their gains in coquetry; so that the shop fronts stood along that thoroughfare with an air of invitation, like rows of smiling saleswomen. [The street] with its freshly painted shutters, well-polished brasses, and general cleanliness and gaiety of note, instantly caught and pleased the eye of the passenger."[131] But fog soon shrouds this bright and airy scene too. It is denser the next day, and "even in the houses the fog began to lie thickly."[132] This presages Utterson's invasion of Jekyll's secret den, with the assistance of the butler Poole. A fire is burning in the hearth as they enter the room, and a lamp has been lit on the chimney shelf; but this does not protect Jekyll's privacy.[133]

These domestic images recur in a more comforting form in the description of Utterson's hearth on the evening of the same day as the murder, with Mr. Guest, his head clerk, his "guest" for the evening. The outside horror is not forgotten: "The fog still slept on the wing above the drowned city, where the lamps glimmered like carbuncles; and through the muffle and smother of these fallen clouds, the procession of the town's life was still rolling in through the great arteries with a sound as of a mighty wind."[134] Utterson and his guest partake of some fine wine "that had long dwelt unsunned in the foundations of his house," recalling "acids . . . long ago resolved; the imperial dye [which] had softened with time, as the colour grows richer in stained windows; and the glow of hot autumn afternoons on hillside vineyards."[135] The picture helps their imaginations "to disperse the fogs of London." Under the influence of the hearth and the wine, "insensibly the lawyer melted."[136] The good chemicals of the wine contrast with the bad chemicals used by Jekyll to transform himself and also provide a contrast with the chemically constituted fog outside. Utterson's own home seems immune from the fog, penetrated only by the sounds of the city, which are themselves muffled by the fog.

It is important for the plot that at the time of the murder of Carew the night is bright, since this gives credence to the clear view of events witnessed by a maid when she gives evidence to the police. Ironically, even though the night is bright and clear, Dr. Jekyll, when he describes the murder in a letter, recalls, "A mist dispersed."[137] This is of course a psychological mist, seen from the viewpoint of Mr. Hyde, Jekyll's evil alter ego. It is only self-preservation which causes the mist to clear: "I saw my life to be forfeit; and fled from the scene of these excesses, at once glorying and trembling."[138] Only after the murder does the real mist, in the form of the "great chocolate-coloured pall" of fog, descend to obscure events. Of course mists are used in a more conventionally metaphorical way, towards the beginning of the novel, to describe Utterson's initial ignorance of Hyde—"out of the shifting, insubstantial mists that had so long baffled his eye, there leaped up the sudden, definite presentiment of a fiend."[139] But when, after Utterson has searched for Hyde even "at night under the face of the fogged city moon," he finally meets Dr. Jekyll's evil alter ego, it is on another of those fine clear nights (like the night of the murder), so Hyde can be clearly recognized.[140] Yet although Utterson thinks he can glimpse the true Hyde out of these metaphorical mists, he does not gain the full picture. Hyde never appears out of a real fog or mist within the story. When Utterson travels through the fog with Newcomen to track Hyde down, he finds that the doctor's alter ego has disappeared.

The Strange Case of Dr. Jekyll and Mr. Hyde is above all a novella of contrast, of public and private, reason and passion, respectability and degradation. Hyde commits his crimes in public, yet Jekyll's friends, including Utterson, want to keep his disastrous experiment private once they have discovered it. Respectability, a key theme of the novella, is a public virtue, yet Hyde completely negates it. The mist of uncontrolled urges obscures Jekyll's reason when he is transmuted into Hyde and is easily dispersed by apprehension of danger; a far denser, darker fog descends on the other characters when they try to use their powers of reason to penetrate the mystery of the two men's relationship to each other. Utterson is first introduced to us as a great walker of the city. Yet when Utterson takes the cab journey through the fog with Newcomen, he seems unprepared, even shocked, at what he glimpses through it. The fog is not used in this novel to hide the murderer or his actions, but it does conceal the moral depravity of some parts of the city. Finally, there is also a personal, psychological angle to these descriptions. Stevenson uses his description of the fog to explore his own personal nightmares, which, he wrote, "haunted, for instance, by nothing more definite than a certain hue of brown."[141] This would then take on the form of nightmarish "Brownies," the depressions which caused his periodic breakdowns and had contributed to his leaving for France in 1873.[142]

VI

Stevenson's *The Strange Case of Dr. Jekyll and Mr. Hyde* is ostensibly about a single individual, but the Soho scenes make it clear that there is a wider process of moral decay at work in the capital. In this sense the novel is part of a wider discourse characteristic of the decade in which it was written. In his semi-fictionalised autobiography, *The Private Papers of Henry Ryecroft*, George Gissing described the following picture: "After a sleepless night, I fell into a torpor, which held me unconscious for an hour or two. Hideous cries aroused me: sitting up in the dark, I heard men going along the street, roaring news of a hanging that had just taken place. 'Execution of Mrs.'—I forget the name of the murderess. 'Scene on the Scaffold!' It was a little after nine o'clock; the enterprising paper had promptly got out its gibbet edition. A morning of mid-winter, roofs and ways covered with soot-grimed snow under the ghastly fog-pall; and, whilst I lay there in my bed, that woman had been led out and hanged—hanged. I thought with horror of the possibility that I might sicken and die in that wilderness of houses, nothing above me but a 'foul and pestilent congregation of vapours.'"[143] This is based on Gissing's own memory of the

Figure 3.10 "November Mourning!," by William Luker. The link is made directly between London fog and death in this punningly titled illustration. This is from the popular book *London City* (1891), by W. J. Loftie. Reproduced by kind permission of the Syndics of Cambridge University Library.

execution of the murderess Mrs. Mary Pearcey on the morning of 23 December 1890.

A sketch by William Luker (1867–1951) the following year, titled "November Mourning!," makes the connection between fog and death in a very direct way (Figure 3.10). The title suggests that the horse is drawing a hearse; it has to be led by a man with a flare because it cannot see where it is going, and the lamps are of no use. The blinkers that the horse is wearing cannot make things any easier for it. The other man in the picture can advance only by gingerly using a stick like a blind man to feel his way; he may even be blind himself. The whole scene seems to be enveloped in a canopy of black. For many London fog was associated with suicide: "A LONDON Fog, 'tis always here/At this inclement time of year!/ When people hang themselves or drown."[144]

The association of fog with death was not accidental. The fog of 1873 provided seemingly irrefutable evidence that it could kill not just animals but people. Moreover, by the 1880s a metaphorical relationship between social conflict and fog became apparent—a fear that the most brutal members of the residuum could spread across London, moving from east to west, like the fog, to upset the social balance and wreak havoc and destruction. In the West End disturbances of 1886, indeed, this threat for a time became a reality, further stoking the fires of social tension and anxiety. But the threat posed by fog had a more specific target than society as a whole, and that was women, as we shall now see.

CHAPTER FOUR

Women in Danger

I

On Friday, October 12, 1888, the *Daily Telegraph* reported on the closure of the stage version of *Dr. Jekyll and Mr. Hyde*. It made explicit a connection between the closure and the recent "Jack the Ripper" murders: "Mr. Richard Mansfield has determined to abandon the 'Creepy Drama,' evidently beloved in America, in favour of wholesome comedy. The murderous Hyde will peer round the drawing-room windows and leap at his victim's throat for the last time during the forthcoming week. . . . Experience has taught this clever young actor that there is no taste in London just now for horrors on the stage. There is quite sufficient to make us shudder out of doors."[1] Fact and fiction were beginning to merge in the public's mind. The Whitechapel murders that took place between the months of August and November 1888 became inextricably linked to the stage version of the story, to the point where an American newspaper claimed that "the Whitechapel murders are the result of a case in real life of 'Dr. Jekyll and Mr. Hyde.'"[2] Richard Mansfield (1857–1907), an actor-manager best known for his Shakespearean roles, opened in the dual roles of Jekyll and Hyde at the Lyceum Theatre, London, on Saturday, August 4, 1888. As a homage to the impact of the murders on the East End, and possibly to the play, Mansfield gave the final performance in aid of the homeless of the East End. Its only lasting legacy for its actor was that he was to be named by some later Ripperologists as one of the possible suspects in the real murder case, since he was accused by letter of having committed the murder at the time.

The Ripper murders were never solved, though there has been persistent and often ingenious speculation about the killer's identity ever since. The most successful account of the Ripper murders before the First World War was fictional: *The Lodger,* written in 1911 by Marie Belloc Lowndes (1868–1947), the daughter of a French lawyer, Louis Belloc, and

Figure 4.1a The actor Ivor Novello in a still from Alfred Hitchcock's early silent movie *The Lodger: A Story of the London Fog,* released in 1927. It was adapted from the novel of the same name, by Marie Belloc Lowndes, which was also filmed on four further occasions. Novello's casting meant that the role had to be rewritten so there would be no doubt of his innocence—a major difference from the novel. Gainsborough Pictures / ITV Global Entertainment Ltd.

Bessie Rayner Parkes, the campaigner for women's rights.[3] Her brother was the well-known writer Hilaire Belloc. *The Lodger* was the best-selling title of all her more than sixty books. It has been in print since its publication and has been turned into a play, an opera, and several movies—one film version being an early Alfred Hitchcock silent movie, starring Ivor Novello (see Figures 4.1a and b). *The Lodger* began life as a short story in *McClure's Magazine* and was then published, two years later, as a novel. Lowndes had become a journalist in the late 1880s, writing for, amongst others, the *Pall Mall Gazette,* at that time under the editorship of W. T. Stead (1849–1912), a champion of equal opportunities for women. Stead had taken the lead in reporting the Whitechapel murders in the press. He compiled and summarised accounts of the murders from the morning papers and represented them in his evening paper with a few twists of his own. Lowndes's proximity to Stead at this time may have sown the seeds for *The Lodger.*

Figure 4.1b Title screen from *The Lodger*. Gainsborough Pictures / ITV Global Entertainment Ltd.

The story centres on a respectable landlady, Mrs. Bunting, who begins to suspect that her lodger is a serial murderer known as "The Avenger." "The Avenger," the author notes, "comprises in his own person the peculiarities of Jekyll and Hyde, Mr Louis Stevenson's now famous hero."[4] The effect of Bunting's growing suspicions and what she might do with them creates the dramatic tension within the novel. The novel opens on a day described as "so cold, so foggy, so-so drizzly." The "fog-laden, drizzling atmosphere of the Marylebone Road" is securely shut out by a pair of "red damask curtains."[5] The curtains have a double function: they keep out the bad weather both physically and visually, but they also guard the room from the gaze of strangers. The Buntings want to retain the façade of being comfortably off, though their "carefully-banked-up fire" makes it clear they are not.[6]

The boundary that the Buntings try to erect between public and private is breached, in the course of the novel, in several ways. Most obviously, the couple needs to take in a paying guest so their privacy will not be invaded in a more violent way by the bailiffs because they cannot pay their bills. Their sense of being intruded upon becomes even more acute with their growing certainty that the lodger is the murderer. In Mrs. Bunting's mind, though, he only takes on the attributes of The Avenger when he is out of her sight; when they are in the same room, he becomes a gentleman again—Hyde gives way to Jekyll. By moving the murders closer to the Buntings' home in the West End—the Ripper murders took place in the poorest parts of East London—Belloc Lowndes increases the contrast between safe domestic space and the dangers outside. The contrast is present too in her repeated metaphorical use of fog. Nearly all the murders that take place within the novel (four have already occurred before it begins) are committed on foggy nights; only the final murder does not. The connection is underlined by a letter in the correspondence column of a newspaper, speculating that the murderer might be a middle-class gentleman: "On foggy nights, once the quiet household is plunged in sleep, he creeps out of the house." The fog obstructs the police force's view; their hunt for the killer is likened to "a game of blind man's buff, in which the detective has his . . . eyes bandaged."[7]

This is a reference to a cartoon in *Punch* at the time of the actual Jack the Ripper murders in which a policeman's sight is obstructed, not by fog but by a blindfold representing his ignorance and lack of progress. The cartoonist, Sir John Tenniel, shows the policeman surrounded by degenerate, simian representatives of the underclass, throwbacks to an earlier stage of human evolution, much as Mr. Hyde is depicted by Stevenson or as criminals were supposed to be in the influential system of criminology developed by Cesare Lombroso in the 1870s. Just as the police were widely regarded as ineffectual during the real Ripper murders, so too the detective in Belloc Lowndes's story, Joe Chandler, the only official member of the police force represented within the novel, never questions the appearance of the lodger in the house. It is ironic that Chandler, whose name represents candles, should contribute so little to the illumination of the mystery. The lodger himself goes by the name of "Sleuth," though he is a major suspect. The true detective in the novel is Mrs. Bunting. She ferrets out clues—such as the whereabouts of Sleuth's holdall—and matches the timing of the murders with Sleuth's walks in the fog. But she does this only to try to ease her anxiety, to try to establish that he is not the murderer. Even when she does suspect him, she makes it quite plain that she will never tell the police. She even keeps her suspicions from her husband throughout most of the novel.

The reader of the novel is led by the author to suspect that the lodger is the murderer long before Mrs. Bunting does. Her suspicions of Sleuth are only aroused when she observes his "funny habit . . . of going out for a walk after midnight in weather so cold and foggy." The fifth murder, which takes place after the lodger has come to stay, takes place on a night with such an "awful fog" that the murderer can hardly be seen. He is described as just "a tall, thin shadow of a man—with a bag." Mrs. Bunting's view of the unknown Avenger is similarly indeterminate: "[She] always visioned The Avenger as a black shadow in the centre of a bright, blinding light—but the shadow had no form or definite substance. Sometimes he looked like one thing, sometimes like another."[8] Dramatic tension occurs one afternoon, when "a yellow pall of fog had suddenly descended on London." By this time Mrs. Bunting has begun to sense a connection between the London fog, the brutal acts of The Avenger, and the lodger, Mr. Sleuth (see Figure 4.2). When Sleuth indicates that he is going out in the fog that same afternoon, she tries to prevent him: "She moved back, still holding the tray, and stood between the door and her lodger, as if she meant to bar his way—to erect between Mr Sleuth and the dark, foggy world outside a living barrier." Mrs. Bunting wants to perform the same function as the red damask curtains in order to keep Sleuth safe within her home. When the lodger notes the sudden lifting of the fog—"rolling off in that sudden, mysterious way in which local fogs sometimes do lift in London"—there is "no relief in his voice, rather was there disappointment and dread," which rouses the suspicions of Mrs. Bunting, and the reader, still further.[9]

Yet Mrs. Bunting is determined to keep quiet, pushing sympathy for the victims out of her mind when she returns home from an inquest on one of them: "Her spirit suddenly lightened. The narrow, drab-coloured little house . . . looked as if it could, aye, and would, keep any secret closely hidden. . . . For a moment, at any rate, The Avenger's victims receded from her mind. She thought of them no more. All her thoughts were concentrated on Bunting—Bunting and Mr Sleuth."[10] As in *Dr. Jekyll* the house is the domain of secrecy. To Mrs. Bunting the idea that a gentleman like Sleuth might be a murderer is in any case too much of a contradiction.

Figure 4.2 A still from Hitchcock's movie *The Lodger: A Story of the London Fog,* showing the scene in which fog enters the hallway of Mrs. Bunting's house. This was a common problem for householders, who had to live with the dirt created by fog that entered homes and left dirty marks on white linen. This scene is directly described in the novel on which the film was based. Gainsborough Pictures / ITV Global Entertainment Ltd.

She tries to resolve it by keeping Sleuth within doors so that he will not be contaminated by the fog and become a murderer. As Mr. Bunting says, "It isn't safe for decent folk to be out in such weather."[11] Even when Mrs. Bunting thinks of the horror of The Avenger's crimes, it is always overshadowed by her lodger's genteel background: "Somehow, a great rush of pity, as well as of horror, came over Mrs Bunting's heart. He was such a—a—she searched for a word in her mind, but could only find the word 'gentle'—he was such a nice, gentle gentleman, was Mr Sleuth."[12] So it is a shock when she reads a letter to a newspaper by a reader who calls himself "Gaboriyou" that suggests the murderer may be someone who lives in West London and is, therefore, a gentleman.

One afternoon, when the Buntings' daughter, Daisy, goes for a walk with Joe Chandler, fog comes through the open door: Mrs. Bunting "found herself downstairs in the fog-laden hall, for it had drifted in as she and her husband had stood at the door seeing Daisy off." Not coincidentally, it is then that she feels "her secret suspense and trouble was becoming intolerable."[13] When Mr. Sleuth returns from his walk out into the fog, Mrs. Bunting imagines his progress—"'stealthy' she called it to herself-through the fog-filled, lamp-lit hall." Mr. Sleuth himself brings in a sort of fog into the house, creating noxious vapours with "experiments," performed in the cold room at the top of the house, which he has chosen because it has a gas ring and sink. What these experiments are never becomes clear, but the suggestion is that he is in fact burning his own clothes after each murder. Mrs. Bunting thinks one evening, "'Twas odd he chose tonight, when it was so foggy, to carry out an experiment."[14] On finding that his own gas ring is not working, Sleuth asks Mrs. Bunting for the use of her kitchen. Although she tries to stay awake to listen out for Sleuth coming downstairs to use her kitchen, she falls asleep. Later, in her bedroom, she is awakened by the "faint acrid odour" of Mr. Sleuth's experiment down below. It is "elusive, intangible, it yet seemed to encompass her and the snoring man by her side, almost as a vapour might have done."[15] When Mrs. Bunting descends to her kitchen the following morning, expecting the acrid smell to be there, "the cavernous, whitewashed room was full of fog," as the windows have been left open, presumably to rid the room of the smell.[16] The fog itself has now entered beyond the hall, into the private space of the Buntings' kitchen, in the same way that the suspected murderer has infiltrated their home as a lodger.

Mr. Bunting's surprise that the lodger has gone out in the fog brings on an affectionate lament: "We don't get the good old fogs we used to get—not what people used to call 'London particulars.'" He then recalls a former employer who loved living in London so much that she would go out in foggy weather without being afraid. Fog has become more dangerous, he implies. It has become, as in *Dr. Jekyll and Mr. Hyde,* a cloak for moral degeneracy, deviance, and murder. Fog even reduces light to a signifier of bloody violence: "She could see the lamplights on the other side of the Marylebone Road, glimmering redly."[17] When Sleuth gives Mrs. Bunting some money for the use of her kitchen, the light from the winter sun, "a scarlet ball hanging in the smoky sky, glinted in on Mr Sleuth's landlady, and threw blood-red gleams, or so it seemed to her, on to the piece of gold she was holding in her hand."[18] Mrs. Bunting's acceptance of the money and her continuing protection of Sleuth as her lodger make her an accomplice in his bloody deeds. When Mr. Sleuth eventually

Figure 4.3 "The Nemesis of Neglect," by Sir John Tenniel. This appeared shortly after the Jack the Ripper murders. The biting satire is partly aimed at "slum's foul air" as well as poor housing and other aspects of poverty. (*Punch*, 29 September 1888, p. 151). Courtesy of the President and Fellows of Wolfson College, Cambridge.

disappears, the murders abruptly cease; Mrs. Bunting acknowledges her complicity by anonymously donating the money Sleuth has left on his dressing table to the Foundling Hospital.[19]

The Ripper's five or more victims were all impoverished prostitutes living in the East End of London; the fact that the internal organs of at least three of them were removed by the murderer was what gave rise to the epithet "Jack the Ripper," along with a number of letters addressed, ostensibly by the murderer, to the police. Contemporary commentators linked the murders to poverty and deprivation in the East End. A cartoon by Sir John Tenniel (Figure 4.3) depicted the murderer as a "phantom upon the slum's foul air," a fog that kills not merely with the knife but also through the social indifference and political neglect of the middle classes, a theme much discussed in the press at least since the invasion of the West End by the dockland "roughs" of "outcast London" during the fog of February 1886. Tenniel's phantom is very similar to his Fog Demon, produced in November 1880 also for *Punch* and illustrated in Figure 3.6. Fog-bound Whitechapel was depicted in the innumerable press reports of the murders as a decaying slum, the haunt of the casually employed, of criminals and prostitutes, of foreign refugees and immigrants, much like the Soho quarter glimpsed through the fog by the hero of Stevenson's *Dr. Jekyll and Mr. Hyde*. Some contemporaries ascribed the murders to the malign influence of Whitechapel's environment, the filth and squalor of the East End creating a moral degeneracy that found its expression both in the activities of the murderer and in the profession of his victims.[20]

II

The murders committed by Jack the Ripper were not merely, as contemporaries saw them, outbursts of pure evil fastening on social misery; they were also an expression of the threat seen to face Victorian women of all classes who ventured out alone. This is referenced in a little-known novel, *Out of the Fog* (1888), by William Hardinge, published in the year of the Ripper murders. In the novel the female protagonist feels imprisoned by the fog. The possibility of a walk outside will be determined by the thickness of the fog, "and if the fog should not thicken, she might, perhaps, be able to walk the length of the street to where those great iron gates shut off the Bloomsbury Squares."[21] The fog that constrained the movement on the streets of Hardinge's heroine may be seen as a metaphor for the constrictions under which lone women existed when they appeared on the streets of the capital city (Figure 4.4).[22] Such was the level

Figure 4.4 *Fog: Ladies Crossing Piccadilly,* by Yoshio Markino, a Japanese artist who came to London specifically in order to paint its fogs, which he found fascinating, mysterious, and unique. His works reveal the beauty as well as the dangers of London fog especially to women. First published in *The Colour of London: Historic, Personal, & Local,* by W. J. Loftie, illustrated by Yoshio Markino (London: Chatto and Windus, 1907), p. 2. Author's own copy.

of social threat posed in the 1880s by working-class men on the streets of London that middle-class women could not feel safe on their own. Equally, for all the temporal and geographical specificity of the newspaper panic about "the Whitechapel murders," crimes of violence were being committed against prostitutes all over London and throughout the century.[23]

Prostitution was widely considered by the respectable middle classes and the ruling elites in Victorian England as the central vice of the age, and attempts had been made to restrict its visibility by the introduction of close police controls in the Contagious Diseases Acts. But in 1886 the Acts were repealed, following a lengthy and impassioned campaign by feminists who objected to their imposition of sanctions on the women but not on their male clients. The failure of regulation sharpened fears of social and sexual contagion as "fallen women" escaped male control. Prostitutes had been figures in many works of literature, not least in those by Charles Dickens, most notably Nancy in *Oliver Twist,* and were a familiar sight in the streets not just of the East End but of central London too. Victorian morality denied respectability to unaccompanied women walking the streets; merely to appear on one's own was to invite suspicion of immorality. At a time when women were in most respects still legally minors, unable to sign contracts or represent themselves in law, beholden to their father or, if married, their husband to act on their behalf, the absence of a male companion was a virtual impossibility for the respectable lady. If the Ripper's victims were lone women who should have been given male protection, then the implicit threat of the murders extended to all women venturing onto the streets of the capital on their own.[24]

Yet there were countercurrents emerging in the 1880s as well. The campaign that had abolished the legal and medical regulation of prostitutes had been led by women, notably Josephine Butler; women were taking a leading role in charitable activities, entering the East End as social investigators; social reformers such as Annie Besant and Beatrice Webb were making their influence felt; moral purity societies led by women were calling upon men to exercise sexual restraint.[25] In this changing and contested social and political world, novelists began to portray women making their own way, independently of men; and for Henry James as well as William Hardinge, London fog presented itself as a suitable metaphor with which to describe the process. As might be expected, however, James's metaphorical appropriations of fog were far more complex and subtle than those of the lesser-known author.

Henry James was no stranger to London fog. He came to the capital in 1876 and stayed for most of the rest of his life. Within a few weeks of his arrival he began to reflect on the city and its atmosphere. A letter written to his mother after two weeks in the city gave a far from positive picture of his surroundings: "The weather is, and has been, beyond expression vile—a drizzle of sleet upon a background of absolutely *glutinous* fog, and the deadly darkness of a London holiday brooding over all . . . to plunge into darkness, solitude and sleet, in mid-winter—to say nothing of the sooty, woolsy desolation of a London lodging—to do this, and to like this murky Babylon really all the better, is to feel one is likely to get on here."[26] His "London" essay, written twenty years later, describes the "murky modern Babylon" in much the same way.[27] Yet he saw advantages too: "Those to whom it is forbidden to sit up to work in the small hours may, between November and March, enjoy a semblance of this luxury in the morning. The weather makes a kind of sedentary midnight and muffles the possible interruptions. It is bad for the eyesight, but excellent for the image."[28] Fog dampens the sounds coming into his study from outside, and the fact that it is difficult to see beyond the pages of the book acts as a stimulus to the imagination.

Henry James could afford the oil to light the lamps and the coal to provide heat; for the less successful writer, such as George Gissing, fog had a different effect: "I think of fogs in London, fogs of murky yellow or of sheer black, such as have often made all work impossible to me, and held me, a sort of dyspeptic owl, in moping and blinking idleness. On such a day, I remember, I once found myself at an end both of coal and of lamp-oil, with no money to purchase either; all I could do was to go to bed, meaning to lie there till the sky once more became visible."[29] Gissing was in the process of writing *New Grub Street* (1891) when James's essay on London was printed in the *Century* magazine in 1888, the same year in which Hardinge's novel was published. For Gissing the act of writing was a solitary, agonising affair in which the role of a spectator was desired only in order to reveal the pain of authorship. The protagonist of *New Grub Street* is an author, Edwin Reardon, who delights at the receipt from the publishing house of six bound copies of his latest work, which "people will skim over . . . without a suspicion of what it cost the writer!"[30] For

Reardon, whose first work was published with great critical success, the act of writing subsequent pieces has become torturously difficult: "What hellish torment it was to write that page! I did it one morning when the fog was so thick that I had to light the lamp."[31] He longs to gain the form that enabled him to write his first successful novel: "How full my mind was in those days! Then I had only to look, and I *saw* something; now I strain my eyes, but can make out nothing more than nebulous grotesques."[32] Physical fog not only makes the act of writing difficult with its unnatural darkness, but it also becomes a metaphor for the inchoate formlessness of his defective imagination.

Earlier in *New Grub Street* an unwilling worker in the world of literature, Marian Yule, is forced to work in the British Museum on a foggy day. The inconvenience of the fog which intrudes into the Reading Room is both an insight into the practical disadvantages of the thick fog whilst working and the basis for two magnificent metaphors for the pain caused by the act of writing:

> The days darkened. Through November rains and fogs Marian went her usual way to the Museum, and toiled there among the other toilers. . . . One day at the end of the month she sat with books open before her, but by no effort could fix her attention upon them. It was gloomy, and one could scarcely see to read; a taste of fog grew perceptible in the warm, headachy air. Such profound discouragement possessed her . . .
>
> The fog grew thicker; she looked up at the windows beneath the dome and saw that they were a dusky yellow. Then her eye discerned an official walking along the upper gallery, and in pursuance of her grotesque humour, her mocking misery, she likened him to a black, lost soul, doomed to wander in an eternity of vain research along endless shelves. Or again, the readers who sat here at these radiating lines of desks, what were they but hapless flies caught in a huge web, its nucleus the great circle of the Catalogue? Darker, darker. From the towering wall of volumes seemed to emanate visible motes, intensifying the obscurity; in a moment the book-lined circumference of the room would be but a featureless prison-limit.[33]

For Marian the agony of writing is connected with her feeling that she is simply a machine supplying material for her father's unsuccessful works of criticism. Here too the intellectual world dissolves into formless chaos: "This huge library, growing into unwieldiness, threatening to became a

Figure 4.5 *London from the Monument, England, 1870,* by William Lionel Wyllie, addresses the modernity of the city, showing Cannon Street Station and the smoke of a train heading towards it. The Palace of Westminster disappears behind a thickening yellow haze in the background. It is both a tribute to a bustling industrial city and an acknowledgement of its polluting tendencies. Fine Art Photographic Library.

trackless desert of print."[34] Her feelings of entrapment, increased by the fog and the book-lined shelves, lead her as much as the heroine of *Out of the Fog* to a sense that she is imprisoned.

Fog, in Henry James's vision, on the other hand, not only constrained women's behaviour in public but on occasion revealed their misbehaviour: "London, in December, was livid with sleet and fog, and against this dismal background was offered me the vision of a horrible old woman in a smoky bonnet, lying prone in a puddle of whisky! She seemed to assume a kind of symbolic significance and almost frightened me away."[35] The woman seems almost a product of the fog, extruded by it onto the street. James's experiences an "attraction of repulsion" in his view of London and more especially its strange and obfuscating atmosphere, creating a con-fusion of form and blurring boundaries. London, he wrote, was a place "where the smoke and fog and the weather in general, the strangely un-defined hour of the day and season of the year, the emanations of indus-tries and the reflection of furnaces, the red gleams and blurs that may or may not be of sunset—as you never see any *source* of radiance you can't

THE FOG IS SO VERY THICK THAT FREDERICK AND CHARLES ARE OBLIGED TO SEE CLARA AND EMILY HOME.

Figure 4.6 "The Fog Is So Very Thick…" This sketch is by John Leech, a regular contributor to *Punch* and also an illustrator for a short time for Charles Dickens. The linklighters look characteristically impish and disorderly. (*Punch's Almanack* 28 [1855]). Courtesy of the President and Fellows of Wolfson College, Cambridge.

in the least tell—all hang together in a confusion, a complication, a shifting but irremovable canopy."[36]

James's attitude towards London's atmosphere had been partly conditioned by his reading of Dickens and Thackeray as a young boy. He also perused *Punch,* and he was particularly impressed by one of its main illustrators, John Leech, who, he wrote, "conveys at times the look of the London streets—the colour, the temperature, the damp blackness. He does the winter weather to perfection."[37] James dates his acquaintance with Leech's sketches from about 1850 to 1855.[38] The only example of work explicitly on fog by Leech appeared in *Punch's Almanack* of 1855 (Figure 4.6). The sketch suggests that women could not be left alone on the streets in a fog. There are threats all around. The background figure of the hirsute gentleman looming towards the two couples looks menacing and threatening. The misty outline of the horse's heads, the street lamp, the carriage driver, and a linkboy hover as if they are phantoms in midair. The maidservant holds a cloth over her mouth to block the dampness and the disagreeable taste of the foggy evening. The impish linkboy guiding the couple appears to be enjoying the scene, a sinister grin on his face which seems to reflect the malevolent leer on the face of the young man accompanying the girl in front. This is, as James wrote in another context, "like the late afternoon light of a foggy winter Sunday, when even inanimate objects have a kind of wicked look."[39]

We do not know whether James was familiar with this sketch. But the theme of women in fog occurs more than once in his fiction. In his novel *The Portrait of a Lady* (1881) he writes about a wealthy young American in Europe, Isabel Archer, and her internal struggles over whether to remain single and independent or to marry and, if the latter, whom to marry. Isabel is independently wealthy and rejects all proposals of marriage, even though she feels some attraction to the proposers. In Florence, however, Isabel meets an American widower, Gilbert Osmond, who woos her. She accepts his proposal of marriage, only to realize too late that she is victim to a Machiavellian plot engineered by Osmond and his mistress, Madame Merle, who only want her fortune.

James uses London fog as a metaphor for the heroine's state of mind. Isabel Archer has just said goodbye to her sister, Lily, and her family at Euston Station. Lily has been criticising Isabel for deciding to remain in Europe, unmarried, rather than settling down in New York. Lily for her part is puzzled by Isabel's silence regarding her private life and concludes "that she had lost her courage"—a trait connected with Isabel.[40] In fact her family's departure leaves Isabel feeling that "she had never had a keener sense of freedom, of the absolute boldness and wantonness of liberty."[41] She is not lacking in courage at all: "The world lay before her—she could do whatever she chose. There was a deep thrill in it all, but for the present her choice was tolerably discreet."[42]

Isabel's immediate choice is to walk back from the station through the fog to the hotel. James lists the reasons why this is an act of "absolute boldness" in a mock-romantic style: "The early dusk of a November afternoon had already closed in; the street lamps, in the thick, brown air, looked weak and red; our heroine was unattended and Euston Square was a long way from Piccadilly."[43] Her lack of an escort on such a long walk and under such conditions placed her in danger as a woman alone on the street. It is this boldness which she earlier proclaimed to desire when she resisted a proposal of marriage from the wealthy young Bostonian Caspar Good-wood: "I wish to choose my fate and know something of human affairs beyond what other people think it compatible with propriety to tell me."[44] In fact her walk is uneventful, and Isabel's deliberate attempt to make it more dangerous by losing her way is thwarted by a kindly policeman who gives her clear directions back to her hotel.

Yet Isabel's feeling that the world is before her as her sister's train leaves the station is an illusion because precisely at that moment her vision is diminished by the fog. She is already contemplating marriage with Gil-bert Osmond and feels she knows what her future will hold. Her cousin Ralph Touchett suggests that she "wait a little longer . . . for a little more light."[45] The fog is a metaphorical representation of this lack of light in her life, the obscurity of her emotional future. In her desire to control her fate, Isabel seeks a sense of danger; she is disappointed by her failure to find it. In her marriage to Osmond, by contrast, she senses little danger; but in the end it brings a confinement, a narrowing in of her emotional and spiritual freedom, just as fog causes the physical world to shrink round the beholder like a prison.

Isabel's feelings of liberty and boldness at Euston Station are in direct contrast to her feelings after her marriage as she returns to England. Even though the countryside on her journey through Europe is blossoming in the spring weather, Isabel sees only "strange-looking, dimly-lighted, pathless lands, in which there was no change of seasons, but only as it seemed, a perpetual dreariness of winter."[46] Whereas she had felt that she could see that "the whole world lay before her," now she undertakes this return to London "with sightless eyes." "Her mind had been given up to vagueness; she was unable to question the future."[47] Just as Ralph had warned her five years earlier that she would "be put into a cage" by her marriage, Isabel now feels that "she should never escape; she should last to the end. Then the middle years wrapped her about again and the grey curtain of her indifference closed her in."[48] The "grey curtain" reminds the reader of the foggy day at the train station and her own thoughts wander back to that day: "She remembered how she walked away from Euston, in the winter dusk, in the crowded streets, five years before. She could not have done that to-day, and the incident came before her as the deed of another person."[49] Her confidence five years earlier contrasts with her passivity at Charing Cross Station: "She asked nothing; she wished to wait. She had a sudden perception that she should be helped."[50] This is in direct contrast to her disappointment in being helped by the "obliging policeman" before: "The dusky, smoky, far-arching vault of the station, the strange, livid light, the dense, dark, pushing crowd, filled her with a nervous fear."[51]

In the conclusion of the novel the physical fog experienced by Isabel during her November walk has turned into a metaphysical sea of water; James employs both fog and water imagery, connecting them to each other with thematic strands through the novel. The final scene refers back to Isabel's walk through the fog to show her understanding and final acceptance of her situation. Ralph Touchett has died, and her close friend Henrietta Stackpole is to be married and will move to America. Caspar Goodwood, still in love with her, urges her to leave her husband. She now comprehends that "the world, in truth, had never seemed so large; it seemed to open out, all round her, to take the form of a mighty sea, where she floated in fathomless waters. She had wanted help, and here was help; it had come in a rushing torrent."[52] The false illusion of clarity which she had experienced in the fog is now replaced by the clearer "train of images" that she has heard appear to "those wrecked and under water . . . before they sink. . . . She had not known where to turn; but she knew now. There was a very straight path."[53] Her desire to be lost earlier and her willingness to be directed five years later have now been replaced by a certainty of direction to return to her husband, finally accepting the limits to which she is subjected in life. The fog had obscured the contours of conventional behaviour; now clarity had been restored.

III

"The friendly fog seems to protect and enrich," wrote James in 1888: "Then it is that I am most haunted with the London of Dickens, feel most as if it were still recoverable, still exhaling its queerness in patches perceptible to the appreciative."[54] Thinking perhaps of his novel *The Princess Casamassima*, published in 1886, James knew that any writer who wrote a social novel of London would have in some way to reference himself or be compared to Dickens. For James, as for other post-Dickensian writers, fog

Figure 4.7 "A London Fog." Another sketch of London on a foggy day, with two horse-drawn carriages about to crash into each other. The linklighter's torch shows the near collision but also seems to be frightening the horse. A man on the left holds a handkerchief to his mouth. (*Illustrated London News*, 22 December 1849, Supplement). Author's own copy.

was a key signifier of London, as he makes clear when the novel's hero fixes his "eyes on the distant atmospheric mixture that represented London."[55] In James's view the general attitude towards the atmosphere represented one's view of the city: "One doesn't test these truths every day, but they form part of the air one breathes (and welcome, says the London-hater—for there be such perverse reasoners—to the pestilent compound)."[56]

Nevertheless, fog has not been reduced to a mere cliché; on the contrary, James uses it in complex and subtle psychological ways. James saw that to a generation born in the city, London could never be seen as outsiders saw it, as an entity separate from themselves. In *The Princess Casamassima*, Millicent Henning is one of these, "a daughter of London, of the crowded streets and hustling traffic of the great city; she had drawn her health and strength from its dingy courts and foggy thoroughfares, and peopled its parks and squares and crescents with her ambitions; . . . she understood it by instinct and loved it with passion."[57] Unlike Isabel Archer, who thrills at the sensation of the crowded London streets but can only enjoy it as a "spectacle of human life," Millicent is part of the spectacle herself—lively and spirited but of humble and common origins, coarse, and lacking in refinement.[58] Millicent's friend Hyacinth Robinson, the "hero" of the novel as James often terms him, is born and brought up in London, but he has a more cerebral and artistic appreciation than Millicent does. His view is more that of a spectator: "He liked the reflection of the lamps on the wet pavements, the feeling and smell of the carboniferous London damp; the way the winter fog blurred and suffused the whole place, made it seem bigger and more crowded, produced halos and dim radiations, trickles and evaporations, on the plate of glass."[59] The blurry formlessness created by the fog is congenial to Hyacinth, who is suspended between social classes, both a denizen of London and trying socially and spiritually to move beyond its confines; its effects show that he is delighted by illusion, rather than by the realities of the world as it is.

Millicent and Hyacinth's rather strained courtship illustrates the dilemma of working-class couples who could not enjoy privacy in their own small homes and who also could not afford to go regularly to the theatre or a restaurant together: "Their conversation was condemned, for the most part, to go forward in the streets, the wintry dusky, foggy streets, which looked bigger and more numerous in their perpetual obscurity, and in which everything was covered with damp, gritty smut, an odour extremely agreeable to Miss Henning."[60] The city again appears to expand in the fog, but it also remains perpetually obscure. Even when accompanied by a man, Millicent is still imprisoned by the fog. Without doubt James is making fun of Millicent's aspirations by referring to her as Miss Henning whilst also showing her to be working class in her tastes.[61] Hyacinth is an outsider, whose personality is described in fog-like terms: "He was liable to moods in which the sense of exclusion from all that he would have liked most to enjoy in life settled upon him like a pall."[62] It is his lack of money but just as significantly his position within the working classes which excludes him from the cultured life he most desires, just as fog could, in some representations, act as a barrier.

Yet Hyacinth is no ordinary young man from the working classes. His birth is illegitimate, and he has been brought up by a poor seamstress, Amanda Pynsent ("Pinnie"), who had adopted him after his mother, Pinnie's friend, the passionate Frenchwoman Florentine Vivier, had murdered his father, an English lord. While working as a bookbinder, Hyacinth makes friends with the revolutionary Paul Muniment, who pulls him into the orbit of a revolutionary group that meets at a public house, the 'Sun and Moon' (neither of which is visible in the fog). In the early part of the novel Hyacinth wonders when the revolution is going to happen: "Hyacinth only wished that day would come; it would not be till then, he was sure, that they would all know where they were, and that the good they were striving for, blindly, obstructedly, in a kind of eternal dirty intellectual fog, would pass from the stage of crude discussion and mere sharp, tantalising desirableness into that of irresistible reality."[63] Muniment, the men at the Sun and Moon admit, "could see further than most. But it was suspected that he wanted to see further than was necessary."[64] The foggy world of London is transferred metaphorically to differing visions of the working man in the varying extent of his radical ambitions. Meeting the beautiful Princess Casamassima during a visit with Millicent to the theatre, Hyacinth is impressed by the fact that she also has revolutionary convictions, and he confides his parentage to her. Gradually he is converted to an acceptance of life as it is. He comforts Pinnie on her deathbed and uses the small legacy she left to him to travel to France and Italy, where he realizes the beauty of the real world and the futility of the revolutionaries' anger against it. When the moment comes for him to carry out an assassination commissioned by the revolutionaries, he turns the gun on himself, unable to eliminate the chosen victim but knowing that the revolutionaries will kill him if he does not.

Here the fog is identified with Millicent, as Hyacinth is unable to see when he is with her that his revolutionary commitment is blinding him to the beauty of life. The fog blurs moral distinctions and obscures social boundaries. In the end Millicent and the Princess both escape the confines of convention, the shopgirl by conducting what seems to be at least one affair with another man, and the aristocrat, who has left her dull husband and lives on her own, by conspiring with the other revolutionaries to persuade Hyacinth to take part in a political murder plot. They are independent women whose influence on men is by no means innocent or harmless. Both are trapped within the fog of a false ideology and false moral values.[65] For Hyacinth, however, the reality that he accepts when the intellectual fog of revolutionary ideology lifts is not what he expected but a realization that his political activities have been pointless and immoral.

The friendly fog, to use James's expression, "could protect and enrich" illicit love affairs as well, protecting women's reputation in a world where the consequences of discovery were far more serious for women than for men. In *Love and Mr. Lewisham,* a novel written in 1899 but set in London in the 1880s, H. G. Wells (1866–1946) uses fog as a device to conceal a love affair. The eponymous hero, involved in a somewhat intellectual relationship with a fellow student, Alice Heydinger, encounters an old flame, Ethel Henderson, at a séance held by her father. Their love is rekindled, concealed by

> thick fogs . . . turning every pavement into a private room. Grand indeed were these fogs, things to rejoice at mightily, since then it was no longer a thing for public scorn that two young people hurried along arm in arm, and one could do a thousand impudent, significant things with varying pressure and the fondling of a little hand. . . . And the dangers of the street corners, the horses looming up suddenly out of the dark, the carters with lanterns at their horses' heads, the street lamps, blurred smoky orange at one's nearest, and vanishing at twenty yards into dim haze, seemed to accentuate the infinite need of protection on the part of a delicate young lady who had already traversed three winters of fogs, thornily alone.[66]

Here again is fog as danger to a woman out alone, experienced as excitement only when she has a man to protect her. Realising that Lewisham has a lover, Alice Heydinger breaks down. "She saw herself alone and small in a huge desolation . . . standing, lost in thought, staring at the December fog outside the laboratory windows."[67] For her the future has become an impenetrable mystery, full of uncertainty. For one woman the fog could turn dangerous public spaces into protective private rooms; for another it could block an imagined future that has suddenly come to nothing.

In other fictions fog could lead towards love rather than away from it. "Love in a Fog," a short story by the American writer Hester Caldwell Oakley (?–1905), published in the *Illustrated London News* in June 1899, advertised this fact on the frontispiece, where the title was set within an illustration in which Cupid, complete with wings and bow, is portrayed

Figure 4.8 "Love in a Fog." The title of this short story was illustrated by A. Forestier and uses the figure of the linklighter as Cupid—a more positive view than appears in other representations of these urchins. (*Illustrated London News,* 10 June 1899, p. 831). Reproduced by kind permission of the Syndics of Cambridge University Library.

as a linklighter leading a couple through the murk with a lighted torch and using his bow to point out an approaching kerb (Figure 4.8).[68] The story is told from the point of view of a young American. Walking in the fog, he perceives the shadows of people about him and likens them to "unreal phantoms of a lantern-slide." He quotes to himself, "We are no other than a moving row/Of magic shadow-shapes that come and go."[69] But "now he noticed that the occasional passer-by had ceased to cross his path, and the first doubt of his strongly developed bump of locality assailed him suddenly, and—instantly he was at sea, beyond his depth, in the treacherous ocean of fog." Once more the world seems to be returning to a prehistoric era, as so often in depictions of fog. He, "Ralph Brewster, hunter and ardent woodsman, was more hopelessly turned about in the most familiar part of London than he had ever been in the depth of the forest primeval."[70]

Brewster's reverie is broken by a woman's cry for help. It is a refined voice but also a voice of command that has within it "an imperative note." He attempts to locate the owner of the voice with "outstretched groping arms"—and here we return again to a familiar watery metaphor—"which gave him the effect of a submarine swimmer, moving far down in some deadly calm of heavy untranslucent waters." In the end he finally bumps unceremoniously into the girl, causing her to giggle—an emotion she quickly suppresses. She is obviously a girl of spirit, as she had tried to move towards Brewster rather than waiting for him to come to her. Brewster wonders why she should be out alone in the fog: "It is a frightful night for a woman to be out alone, and dangerous as well." She explains that she had lost her original companion in the gloom. Brewster continues to think her foolhardy. "But the fog—surely by that time it must have been very thick. You should never have attempted—." The girl feels safe with Brewster, and this brings out in him a sense of chivalry: "He felt all at once an immeasurable desire and capacity to move mountains, in order that this delicate, high-bred girl beside him might walk unobstructed henceforth. Unfortunately, no mountains were at hand—only the fog, grim, relentless, omnipresent, like a melodramatic ghost, the clutch of whose clammy fingers no power other than the elements could shake off." Brewster is able to lead them to Trafalgar Square, which they recognise when they bump into one of Landseer's lion statues. But of course they have no idea which side of the Square they are on, so they move out from the lion in different directions, she holding the crook of his umbrella and he stabbing out to the front with his cane (Figure 4.9).[71]

The journey of Brewster and the girl through the fog creates a sense of camaraderie, and the fog as a subject leads them to discuss themselves. The girl, who is a foreigner too and thinks her companion is an Englishman, playfully needles him: "Oh, what a country, this England of yours! It would kill me; I could not breathe in it! Faugh!" She clearly feels the restrictions placed on female independence by the conventions of Victorian England. When Brewster tells her that he is not English but American, she expresses her surprise that he should have been so critical of her being out alone: "I thought it was the custom over there for women to do exactly as they please; to go out and about, alone and unprotected at any hour. Oh, how I have longed for the freedom of it all, at times!" In fact the girl, who remains unnamed, turns out to be from Germany—a country no more known for the freedom of its women than was England at the time.[72]

Meanwhile, the two are brought closer together when a large dray suddenly lumbers out of the fog and Brewster has to pull the girl out of its

He grasped one end of her slim little umbrella, telling her to hold to the crook behind him.

Figure 4.9 Another illustration from the short story "Love in a Fog," showing the man and woman struggling to make their way through the fog. She holds on to his umbrella as he waves his stick in front like a blind man. (*Illustrated London News*, 10 June 1899, p. 831). Reproduced by kind permission of the Syndics of Cambridge University Library.

path. Now, instead of being held apart by the crook of an umbrella, they link arms, and the fog takes on a kindlier hue: "the blessed, the kindly fog shut down again, separating them from the rest of the world; leaving him in a new world of his own, with this one woman." The malicious ghostliness of the fog earlier is replaced by a dream-like world of emotion: "The isolation; the unreality of past or future, of anything but the intense, all-sufficing present; the complete disconnection with any fellowship beyond the limitless one of the other dream-figure at this side—that figure so vital and real, where it touched him closely, her fading itself at the further points into unsubstantiality." The fog now provides "still, deep harbours" of affection: Brewster has fallen in love with the girl. Yet when he finally catches sight of her face, he realises that all is not well with her. He sees "a sort of hopeless weariness, inconsistent with its youth and extreme fairness." The sight of the lamps of the linklighters brings Brewster back to reality. The girl wonders what they are, and Brewster has to describe their role in guidebook fashion: "men who carry about lighted torches, and make it their business to find people who are lost in the London fogs, and show them to their destination"—a rather more positive definition than the one many Londoners of an earlier time would have given.[73]

Brewster realises that the sight of the linkboys raises the question as to why he had not just hailed one earlier and got back to the hotel in half the time. He had been too fascinated by his chance companion, who forgives him his deceit, even saying that she had preferred his company to being in "a torchlight procession." However, the realisation of the deceit has broken the dream: "His glorified cloud became only a murky, yellow London fog once more, lit by the approaching electric lamps, whose dim aureoles slowly grew denser, for the hotel was close at hand." They are brought back to reality. "Behind them lay the fog, in the sphinx-like depths of which the man fancied that he had found an answer to the riddle of his life." The girl has become indelibly associated with the fog, transformed in Brewster's imagination into a creature from a fairy tale: "What was to hinder if he chose to follow his fog-maiden, his will-o'-the-wisp through all the world." Overnight and on the following morning Brewster begins to make plans to see her again. He goes out into Hyde Park to kill time before he can call on her "in the mellow October sunshine, whose hazy quality was the sole legacy of yesterday's fog." He can see clearly, and when a carriage with a "curiously familiar coat-of-arms" passes by, he can make out the Princess of Wales beside a stately old individual; and opposite them sits the "fog-maiden" from the previous evening. She recognises him also, and immediately her bored look vanishes. Yet her gesture of recognition is expressed as "indescribably pathetic." He asks someone who stands next to him who she is, and the man, believing Brewster to be "one of those 'aristocracy-worshippers from the other side,'" tells him that she is her Serene Highness Alexandrine, Princess of Saxe-Weisenach and Countess of Hennebourgh. She is beyond his reach, completely unobtainable for an American commoner, and the love story is over with no further explanation.[74]

In Oakley's story fog briefly connects strangers who, in a clearer light, are forced to remain apart. The 1908 novel *The Suspicions of Ermengarde* uses fog in a diametrically opposite fashion to spur a separation that helps keep a husband and wife together. Its author was Maxwell Gray, the penname of Mary Gleed Tuttiett (1846–1923), a native of the Isle of Wight who visited London as a young adult and eventually settled in West Richmond after the death of her father. The novel opens with an artistic view of a dense London fog:

> Fog of the colour known as pea-soup—in reality amber mixed with lemon-peel and delicately tinted with smut—pervaded the genial shades of Kensington Gardens and cast a halo of breathless romance over many a "long, unlovely street" and many a towering pile of crudely hideous flats in the regions round about. It sneaked down chimneys, stalked insolently through front doors, regardless of locks, curtains and screens; it wandered noiselessly about houses, penetrating even to my lady's chamber; it permeated cosy drawing-rooms and snug dining-rooms with gloom like that of an ancestral ghost, or an unforgettable sorrow, or—the haunting horror of unpaid bills.[75]

These are the thoughts of Ermengarde Allonby, the eponymous centre of the book, a woman with a romantic and artistic but melancholy disposition. The fog haunts London just as Ermengarde is "haunted" by the knowledge that she has spent too much money on herself—a fact that will irritate her husband—and that a bout of influenza has left her weakened, depressed, and feeling aged. The suspicion that her husband might be having an affair adds to her unhappiness. She hopes that the fog will allow her some time alone, but in fact "people came trooping in, all breathing visible breath and complaining of the fog, each alluding to its density, dirt and inconvenience, as if it were an entirely new and startling experience, peculiar to each separate individual. . . . An elderly woman . . . had to sit and cough in a corner for five solid minutes before she was capable of receiving or imparting instructions in the natural history of fog."[76] Ermengarde wonders "if civilization was worth that last, worst penalty of a real London fog—an ideally high and gamey one like this, that you might smell all the way across Dover Straits—at least."[77] This idea of whether the fog is worth the price of civilization leads her to wonder whether her husband is worth the pains of marriage. The fog, whilst giving her an opportunity to stretch her artistic metaphors, also encourages her to seek a much-needed holiday in the sunshine of the south of France. It is a holiday that her husband refuses to sanction by accompanying her, and thus she sets off on her own. While on holiday she is shadowed by a mysterious stranger, who is in fact her husband. They are reconciled—he has not been having an affair—and she declares herself a much wiser woman at the end. In Oakley's story the American visitor and the German princess are forced to leave their hopes behind for a world of social limits when the fog clears. In James's *The Portrait of a Lady* Isabel Archer similarly feels liberated by the fog and oppressed by the stark outlines of married propriety. In *The Suspicions of Ermengarde,* by contrast, the heroine needs to escape from the fog of doubt to see clearly what she already has. Fog represents for all three women another world. It may be a refuge for hope or a claustrophobic prison of doubt, but as long as it lasts, it is an agent of change.

IV

The complex interrelationships of female virtue, the search for emotional fulfilment, and moral convention, as expressed metaphorically by London fog, are present in yet another way in "The Fog," a short story published in the *Strand Magazine* in 1908 by Morley Roberts (1857–1942), a popular author best known for his 1912 novel *The Private Life of Henry Maitland,* a fictional account of the life of George Gissing. Roberts's short story returns us to the apocalyptic tales of William Hay and Robert Barr. "The fog," the story begins, "had been thickening for many weeks, but now, moving like a black wall, it fell on the town."[78] The story centres on a blind beggar, Tom Crabb, who is the only one who can find his way around. He remembers the voices of all those who have given him money, and when he bumps into Bentley, a chauffeur and engineer, he remembers that Bentley had given him "many a copper" in the past. Bentley is trying to get his employer, Lord Gervase North, his Lordship's fiancée, Julia Semple, and her mother shelter from the fog. Tom Crabb offers to lead them, but he does not know the more affluent areas of London where they live; he can, however, lead them to Bentley's home, where all can stay the night until the fog disappears. "He had a sense of power in him. All the rest of the world were blind. He alone had some sight."[79] Lord Gervase offers Crabb five pounds for his help, but the blind man recalls that Gervase had given him a shilling once and offers to take them for free. In an ascending hierarchy of donations Crabb soon discovers, on hearing the voice of Julia Semple, that she is the girl who five years previously gave him a sovereign and said gently, "Poor blind man." Her kindness had touched Crabb, and it makes him feel even more protective of the group under his wing.

As the group gropes its way to Bentley's home, led by the blind beggar, the fog provides the cover for a breakdown of order on the streets. "There were many people in the street; some were drunk, and many wild, but most were fearful. Yet the darkness released some from fear and let loose their devilry. It seemed that two men in front of them smashed every window as they passed, and laughed wildly."[80] Crabb seems to relish the mayhem: "I can't tell you all that's going on. 'Tis madness. There are awful things being done; fires, murders, and horrible screams about. . . . Terror is in us all, but many have broken into liquor shops and are drunk. . . . Folks are going mad and jumping into the river. . . . And I heard women shrieking awfully. Wicked people are about."[81] As in the apocalyptic novels of the 1890s the moral and social order breaks down completely under cover of the fog's darkness:

> Horses lay dead; others wandered loose. There were fires in the streets, made of smashed vehicles; gloomy shadows burnt themselves and cooked horseflesh by the leaping hidden flames; some danced drunkenly and fell in the fires. Many offered golden loot for food. . . . Out of the night came the mad shrieks of women and the wildest laughter. Dying men played with death and fell on fire and crime and the awfullest disasters. . . . A blind organist made mad music to Heaven in a church that Crabb passed. . . . Wild crowds were marching east and west and south and north or trying to march.[82]

Horrible Apparition which appeared to a benighted Elderly Female during the Fog of Tuesday, February 1.

Figure 4.10 "Horrible Apparition…" A Mrs. Gamp–type figure is startled by a linklighter, who is transformed by the fog. The light behind is far from reassuring. (*Punch,* 12 February 1853, p. 68). Courtesy of the President and Fellows of Wolfson College, Cambridge.

Why the women were shrieking is suggested when someone steals a kiss from the young Julia Semple. Her fiancé, appalled by the audacity, reacts violently, and in a moment of surreal description we are told, "He leapt at the laugh, caught it by the throat, and dashed the laughter on the pavement."[83] Once more the man is the woman's protector; but such protection is evidently unavailable to the women heard crying out in the gloom out of view.

Eventually the party reaches Bentley's abode, and Mrs. Bentley suggests that they break into the flat next door. She knows the owners are away and unlikely to come back in the fog, and they need the extra beds to make the guests feel more comfortable. Lord Gervase and Bentley turn "housebreakers inside five minutes."[84] But they clearly cannot stay in the disintegrating city. Gervase knows where a gas-fired balloon is moored, on the outskirts of the city. Making their way to it, guided by Crabb, they secure the help of a watchman, who turns off the supply of gas to the whole of London in order to secure it for the hot-air balloon (neither the author nor any of his characters comments on this staggering act of selfishness). The situation meanwhile has grown more desperate, especially for Julia's mother, Lady Semple, whose lungs are seriously affected by the fog. She is near to death by the tenth day, when they locate the balloon. Crabb carries Lady Semple to the balloon, but she is convinced that she will not survive. "Am I blind, Crabb? I see nothing—nothing! I choke!"[85]

The balloon can only take five people, and with the watchman who has helped them, they total seven. Crabb selflessly volunteers to stay, as does Bentley. In the end the balloon carries only four aloft, as Bentley's wife refuses to leave her husband. The balloon's first ascent is marked by the change in colours as they go higher above London: "a dimness, a blur, a space. It was almost black, but visible; it was brown, it was yellow, and then grey. There was a dash of wonderful blue in it, and then they shot out into a magic and intolerable day of noon!"[86] They look down to the variation in colour: "The far cloud was white, and yet in places a strange dun colour. It heaved and moved and rose and sank. Out of it came strange pillars of yellow clouds." Despite doom-laden claims that the whole world was affected by the fog, it becomes clear to the balloonists that "the great cloud rested only on the town; far away was peace. . . . The outside world had deserted London and cut it off. It was sunk in a pit; it lay at the bottom of a well."[87] But they cannot escape, for there is no wind to carry them away, and the balloon slowly descends to the same spot from which it had started. It also has a slow leak. The watchman, who has already shown signs of madness, flings himself from the balloon and falls dead beside the waiting Crabb. When the balloon reaches the ground, the survivors discover that Lady Semple is also dead. They fill the balloon again with the last remaining gas. Crabb is now persuaded to come and is joined by Bentley and his wife. They ascend again but cannot go high enough to catch the wind that will move them away from London. Having thrown everything out, including food to lighten the load, it looks as if their last attempt to escape will fail. Crabb, having fallen in love with Julia, asks to touch her face, to appreciate her beauty, and then he throws himself out of the basket, sacrificing himself to save the others. The story ends with the balloon drifting away from London to the west.

Roberts was a biologist as well as a writer of fiction, and part of the point of "The Fog" is to show that physical strength and inherited qualities play a larger role in society than do class distinctions, which he clearly regarded as artificial. Crabb, the blind man, is able to lead the sighted, who are blinded by the fog. He is a beggar, but he proves his strength of leadership. "Lord Gervase . . . yearned to live. . . . But he found Bentley a bigger man than himself; and Crabb was bigger than either, though he had been no more than a soldier, wounded in a foolish fight in far-off India."[88] Crabb makes the ultimate sacrifice, flinging himself from the basket, with the knowledge that this will help the others to survive. Lady Semple also deserves to die because she is weak; she moans and longs for her home while looking down her nose at the shelter that the Bentleys offer. But towards her end there is redemption as she realizes Crabb's true strength in spite of his lowly status, and she significantly asks him to save her daughter and not her daughter's fiancé, Lord Gervase; her daughter represents the future of the race more than the noble lord does. Both Lady Semple and her daughter require the protection of strong men like Crabb because the breakdown of order on the streets threatens women more than men.

This image runs through all the depictions of women in the fog, from representations of the Jack the Ripper murders by Marie Belloc Lowndes and contemporary newspaper reporters to Henry James's account of Isabel Archer plunging into the fog in *The Portrait of a Lady*. For women London fog posed a threat, increasing the risk of male violence, of murder and rape. It blurred social and moral distinctions, and if for some, such as

Ethel Henderson in *Love and Mr. Lewisham* or the Princess in Hester Oakley's short story, it provided a welcome anonymity for love and romance, it still contained dangers that required the presence of a male protector. In a world reduced to a state of nature or regressed by fog to prehistory, the strong man was king.

CHAPTER FIVE

The View from Abroad

I

As a ship steamed into the Port of London early in November 1880, carrying a group of French radicals who had been transported to the remote Melanesian islands of New Caledonia following their conviction for participating in the Paris Commune of 1871, it entered a very different atmosphere from the tropical warmth and humidity of the penal colony. Thick fog enveloped the River Thames as the vessel proceeded slowly up the estuary. So dense was it that even experienced river pilots refused to take charge of it and steer the ship into port. The émigrés were forced to charter small boats to make their way to shore.[1] The anarchist Louise Michel, to whose writings we owe this description of the revolutionaries' arrival in the British capital, was far from the only foreigner to be confounded by the turbid atmosphere of the city in the winter months. The city provided a refuge for many Continentals who had run into political difficulties in their own country; but it did so only reluctantly, and its inhabitants were notoriously unwelcoming to foreigners, speaking, as one observer complained, of Europeans "continually emptying and discharging themselves into this grand Reservoir, or common-Sewer of the World."[2] The murky gloom that greeted political refugees both symbolised and deepened their sense of exile. Trying to make sense of the strange manners and habits of the English, exiles expressed their bewilderment and alienation through elaborate depictions of London fog.

Among the many political exiles fleeing the French police in the wake of the suppression of the Paris Commune was the twenty-seven-year-old poet Paul Verlaine (1844–1896), who had acted as a newspaper censor for the Commune. Verlaine had an additional reason for leaving his native land, however, for he had fallen in love with a young fellow poet, Arthur Rimbaud (1854–1891). In September 1872 Rimbaud persuaded Verlaine to escape from the restrictions of life at home with his young wife, Mathilde, and their new baby, and to go to London in order to avoid the pursuit of her parents, as well as the many police officers who were spying on them. The move was not a success. Both men were extremely poor, and their English was limited; but they tried to continue their dissipated lifestyle fuelled by ale, gin, and absinthe in Soho, while working in the Reading Room of the British Museum. The weather was not good for their health. In early October, Rimbaud complained, "yellow fog added the constant sound of coughing to the roar of traffic."[3] "The fog," Verlaine agreed, "is beginning to show the tip of its filthy nose. Everyone is coughing here, except me."[4] "Imagine a setting sun seen through grey crêpe," he wrote.[5] In May 1873 they moved to 8 Great College Street in Camden Town. They largely survived on a small income from Rimbaud's mother. They argued bitterly, and Verlaine returned to France by himself in June 1873. Missing Rimbaud intensely, Verlaine telegraphed him to meet in Brussels. The reunion went badly. Verlaine, drunk and angry, fired two shots at Rimbaud, wounding him in the wrist. Verlaine was arrested and imprisoned. In March 1874 Rimbaud returned to London with another young poet, Germain Nouveau (1851–1920). "Far, far above my subterranean sitting room," he wrote gloomily, houses settle and spread, fog gathers. Mud is red or black. Monstrous city, endless night!"[6] He did not feel at home in the city, whose anonymity—filled with "millions of people who have no need to know one another"—left him feeling no more than a "transient" visitor.[7] Another exiled Communard journalist, Jules Vallès, penned a lengthy and splenetic denunciation of the city, La Rue à Londres (1876), in which he railed against "the black city" and "the furious fog that resents the sun."[8]

Earlier in the century, like Rimbaud and Verlaine, the Franco-Peruvian feminist and utopian socialist Flora Tristan (1803–1844) was struck by the gloomy atmosphere. Arriving in London in 1839, she noted "the domes, the towers, the edifices strangely deformed by the mists; the monumental smoke-stacks which belch their black smoke into the sky and reveal the existence of the great factories; the blurred look of the things around one."[9] She was both fascinated and appalled by the monstrous size and activity of the city and considered its fogs an element in their own right in the oppression of London's industrial workers. "To the enormous mass of soot-laden smoke exhaled by the monster city's thousands of chimneys is joined a thick fog, and the black cloud which envelops London admits only a wan daylight and casts a funeral pall over all things."[10] Aware of the atmosphere's dangers to health, she blamed it for what she saw as a lack of vitality in Londoners and indeed in visitors and exiles as well: "Ah, there is nothing so lugubrious, so spasmodic as the look of the city on a day of fog. . . . When one is in the grip of such influences, one's head is heavy and aching, one's stomach has trouble functioning, breathing becomes difficult for lack of pure air, one feels an overwhelming lassitude, . . . finally a loathing for everything and an irresistible desire for suicide." She concludes, like many others, that the atmosphere of London caused among its inhabitants an alarming level of drunkenness, because "the London climate would drive the soberest Spaniard to drink."[11]

Tristan was only on a brief visit to London, but many other Continental Europeans were forced to stay there longer after fleeing persecution at home for subversive political activities, whether socialist, anarchist, or nationalist. Southern Europeans were brutally reminded by London's fog of the clear skies and warm climate from which they had been forcibly parted. Francesco Crispi (1818–1901), a nationalist who later served with Garibaldi's "thousand" in the wars of Italian unification and subsequently became Prime Minister of his country, was forced to come to London after the failure of the 1848 revolution. He wrote to his father on January 17, 1855: "It is a frighteningly cold country. The fog is constant. You know the sun rises and sets, but it does not give out any light."[12] Max Schlesinger (1822–1881), an Austro-Hungarian physician and nationalist, complained bitterly in a similar vein. Politically active in his homeland, he had taken part in the Viennese 1848 revolution, publishing many articles in German and Austrian newspapers in favour of a republic and in support of Hungarian autonomy. His views came under scrutiny in the counter-revolution, and in 1850 he had to flee for London, where he became a correspondent for the *Kölnische Zeitung* (a major liberal newspaper in Cologne). He wrote a memoir of his impressions of the great city for the German market under the title *Wanderungen durch London* (*Saunterings in and about London*), published in Berlin in two volumes and subsequently translated into English.

Schlesinger too linked London's gloom with his political exile: "The London sun, like unto German liberty, exists in the minds of the people, who have faith in either, and believe that either might be bright, dazzling and glorious, were it not for the intervention of a dark, ugly fog, between the upper and nether regions."[13] He could see no redeeming feature in the gloom cast by atmospheric pollution in the English capital:

> The winter-fogs of London are, indeed, awful. They surpass all imagining; he who never saw them, can form no idea of what they are. He who knows how powerfully they affect the minds and tempers of men, can understand the prevalence of that national disease—the spleen. In a fog, the air is hardly fit for breathing; it is grey-yellow, of a deep orange, and even black; at the same time, it is moist, thick, full of bad smells, and choking. The fog appears, now and then, slowly, like a melodramatic ghost, and sometimes it sweeps over the town as the simoom over the desert. At times, it is spread with equal density over the whole of that ocean of houses on other occasions, it meets with some invisible obstacle, and rolls itself into intensely dense masses, from which the passengers come forth in the manner of the student who came out of the cloud to astonish Dr. Faust.[14]

II

American visitors came to London for very different reasons: many of them could be regarded as tourists of one kind and another. One such was the traveller, poet, and literary critic J. Bayard Taylor (1825–1878), who abandoned his apprenticeship to embark on a tour of Europe. He made ends meet financially by negotiating a small deal with newspapers such as the *Tribune* and the *Saturday Evening Post* to write letters describing his travels. The letters then formed the basis of a book titled *Views A-foot; or, Europe seen with Knapsack and Staff,* published in two volumes in 1847, which reached its sixth edition by 1855. When he arrived in London in 1844, he noted: "The morning sky was as yet but faintly obscured by the coal-smoke."[15] And as he left, a major fog became part of his last glimpse of the city:

> A few days ago we had a real fog—a specimen of November weather, as the people said. If November wears such a mantle, London, during that sober month, must furnish a good idea of the gloom of Hades. The streets were wrapped in a veil of dense mist, of a dirty yellow colour, as if the air had suddenly grown thick and mouldy. The houses on the

opposite sides of the street were invisible, and the gas-lamps, lighted in the shops, burned with a white and ghastly flame. Carriages ran together in the streets, and I was kept constantly on the look-out, lest some one should come suddenly out of the cloud around me, and we should meet with a shock like that of two knights at a tournament. As I stood in the centre of Trafalgar Square, with every object invisible around me, it reminded me, (hoping the comparison will not be accepted in every particular) of Satan resting in the middle of Chaos. The weather sometimes continues thus for whole days together. . . . I shall take a last walk through the Minories and past the Tower yard, and as we glide down the Thames, St. Pauls, half-hidden in mist and coal-smoke, will probably be my last glimpse of London.[16]

Here was a characteristically negative view of the fog, smoke, and pollution of the city in these years, yellow and sulphurous, a vision of Hell.

European tourism was, however, still a relatively unusual enterprise for Americans in the middle decades of the nineteenth century. More commonly, we owe our knowledge of what they thought of London and Londoners to men who came as diplomats in the service of the Federal Government. One of these was Nathaniel Hawthorne (1804–1864), who came to England with his family in 1853 for a four-year appointment as U.S. consul at Liverpool. He was already approaching his forty-ninth birthday and was a well-known and published writer, author of such works as *The Scarlet Letter* and *Tanglewood Tales*. His consular post offered him a much higher income than he had earned from his writings— indeed it was regarded as the most lucrative in the entire American foreign service at the time—and gave him an opportunity to visit a country he had always longed to experience. While based in Liverpool, Hawthorne visited London several times for short periods both by himself and with his family.

On November 12, 1857, the family arrived in the capital for a visit. Hawthorne was immediately struck by the atmosphere, in which fog and smoke were drifting along, propelled by a wind: "It kept alternately darkening, and then brightening a little, and darkening again so much that we could but just see across the street."[17] A slight lifting of the fog encouraged the party to explore London further, but then "the fog darkened again": "the Duke of York's Column was but barely discernible, looming

IN A NOVEMBER FOG.

Frenchman (just arrived on his first visit to London). "HA, HA ! MY
FRIEN', NOW I UNDERSTAN' VOT YOU MEAN VEN YOU SAY ZE SUN
NEVAIRE SET IN YOUR DOMINION, MA FOI ! *IT DOES NOT RISE !"*

Figure 5.1 "In a November Fog." This French theme was a continuation from an earlier page
of this issue of *Punch's Almanack,* where a short article titled "Fashions for November" described the main fashion as "Fog *à la mode du potage des pois.*" (*Punch's Almanack for 1897,*
1 January 1898, p. 310). Courtesy of the President and Fellows of Wolfson College, Cambridge.

vaguely before us; nor, from Pall Mall, was Nelson's Pillar much more
distinct, though methought his statue stood aloft in a somewhat clearer
atmosphere than ours."[18] The party entered Westminster Abbey, "which
looked very dusky and grim in the smoky light."[19] They found themselves

"looking upward at the fog which hung half way between [them] and the lofty roof of the Minster."[20] Like many others, Hawthorne was oppressed not only by the fog but also by the restless anonymity of the teeming streets: "It is really an ungladdened life, to wander through these huge, thronged ways . . . jostling against people who do not seem to be individuals, but all one mass, . . . everywhere, the dingy brick edifices heaving themselves up, and shutting out all but a strip of sullen cloud that serves London for a sky; . . . and, at this season, always a fog scattered along the vista of streets, sometimes so densely as almost to spiritualize the materialism and make the scene resemble the other world of worldly people, gross even in ghostliness."[21] The foggy, damp weather made the family ill, and all had colds for several weeks. This, and the further inconvenience of the children catching the measles, delayed the Hawthornes' plans to travel to Paris to make an onward journey to the warmer climate of Italy for what they thought would bring an end to their stay in England.

December 8, 1857, brought yet another fog, a real specimen of the traditional pea-souper, which further delayed their travel plans:

> This morning, when it was time to get up, there was but a glimmering of daylight; and we had candles on the breakfast-table, at nearly ten o'clock. All abroad, there was a dense, dim fog, brooding through the atmosphere, insomuch that we could hardly see across the street. At eleven o'clock, I went out into the midst of this fog-bank, which, for the moment, seemed a little more interfused with daylight; for there seem to be continual changes in the density of this dim medium, which varies so much that now you can but just see your hand before you, and, a moment afterwards, you can see the cabs dashing out of the duskiness, a score of yards off. It is seldom or never, moreover, an unmitigated gloom, but appears to be mixed up with sunshine in different proportions; sometimes, only one part sun to a thousand of smoke and fog, and sometimes sunshine enough to give the whole mass a coppery hue. This would have been a bright, sunny day, but for the interference of the fog; and before I had been out long, I actually saw the sun looking red and rayless, much like the millionth magnification of a new half-penny.[22]

Undeterred by the fog, Hawthorne made his way, rather appropriately, to an exhibition of Turner paintings at Marlborough House and then to another exhibition of the same painter's works at the National Gallery. After this artistic detour he went out again to meet an old friend. Ever the moralist, he transmuted the continuing dense fog into a religious experience, a vision of Hell, contrasting the gloom of the dirty city with the light and airiness of the biblical New Jerusalem:

> I went home by way of Holborn; and the fog was denser than ever—very black, indeed, more like a distillation of mud than anything else; the ghost of mud, the spiritualized medium of departed mud, through which the departed citizens of London probably tread in the Hades whither they are translated. So heavy was the gloom, that gas was lighted in all the shop-windows; and the little charcoal furnaces of the women and boys, roasting chestnuts, threw a ruddy, misty glow around them. And yet I liked it. This fog seems an atmosphere proper to huge, grimy London; as proper as that light, neither of the sun nor moon is to the New Jerusalem. On reaching home, I found the fog diffused through the parlour, though how it could have got in is a mystery.[23]

Prosperous, happily married, and celebrated as a successful author, Hawthorne did not need to link London fog in his mind to melancholy and despair, as so many of the political exiles did; yet the picture he painted of London was still in the end one of darkness and gloom, relieved only by the Christian vision of the invisible cathedral and the imagined heavenly city of New Jerusalem.

While Hawthorne found London fog a stimulus to moralistic reflection, the humourist Mark Twain saw in it, by contrast, an opportunity for joking. Twain experienced thick fog whilst in London on December 9, 1873, on a lecture tour organised by George Dolby (1831–1900), the theatrical manager who had escorted Charles Dickens on his reading tour in Britain in April–June 1866: "The fog was so thick to-day at noon that the cabs *went in a walk, & men went before the omnibuses carrying lanterns.* . . . It was the heaviest fog seen in London in 20 years. And you know how the fog invades the houses & makes your eyes smart. To-night, the first thing I said on the stage was, 'Ladies & gentlemen, I *hear* you, & so I know that you are here—& I am here, too, notwithstanding I am not visible.' The audience did look so vague, & dim, & ghostly! The hall seemed full of a thick blue smoke."[24] Twain had been giving a popular lecture on "roughing it," and he certainly appeared not to have been put off by the weather, even using it in a light-hearted manner at the beginning of his lecture. However, at the end of this letter to his wife, he acknowledged the discomfort caused by the fog: "But I *must* quit, my eyes smart so."[25] Even *Punch* felt compelled to encourage its readers to come to the lectures, where "Mr Mark Twain is to be visible to the naked eye, (fog permitting) in Hanover Square."[26]

Charles Warren Stoddard (1843–1909), Mark Twain's secretary and companion, recalled the same fog in his book *Exits and Entrances: A Book of Essays and Sketches*. His description has greater dramatic impact than that of Twain, who was simply describing it in a letter. Stoddard was particularly struck by the activity of the linkboys, who offered to accompany people along the streets during the fog, lighting their way with torches:

> There was an evening of fog at the close of a day during which the street-lamps had in vain struggled to light the bewildered citizens through the chaotic city. At high noon linkboys bore their flaming torches to and fro; and the air was burdened with the ceaseless cries of cabmen who were all adrift, and in danger of a collapse and total wreck at the imminent lamp-post. That night the Queen's Concert Rooms were like a smoke house; and I saw from my chair in the royal box a shadowy dress coat, supported by a pair of shadowy trousers girdled by the faint halo of the ineffectual footlights. A voice was in the air, but it was difficult to locate it with any degree of certainty. The apparently headless trunk of the lecturer told what he knew of our fellow savages, the Sandwich Islanders; and at intervals out of the depths ascended the muffled murmur of an audience invisible to the naked eye.[27]

Lecturing in such conditions was virtually impossible. People knew it and stayed away. Many must have found it impossible to travel to the venue anyway. "The fog got so thick, & so depleted my audiences," Twain complained, "that I got desperate. I *can't* talk to thin houses; I would so cheerfully have paid half a crown to every man who would come—but I couldn't *say* that, & so I had to talk, & go on suffering."[28] He longed to return home to America. He was contracted for further lectures throughout the country, so his return home to America was not possible; but he did cancel the rest of his tour in London:

I ought to keep on lecturing in London, but the fog nearly broke my heart, & on the foggiest night I lost faith & Dolby advertised the early close of my season. It was rash & wrong, but I could not help it. Day & night the streets were void of people; all day long the street lamps burned, yet they only looked like rows of dull embers, half-dead sparks, extending up Portland Place—& you see them only *half way* up Portland Place, at that. There were but few cabs about. The steeple opposite the parlor window was visible only as a dreamy, unformed, spectral thing. My houses fell right down till they contained only £14 & £17! It said "It is going to last forever & ever—cut my season short!"[29]

London seemed a city of the dead, with few people abroad, nothing to see or do, and sounds dampened by the fog.

Two decades later another American visitor, Mary Hannah Krout (1851–1927), a journalist and staff correspondent for a Chicago-based daily paper, wrote with feeling about the "ill-smelling mixture of smoke and vapor, changing from yellow to deep brown and greenish grey, through which the sun appears like a brazen ball," that descended upon London in the winter months:

As more fuel is consumed and thicker and blacker smoke ascends from millions of chimneys, it changes its complexion and becomes thick dark-ness. Night appears to be pressing close against the windowpanes at noon-day; lamps are lighted upon passing cabs, in houses, in the shops and along the streets. Traffic is not interrupted, although daylight is completely extinguished—so long as the pall remains above the housetops. When it descends to the surface of the ground, the discreet remain indoors; belated pedestrians are conducted home by link-boys, like fine ladies and gentlemen in the days of the Stuarts; cabmen lead their horses, and vehicles moving at a snail's pace frequently come to grief; the driver of the tram-car is often unable to see his horses, and the conductor is hardly able to distinguish the hand that passes the fare. It is estimated that a black fog of this description costs many thousands of pounds per day for additional gas, which can do little more than make darkness visible; and there is an immediate increase in the death-rate, especially among people predisposed to pulmonary disease.

Exuding the optimism, the confidence, the can-do approach, and the feeling of superiority that were becoming widespread among Americans as the United States grew in power and prosperity, she declared, "There is little doubt that had Americans to contend with such conditions, some means of lessening the difficulty would have been found."[30] From the middle decades of the century, when writers such as Bayard Taylor and Nathaniel Hawthorne likened a fogbound London to Hades or Hell, to the 1870s, when Mark Twain dwelt on the chaos and bewilderment of the urban fog-scape, to the 1890s, when Mary Krout saw it as evidence of the supine indolence of the Old World, American writers saw London fog in negative terms, a confirmation of the superiority of American nature and American mores.

III

As early as the 1840s Flora Tristan had dwelt on the effects of foggy days and weeks on the character of London's inhabitants, seeing drunkenness, indolence, and melancholy among its principal effects. By the latter part of the century this linking of meteorology and psychology had become both firmer and more ambitious. The influence of Charles Darwin (1809–1882) and his doctrine of the evolution of species through natural selection came together with the racial theories of Count Arthur de Gobineau (1816–1882) to make the propagation of racial and national stereotypes more popular and respectable. If animal species had acquired group characteristics, the same might also hold good for humans. One of the first to link London fog to the English national character was the French writer and historian Hippolyte Adolphe Taine (1828–1893). Taine believed that works of literature were formed by the threefold influence of what he called "race, milieu, and moment." Writing a history of English literature, he felt a strong need to visit the country "to study the life and customs of the race on the spot, and to see with his own eyes the soil from which it had grown."[31] The first thing that struck him was London fog. On June 25, 1860, during his first visit to London, he wrote despairingly to his mother: "This great London wearies and saddens me; I am actively pursuing my task as an anatomist, but that is all. Everything here is too large, too black, too much heaped up."[32] In May 1871 his impressions were if anything even more negative: "Mean alleys at the back of sumptuous streets, massive trees and beautiful verdure in streets full of sooty fog that chokes up one's throat and nose."[33] Like Flora Tristan before him, he thought that fog caused melancholia and suicidal thoughts:

> A thick, yellow fog fills the air, sinks, crawls on the very ground; at thirty paces a house or a steam-ship look like ink-stains on blotting-paper. In the Strand, especially, and the rest of the City, after an hour's walking, one is possessed by spleen and can understand suicide. The tall, flat, straight façades are of dark brick; fog and soot have deposited their secretions on these surfaces. . . . The vast space which, in the south, lies between earth and heaven, is missed, here, by the seeking eye; no more air, nothing but the flowing fog. In this livid smoke, objects are no more than phantoms and nature looks like a bad drawing in charcoal on which someone has rubbed his sleeve. I have just spent half an hour on Waterloo Bridge. Parliament House, indistinct, outline washed out, seems, in the distance, no more than a wretched huddle of scaffolding; nothing perceptible, above all nothing alive, except the small steam-boats moving on the river, black, smoky, indefatigable insects.[34]

For Taine the fog symbolised the complete denaturing of the urban-industrial landscape, the triumph of soulless English materialism and the prosaic English national character. To the familiar French cliché of foggy London he joined the even more familiar French cliché of the nation of shopkeepers.[35]

London fog was similarly linked to the English national character by Eça de Queirós (1845–1900), a Portuguese writer who survived financially by acting as a consul for the Portuguese Foreign Service in England from 1874, based in Newcastle-upon-Tyne and later Bristol. He sent his *Letters from England* beginning in 1879 to the *Gazeta de Noticias* of Rio de Janeiro. He was honest about his view of England: "I loathe England, but that does not prevent her from being probably the first among thinking nations. Taine said she was the second—but then Taine was French."[36] He was an inspired choice as a consul since he was already well read in English literature and culture. He knew the works of Shakespeare, was a fan of George Meredith, as well as of Dickens and Thackeray, and had read Tennyson and Macaulay's essays. Eça was a compulsive writer, and his newspaper and journal articles enabled him to travel around England and gave him the opportunity to visit London during the "season" from October to June. Eça was critical of everything he saw around him, but he was

Figure 5.2 *Westminster* (1878), by Giuseppe de Nittis. Here, as the artist noted, the Palace of Westminster's "high spires are veiled by a thin layer of fog and low clouds which give us a sense of insurmountable distance, as if imperial institutions were out of reach and only visible from afar." Edmond de Goncourt, *Diario. Memorie di vita letteraria 1851–96,* 17 February 1884, p. 283. Trans. by Dr. Bianca Gaudenzi. De Agostini Picture Library / A. Dagli Orti / Bridgeman Images.

also fascinated because, like Taine, he perceived a connection between the climate and character. In a humorous mock-letter from his dog, staying with his master in France, to his cat, who has remained in England, Eça describes the influence of climate on character by comparing France and England: "I left England that foggy, miserable morning. . . . Here there's no fog—that's the first point where France is superior to our glorious but gloomy homeland. Under this cloudless sky, the spirit also remains unclouded. In England, ideas (and as you know, mine are not complicated) always seem to me vague and indeterminate, like our brick buildings when seen through damp mist. . . . It's this temperate sky which gives the French their gentle manners. At home the freezing fog has the same effect on our characters as it does on our skin. It chaps and roughens."[37] The dog goes on to describe how Englishmen "smell the same: a mixture of Windsor soap, Maryland tobacco, *eau de cologne* and coal."[38] Eça is very aware of the importance of coal to the nation, reporting that a "sooty youth with an old cap . . . out there in the street, in the gloomy fog of late October with his plaintive, muted voice," was calling out "from door to door his melancholy cry: 'Coals! Coals!' "[39]

One of the pieces in Eça's *Letters from England* is titled "Winter in London," printed in 1879, and describes the London fog in great detail:

> One wakes in the morning to find a thick, grey, chilling shadow enshrouding everything outside the window; one must shave by gas-light and take breakfast with all the candles of the candelabra alight; and the carriage which transports us is preceded by a torch. By midday this scene changes; the shadow loses some of its greyness and by slow odious stages changes to ochre yellow and begins to exude a malodorous vapour. Breathing becomes difficult, one's clothes feel clammy against the skin; the buildings that surround us have the vague, ghostly lines of the cursed cities of the Apocalypse, and the thunder of London's streets, that tumultuous din which must disturb the court of Heaven, becomes a low rumble like a noise echoing from under the group.[40]

This piece, like many other writings from foreign hands, links the climate to the English habit of drunkenness: "Everyone drinks heavily and incessantly to combat this freezing, fatal fog, there is a vague smell of alcohol in the streets, which is exuded upon the breath." Eça too saw fog as the expression of the unnatural character of the English capital: "The constantly black sky and the ever-present mud are not natural—it's just that the thousands of feet are trampling the ground, while thousands of chimneys are belching out smoke."[41] London presented apocalyptic scenes to the visitor, visions of hell that also struck other writers who came to the city from abroad.

One such writer was Rudyard Kipling (1865–1936), well known for stories set in India, such as *The Jungle Book* and *Kim*. Kipling was born in India, sent to school in England, and returned to India at the age of sixteen to start life as a journalist. In October 1889, as a young man of twenty-three, he arrived back in England. He had already enjoyed a career in journalism in India and a successful tour of America.[42] He chose to live in central London on an upper floor in Villiers Street, just off the Strand, where one window looked east across Embankment Gardens, towards the River Thames, and another window looked into that symbol of modernity, Charing Cross Station, with all its smoke and noise.[43] Kipling saw London through the eyes of someone who had spent much of his life in the hot and fog-free climate of the Raj. He quickly felt alienated and ill at ease in the northern metropolis. "Rose up in the morn at 9," he wrote to Edmonia Hill, an American friend on November 11, 1889, "and found the gloom of

BE-FOGGED.

Polite Old Gentleman (in the Fog). " PRAY, SIR, CAN YOU KINDLY TELL ME IF I'M GOING RIGHT FOR LONDON BRIDGE?"

Shadowy Stranger. "LUM BRI'GSH! GOO' JOKE! 'NOTHER MAN 'SHAME SHTATE'S MYSHELF! I WAN' T' FIN' LUM BRI'GSH, TOO! TA' MY ARM——"
[Old Gent hurries off!

Figure 5.3 "Be-Fogged." Here the association between drink and fog is made clear: a drunk presumes that a man lost in the fog must also be inebriated. (*Punch,* 14 February 1880, p. 70). Courtesy of the President and Fellows of Wolfson College, Cambridge.

the Pit upon the land, a yellow fog through which the engines at Charing Cross whistled agonizedly one to the other."[44] The "fiendish darkness" worsened, "darker than any dust-storm": "I had to light my reading lamp before lunch."[45] He immediately turned this despairing experience into a "doleful ditty." Entitled "In Partibus Infidelium" (In the Lands of the

Heathen), the poem "was the wail of a fog-bound exile howling for sun-light."[46] London was full of vice and immorality, he complained; Christian conduct was nowhere to be seen. "Earth holds no horror like to this / . . . And 'twas to hide their heathendom / The beastly fog was made." Much of the poem dwells on the dirt and inconvenience of the foggy atmo-sphere: "I see the smut upon my cuff / . . . I cannot leave my window wide / When gentle Zephyr blows, / Because he brings disgusting things / And drops 'em on my clo'es." The sky, in another version of fog's nickname as a pea-souper, is described as "a greasy soup-tureen." Later, in 1892, on announcing his marriage to Caroline Balestier, he also states his desire to "get out of this pea soup air as soon as [he] can."[47]

For Kipling fog abolished not only the contours of the buildings but also the certainties of time. "I cannot tell when dawn is near, / Or when the day is done, / Because I always see the gas / And never see the sun." When he does get a glimpse of it, uncertainty prevails once more:

> But stay, there was an orange, or
> An aged egg its yolk;
> It might have been a Pears' balloon
> Or Barnum's latest joke:
> I took it for the sun and wept
> To watch it through the smoke.

Kipling's feelings of homesickness and depression at this time, like those of political exiles earlier in the century, were aggravated by the fog, which seemed to symbolise the bewilderment and uncertainty of his new life. "My spirits were most awful low," he remarked. Another letter, also to Edmonia Hill, opens with "A day of Death and Fog"; the following day "weather black as Pit," and a few days later, on December 9, 1889, he is writing to the poet and critic John Addington Symonds (1840–1893), who had gone to live in Davos for health reasons, begrudgingly wishing him a merry Christmas because he has "the sun over there": "I shall eat the plum pudding of the British in fog."[48]

Besides complaining about the fog in letters and poems, Kipling also wrote a short comic story titled "The Adoration of the Mage" in De-cember 1889 and published in an English-language newspaper in Lahore, India, called the *Civil and Military Gazette*. The tale is a story within a story

Figure 5.4 "Fogged." Even London cabbies were confused by the fog. The linkman seems rather older than the boys usually depicted. The men in the image are conversing: *"Cabman (who thinks he has been passing a line of linkmen):* 'Is this right for Paddington?' *Linkman:* ' 'Course it is! First to the right and straight on. 'Aven't I told ye that three times already? Why, you've been drivin' round this Square for the last 'arf hour!'" (*Punch,* 7 December 1904, p. 411). Courtesy of the President and Fellows of Wolfson College, Cambridge.

and recounts a narrative told by one of four men who share a cab when they leave together from the London house of a highly distinguished politician during a very thick fog, referred to as a "London Particular." We are told that the fog has nothing whatsoever to do with the story and is interesting for only one reason: "that little fact that we could not see our hands before our faces." Even so the fog is described as "black brutal" and "the gloom of Tophet," and it has turned "each gas-jet into a pin-prick of light, visible only at six-inches range. There were no houses, there were no pavements. There were no points of the compass." A burst of swearing heard in the gloom indicates that a cabby has lost his way. In comic style he drives the cab gracefully onto the pavement in front of them. He promises to take them on board for a half a crown apiece, although he does not promise to take them to a specified destination, as the narrator relates:

"The cabby kept his word nobly. He did not find anywheres in particular, but he found several places. First he discovered a pavement kerb and drove pressing his wheel against it till we came to a lamp-post, and that we hit grievously. Then he came to what ought to have been a corner, but was a 'bus, and we embraced the thing amid terrific language. Then he sailed out into nothing at all-blank fog—and there he commended himself to heaven, and his horse to the other place."[49] At this point one of the passengers, an eminent novelist, begins to give directions to the cabby. Conversation follows on the subject of the weather.

Soon the characters are discussing Mr. Gladstone, the Liberal Prime Minister, famous for his long and complicated sentences. While the eminent novelist defends Gladstone—"he moves in an atmosphere that you and those like you cannot breathe"—another passenger takes up the metaphor: "Yes, I always said it was a pretty thick fog. Now I know it is as thick as this one." The cab finishes by landing them in the drinking fountain in High Street Kensington with the horse falling down and the cabman taking his money. The narrator eventually gropes his way home.[50]

Kipling, like Henry James before him, came to London with high expectations but found the reality disappointing. His feelings of loneliness were accentuated when the fog descended. It created a psychological and physical wall between the aspiring writer and the society he hoped to join. Kipling approached the metaphor of fog as a cover under which the immorality of London life and society was hidden, but as so often, he was unable to resist the temptation of using it for humorous purposes. Perhaps this indicated that he was beginning to get used to it. Nevertheless, here was another example of a recent arrival from abroad finding London fog adding to the dismal experience of exile.

IV

Picturing a city so frequently obscured by fog and smoke struck the majority of native British artists as well-nigh impossible. John Ruskin (1819–1900), the most influential critic of the age and author of the classic *Modern Painters* (1843), confessed in old age, "had the weather when I was young been such as it is now, no book such as 'Modern Painters' ever would

A BLACK FOG.

Figure 5.5 "A Black Fog." An artist attempts to improve visibility in his studio by cleaning his skylight. His model also seems to be in a "black fog." Depression was common on foggy days, and November was reputed to be the leading month for suicides. (*Punch,* 14 February 1863, p. 68). Courtesy of the President and Fellows of Wolfson College, Cambridge.

or *could* have been written."[51] Many English artists, especially those based in London, felt the same about the murky atmosphere as Ruskin did. To them it was a nuisance that affected the light and prevented them from painting. David Roberts (1796–1864), a Fellow of the Royal Academy, acknowledged the problem in 1862: "I break new ground with my 'London from the Thames'; but I have still two weeks, and if the weather keeps from fog I shall be all right and ready."[52] In October 1880 another artist, Samuel Luke Fildes (1844–1927), complained, "We have endured and still endure the most awfully dark and hopeless winter that has ever been known in London, consequently the civilized globe. We had uninterrupted heavy fog for 5 consecutive days last week . . . . it is too dark for painting and so dense that we have had to burn gas to get our meals by. . . . Nobody is doing any work except a few at Hampstead."[53] Some artists tried to get around the problem by having winter studios built. These were made of glass or equipped with floor-to-ceiling windows. Artists would do all that could be done to allow the light to come through. Others, who could afford to do so, ended up going abroad to paint. In the south of France or above all in Italy, the light gave painters the clarity they sought. Fildes himself reluctantly came to this conclusion but considered it a second-best solution to remaining in London, since the subjects he painted could not be found in the Mediterranean.[54] Roberts went instead to Egypt, from where he enthusiastically wrote to his daughter about "the moonlights such as you cannot conceive in your dismal foggy atmosphere."[55]

Fog obscured and distorted, blurred the sharp contours of buildings, and confused lines of perspective. The meteorologist Luke Howard, writing about the great fog of November 11–12, 1828, tried to provide a scientific explanation for these effects: "On the Thames, as on land, the tendency which fog has to enlarge distant objects, was strikingly illustrated; the smallest vessels on their approach seemed magnified to thrice their usual dimensions. St. Paul's had a prodigious effect through the mist, though neither that nor the Monument were visible above the height of the houses. This optical illusion is said to arise from the fog diminishing the brightness of objects, and consequently suggesting a greater distance; since while the visual angle remains the same, the greater the distance the greater the [real] magnitude."[56] Whatever the source of the illusion, this disruption of form and perspective compounded the effects of fog on visibility to frustrate many English artists. Frederick Leighton (1830–1896), one of the most popular of all Victorian painters and sometime President of the Royal Academy, felt so incensed about the problem that he made a public speech at the Lord Mayor's dinner on the subject of London fog in 1882:

> We are further and especially attacked and paralysed in the heart and centre of our intellectual activity; for we live by the suggestive imitation and presentment of that which is revealed to us by light,—and by light alone,—and made lovely by its splendour. To us, therefore, the quenching of light, the blotting out of colour, is an approach to the drying up of the very life springs from which we are fed and set in motion. . . . Many a brother painter must regret with me the interminable hours, days and weeks of enforced idleness spent in the continuous contemplation of the ubiquitous yellow fog, depressing the spirits all the more.[57]

It was not just that the fog obscured the painter's subjects; its impact on the townscape rendered it dull and unpaintable. "As regards colour and light," declared the *Art Journal* in 1888 in a discussion of painting in London, "there is the standing grievance of the smoke. . . . The blackness that comes from soot has neither depth nor lustre; it is opaque, gritty shallow, grey—a denial of everything that the colourist loves."[58]

Yet a handful of English artists recognised the potential of fog and smoke as a basis for art. "So far from the smoke being offensive to me," wrote Benjamin Robert Haydon (1786–1846), "it has always been to my imagination the sublime canopy that shrouds the City of the World. Drifted by the wind or hanging in gloomy grandeur over the vastness of our Babylon, the sight of it always filled my mind with feelings of energy such as no other spectacle could inspire."[59] All the same, he produced very few London paintings and mainly specialised in historical subjects. A less conventional painter, such as Joseph Mallord William Turner (1775–1851), whose dramatic cloud and seascapes so impressed Ruskin, might have been expected to appreciate the play of light and dark, colour and density, created on occasion by London fog, but industrial London was not really considered a suitable subject for an artist; rural landscapes, portraits, or the Classical subjects preferred by the Academies were what appealed and, crucially, what sold. One of the few oil paintings Turner produced of urban London in 1835, *The Thames above Waterloo Bridge* (see Figure 2.2), had this verse appended to it:

> Where burthen'd Thames reflects the crowded sail,
> Commercial care and busy toil prevail,
> Whose murky veil, aspiring to the skies,
> Obscures thy beauty, and thy form denies,
> Save where thy spires pierce the doubtful air,
> As gleams of hope amidst a world of care.

Indeed Turner never actually bothered to finish the painting, realising that a picture of London complete with smoke-belching chimneys and clouds of atmospheric pollution was unlikely to find a buyer.

Wealthy patrons preferred a picture of a light, clean-looking London to one that depicted the often dirty-grey reality. In the eighteenth century a foreign visitor, Giovanni Antonio Canal (1697–1768; better known as Canaletto), painted London's atmosphere as if it was Venice's: clear, pellucid, without even the merest hint of smoke or pollution. Every building was observable in the sharpest contour and detail. Canaletto was offering English collectors what he thought they would be willing to buy. Fog and smoke simply did not appeal, associated as they were with work, poverty, grime, pollution, and the sordid realities of everyday life.

Nevertheless, by the 1880s fog had become too much a part of the London townscape for artists and their customers to ignore. In 1884 a large-scale oil painting titled *From Pentonville Road Looking West: London, Evening,* by John O'Connor (1830–1889), an Irish artist who earned his living mainly from painting theatre scenery but sometimes tried his hand at something more ambitious, was exhibited at the Royal Academy (Figure 5.6). It is painted from the viewpoint of a rooftop on the corner of Rodney Street and Pentonville Rise. Nobody who knew the area in this period would have been convinced by a representation of it that showed the scene in the bright, Italianate light pictured by Canaletto a century before.[60] O'Connor therefore painted a thick haze above the city. The people and horse-drawn trams are descending from foreground clarity into the background murk, passing by unawares an unsettling scene of mess and debris on the rooftop at bottom right, suggesting the chaos that lay behind the orderly street façades below, a reflection, perhaps, of the social anxieties

Figure 5.6 *From Pentonville Road Looking West: London, Evening* (1884), by John O'Connor. This romantic view of London's skyline has become a staple for use as a cover illustration on many books on the Victorians. It is often popularly marketed under the title of *Sunset*. © Museum of London, UK / Bridgeman Images.

of the decade. A yellow atmosphere hangs over the whole scene and suggests the essential characteristics of the "pea-souper." Yet although the fog here is genuine, it is not dense or all obscuring; it is discreetly suggested rather than openly acknowledged. The edifice of St. Pancras Station in the middle background retains its clear contours. London fog is hinted at without being in any way the centre of the artist's attention.

The problems that English artists faced in attempting to represent the smoky, frequently fogbound city were experienced in 1870 by William Wyllie (1851–1931), when his *London from the Monument* (1870; see Figure 4.5) aroused fierce criticism for its "disagreeable" representation of fog, despite its adherence to established topographical conventions. It not only did not sell; worse was to follow when a picture dealer known as "little T'" came into the Wyllies' bedroom, where the painting was hung. Mrs. Wyllie takes up the story: "He looked at the picture for some time and said, 'What d'ye want for it?' Bill named his price. T. said, 'I'll tell you what I value it at.' He took out his penknife, opened it, reached over me, and stuck the blade right into the middle of the canvas."[61]

For some years Wyllie turned away from picturing the dirtier aspects of London life, and indeed following a rejection of some of his work by the Royal Academy he went to sea, declaring that he would never paint again. However, the experience brought him back to the artistic life, above all as a painter of marine scenes, a genre which brought him considerable success. In 1883 his *Toil, Glitter, Grime and Wealth on a Flowing Tide* not only was exhibited at the Royal Academy, with a buyer waiting in the wings to take it after the exhibition, but also gained the attention of the prestigious Chantrey Bequest, which purchased it for the nation.[62] One trustee of the Chantrey Bequest was none other than Sir Frederick Leighton, who had railed against fog in a public speech a year earlier. The picture's title signifies the contrast that Wyllie wished to portray, the toil of the workers set against the value of the cargo and the wealth to its owners. The painting is filled with broad contrasts of light and dark. Smoke rising from the steamboats and factories in the background creates a yellow, brown, and black murk that obscures the view in the distance.

Nevertheless, here too London fog was portrayed tastefully, as background rather than as a subject in itself. As the *Art Journal,* which had been so critical of Wyllie's *London from the Monument,* suggested, "Painters are making an energetic effort to give London a good character as a paintable city, by turning its very blemishes to pictorial purpose. If they cannot have lucid horizons, they make good effects of the lurid skies; . . . Mr. Wyllie, for instance, has lately been bold to present to us coal-barges floating down a dreary river, with an imp-like body of smoke hanging over them in a chilly sky."[63] Like O'Connor, Wyllie did not allow his fog to soften or blur the outlines of his subjects. Even in the middle background the ships and buildings have clear contours and sharp, easily recognisable forms. The yellowness of fog is merely suggested by the colouring of the sky. More daringly, the artist chose to foreground in his title the social antagonisms that caused such concern in the 1880s. But grime rather than fog was the chosen means of conveying poverty and toil in visual terms. It would take a revolution in art, inspired by new developments across the Channel, before fog could become a subject for representation in itself.

V

It took foreign writers and painters to see the positive side of London's vaporous atmosphere and the unusual light effects it created. Eugène Delacroix, France's leading Romantic painter, arrived in London in May 1827 and reported with enthusiasm: "The daylight too is here of a special kind, always as on the day of a solar eclipse."[64] In 1833 the Italian writer Guiseppe Pecchio (1785–1835), who had fled Italy after being involved in an unsuccessful uprising in 1821, confessed himself, like other political exiles, terrified by the constant darkness created by London fog, but could not help but acknowledge its aesthetic appeal: "An eternal cloud of smoke which involves and penetrates every thing; a fog which, during the months of November and December, now grey, now red, now of a dirty yellow, always obscures, and sometimes completely extinguishes, the light of day, cannot fail to give a lugubrious and *Dantesque* air to this immeasurable and interminable capital. . . . In fact, for several days the sun only appears in the midst of the darkness visible, like a great yellow spot."[65] Even Taine, in his *Notes sur l'Angleterre,* occasionally waxed lyrical about London fog. While decrying its unnatural effects, he saw the Thames "enveloped in a fog of smoke irradiated by light. The sun turns it to golden rain, and the water, opaque, shot with yellow, green and purple, gleams and glitters as its surface lifts and falls, with strange and brilliant lights. . . . Nothing here is natural: everything is transformed."[66] In 1877 Henry James, likewise enthused about the "damp-looking, dirty blackness" of London in a fog, which lent "an harmonious grayness" to the townscape until "the whole picture, glazed over with the glutinous London mist, becomes a masterly composition."[67] In similar vein the American poet James Russell Lowell (1819–1891), ambassador to London from 1880 to 1885, wrote from London on a brief return visit to England in 1888: "We are in the beginning of our foggy season, and to-day are having a yellow fog, and that always enlivens me." Fog, he said, "has such a knack of transfiguring things. . . . Even the gray, even the black fogs, make a new and unexplored world not unpleasing to one who is getting palled with familiar landscapes."[68]

Fog's ability to transform the cityscape was expressed most powerfully perhaps by two of the most influential painters of the nineteenth century, one American and one French, both exponents of a new way of depicting the world. Just as some English artists moved to the Mediterranean for the different clarity of the light, so both of these artists found a new and exciting kind of light in London. The first was James McNeill Whistler (1834–1903), who claimed to have been the first painter to make fog his special subject.[69] An American, Whistler had been trained at the St. Petersburg Academy while his father was working on the extension of the railway system in Imperial Russia, and later moved to Paris, where he came into contact with the poet Charles Baudelaire, whose theories of art had a strong impact on him and helped him to break free of the conventional academic focus on Classicism and allegory. For Whistler art came to parallel music, and while he always worked figuratively, he began to give his paintings abstract titles such as "Nocturne" or "Study in Grey and Black." From 1859 he based himself in London, while maintaining regular contact with his friends in Paris. From the early 1860s, fascinated by the effects of fog on light and form, he began to incorporate it into his paintings of the English capital.[70]

Whistler chose to paint the Thames at quieter times, at night, or when the river turned to ice, or during periods of fog. His painting *Battersea Reach from Lindsey Houses* (1864–1871) shows a Thames smothered by fog; the many years it took Whistler to complete it suggest the difficulty he had in finding a means of representing fog, which appears in the painting particularly through blurred outlines of buildings and objects. *Nocturne in Grey and Gold—Piccadilly* (1881–1883) went much further, revealing a world disappearing into formlessness beneath the weight of the yellow-grey fog (Figure 5.7). In trying to capture how the scene would appear to the human eye, Whistler painted the lights and the brighter windows so as to make them seem to loom towards the viewer, as in fact they often appeared to on a foggy night. The horses and the people are ghostly silhouettes whose form appears to be dissolving before our eyes. The people on the top of the carriage in the foreground appear to be floating on air. As the *Standard* wrote: "The horses are 'understood.' "[71] The eeriness and the ghostliness are further enhanced by the flares of the linklighters. The *Kensington News* described this painting as "one of the most enchanting little atmospheric gems one could well desire to possess."[72]

Figure 5.7 *Nocturne in Grey and Gold—Piccadilly,* painted by James McNeill Whistler between 1881 and 1883. Whistler wrote of the London fogs, "I am their painter" in a letter to his sister-in-law Helen Euphrosyne Whistler ("Nelly") in 1879. Here he suggests shapes behind the fog and, within, a sensation of movement. Photograph © National Gallery of Ireland.

By this time Whistler was a well-known and somewhat controversial figure. Appalled by his insistence on art for art's sake and his rejection of any moral intent in painting, Ruskin had damned his *Nocturne in Black and Gold* in 1877 as an impudent example of a man asking for money "for flinging a pot of paint in the public's face."[73] Whistler sued for defamation, but neither the judge nor the jury appreciated the painting; and while the artist won his case, he was awarded the derisory sum of a farthing in damages. A sketch from *Punch* in 1886 showed that the public incomprehension of his work had still not been overcome a decade later. The fog has seeped into the gallery, blinding the visitors so that they cannot see the art at all (Figure 5.8). It adds to the general confusion raised by artists like Whistler.

Whistler was undeterred. He declared it his aim to aestheticise London fog. He loved the transformative effect it had on shape and form, turning the prosaic into the poetic, as "the poor buildings lose themselves in the

THE WINTER ART EXHIBITIONS

OPENED LAST WEEK, TO THE DELIGHT OF ALL.   OUR ART-CRITIC, WHO SENDS MR. PUNCH
THE ABOVE, HAS NOT SENT ANY NOTES OR SKETCHES!

Figure 5.8 "The Winter Art Exhibitions" shows the effect that London fog had on exhibitions and other forms of entertainments when it made its way inside. The same page also has a poem titled "Ode to an Expiring Fog, *Mrs. Leo Hunter Improved,*" which is taken from Charles Dickens's *The Pickwick Papers* (1836), in which Mrs. Hunter reads her "Ode to an Expiring Frog." (*Punch,* 4 December, 1886, p. 274). Courtesy of the President and Fellows of Wolfson College, Cambridge.

dim sky, and the tall chimneys become *campanili,* and the warehouses are palaces in the night, and the whole city hangs in the heavens, and fairyland is before us."[74]

Whistler was joined by others in praising the aesthetic potential of London fogs as they reached their greatest frequency and density in the 1880s. In 1883 the writer George Gissing, whilst standing on Battersea Bridge, wrote of the fog

obscuring, but not hiding; blotting out all meaner details, shading off the harsher intermediate lines, leaving only the broad features of buildings massed darkly against the grey background . . . [Now] the eye loves to dwell on what would offend it in the clearer light; the rude blocks of new houses on the north bank show only a glimmering window here and there on the surface of what looks like a lordly pile; to the left, the group of factory chimneys does not lack its suggestive beauty in the murkier air which hangs about it; the brief spire of St. Mary's of Battersea has lost its commonplace ugliness; the railway bridge which remotely spans the river is only a faint vision of arches, bounding the prospect not ungracefully.[75]

As the passage suggests, sensibilities had been affected by the emergence of Impressionism, of which Whistler was one of the harbingers.

The Impressionist movement began in 1862, when a group of young French artists rejected the Classicism of the Academy and began to paint not in a supposedly objective way but in a manner that tried to represent the subjective effect of light and form upon the observer. The second great painter of London fog was one of the movement's leaders, Claude Monet (1840–1926), whose work *Impression, Sun Rising* (1872) led a critic to coin the word for the movement. Monet's growing focus on the effects of atmosphere and light found an ideal subject in the Thames, shrouded in a winter fog, which he initially encountered when he fled Paris after the outbreak of the Franco-Prussian War in 1870. *The Thames and the Houses of Parliament* (1871) showed a thick yellowy, purply overcast sky, the colour of the haze reflected in the water of the Thames. In order to study the impact of the changing atmosphere of London, he took a room on the sixth floor of the Savoy Hotel from September to November 1899, returning to the hotel twice more in order to complete his work. During his second stay he was unable to use the same room and had to content himself with a room with a similar view on the fifth floor. From here he painted Charing Cross Bridge and Waterloo Bridge, producing a total of thirty-four and forty-one paintings respectively of each bridge. He used a room in St. Thomas's Hospital to paint a series of pictures of the Houses of Parliament, of which nineteen examples are known to have survived. Views of Leicester Square, which he also worked on, were painted from the green room of a club in St. Martin's Street.

Monet started many sketches at this time; but the effect that so impressed him—the changing colours of the light and atmosphere—proved an immense problem, as the changes were so rapid that it was difficult to finish any one painting at a time. So he started on several canvases and went back to them when he figured the light was similar. In this way he started over a hundred paintings, many of which he destroyed or never finished. In the end he took them back to his studio in Giverny to complete them. In 1903 he informed Paul Durand-Ruel, his Parisian art dealer, "I cannot send you a single painting of the London series as it is absolutely necessary for the work I am doing to have them all in front of me and, to be honest, not a single one is completed yet."[76] Monet did not want each to illustrate a state of the atmosphere individually, standing alone, but wanted to see them all in continuity with each other. His stay in London resulted in the largest series of paintings that he had yet produced. From this period he exhibited thirty-seven paintings in 1904, many showing the same London scenes in different atmospheric conditions but most portraying them through a veil of fog (unlike the 1871 painting, which shows the yellow haze of the fog merely as a backdrop to the scene). The paintings have a similar structure, a bridge dividing the picture between the water of the Thames below the bridge from the line of the buildings appearing against the sky above. Many of the paintings have the word *"effet"* in the title to indicate the impression of the changing atmosphere on the artist's eye.

In Monet's *Waterloo Bridge in Fog* (1899–1901; Figure 5.9) we are given a view of foggy London much more highly coloured than his earlier painting *The Thames and the Houses of Parliament* (1871). The sky and the river are made up of shades of purple. On the bridge there is a sense that people and omnibuses have been merged into a cluttered confusion. Through the purple sky can be seen the smoking chimneys, the source of the fog. Boats continue working on the river. Monet subsequently visited London solely to see the fog. He once wrote, "When I got up, I was terrified to see that there was no fog, not even the least trace of a mist; I was in despair, it seemed all my canvases were going for naught, but then little by little, as the fires were lit, the smoke and the mist returned."[77] Industrial smoke also enthralled him, and he complained of its absence on Sundays: "What a dreary day this damned English Sunday is. Nature feels the effects, everything is dead, no trains, no smoke, no boats, nothing to inspire me."[78]

Monet's paintings of the Houses of Parliament illustrate the synthesis of atmospheric impression he was trying to represent. In *The Houses of*

Figure 5.9 *Waterloo Bridge in Fog,* by Claude Monet, dated 1903. This is part of a series of paintings by Monet on the subject of London fog. Commenting on these works, the critic Wynford Dewhurst observed that fogs were "to the foreigner London's greatest charm, although to the inhabitant they are a deadly infliction" in his *Impressionist Painting, Its Genesis and Development,* 1904, p. 40. Museum of Fine Arts, Moscow, Russia / Bridgeman Images.

Parliament, London, with the Sun Breaking through the Fog (1904), reproduced on page 235 below, the sun is trying to appear through the clouds, its reflection showing itself in warm oranges and yellows on the river. The Parliament buildings are virtually lost in the purple haze of fog; their outlines have almost disappeared, except for the towers. Monet is using the fog deliberately to distort the Neo-Gothic building. He elongates St. Stephen's tower vertically to provide a greater impact, so that it rises like a phantom through the mist. But the buildings are also in a process of dissolution. Monet consistently liked to show the eye's impression of the dematerialization of matter in his paintings.[79]

Whilst talking to René Gimpel in 1918, the artist commented, "I adore London, it's a mass, a whole, and it's so simple. But what I love more than anything in London is the fog. . . . Without the fog London wouldn't be a beautiful city. . . . It's the fog that gives it its magnificent breadth." The city's "massive, regular blocks," he added, "become grandiose within that mysterious cloak."[80] Without the fog he saw the buildings as foursquare, unappealing to the imagination. Octave Mirbeau, an influential French art critic and friend of the artist, commented on Monet's London series of paintings in the 1904 exhibition catalogue, highlighting the relationship between the fog and the smoke:

> Smoke and Fog; forms, architectural masses, perspectives, a whole dull, rumbling city in the fog, composed of fog itself; the struggle of light and all the phases of that struggle; the sun held captive in the haze or breaking through the coloured, irradiant, swirling depths of the atmosphere in separate beams; the complex drama of reflections on the surface of the Thames, infinitely transient and subtle, sombre, or magical, disturbing, delicious, blossoming or chaos, floating gardens, the invisible, the unreal, and all of these together forming a nature, the nature particular to this prodigious city—which was created for painters, but which painters before M. Claude Monet have never learnt to see, have never been able to express.[81]

Charing Cross Bridge, Smoke in the Fog (1902; Figure 5.10) brings to the fore the relationship between the smoke and the fog. They are separate but related. The smoke pushes a sense of energy into the highly coloured sky, and all is reflected in the equally highly coloured river. There is a real sense of movement in this painting.

Monet may have chosen such well-known objects as the Houses of Parliament or the bridges spanning the Thames in order to play with the preconceptions of the viewer and to suggest the transience of apparently fixed impressions dissolving time as well as space. The changing nature of the fog imposed constantly varying impressions on the artist's, and hence the viewer's, eye. "London," wrote Monet, "is the more interesting that it is harder to paint. The fog assumes all sorts of colors; there are black, brown, yellow, green, purple fogs, and the interest in painting is to get the objects as seen through all these fogs. My practised eye has found that objects change in appearance in a London fog more and quicker than in any other atmosphere, and the difficulty is to get every change down on canvas."[82] From treating fog not as an objective phenomenon but in terms of its impact on the perceptions of the observer, it was only a short step to divorcing it from reality altogether, as writers would soon learn to do.

Figure 5.10 *Charing Cross Bridge, Smoke in the Fog* (1902), by Claude Monet. Another repeated motif in Monet's *London* series of paintings is that of Charing Cross Bridge. Monet was a great admirer of J. M. W. Turner, especially his *Rain, Steam, and Speed—The Great Western Railway* (1844), displayed in the National Gallery of London. Musée Marmottan Monet, Paris, France / Bridgeman Images.

For fog transformed the city into a work of the imagination: a transformation that can be found at its most extreme in the work of the "decadent" French writer Joris-Karl Huysmans (1848–1907), who rebelled against the nineteenth-century realist novel in works such as his notorious *Against Nature (À Rebours),* published in 1884.[83] Des Esseintes, the book's protagonist, is a bored aesthete who cannot derive true pleasure from any part of his life, even though he is wealthy, intelligent, and cultured. Des Esseintes controls his environment by carefully placing objects within his grand home that will stimulate his inner fantasies to "evoke pleasurable imaginings."[84] However, inspired by the works of Dickens and by the appalling weather he is experiencing in France, he walks outside and begins to imagine the Paris around him as if it is London: "The abominably foggy and rainy weather fostered these thoughts by reinforcing the memories of what he had read, by keeping before his eyes the picture of a land of mist and mud." And later he views "the appalling weather" in financial terms, "as an instalment of English life paid to him on account in Paris."[85]

Des Esseintes's imaginative view of London is one of "an immense, sprawling, rain-drenched metropolis, stinking of soot and hot iron, and wrapped in a perpetual mantle of smoke and fog."[86] The dockyards may be hives of activity, but "all this activity was . . . washed by the dark, slimy waters of an imaginary Thames. . . . Up above, trains raced by at full speed; and down in the underground sewers, others rumbled along, occasionally emitting ghastly screams or vomiting floods of smoke through the gaping mouths of air-shafts. And meanwhile, along every street, big or small, in an eternal twilight relieved only by the glaring infamies of modern advertising, there flowed an endless stream of traffic between two columns of earnest, silent Londoners, marching along with eyes fixed ahead and elbows glued to their sides."[87] As he imagines this nightmarish scene, the actual physical scene about him in Paris is remarkably similar to his vision and one that is linked through the fog and the damp: "He looked out of the windows and saw that night had fallen; the gas lamps were flickering in the fog, each surrounded by its dirty yellow halo, while strings of lights seemed to be swimming in the puddles and circling the wheels of the carriages that jogged along through a sea of filthy liquid fire."[88] A peek into a French bookshop's window reveals comic scenes by British artists such as George du Maurier and John Leech, as well as by Randolph Caldecott.

Des Esseintes hails a hansom cab. The cabby seems to have no problem in driving Des Esseintes wherever he wishes to go despite "the pestilential fog."[89] This would have amazed most cabbies in London, used as they were to the impossibility of navigation through a pea-souper. But we have to remember that we are still in Paris, where the fog was in no way as dense as it was in the British capital. Des Esseintes is driven to an underground bar, largely inhabited by English tourists.[90] The chatter of English and the effects of drink lead him to daydream that the cellar is in fact peopled by Dickens's characters, "who were so partial to the rich red port he saw in glasses all about him." These include Mr. Wickfield, from *David Copperfield,* and Tulkinghorn, the sinister lawyer from *Bleak House.* He pictures their homes in London "in the guise of a cosy ark sailing snugly through a deluge of soot and mire."[91] The restaurant in which he later dines is also filled with English people "discussing the weather." At this point, after a large meal accompanied by ale and then brandy, he decides that he has travelled sufficiently in his imagination: "When you come to think of it, I've seen and felt all that I wanted to see and feel. I've been steeped in English life since I left home, and it would be madness to risk spoiling such unforgettable experiences by a clumsy change of locality."[92] He returns home "feeling all the physical weariness and moral fatigue of a man who has come home after a long and perilous journey."[93] Fantasy not only takes precedence over reality; it actually replaces it.

For the Irish poet, dramatist, and wit Oscar Wilde (1854–1900), fog only became perceptible when the Impressionists reinvented it as a thing of beauty, transforming London's prosaic contours into ones of magic and mystery. In one of his characteristically paradoxical essays, "The Decay of Lying," published in 1891 in the form of a dialogue, he wrote,

> Where, if not from the Impressionists, do we get those wonderful brown fogs that come creeping down our streets, blurring the gas-lamps and changing the houses into monstrous shadows? To whom, if not to them and their master, do we owe the lovely silver mists that brood over our river, and turn to faint forms of fading grace curved bridge and swaying barge? The extraordinary change that has taken place in the climate of London during the last ten years is entirely due to a particular school of Art. . . . Things are because we see them, and what we see, and how we see it, depends on the Arts that have influenced us. To look at a thing is very different from seeing a thing. One does not see anything until one sees its beauty. Then, and then only does it come into existence. At present, people see fogs, not because there are fogs, but because poets and painters have taught them the mysterious loveliness of such effects. There may have been fogs for centuries in London. I dare say there were. But no one saw them, and so we do not know anything about them. They did not exist until Art had invented them. Now, it must be admitted, fogs are carried to excess. They have become the mere mannerism of a clique, and the exaggerated realism of their method gives dull people bronchitis. Where the cultured catch an effect, the uncultured catch cold.[94]

And indeed Londoners, and others too, may well have been made more aware of London fog by looking at the paintings of Whistler and Monet and also indeed by reading the works of Dickens and other authors. This awareness in turn found its way into the discourse of the day, feeding on itself. Another poet and dramatist, the symbolist Arthur Symons (1865–1945), echoed Wilde in writing of the impact the Impressionists had on perceptions of London. In what was to prove virtually the last thing he wrote before a psychotic breakdown silenced him for the best part of two decades, Symons described how fog in effect turned the great city from a collection of buildings into a painting: "The English mist is always at work like a subtle painter, and London is a vast canvas prepared for the mist to work on. The especial beauty of London is the Thames, and the Thames is so wonderful because the mist is always changing its shapes and colours, always making its lights mysterious, and building palaces of cloud out of mere Parliament Houses with their jags and turrets. When the mist collaborates with night and rain, the masterpiece is created." This, Symons wrote, was not an illusion or a work of art: it was nothing less than "English air, working upon London smoke, . . . the real London."[95]

VI

By the time Symons was writing, London had long since become a global city, the capital of a great empire, with connections all over the world. The impact of imperialism on the Far East, the advances made by European industry, science, and culture, proved an increasingly powerful magnet for Chinese and Japanese students and intellectuals. From the mid-1860s Japan and then, around the turn of the century, China opened up to Western influences as the need to close the gap with Europe became ever more urgent. In the early twentieth century many Chinese students went to Japan, the United States, France, and of course Britain to study. One such was Min-ch'ien T. Z. Tyau, who arrived in London on March 28, 1909, and stayed for seven and a half years. He studied international law at the University of London but became a journalist on his return to China and set up one of its most influential English-language newspapers, The *Peking Leader,* published between 1917 and 1930. Inevitably, when Tyau arrived in the capital, he was immediately struck by "the fog one sees in London," which, he averred, "is obtainable nowhere else. And if ever there is to be an exhibition of weather conditions of all countries, the London fog will no doubt be unanimously awarded the Grand Prix d'Honneur!"[96] While walking back from Kingston to Kensington, he was suddenly "enveloped by a thick yellowish shroud, which gradually thickened with the darkness of the gathering twilight": "A feeling of dread and anxiety slowly crept over me, and I began to think of Kingston as a modern Pompeii."[97] A passing omnibus meant that he could at least experience the fog with other people, and in a scene replayed during many foggy spells, he wrote, "Our vehicle slowed down and crawled along at a snail's pace. The conductor walked along the edge of the pavement with a lamp and in this way warned the driver to keep away from the kerb."[98] Tyau was aware of the possible dangers of walking through a London fog. "If you can stumble upon a police constable," he wrote, "well and good, for he is sure to pilot you home. But if you happen to come across a footpad, then your fate is sealed!"[99]

Tyau did not in any way see the fog in aesthetic terms. For him it was little more than a curiosity, an inconvenience or at worst a threat. But for another visitor from the Far East, the Japanese artist Yoshio Markino (1869–1956), London fog was an answer to a long quest. Markino came over to England in 1897. Originally from Japan, he had spent four and a half years in San Francisco trying to paint the thick fog that rolled in from the sea at certain times of the year to cover much of the city. Dissatisfied with its effects, he came to London to produce "a study of London mists."[100] Heavily influenced by Turner, Markino, like Monet, could not perceive London in any other atmosphere: "Age and the fogs have made the buildings so beautiful. . . . The colour and its effect are most wonderful. I think London without mists would be like a bride without a trousseau. I like thick fogs as well as autumn mists. Even on a summer day I see some covering veils. When I came to London first, I thought the buildings, figures, and everything in the distance, looked comparatively large, because in Japan the atmosphere is so clear that you can see every small detail in the distance, while here your background is mystified abruptly, which has a great charm to me."[101] Like Monet, Markino appreciated the way London fogs transformed the bricks of London: "For instance, that house in front of my window is painted in black and yellow. When I came here last summer I laughed at its ugly colour. But now the winter fogs cover it, and the harmony of its colour is most wonderful."[102]

Markino's delicate watercolours and sepia drawings are a good contrast to Monet's much denser treatment in oils of the subject of the atmosphere. The introduction to a reprint of his autobiography, by Sammy I. Tsunematsu, is titled "Yoshio Markino,—the painter of fog."[103] Markino was nicknamed "Heiji, painter of fog, in London."[104] He initially found it difficult to find a market for his paintings. But things changed when the Northern Irish clergyman and writer on London-based themes William Loftie (1830–1911) chose many of them to illustrate his book *The Colour of London* (1907).

In Markino's sepia drawing *Feeding the Gulls, Blackfriars Bridge* (1907) the buildings in the background are blurred beyond recognition (Figure 5.11). In spite of the lack of colour the artist manages to show the different densities of the fog, not only in the distance but as it swirls around and through the bridge. In his painting *Fog. Ladies Crossing Piccadilly* (see Figure 4.4) the fog in the background appears as layers of delicate shades of pink, blue, and yellow. People are blurred into indistinction by the fog, except for two ladies in the foreground. The art critic Marion Spielmann (1858–1948), editor of the *Magazine of Art* for seventeen years, noted in her introduction to *The Colour of London* how Markino managed to convey the quality of a city "whose greyness is built up of every colour of the rainbow, whose murkiness gives quality to the silvery greys, and tinges the yellow fog with auburn gold, whose mists and moisture lend height and added dignity to the buildings, and close in the shortened vistas with poetic mystery."[105] For Markino the fog transformed the city from the grey reality into a "poetic mystery." In his autobiography Markino confessed: "At first I was so frightened with London fogs. I thought, if I live in such dreadful fog I will soon become consumptive. So I bought a respirator at a drug store, and used to wear it whenever I went out." Yet, he added, "This 'dreadful fog' has become my greatest fascination, only a few years later!"[106]

The Irish painter Rose Barton (1856–1929) is perhaps the only well-known female painter of foggy London. Her often soft and subdued rendering of the city creates a picture of a misty atmosphere and demonstrates the influence of Impressionism on her work. She was fascinated by the atmospheric tones of both Dublin and London, but of the latter she wrote, "what can be more striking than the blue-grey fog that turns the end of a London street, as you look down it, into mystery and beauty

Figure 5.11 *Feeding the Gulls, Blackfriars Bridge* (1907), by Yoshio Markino. The *Academy* commented on one London fog on 15 January 1910 (p. 61): "It is as though one walked at the bottom of a muddy sea." Here the muddy sea is beneath the pedestrians on the bridge. From *The Colour of London* by W. J. Loftie. Author's own copy.

that give to the present a tinge of the uncertainty of the future, and throw a halo of poetry over the most commonplace home?"[107]

Barton's work is more highly coloured than many of Whistler's paintings, but the American artist's influence is nonetheless visible. She admits that her love of London fogs is not shared by everyone and rather ironically notes that she had only found one person who shared her enthusiasm, and he happened to be the chairman of a gas company. Like many people on the subject she makes her own distinctions between different types of fog. Thus she does not like "a fog that gets down the throat, and makes the eyes smart—when, if you do venture out, it is with the feeling that you may be robbed, or even murdered," but in the "fog that is fairly thick, yet not dense enough to stop the traffic, it is wonderful to see the shrouded forms looking gigantic as they come towards you. The scene is weird, ghostly, almost silent. The fog deadens sounds, and you hear little more than the shouts of charioteers."[108]

Barton's first major show was in February to March 1893 at the Japanese Gallery on New Bond Street, where she exhibited sixty views of London, and later, in June 1898, she exhibited illustrations of London at the Clifford Gallery. A reviewer of this particular show noted at the time: "Miss Barton realises the artistic possibilities of the perennial fog of London vistas admirably; its attractiveness and mystery which so many obtuse people refuse to see are well rendered in her drawing."[109] Many of these views of London were included in the 1904 publication *Familiar London*. This was part of a series of up-market books published by A&C Black, priced at twenty shillings, with intricate blocking, often in three or four colours, on the cases, which were designed by the talented Albert Angus Turbayne. Barton, unlike Markino, supplied her own text, thereby ensuring total control of the project.

In *Familiar London* she included a subsection on the fogs of London that significantly followed passages on the East End and on the police, thereby associating the fogs with poverty and crime. She begins by praising London fog, whose "opaque density . . . is at times very wonderful," and then recounts the story of a man lost in the fog who on being informed where he was exclaimed, "Good heavens! I've been groping my way about here for half an hour at least, trying to find the house, and I've lived there for over ten years." Fogs are divided into those "when the sounds . . . are

Figure 5.12 *Nelson's Column in a* Fog (1904), by Rose Maynard Barton. Here the sky appears heavy with cloud, but life continues beneath this canopy. There is a similarity in style between Markino and Barton. Both use the fog to introduce a softening of colours. From *Familiar London* by Rose Barton (appears opposite p. 118). Private Collection. © Look and Learning / Bridgeman Images.

all muffled, and the people one meets are seen only for a moment, and then vanish completely, as if they had walked through a wall," and those "strange fogs that float in the upper air above the houses—dense and black, shutting out all light from the sun—when the gas and electric lights rapidly shine out and one can almost fancy that midnight is over us, whereas it is only 10 or 11 A.M." The former fog she calls a "London particular," and she mistakenly associates this with the Dickens character Sam Weller from *The Pickwick Papers,* whereas it is that other well-known cockney character, Mr. Guppy in *Bleak House,* who actually uses the term.[110]

It is the latter type of fog, however, that she concentrates on when painting, unlike Whistler, in whose works everything seems to be caught up by the fog. In her *Nelson's Column in a Fog* Landseer's lions and the buildings beyond disappear into a foggy soup (Figure 5.12). Only the lights show through, and the faces are curiously highlighted. Nelson's Column, framed by a canopy of fog, highlights the sense of isolation. The foreground is very clear with the paving-stones reflecting the light of the sun trying to penetrate through the fog. It looks more wet than foggy. This painting was owned by George, Prince of Wales at the time. Another painting of the same name appears in a catalogue from an exhibition of Barton's work in 1987.[111] It shows Nelson's Column from another angle. The lions are clearer, whereas the background disappears under the weight of yellow clouds. There are more people in this version, signed and dated 1891, which reduces the feeling of isolation. Both paintings illustrate those "strange fogs that float in the upper air above the houses," but neither shows the clouds to be black in colour; they are both more yellow. Barton's *Brompton Road on a Foggy Evening* depicts London's prime fashionable shopping centre under another murky yellow haze.[112] There is no sense that the fog is inconveniencing those who are driving carriages along the road, and in the foreground a pram is even being pushed by a female, seemingly undaunted by the weather. The pinkish hues in the painting and the bright yellowness of the lamps give it a significantly warm feeling. Another of her paintings *Big Ben* (1904) is reproduced on page 112, above.

In Barton's opinion it was the foreigner who was "perhaps naturally, the most severe observer of our atmospheric changes, and he does not seem to appreciate the sombre beauty that is given to our streets by the fogs and soot of centuries."[113] This is a surprising statement since she admired the work of Whistler and Monet and knew their paintings of London fog. She became less able to paint London in bad weather such as fog or rain when she grew older. She wrote ruefully in 1924, "Unfortunately all the effects my soul loves mean more or less bad weather and I have a beloved dragon of a nurse who lives with me and prevents my doing anything rash."[114]

Markino's delicate drawings and paintings gave London fog an exotic, Oriental tinge, seen through a distinctively Japanese lens. Barton's paintings also depict a softer and less threatening aspect of a foggy day. By the time they were painting, photography had already exerted a powerful influence on art, with its claim to an accuracy of representation that the painter could never hope to achieve. Representing London fog, however, posed a particularly strong challenge in the state that the technological development of photography had reached before the First World War. One who tried it was Alvin Langdon Coburn (1882–1966), an American known for his portraits of literary figures, such as Henry James, George Meredith and W. B. Yeats, collected together in two books, *Men of Mark* (1913) and *More Men of Mark* (1922). In 1909 Coburn initiated a book of photographs on the subject of London with a text written by the Anglo-French writer and man of letters Hilaire Belloc (1870–1953), whose sister wrote *The Lodger* and whom Coburn had photographed in 1908.[115] Belloc devoted much of his attention to London fog, insisting that it was "not wholly produced by modern industrial conditions. The mists of the Thames estuary, the murkiness of the North Sea fog, were there long before London arose."[116] Coburn was not keen on Belloc's text. He later explained, "The introduction by Hilaire Belloc concerning the city completely ignored my pictures!"[117] He actually preferred a foreword written by the Irish playwright George Bernard Shaw (1856–1950), rejected by the publisher in favour of Belloc's text. Perceptively, Shaw saw the relationship to another American's work: "Like Whistler, Mr. Coburn has the advantage of looking at London much more imaginatively than any born Londoner could. What he shews us is there, as the camera testifies; but few of us had seen it until Mr. Coburn shewed it to us."[118] Shaw knew that it took the foreigner to appreciate the beauty of the London atmosphere. In a later book of Coburn's photographs a preface by the novelist and science fiction writer H. G. Wells (1856–1946) predicted optimistically that a future

Figure 5.13 *Kensington Gardens, November.* This is one of a series of photographs taken by the American photographer Alvin Langdon Coburn of a foggy day in London in 1909, though it concentrates more on the atmospheric wintry scene than on the fog and its consequences for traffic. © Royal Photographic Society / Science & Society Picture Library.

generation "will know nothing of carbon-laden fog-veils and sooty bricks and the blackened stems of trees against the spring."[119]

Coburn's pictures highlighted the mysteriousness and isolation produced by the fog. In his photograph *Hyde Park Corner* the lack of clutter, with the horse-drawn bus dimly visible in a solitary position between the trees, provides a sense of melancholy isolation. Everything behind the trees has lost its contour and shape.[120] Another picture, *Kensington Gardens, November,* (Figure 5.13) produced in 1909, has a similar effect. Belloc's text describes "the curious way in which London engulfs village after village, creeping round it as a flood of lava might creep round a temple or a walled enclosure," creating an unspoken parallel to the way fog submerged the built environment.[121] Whistler had complained some years before: "If the man who paints only the tree, or flower, or other surfaces he sees before him were an artist, the king of artists would be the photographer. It is for the artist to do something beyond this."[122] Coburn presented photography as art, using fog for aesthetic effect.

From finding fog oppressive, hellish, Stygian in its gloom, leading people to contemplate suicide or forcing them to leave for clearer skies elsewhere, foreigners who visited London had come to see in it an object of curiosity, even beauty. Nothing like it, as they frequently attested, could be found anywhere else in the world. Fog was London, and London was fog. As Monet painted, Coburn photographed, and Wilde and Symons wrote, fog seemed to have lost its earlier terrors. This was not merely a product of changing aesthetic fashion, though this of course had a lot to do with it. It also, as we shall now see, reflected changes in the nature of London fog itself.

CHAPTER SIX

London Apocalypse

I

In a novel published in 1873, the year of one of the most disastrous fogs of the nineteenth century, the theosophist Edward Maitland (1824–1897) imagined Victorian London from the point of view of an observer looking back on the period from the distant future: "Who now that sees our flat and commodious roofs, with their friendly gatherings, and elegant adornments, can realise the time when for an aerialist to pass over a large town, at a moderate height, would have been to court destruction by suffocation! For then every house was a volcano, and every chimney a crater, in a state of perpetual eruption, vomiting forth fire and smoke that made the atmosphere lurid, and loaded it with darkness and poison."[1] Since the early 1870s, the imaginary narrator remembered, a growing shortage of coal had driven people to discover alternative sources of energy, producing a time when, finally, "the freshest air and the quietest repose are to be found, and not a 'London black,' once so proverbial, comes to soil their garments."[2]

Maitland's fantasy started to come true sooner than he thought. London never managed to become a place of "the quietest repose," but already by the beginning of the twentieth century fogs were becoming less frequent and less intense. The main reason for this development was most probably the emergence in the 1880s, when London fog reached its murky peak, of a sustained campaign to address its root causes. Alarmed by the growing frequency and intensity of fogs in London and elsewhere, Ernest Hart (1835–1898), an eye surgeon, medical journalist, and public health activist, joined forces with Octavia Hill (1838–1912), a social reformer concerned with the health and well-being of the urban poor, to mount a campaign for cleaning up the air of the capital city. Hill was a powerful advocate for the provision of open spaces in London—the "lungs of London" such as Hampstead Heath—and coined the term "green belt"

Figure 6.1 "An Electric Link Boy"—an updated version of the linklighter, here seen holding an electric light rather than a blazing torch to guide people through the fog. He seems less sinister than most of his kind, and his customers appear grateful to follow him. (*Punch,* 19 November 1898, p. 229). Courtesy of the President and Fellows of Wolfson College, Cambridge.

to refer to the country areas surrounding the capital. She was a friend of John Ruskin, who was similarly concerned with the effects of a dark and dingy atmosphere on the moral and social condition of the poor. Hill and Hart, who was by now editor of the *British Medical Journal,* joined forces in founding the Fog and Smoke Committee in 1880.[3] According to other supporters of the movement, the dangers that fog and smoke posed for health seriously threatened Britain's position in the world, not just the inhabitants of its capital city. Lord Reginald Brabazon, twelfth Earl of Meath (1841–1929), a former diplomat who devoted himself to patriotic causes (he invented "Empire Day") and social and charitable work among the poor, spoke for an increasing number of imperialist enthusiasts when he warned in 1887 that fog was weakening the constitution of Londoners and rendering them unfit for military service. Brabazon became even more seriously alarmed when British forces suffered a series of defeats in the second Boer War (1899–1902), noting that many of the men who volunteered for service were not accepted because of their physical weakness.[4] He urged a redoubling of efforts to bring the capital's atmospheric pollution under control.

The committee appointed a number of inspectors who went round factories and industrial plant in the capital measuring smoke pollution from chimneys and getting the provisions of Palmerston's Act and its successors enforced as far as possible. The inspectors were aided over time by the development of new and more accurate instruments with which to measure the concentration of soot in the atmosphere and the deposits of sulphur dioxide on the capital's buildings.[5] With the committee's emergence, however, the focus was for the first time primarily on the pollution of the air not by factory chimneys but by domestic coal fires. The committee did not think that legislation to control emissions from domestic fires was practicable, so it decided that the best way to reduce them was by publicity rather than by going down the parliamentary route taken by William Mackinnon in the 1840s (indeed it was advised by a government minister that there should not be "any hasty attempt to legislate").[6] It enlisted prominent scientific experts to write a report on the causes of the smoke and fog problem; it organized a public meeting at London's Mansion House, attended by the Earl of Aberdeen, the President of the Royal Society, and the President of the British Medical Association; and it ensured that all of this received publicity in the pages of *The Times*. In true Victorian style it also staged a Smoke Abatement Exhibition, opened in South Kensington on November 30, 1881, with 230 exhibits, most of them on smoke-reduction devices for domestic fires, and a series of lectures; 116,000 visitors came to view the exhibits, and after it closed, it was transferred to Manchester at the request of another, similar organization, the Manchester and Salford Noxious Vapours Abatement Association. The exhibition gave enormous publicity to the dangers of smoke pollution, aided by the occurrence of two severe fogs, on January 18 and February 3–4, 1882, when trials were suspended because witnesses were unable to find their way to the court, and a theatre performance was abandoned because the fog got into the building and "rendered it difficult for the actors and the audience to see each other."[7]

The exhibition had some success, and one company in South Kensington sold 14,000 cheap closed stoves burning anthracite over the following two years. Continental-style stoves, however, did not provide the blazing fires that made for a cheerful domestic hearth, and the overall take-up was slow. Meanwhile, the Fog and Smoke Committee transformed itself into the National Smoke Abatement Institution (and from 1889 Society), which held further public meetings and began to campaign for a Royal Commission on smoke and fog pollution.[8] At this point, however, unprompted by the campaigners, Lord Stratheden and Campbell introduced a Bill into the House of Lords empowering local authorities to regulate the emission of smoke from domestic chimneys. "The ordinary fireside," the noble lord complained, ". . . only burns for the advantage of the circle who surround it"; the time had come to take action against such selfishness. He somewhat undermined his arguments by the hyperbolic suggestion that if fogs continued to get worse, London might have to be abandoned altogether and another capital city built elsewhere, a proposal worthy of the apocalyptic fog literature of the era.[9] Nevertheless, his Bill passed its second reading, only to be lost through government inaction, as were further Bills introduced by the persistent peer until his tenth attempt, in 1892. The Bills were lost because public opinion, backed by a substantial proportion of the legislature, feared the higher cost of burning anthracite instead of coal, opposed the interference of government inspectors and agents in what people did in their own homes, and wanted, as an eminent engineer put it, "an open, pokeable, companionable fire."[10] More significant was the inclusion of smoke-control measures in the Public Health (London) Act of 1891, which required factories and workshops to consume their own smoke and declared that "any chimney sending forth black smoke might be deemed a nuisance." In 1907, however, when Chelsea Borough Council sued the underground railway company because of the smoke emitted from its power-generating station, the company mounted a successful defence on the grounds that the smoke was only brown, not black.[11] Outraged, the Smoke Abatement Society promoted fresh legislation in Parliament, which passed in 1910 but was effectively emasculated by objections from representatives of the railways, the Chambers of Commerce, and the gas and electric-generating companies.[12] Ian O'Neill of Cambridgeshire found in his family records details of his grandmother Harriet Eliza Slope (born 1876), who lived in London near a large railway terminus: "She ran the business of this restaurant which was about 100 yds downwind of multiple railway tracks of mainline services raised on brick viaducts. The smoke and fumes from the engines added to that from domestic and other industrial use. Over several years, her health deteriorated to the point that she was forced to use a wheelchair. Eventually, with her health getting worse, a doctor told my

Figure 6.2 *The Wood Lane Power Station,* by Charles John Holmes (1868–1936). Holmes painted this from his own home at 73 Ladbroke Grove in 1907. The power station was opened in 1900 and supplied electricity to the Kensington area. It was closed down in 1928 and demolished in 1979. There were many complaints about the amount of smoke produced by power stations of this kind. © Museum of London, UK / Bridgeman Images.

grandfather that unless she was removed from the smoky atmosphere, she would die soon."[13] The Slopes moved to Hove, Sussex, in 1910, and although it took six months, Harriet's health recovered fully.

Yet the 1891 Act was a measure of real significance in the campaign to reduce the incidence of fog in London. In November 1898 a particularly noxious, black smoke-fog "in many parts of the town on Thursday morning at 10 o'clock, [when] it was too dark to permit the reading of letters," sparked an impassioned correspondence in *The Times,* in which the lack of action by local government was widely criticised.[14] The moving spirit of this correspondence was Sir William Richmond (1842–1921), a distinguished artist who clearly considered London smoke an obstacle to his profession, not to mention his wider concerns for the population at large. Richmond was a successful portrait painter, but he also worked on stained glass, designing the glass mosaics covering the spandrels and choir of St. Paul's Cathedral, a building that clearly suffered from the impact of the smoke-filled fog. In his first letter to *The Times* he argued, "The law is clear; the enforcement of it is all that is needed."[15] With the support of veteran campaigners such as Rollo Russell, Richmond founded a new organization, the Coal Smoke Abatement Society, in 1899, with the principal aim "to aid in enforcing to its utmost the existing law dealing with the smoke nuisance which is contained in the Public Health Act 1891."[16] The society set up training courses for stokers, mobilised ratepayers to bludgeon their local authorities into prosecuting offenders, and appointed an inspector to record smoke emissions from factory chimneys. From May to November 1899 the inspector reported 500 separate smoke nuisances of black smoke emitted for more then ten minutes in an hour. Local authorities were persuaded to take action in sixty cases; twenty-three were solved when the factory owners took immediate action, sixteen summonses were issued, and £200 worth of fines were levied. Prosecutions, though hampered by the reluctance of some local authorities to press charges and weakened by the minimal fines usually imposed, continued until the First World War.[17]

The activities of the society gave a significant boost to the already substantial impact of the 1891 legislation. The Meteorological Office observed in 1904 that the number of foggy days had been declining steadily since 1890; 1900 indeed was the least foggy year since 1871, with a mere twenty fogs; 1901 and 1902 each had forty and 1903 fewer than thirty. This compared with more than sixty at the height of London fog's career, in the 1880s.[18] In 1886 there had been eighty-six foggy days in London, and in 1887 there were eighty-three. But in 1905, 1906, and 1908 there were fewer than twenty.[19] In 1910 *The Times* reported that the amount of winter sunshine in London had risen by 40 percent over the previous decade.[20] The Meteorological Office attributed the decline in the first place to the efforts of the Coal Smoke Abatement Society in getting the 1891 Act more rigorously enforced. The society's inspectors had caused sixty-eight factories that had previously emitted large volumes of smoke to change their practices. In addition, many homes had fitted better grates or stoves, and perhaps most important, penny-in-the-slot gas cookers had spread rapidly among the working classes, replacing cooking on coal-fired kitchen ranges. In 1899 already it was reported that more than 150,000 working-class houses had been supplied with gas heating since 1895, and the number of gas fires and stoves rented out by one company in London, "placed side by side, would reach from Charing Cross to the West pier at Brighton and 50 miles back again."[21] Gas ovens and hobs were more efficient and easier to use as well as cleaner and more attractive, and their use had become very widespread by the outbreak of World War I.[22] By 1910, according to the Coal Smoke Abatement Society, "over 750,000 gas-cookers [were] in use in the metropolis alone, and their aggregate effect in preventing the emission of smoke from kitchen chimneys must [have been] very great."[23] Industry, moreover, was starting to move out of the central boroughs of the city into the suburbs or even further afield.[24] Finally, electric motors had started to replace coal-fired steam engines in small workshops and factories in the city itself. Other observers pointed out that there had been a decline in westerly winds and thus in the amount of water vapour precipitating over the capital. At the same time, the weather, according to some, had become windier, thus avoiding the still conditions necessary for the formation of a "London particular."[25]

Fog also appeared to be declining in intensity. An article written in 1899 noted that the latest fog had "but a slight approach to the proverbial pea-soup hue, and the Egyptian darkness in which on such occasions London has been invariably plunged was conspicuous by its non-occurrence."[26] In 1901 Sir Charles Alfred Cookson commented that a "great difference has taken place in the atmosphere": "we had more than the normal number of misty days, but not one of those black fogs with which we are annually plagued during the winter."[27] Looking back at the turn of the century from the vantage point of the early 1930s, R. Morton Rowe, technical and chemical adviser of the Manchester Public Health Department, suggested that London fog had changed colour over time because of a decline in emissions from industrial sources: "Thirty years ago the fogs were absolutely black. I have known it, at midday, be as black as night and impossible to see across the pavement. To-day the character of the fog has altered,—they are more yellow and not so densely black. But on the other hand I am inclined to think that they are quite as venomous as the black. The old fogs were black owing to the carbonaceous matter present, while the modern yellow fog is more characteristic of household smoke."[28] London fog, then, had declined from its high point of the 1880s and was becoming less of a nuisance. This did not prevent writers from using it as a metaphor in the Edwardian period just as they had done in the

Victorian era; but it did begin to change the way they perceived it, especially as social concerns began to mutate in response to the new threats that were seen to emerge after the turn of the century.

II

Already in 1903 the subject of London's fog was being treated in a more optimistic manner by some authors and commentators. A positive outlook of this kind is discernible in a series of short stories published in *Pearson's Magazine* by Frederick Merrick White (1859–1935). The stories imagine a variety of disaster scenarios in the capital city. "The Four White Days" subjected London to the grip of an arctic winter, for example. Another of these stories, "The Four Days' Night," published in 1903, tells "the story of a London fog that turned daylight into darkness for four days."[29] The initial disaster described in the story is created not by the fog but by a fire that breaks out in large petroleum storage tanks stationed on the Thames. A scientist, Martin Hackness ("B.Sc., London"), has been convinced that an accident of this nature, which creates black plumes of smoke wafting over the capital, will lead to the smoke being pressed down on to London if it happens on a foggy day, suffocating those who are unfortunate enough to be caught up in it: "I pictured that awful canopy of sooty, fatty matter suddenly shut down over a great city by a fog. A fog would have beaten it down and spread it."[30]

Inevitably, of course, a thick fog descends on London at the same time as the conflagration takes hold. It takes on the yellow hue typical for the time of year. When the fog restricts the movement of the smoke and presses it down to ground level, it forms a "black wall, . . . greasy and oily and grimy." Noxious and reeking of petroleum, it makes breathing difficult. The Cimmerian darkness it imposes means that people walk into the river and drown as well as suffer numerous other accidents of a kind familiar in a normally dense London fog: "No bread could be baked, no meal could be carried round, no milk or vegetables delivered so long as the fog remained. Given a day or two of this and thousands of families would be on the verge of starvation."[31] "One of the plagues of Egypt with all its horrors had fallen upon London."[32] Yet the people of London are not accused of moral degeneration in White's tale, as they were in other apocalyptic stories. There is no panic, and although there are some criminals who attempt to take advantage of the situation, even they realise that they cannot escape the city with their stolen goods. Overall, we are told, "London was holding out doggedly and stolidly."[33] And because people are unable to reach their own homes, they are forced to stay wherever they are made welcome: "Belated women, frightened business girls, caught in the fog had sought the first haven at hand, and there they were free to remain. There were sempstresses in Mayfair, and delicately-nurtured ladies in obscure Bloomsbury boarding-houses. Class distinction seems to be remote as the middle ages."[34] The fog brings out a strong sense of community, transcending class divisions.

The situation appears to be deadly, with alarmists predicting disaster: "Every hour the air, or what passed for air, grew more poisonous. Men fancied a city with six million corpses!"[35] But the crisis is in the end resolved by Hackness himself, who lets off explosions through the fog from a flying machine, thus opening channels through which the deadly smoke can escape into the upper air, to dissipate over the sea. Inventions to disperse fog were indeed proposed in the early twentieth century. One, from as early as 1907, was labelled a "Fog Dispersing Machine" (see Figure 6.3), a large cannon that could be fired to disperse the fog into the atmosphere. As a tribute to the designer's sense of neatness, the cannon could be retracted into an elaborate monument.[36] Four years later another new invention was being tried out by the London General Omnibus Company, in which fog was dispersed by a current of air. The hope was that it could be fixed to all London buses and trams. It does not seem to have got any further than the initial trial (Figure 6.4).

After the fog in "The Four Days' Night" has been dispersed through Hackness's ingenuity, White reflects on how such a disaster might be avoided in future: "No great mass of people would ever dare to congregate together again where manufacturers made a hideous atmosphere overhead. *It would be a great check upon the race for gold.*"[37] Yet this is the only statement of moral condemnation in the story. White leaves it to one of his protagonists, a character called Eldred, to apportion the blame and suggest a remedy: "Abolish all fires throughout the Metropolitan area. . . . In time it will *have* to be done. All London must warm itself and cook its food and drive all its machinery by electric power. Then it will be one of the healthiest towns in the universe. Everything done by electric power. No thousands of chimneys belching forth black poisonous smoke, but a

Figure 6.3 This "Fog Dispersing Machine," depicted here in 1913, was devised by Professor M. Demitrio Maggiora, a prolific Italian inventor. This machine is mentioned as early as 1st December 1907 in the *Washington Post* (Miscellany Section, p. 4), in which Maggiora suggested that the London County Council was willing to test it. There is no evidence, however, that it ever existed in reality. Artist unknown. Source: London Metropolitan Archives (Unidentified monogram; City of London Ref: SC/GL/WUL/001/013).

clear, *pure* atmosphere. In towns like Brighton, where the local authorities have grappled the question in earnest, electric power is half the cost of gas."[38] White accepts that this must be done through government interference in the home, reflecting perhaps the growing willingness of liberals as well as conservatives to allow government interference in everyday life. Unlike earlier authors of apocalyptic fog scenarios, White did actually think the problem was capable of solution.

White's story also reflects a greater optimism about relations between social classes characteristic of the turn of the century. The social antagonisms of the 1880s had weakened.[39] Social investigators such as Charles Booth had begun to compile information on the world of the poor. The

Figure 6.4 A new invention for dispersing fog by a current of air was proposed by a London publican, Henry A. Lloyd, and his colleague Frank A. Wright, for attachment to all London buses and trams. Here it is placed on a car in 1929. It would allegedly permit motorists to drive at sixteen miles an hour in the thickest of fogs, but it never caught on. © Planet Pix Ltd—Planet News / Science & Society Picture Library.

underclass of the metropolis was no longer a dark, unknown, uniform mass posing a huge latent threat to civilization but a complex and differentiated social layer in which the respectable working class was as different from the indolent as the middle class was from artisans and shopkeepers. Booth's researches demystified the world of the slum, the casual labourer, and the urban poor, robbing it of many of its terrors for the middle class.[40] Reform and improvement through social welfare began to take the place of panic fears of degeneracy and the threat of violence and revolution that had characterised the 1880s.

More importantly, however, during the Edwardian era fear of social upheaval was increasingly displaced by the growing anxiety about international conflict. The construction from 1898 onwards of a massive German battle fleet; the bombastic utterances of the Kaiser, who backed the Boers in the South African War at the turn of the century and caused considerable offence in Britain with a tactless interview in the *Daily Telegraph* in 1908, the unpredictable but decidedly bellicose intervention of the Germans in a series of international crises—all this made the world seem a more dangerous place and turned public attention to the looming threat of war. Novels about future wars such as William le Queux's *The War of 1910* (published in London in 1906) raised the alarming prospect of German invasion if Britain's defences were not quickly strengthened. Spy scares began to be whipped up by popular newspapers such as the *Daily Mail*, and hostility to the large numbers of German immigrants in London started to grow. The anarchist outrages of the early 1900s, including bomb attacks and assassinations in many European countries and culminating in 1911 with the siege of Sidney Street in London, in which an alleged Latvian anarchist ("Peter the Painter") became involved in a gun battle with the police, fuelled popular concerns about the supposed dangers of immigration and the threat to the security and stability of British life from abroad. The literature of the era began to use fog in connection not with domestic social dangers but with the supposedly disruptive influence exerted on British society and politics from outside.[41]

III

In 1908 a short story with the somewhat unwieldy title "The Poison Cloud: A Record of the Great Fog—with the Story of the Adventures and Sufferings of Some of the Survivors of London's Greatest Disaster," by Hugh Owen, appeared in *Pearson's Magazine* in 1908 (as had White's story in 1903).[42] In many ways it was a continuation of the apocalyptic scenarios of William Delisle Hay and Robert Barr. It certainly made no concessions to the new mood of social harmony, nor did it give any recognition to the decline in the frequency and intensity of London's fogs—rather, if anything, the reverse. The story is told in the first person by one Collinson, travelling from Edinburgh to London by train just as the fog is settling over London. He is keen to meet with his girlfriend, whose stepmother had recently refused permission for them to marry when Collinson had asked her during his visit to Scotland. The first hint of the danger created by the fog is a ten-hour delay to the train on its journey into London because of

Figure 6.5 A hot refreshment stall at Waterloo Station on November 19, 1937. Many passengers would have had to endure long delays to their journey time, and the opportunity to enjoy a warm drink would have been especially welcoming in the cold, foggy weather. © Daily Herald Archive / Science Society Picture Library.

adverse weather conditions. Indeed the train is fortunate to arrive at all, since many trains have collided with each other or been stopped because of debris on the line.

The fog is described as "the densest fog of recorded experience," a "'London particular,' a 'pea-souper,' . . . just the ordinary London fog that the Londoner has always tolerated, and in his heart been secretly proud of."[43] A newspaper article quoted in the narrative reports that "one contributory cause of the calamity may be the huge quantities of inferior foreign coal that have latterly been burned in London owing to shortage of home supplies due to the coal strike."[44] In fact during this period, according to the official history of the British coal industry, "imports [of coal] were negligible, only once exceeding 50,000 tons, which was during the national stoppage of 1912."[45] The narrative taps into a mood of xenophobic nationalism which prevailed at the time of Owen's story, not least in the increasingly insistent calls for tariff reform to reduce the flow of cheap goods entering Britain in the era of free trade.[46] Foreign coal, it seems, is to blame for the fog.

Soon, and without warning, the fog is transformed from an ordinary pea-souper into something much more deadly: "The fog had changed suddenly to the black infliction we felt about us, and had closed in on town and suburbs, blotting London out, as it were."[47] Atherton, a medical man and the scientific hero of the story, exclaims, "Why, a London fog may turn out to be one of the tragedies of history. I've always said that, given the right conditions of barometer and temperature, with a windless, stagnant, and moistened air—conditions always within the compass of probability—and we should paralyse London, and stagger humanity."[48] The doctor likens it to the Great Plague: "Why, every day of it will account for a month's ordinary mortality bill!" The fog was now deadly in itself: "No, I don't mean casualties only. I mean, quite simply, that even the healthy will have a struggle to live through much of this, and that the very young and the very old, and all the weak or ailing, will not possibly be able to survive even three or four days of it. And if we had a week of it, why, London would become a dead city—a gigantic charnel house!"[49] The narrator, caught up in the fog himself, feels the impact on his own health.

The description conveys, in an extreme fashion, what many people must have felt in an ordinary fog: "The cold was intense—it numbed and deadened the limbs, and the fog seemed to soak into one's very bones. My eyes smarted agonisingly, my head throbbed with pain, a dull singing noise began to fill my ears, and my breathing became quick and laboured. The engineer seemed to suffer even more than I."[50] The engineer, who has travelled from Edinburgh in the same carriage as the narrator, Collinson, accompanies him on a frightening journey by car through London. Collinson manages to get the engineer to his flat and calls Atherton, a friend of Collinson's, to come over. The doctor details the engineer's symptoms: "Acute pneumonia, complicated by a distinct state of narcosis, . . . breathing poisoned air."[51] The poisonous air has become a kind of vaporous drug that causes a narcotically induced sleep. Atherton tries to revive the engineer from the coma into which he has slipped by administering pure oxygen, a large supply of which the doctor has acquired precisely as a precaution against the potential dangers of a major fog. Unfortunately it is too late to save the engineer. But it is this oxygen supply that saves the lives of Collinson and his fiancée. The oxygen is used in conjunction with two mining helmets found in the engineer's personal belongings—helmets originally intended to save miners from the effect of choke-damp (carbonic acid gas). The oxygen and helmets enable Collinson and his fiancée to travel southwards to safety beyond the fog. The mining helmets suggest, too, how entering a fog was akin to entering a dark and airless mine gallery.

The doctor describes the situation in the bleakest terms. The fog has caused the virtual destruction of the entire city and its population: "The tragedy gallops to its end. London is almost an obliterated city. Its bricks and mortar are standing, but that is about all that can be said for it. For its population by now must be simply decimated. As an organised city of human existence, London no longer exists. The whole of the East End is a charnel house of horrors. Plague will soon add its terrors to the work of starvation, for all the dead lie above ground and we are all cooped up in a living tomb. The very streets are strewn with the dead."[52] Atherton even fears that an epidemic of smallpox might break out once the fog lifts.[53] This serves as yet another image for the breakdown of society. Epidemics had been brought under control only recently, mainly through state intervention, in the form of compulsory vaccination, quarantines, disinfection, and slum clearances. So the possibility of an epidemic emerging in the wake of a fog that has reached its deadly concentration only because of the state's failure to take preventive measures becomes a metaphor for the overall failure of the state. Here too, as in the issue of tariff reform, the author reveals himself as a champion of increased state intervention in society, in opposition to the traditional liberal proponents of free trade and laissez-faire. Atherton climbs to the top of the Victoria Tower of the House of Lords, one of the highest points in London, in the hope of getting above the deadly fog. There he finds the Speaker of the House of Lords, Black Rod, and others already assembled—physically and symbolically above the people, reinforcing in class terms their superiority and underlining the need for the continuation of government.

The protagonists of "The Poison Cloud"—Collinson; his fiancée, Miss Clarice Heseltine; and the scientist figure of the doctor—are largely calm and practical, as are the professionals with whom they come in contact: nurses, policemen and sailors from the navy. But the impact of the fog on the uneducated masses is one of panic and fear. The poor of the East End are especially vulnerable to the hysteria caused by the fog, as the doctor warns: "All the latent criminality of London will soon be at work, reinforced by the starving hordes of the East End of London. When starvation begins to stalk, and panic and fear go hand in hand with it, and all the restraints of authority are removed, we must look out for trouble. . . . Anarchy is going to take the place of law, chaos of order. We who live in the most law-abiding capital in the world, with law and authority organised on the most perfect basis that civilisation has yet evolved, are suddenly to be thrown back into a vortex of elemental barbarism and passion, each man for himself, and all authority powerless."[54] Reports then follow of "the wild scenes that had taken place, particularly in the East End, where a panic had seized the people to escape to Epping Forest, and of the holocausts that followed, in which hundreds of men, women, and children were trampled to death by surging crowds that moved blindly onwards to their own doom."[55]

Fear and a general lack of order bring looting and riots, and these inevitably lead onwards to still greater destruction by the common people: "Hunger and desperation have converted them into a lawless, fiendish mob."[56] The fog is both a symbol that evolution has regressed and a factor in causing society's rapid degeneration to a primeval state. Even the civilising impact of time is shown to have come to an end: "Big Ben above us was silent, and no longer measured the hours."[57]

In the end martial law is established under the military police and the navy. It is the navy which saves Collinson and Miss Heseltine from convicts who have escaped from Brixton prison and who, under the rules of martial law, are shot immediately. The marines have helmets similar to the ones found in the engineer's case, used to save men trapped in submarines. Their torpedo-boat flotilla is used to clear the Thames, which is filled with debris from crafts which are unable to move or have crashed into each other. The boats also attempt to dispel the fog by sending up rockets (a device successfully utilised in the 1903 story by White), though these fail to work. Since the fog is composed of water as well as smoke, it is hardly surprising that the Senior Service turns out to be the arm of state best equipped to deal with the crisis. It was widely regarded as the key to Britain's global power, and at the time the story was written, a tense naval arms race with Germany was dominating the headlines.[58]

In blaming the fog on the import of foreign coal, backing the Conscription Bill then under consideration, and glamorizing the role of the navy, Owen reflected the growing fear of war prevalent at the time and joined many other commentators who were demanding decisive action to prepare for the prospect of conflict with hostile foreign powers. Fog, seen as a quintessential signifier of London in earlier representations, has here become something *foreign,* to be dispelled by British military action. It was no coincidence that the population of East London was increasing rapidly at this time as a result of the immigration of poor Jews from eastern Europe.[59] A leaflet produced by the Conservative Central Office for the 1905 Mile End by-election revealed growing fears about the East End. If the "alien invasion" remained unchecked, it warned, the East End would see "paupers who fill the streets with profligacy and disorder."[60] The xenophobic mood found expression in the 1905 Aliens Act, designed to control such immigration. Speaking at Limehouse, on December 15, 1904, Joseph Chamberlain told his audience: "You are suffering from the unrestricted imports of cheaper goods. You are suffering also from the unrestricted immigration of the people who make these goods."[61] Owen's "The Poison Cloud," written shortly afterwards, expresses just such fears in metaphorical form.

The conclusion of the story follows the pattern of Hay's 1880 narrative. Clarice Heseltine and Collinson escape from London to a rural retreat in Surrey. By this time they are married. Clarice is even pregnant with their first child, whose forenames will include that of Atherton, now a close friend. The situation has been resolved by the navy, but in the end the fog is dissipated by divine intervention, taking the form of a hurricane: "and the breath of Heaven blew the pall of pollution away—and revealed to London its own horror!"[62] Hordes of immigrants are polluting the air with their fires, using cheap foreign coal. "If I were dictator, I would order every fire in every domestic grate in London to be extinguished. They are all doing their best to contribute to the asphyxiation of London."[63] This is a clear change from literature of the mid-nineteenth century, which still held the open hearth as sacred and central to family life, inviolable from government interference. In Owen's scenario deadly fogs are neither inevitable nor irreversible; they can be prevented by simple acts of government intervention. The British may be morally weak because they let in too many destitute foreigners and cheap and poor-quality imports, but they are not degenerate: it is the foreigners who are beyond redemption.

"The Poison Cloud," then, despite its xenophobia and ferociously apocalyptic depiction of the densest kind of London fog, is in the end more optimistic about the possibility of ridding London of its fogs than were the earlier stories by Hay and Barr. Its most distinctive feature is its underlying argument that London fog of this kind is caused above all by foreign influences. A dramatic illustration of the same point can be found in Sir Arthur Conan Doyle's novella *The Poison Belt,* in which Earth is overwhelmed by a massive band of poison gas through which it passes on its journey through space. Doyle's hero, Professor Challenger, the central figure in his more famous story *The Lost World,* foresees this and invites some friends round to his house outside London, from which, secure from the gas's influence by wearing gas masks, they observe the entire population being struck down as the gas takes hold—characteristically for the age, they are not bothered by the danger posed to their servants, who carry on managing Challenger's household until they collapse. Typical too for the age is the sequence in which the world's peoples succumb, beginning with the "weaker races" and ending with the "superior" Caucasian population. In the end the gas proves to be harmless; it has just sent people to sleep, and they wake up as soon as Earth emerges from its shadow. Although Conan Doyle sees this as a warning to human beings, it is not a warning against their own environmental carelessness, nor does it have any direct application to the way urban society conducts its business.[64]

IV

Fear of foreigners was perhaps at its most acute when Londoners came to contemplate the many political exiles in their midst. Foremost among these were the anarchists, men like the possibly apocryphal Latvian radical Peter the Painter, who saw the destruction of government ministers and representatives of bourgeois society as the means to attaining a new, perfect society without the intrusions of the state and its many individual and institutional agents. Some expression of these fears could be found even in the work of one of the greatest novelists of the era, Joseph Conrad (1857–1924). Conrad was himself a foreigner by origin, a Polish sea captain who had anglicized his name from Korzeniowski. He settled in London, wrote in English, and took on British citizenship. The sea and the exotic places in the world he had visited played a central part in his writing, but unusually *The Secret Agent* is set in London. Written in 1907, it is based on an actual incident that occurred in 1884, at the height of fog's dominance over the atmosphere of the city. The narrative of the novel concerns Mr. Verloc, who not only is a secret agent of an unnamed country (one very like Russia) but also supplies information to the police. Verloc is forced by his new superior at the embassy to agree to commit a terrorist act on a building of scientific worth—it turns out to be the Greenwich Observatory—the blame for which will be placed on a revolutionary group working against the government that the embassy represents. Verloc dupes his simple-minded brother-in-law, Stevie, into carrying the bomb to the observatory to leave it there. Stevie stumbles, and the bomb explodes prematurely, blowing him to bits. When Verloc's wife, Winnie, discovers the death of her beloved brother, she stabs her husband to death.

She starts to make a getaway as the police, led by Chief Inspector Heat, close in but then, realising she cannot escape the horror of her actions, drowns herself in the Channel on the crossing to France.

Fog plays a major part in the novel. Edward Garnett, a friend of Conrad's, wrote of "the murky gloom of old London's foggy streets and squares," which, for him, reflected the novel's preoccupation with "the dim recesses of human motivation."[65] Like Stevenson, Conrad uses fog not simply to signify the setting of the action in Victorian London but in far more subtle and complex metaphorical ways. Stevie's death takes place on a foggy day. Comrade Ossipon, a member of the revolutionary anarchist cell, reads of the events in a newspaper. Yet the report is brief and cryptic: "Half past eleven. Foggy morning. Effects of explosion felt as far as . . . Enormous hole in the ground."[66] This same "fog though not very dense" is an aid to Verloc, helping him to escape without being seen after he has left Stevie within a hundred yards of the observatory walls.[67] Chief Inspector Heat reaches the bomb site so swiftly that the fog has still not been dissipated by the sun. He has not had time to breakfast, and the fog takes on the metaphor of food: "he had swallowed a good deal of raw, unwholesome fog in the park."[68] The world of *The Secret Agent* is very Dickensian, especially in the way it uses fog to sum up the condition of England, more precisely London. Fog and mud are allied in a world where fog is often reduced to its component parts: dirt and water. Even when the sun does appear, it is described as "a peculiarly London sun. . . . It looked bloodshot."[69] More often than not the sun struggles against the mist or fog in the text: "The rusty London sunshine struggling clear of the London mist shed a lukewarm brightness."[70] The fog is rusty because of the amount of dirt in the air and is red tinted like dried blood; as in Marie Belloc Lowndes's *The Lodger,* the red colours of the sun mirror the bloody crimes being committed beneath it.

The atmosphere creates a world in which the inhabitants are imprisoned, like Mrs. Verloc, unable to get out from "the bottom of a black abyss."[71] This is a world without hope. Even a respected professional like Chief Inspector Heat's superior, the Assistant Commissioner, feels trapped by London and his job. His inclination is to return to the colonies, where he will not feel chained to a desk, overwhelmed by administrative duties. He has been forced to move back to London because of his wife's sensi-

Figure 6.6 "The Haymarket, Winter," an evocative photograph by James A. Sinclair (1864–1940), taken in 1913. Its grainy quality and yellow tinge certainly match the reality of the fog. A man in the foreground may be selling hot chestnuts, the fumes adding to the murk. The dome of St. Paul's shows through the smoke and fog with a pale sun shining above. © Royal Photographic Society / Science & Society Picture Library.

tivity to the tropical climate. In the telling final paragraph of the novel the Professor, a member of the anarchist cell who both makes explosives and carries them around on his person to set off should he be caught, cannot look the "odious multitude of mankind" directly in the eye. He is "terrible in the simplicity of his idea calling madness and despair to the regeneration of the world," a world that is still without hope and whose "lofty pretensions" are still "oppressed by the miserable indignities of the weather."[72]

In *The Secret Agent,* in defiance of normal meteorological wisdom, fog often leads to rain; mist is introduced where its moistness can be emphasised. Thus when the Assistant Commissioner looks outside, "it was a very trying day, choked in raw fog to begin with, and now drowned in cold rain."[73] The London that discloses itself to the Assistant Commissioner seems like a scene after a biblical disaster: "The panes streamed with rain, and the short street he looked down into lay wet and empty, as if swept clear suddenly by a great flood. . . . The flickering, blurred flames of gas-lamps seemed to be dissolving in a watery atmosphere."[74] Slightly later, the Assistant Commissioner goes out into a street likened to "a wet, muddy trench." "His descent into the street was like the descent into a slimy aquarium from which the water had been run off. A murky, gloomy dampness enveloped him. The walls of the houses were wet, the mud of the roadway glistened with an effect of phosphorescence."[75] His assimilation into the locality further extends the metaphor of the aquarium: "He might have been but one more of the queer foreign fish."[76] In a symbolic parallel the Assistant Commissioner's own superior, Sir Ethelred, the Secretary of State, is currently pushing through a Bill for the nationalization of fisheries. The Assistant Commissioner is fishing on the state's behalf in the muddy, watery underworld of London, with its foreign terrorists and revolutionaries.

The emphasis on the mud and moistness of London resembles the opening of *Bleak House*. It is well known that Conrad enjoyed Dickens's work and had read this particular novel "innumerable times, both in Polish and in English."[77] The opening of *Bleak House*—"As much mud in the streets, as if the waters had but newly retired from the face of the earth, and it would not be wonderful to meet a Megalosaurus"—harks back to the beginnings of Earth, a postdiluvian swamp.[78] Fog is here reduced to an aspect of a wider liquidity, in which the contours of time and space have been blotted out, reducing humankind to insignificance. At the end of the story, not surprisingly, in a world dominated by water, Winnie Verloc chooses to drown herself: "She was alone in London: and the whole town of marvels and mud, with its maze of streets and its mass of lights, was sunk in a hopeless night, rested at the bottom of a black abyss from which no unaided woman could hope to scramble out."[79] The alliterative *m* words link the seemingly unlinkable—"marvels and mud." This darkness, as throughout the book, represents the condition of London—dark, gloomy, and without hope. After the revolutionary Comrade Ossipon has deserted Winnie Verloc, he is swallowed by the urban gloom: "His robust form was seen that night in distant parts of the enormous town slum-

Figure 6.7 *Reflections on the Thames, Westminster* (1880), by John Atkinson Grimshaw (1836–1893). Grimshaw became known for the misty and atmospheric quality of his paintings. In this work, he only suggested fog rather than directly representing it, thereby masking the unpleasant side of industrialization. © Leeds Museums and Galleries (Leeds Art Gallery) UK / Bridgeman Images.

bering monstrously on a carpet of mud under a veil of raw mist."[80] Neither "carpet" nor "veil" offers the protection or comfort that it usually promises. London, or more precisely London fog, is shown to be fragmenting into its basic parts—mud and water. In the same way, after the explosion Stevie's body is further reduced from the fragments of skin and bones picked up at the scene of the crime to "Blood and dirt. Blood and dirt," a description mumbled by his sister, Winnie, after his death.[81]

Yet the danger posed by the mist should not be overlooked; this is indicated when Mr. Verloc advises his wife to go to bed. "What you want is a good cry," he says to her after she has overheard the details of her brother's death.[82] In a world described in terms of its water content, the significance of crying is not lost on the reader. "This opinion had nothing to recommend it but the general consent of mankind. It is universally understood that, as if it were nothing more substantial than vapour floating in the sky, every emotion of a woman is bound to end in a shower."[83] Verloc misunderstands the depth of his wife's emotions just as the danger of vapour in the sky is misunderstood. Fog has reduced London and its

inhabitants to insignificance, frustrating their aspirations, both imprisoning them and obscuring the moral boundaries that separate sanity
from madness. Fog signifies the blurring of Verloc's and Stevie's moral perceptions and the confusion of identities that they experience, caught between the police and the embassy, a foreign country and their own.

V

Perhaps the most obvious use of London fog in fiction has been as a metaphor for mystery and uncertainty. This could be self-imposed, as in *The
Hill of Dreams* (1907), by the Welsh mystic and horror-story writer Arthur
Machen (1856–1947), best known to posterity for his role in the invention
of the First World War legend of the "angel of Mons." Linked to the
decadent movement of the 1890s, Machen portrayed London as a city of
"unknowable, . . . unplumbed depth," symbolized by the "foggy and dull"
streets through which the hero of his novel wandered, passing "the vague
shapes of houses that appeared for a moment and were then instantly
swallowed up." Clearly influenced by the apocalyptic associations of fog,
Machen writes that his hero thought that he had "strayed into a city that
had suffered some inconceivable doom, that he alone wandered where
myriads had once dwelt. . . . All London was one grey temple of an awful
rite, ring within ring of wizard stones circled about some central place."
It was a "wilderness surrounded by waste places." Fog rendered the city
incomprehensible and underlined the loneliness of the novel's protagonist,
even as he became a kind of seer, moving in a world of imagination created
by the murk.[84]

But while the decadent mystic wallowed in the symbolic stew of fog,
other, more rational creatures sought instead to penetrate it. In some Victorian fiction fog could simply serve as a cloak for mystery and crime, a
plot device to create confusion and uncertainty. In December 1897 the
American journalist and story writer Richard Harding Davis (1864–1916)
took a cab with his childhood friend Ethel Barrymore, the well-known
actress, after a dinner they had both attended. Ethel was staying at that
time with Ellen Terry, another famous actress, some miles beyond Kensington. They left at eleven P.M., and there was a light fog. Davis joked in
the cab "that all sorts of things ought to happen in a fog but that no one

ever did have adventures nowadays." Almost immediately they hit a "bank of fog": "You could not see the houses, nor the street, nor the horse, not even his tail. All you could see were gas jets, but not the iron that supported them."[85] The cabby became lost, and the horse slipped on the frosty road; "We backed into lamp-posts and curbs until Ethel got so scared she bit her under lip until it bled. You could not tell whether you were going into a house or over a precipice or into a sea. The horse finally backed up a flight of steps, and rubbed the cabby against a front door, and jabbed the wheels into an area railing and fell down. That, I thought, was our cue to get out, so we slipped into a well of yellow mist and felt around for each other until a square block of light suddenly opened in mid air and four terrified women appeared in the doorway of the house through which the cabman was endeavoring to butt himself."[86]

Surprisingly, after they warmed themselves at this house, they set off again through the fog, with Barrymore worrying that this might cause her to lose her voice for her performance in *Peter the Great* at the Lyceum on New Year's Day. They heard voices through the fog "like people talking in a dream." Rescued by a man with a strong bicycle lamp, they found a linkboy and went back to the house where they had dined. Leaving Barrymore there, Davis set off to his own home in Jermyn Street. Near his home he heard a voice wailing, "Where am I? I don't know where I am no more than nothing—." On being told that he was in Jermyn Street, "There was a long dramatic silence and then the voice said—'Well, I be blowed! I thought I was in Pimlico!!!'"[87]

Inspired by this incident, Davis wrote a short story called "In the Fog," for the *Windsor Magazine* in 1901, reprinted with illustrations by Frederic Dorr Steele (1873–1944), an American artist who also illustrated some of the Sherlock Holmes stories, including the "The Adventure of the Bruce-Partington Plans." Davis's story is set in a club called The Grill. Four members of the club are sitting together eating supper on a foggy evening. One of them points to Sir Andrew, who is due to speak in the House of Commons in favour of a Navy Increase Bill, and offers £5,000 if someone can delay him from leaving until the Bill is voted on (he obviously wants it defeated). Rising to the challenge, an American member of the club attempts to delay Sir Andrew by telling the story of a murder mystery that even "Sherlock Holmes himself could not decipher." The American reports that he was dining at a friend's house when a fog descended. His friend pulls back the curtains to show his foreign visitor, "You have never seen a London fog, have you? . . . This is one of the best, or, rather one of the worst, of them." The American agrees: "I could see nothing. Had I not known that the house looked out upon the street I would have believed that I was facing a dead wall. . . . Even the light of the street lamps opposite, and in the upper windows of the barracks, had been smothered in the yellow mist. The lights of the room in which I stood penetrated the fog only to the distance of a few inches from my eyes."[88] As a navy man the American is used to fogs at sea, but he notes the difference between a natural sea fog and a London fog: "It is as proper that a fog should spread upon the waters as that steam shall rise from a kettle. But a fog which springs from the paved streets, that rolls between solid house-fronts, that forces cabs to move at half speed, that drowns policemen and extinguishes the electric lights of the music hall, that to me is incomprehensible. It is as out of place as a tidal wave on Hyde Park."[89] He sets out for home, moving forward by feeling his way along a wall; but in allowing other men coming from the opposite direction to pass, he loses the wall: "The further I moved to find it the further I seemed to be sinking into space. I had the unpleasant conviction that at any moment I might step over a precipice."[90]

The light from a street lamp offers little consolation or illumination, but the American grabs the lamppost to try to get his bearings: "For the rest, the mist hung between me and the world like a damp and heavy blanket."[91] Help appears to come from the silhouette of a man standing in an open doorway, and the American rushes forward; but the man rushes rudely out of the light and brushes past him into the fog in spite of his crying out. As the American enters the house, he finds a dead man in the front room. The corpse, he discovers, is Lord Chetney, who has recently returned from Africa after having been presumed dead. In his panic to get help, he rushes out, and the door shuts behind him: "For many minutes I beat the mist with my arms like one at blind man's buff, turning sharply in circles, cursing aloud at my stupidity and crying continually for help. At last a voice answered me from the fog, and I found myself held in the circle of a policeman's lantern." However, they cannot find the house again. The story is then taken up by other club members; and by

The 'cello

A.C. Gould

Figure 6.8 "Patriotism Damped," an example of how fog could transform the most ordinary image. In this case three men carrying cellos appear through the fog to be three soldiers in large bearskin hats, who are being mistakenly admired by some female cleaners. (*Punch*, 10 January 1900, p. 19). Courtesy of the President and Fellows of Wolfson College, Cambridge.

the time they have finished, the vote in the Commons is over, and Sir Andrew, a great lover of mystery stories, has not realized that time has passed. But he had already spoken in favour of the Navy Increase Bill much earlier that evening, and it had been approved. The ruse to delay him from getting to the House was, in fact, pointless.

For Sir Arthur Conan Doyle's fictional detective Sherlock Holmes, the distillation in one individual of the pure spirit of reason, fog was a challenge, an opportunity for the criminal and a challenge for the detective mind. In one story Holmes reflects on the opportunities fog offers to the criminal fraternity:

> The London criminal is certainly a dull fellow. . . . Look out of this window, Watson. See how the figures loom up, are dimly seen, and then blend once more into the cloud-bank. The thief or the murderer could roam London on such a day as the tiger does the jungle, unseen until he pounces, and then evident only to his victim. . . .

Suppose that I were Brooks or Woodhouse, or any of the fifty men who have good reason for taking my life, how long could I survive against my own pursuit? A summons, a bogus appointment, and all would be over. It is well they don't have days of fog in the Latin countries—the countries of assassination.[92]

Here the fog appears in a simple and relatively obvious way as a cloak under which deviants and criminals can carry on their business unobserved. But Conan Doyle used fog in more sophisticated ways too. *The Sign of Four* (1890), an early Holmes novella, begins in fog: "It was a September evening and not yet seven o'clock, but the day had been a dreary one, and a dense drizzly fog lay low upon the great city. Mud-coloured clouds drooped sadly over the muddy streets. Down the Strand the lamps were but misty splotches of diffused light which threw a feeble circular glimmer upon the slimy pavement. The yellow glare from the shop-windows streamed out into the steamy, vaporous air and threw a murky, shifting radiance across the crowded thoroughfare."[93] Holmes himself comments: "Was ever such a dreary, dismal, unprofitable world? See how the yellow fog swirls down the street and drifts across the dun-coloured houses. What could be more hopelessly prosaic and material? What is the use of having powers, Doctor, when one has no field upon which to exert them?"[94] Holmes complains that "crime is commonplace, existence is commonplace, and no qualities save those which are commonplace have any function upon earth."[95]

When Holmes, Watson, and Mary Morstan make their way to the house of Thaddeus Sholto, Watson admits to being affected by the foggy drive, as is the progenitor of the story, Miss Morstan: "Holmes alone could rise superior to petty influences."[96] This fog also provides an effective contrast to the opulence and brightness of Sholto's accommodation. But is it so different from the foggy world outside? They enter Sholto's room: "A blaze of yellow light streamed out" upon them, contrasting with "the yellow glare from the shop-windows" which "streamed out" into the streets.[97] Like humankind on the streets outside, Sholto is also full of movement: "He writhed his hands together," and "his features were in a perpetual jerk."[98] We read from this that Sholto may try to isolate himself within his richly furnished room: a homage to his Indian background and his love of all things Indian. He describes it: "An oasis of art in the

Figure 6.9 "Sandbagging in the Fog," from G. R. Sims's book *Living London.* Sims shows the way that criminals could capitalize on the fog. According to the text, the sandbag was an import from the world of American crime; it left no visible mark, made no noise, and would leave a victim stunned for several minutes. Reproduced by kind permission of the Syndics of Cambridge University Library.

howling desert of South London."[99] The fog remains specifically tied to London, and as they journey away from the city, we are told by Watson, "We had left the damp fog of the great city behind us."[100] Here too fog has become a metaphor for the state of London and its inhabitants; yet the yellow light of Sholto's room and the yellow glare from the shop-fronts creates a similar effect of menace in the suburban world that he lives in and where he commits his crimes.

More obviously, fog can represent Holmes's state of mind before he finally clears up a mystery. The action of "The Adventure of the Copper Beeches" (1892) mostly takes place outside London. The fog appears only at the beginning of the story and is not integral to the plot. Holmes and Watson sit around a "cheery fire" just like an old married couple.[101] The scene is cosy and warm. The gas lamps are lit, and the items on the breakfast table glimmer from the light of the gas and the fire. Holmes complains: "Man, or at least criminal man, has lost all enterprise and originality."[102] This fog is not a winter fog. We are informed that it is "a cold morning of the early spring," and we know by Miss Hunter's appointment time that it is just before 10:30 A.M. Through this spring fog it is possible to see the houses on the other side of Baker Street, although the windows can only vaguely be discerned. The inability to see through the windows reflects Holmes's own mysteries that often seem "dark" and "shapeless" before the great detective throws light on them. "A thick fog rolled down between the lines of dun-coloured houses, and the opposing windows loomed like dark, shapeless blurs, through the heavy yellow wreaths."[103] We are invited to imagine the unimaginative London criminals going about their routine, commonplace transgressions of the legal order under the cover of fog, failing entirely to provide the great detective with the mental stimulus he needs. Only when Miss Violet Hunter arrives to tell her tale does the situation change.

Apart from Holmes, none of the characters in "The Adventure of the Copper Beeches" is affected by the fog; even their visitor, Miss Hunter, appears unperturbed at having had to make her way to Baker Street through the murk. The fog, indeed, is among other things a signifier of Holmes's state of mind when he does not have a case to solve, listless, lacking in focus, dissatisfied, and on occasion moving into the transgressive itself through the use of cocaine. When Holmes's mind finally latches onto a problem, all this vanishes. Only the most difficult of cases ("a three-pipe problem") generate yet more obscuring vapour, sometimes discovered by Watson when he comes into the Baker Street rooms in the morning, through which Holmes slowly moves his mind to a clarifying solution.

In one adventure in particular, "The Adventure of the Bruce-Partington Plans" (1908), fog is integral to the plot. Holmes's brother Mycroft, who works for the British government, visits him in Baker Street to report that a clerk in the Ministry of Defence, Cadogan West, has been found dead on the tracks of the underground railway, with some secret plans for a submarine in his pocket; several other sheets of the plans are missing, enough for a hostile state to build a complete version of the vessel. After ascertaining that West was killed somewhere else and transported to the place where he was found, Holmes visits West's former boss, Sir James Walter, only to find he has died of shock (or shame) after the theft of the plans. He identifies a foreign agent, Hugo Oberstein, whose house backs onto the railway line and determines that he has killed West and placed the body on the top of a train which stopped below the window waiting for a signal to change. By placing a coded advertisement in the papers in the style of messages he recognizes as connected with the case, he lures the thief of the plans to Oberstein's house. It turns out to be James Walter's brother, Colonel Valentine Walter, who was deeply indebted and stole the plans to sell them to Oberstein. West had to be killed by the two men because he had discovered their crime. Another coded message brings Oberstein back to England. He is arrested and the plans recovered.

The story is set in a period when London fog was still somewhat denser and more frequent than it was at the time of writing. The date and weather conditions are directly described: "In the third week of November, in the year 1895, a dense yellow fog settled down upon London. From the Monday to the Thursday I doubt whether it was ever possible from our windows in Baker Street to see the loom of the opposite houses. . . . But when, for the fourth time, after pushing back our chairs from breakfast we saw the greasy, heavy brown swirl still drifting past us and condensing in oily drops upon the window-panes, my comrade's impatient and active nature could endure this drab existence no longer."[104] The "Partington fog" has an imprisoning effect on Holmes and Watson, with their room at 221B Baker Street being described as "fog-girt."[105] They spend the first three days of the fog deliberately employed in indoor activities, much to Holmes's frustration. Yet it is perfectly possible to go out, as Cadogan West and his girlfriend show, when they make their way to the theatre, although the fog does force them to walk since "a cab was useless" in such conditions. In reality it is not the fog which imprisons Holmes and Watson but, again, the lack of a good crime.

As Colonel Valentine Walter says, at the end of the story when admitting to taking part with Oberstein in the murder and disposal of the body, the fog "was so thick that nothing could be seen, and we had no difficulty in lowering West's body on to the train."[106] As usual the plodding police detective Inspector Lestrade is mistaken in his identification of the culprit, assuming that West is guilty, referring to West's plan to take his fiancée to the theatre as a "blind."[107] In fact the fog has left all of the detectives blind apart from Holmes. In order to discover the truth of the matter, Holmes and Watson are forced to break into Oberstein's house through a downstairs window. Watson, who has been instructed to bring the usual tools that would be used to commit a burglary, comments wryly: "It was nice equipment for a respectable citizen to carry through the dim, fog-draped streets."[108] Watson notes, "The fog still hung about and screened us with its friendly shade."[109] Without the fog the crime would have been more risky. Yet in the end, in "The Adventure of the Bruce-Partington Plans," fog provides a conventional cover for criminal activities and a straightforward representation of the mystery that Holmes has to solve. Here again the threat comes not from London itself but from abroad—Oberstein's name suggests that he is most likely German, and the government which seeks to acquire the plans is the Kaiser's.

Fog's role in other Holmes stories is mostly incidental to the plot. It features in "The Red Circle" (1911), in which a fog initially saves the intended victim of the story from his enemies by causing them to mistake the landlady's husband for him in the fog: "It is clear now that some danger is threatening your lodger. It is equally clear that his enemies, lying in wait for him near your door, mistook your husband for him in the foggy morning light."[110] In "The Dying Detective" (1913) Holmes, who pretends to be on his deathbed in order to deceive his enemies, is able to convince Watson and his landlady, Mrs. Hudson, that he is dying partly because of the dull weather: "In the dim light of a foggy November day the sick-room was a gloomy spot."[111] In *The Sign of Four* Holmes and Watson travel to a London suburb in a fog but have left it behind when they arrive.[112]

Most of the Sherlock Holmes stories were written after the turn of the century, when, as we have seen, fog became less significant as a metaphor for social fears. In "The Adventure of the Bruce-Partington Plans" it reflects not merely criminal mystery but also the murky and indeterminate world of traitors and spies, where even a seemingly respectable and honourable military gentleman turns out in the end not to be what he seems. When he is finally trapped by Holmes, the weather is still foggy, reducing a gaslight to no more than a "pin of light," and the traitor Colonel Walter is wearing his cravat over his nose and mouth, not only to protect his lungs against the fog but also to conceal his true identity. The disturbing element in the story is the threat from Germany (far more obvious in 1908, when the story was written, than it was in 1895, when it is set). The normal course of London life is turned upside down by agents of a foreign power; only when they are unmasked does the fog lift.

Five years before writing "The Adventure of the Bruce-Partington Plans," Conan Doyle, weary of the popularity of what he thought of merely as his potboiling stories about the fictional detective, had killed off Holmes at the Reichenbach Falls. After he returned, as one critic remarked: "For Sherlock Holmes, only two years had elapsed. He was now a figure of the past, rooted in the era of gaslight, swirling fog, and hansom cabs, rather than the modern, forward-looking detective who first captured the public's imagination."[113] It is striking that both Joseph Conrad and Arthur Conan Doyle, writing in the mid-1900s, thought it necessary to locate their stories, respectively, in the mid-1880s and the mid-1890s. Marie Belloc Lowndes, writing at the same time, looked back to the 1880s, and H. G. Wells's *Love and Mr. Lewisham,* written in 1899, was also set in the 1880s. Already, perhaps, authors who sought to use a thick London fog in their stories felt they had to situate them in the past, in fog's gloomy heyday. The decline of fog made it difficult to use the present as a backdrop. At its peak, in the 1880s and early 1890s, London fogs had been so frequent and so prominent that they prompted a wide range of novelists to use them in their work, from Robert Louis Stevenson and Henry James to Robert Barr and William Hay. Fewer found them a suitable subject by the mid-1900s. Fog's association with Dickens, and with the 1880s, made it difficult to employ as a metaphorical device in a contemporary setting.

The story of "The Adventure of the Bruce-Partington Plans" not only harked back nostalgically to a lost Victorian past but also looked forward to the war that was to break out between Britain and Germany just a few years later. In that war poison gas soon became a favoured weapon of both sides. Mustard gas, a German invention, was propelled over the front line and blown by the wind towards the British trenches on the Western Front in huge, yellow-brown clouds. If soldiers failed to put on their gas masks in time, they would soon suffer severe burns; if they inhaled it, it could seriously damage their lungs; if it affected their eyes, they would suffer temporary blindness. High doses, often difficult to detect because it took hours for the symptoms to develop, could be fatal. By the final months of the war three-quarters of all German shells fired at the enemy on the

Western Front were gas shells.[114] With poison clouds now a reality, coloured yellow or brown and smelling of sulphur—one of mustard gas's
principal constituents—London fog now faded into insignificance as a
cause of suffering and death. Its power to generate apocalyptic fantasies
was fatally compromised. Even its ability to inspire literary metaphor was
compromised. Yet its history was not yet over. It took another half century
before it was finally vanquished.

CHAPTER SEVEN

Land of the Living Dead

I

After the carnage and destruction of the First World War, Britain found a new determination to create a "land fit for heroes to live in." The war was to end war; the extension of the vote, including to women, was to create a new democratic political system; houses were to be made available to all; and town planning was to create a modern urban environment for people to enjoy. Welfare benefits were extended, and there was a fresh note of optimism in the air, building a consensus that the sacrifices of the millions of dead and maimed of the war should not be in vain. Yet the new mood did not last long. The problems of putting the economy on a peacetime footing added to underlying structural weaknesses to create rising unemployment rates, and relations between employers and unions deteriorated sharply, culminating in the General Strike of 1926. The Liberal Party, dominant before the war, collapsed with terrifying suddenness, as Labour gathered the support of millions at the polls, forming a minority government in 1924. The adjustment to a peacetime society was proving more difficult than anticipated.

The arrival of the first major fog after the end of the war fell into this period of growing disillusion. The decline in the frequency of major fogs since the late nineteenth century was well known. Min-Ch'ien T. Z. Tyau, whose reflections on London fog were discussed in Chapter 5, opined in 1920 that the fog problem of London had improved because of the greater use of electricity: "The amount of smoke in the atmosphere is considerably decreased, and so the city is comparatively cleaner. Moreover, in former days, the fogs were always of the worst imaginable type."[1] Yet this by no means meant that atmospheric pollution had disappeared altogether. On the contrary, it could on occasion be as intense as ever; and indeed the decline in the number of foggy days per year, in progress since

the 1890s, came to a stop for more than a decade in 1920.[2] Three years after
the end of the First World War, London received a stark reminder of the
damage that polluted air could cause. In late November 1921 the city was
visited by the "densest fog for years," according to *The Times*.[3] The fog
lasted for five days. It was very thick on Sunday, when most people could
stay indoors, though of course they would have lit coal fires to stay warm
and cheer themselves, further adding to the pollution. On Monday many
had to leave their homes on their way to work and venture "into the soot-
laden mists, grope a way to railway stations, . . . and endure tedious
journeys at the end of which they found themselves in a ghostly city."[4]
Oil flares were used, even at two P.M., in Westminster to make traffic
islands, and detonators were exploded on the railways as warning signals. The *Pall Mall and Globe* reported that London had been "enveloped
in a shroud of fog" and that Londoners were on "a diet of soot."[5] Uncon-
sciously calling Monet's foggy townscapes to mind, *The Times* described
the fog diminishing later in the day: "the sun could be seen through the
mist, first as a crimson and then as a vermillion ball hanging in the yellowish sky."[6]

The papers were full of anecdotes. Two women were completely
unable to find their way home in Shepherds Bush and were aided by a gentleman going in the same direction. It was only when they turned to thank
him "that they discovered he was an ex-soldier who had been blinded in
the war."[7] The same newspaper reported under the heading "Fog Patches"
that the text of that day at St. Paul's was ironically "I Am the Light of the
World," even though "worshippers could scarcely see the pulpit owing
to the fog" that had penetrated the interior of the cathedral.[8] The 1921 fog
brought forward some literary reflections as well. A tongue-in-cheek piece
in *The Times* complained that classical writers such as Shakespeare, a "Londoner by adoption," would have done justice to the "thickening of the
metropolitan atmosphere" by writing, "Shall I compare thee to a foggy
day?" The writer went on to suggest that Thomas Gray's "Elegy Written
in a Country Churchyard" might have begun, "The fog-horn tolls the
knell." The article opened with a made-up quotation from the cockney
Sam Weller, in Dickens's *The Pickwick Papers:* "'I rather think this is a bit
too thick,' as the gentleman in difficulties said ven he tried to valk home
in the fog, and mistook the Fleet prison for his own willa.' 'Sam,' said

Figure 7.1 *The Houses of Parliament, London, with the Sun Breaking through the Fog* (1904), by Claude Monet. The fogs of the 1920s created effects reminiscent of Monet's earlier paintings. Monet's exhibition of thirty-seven of the paintings from the *London* series in Paris in 1904 was a huge success. Musée d'Orsay, Paris, France / Bridgeman Images.

Mr. Pickwick, 'have the goodness to reserve your comparisons until they are called for.' "[9]

London suffered another great fog on Sunday, January 22, 1922. The *Pall Mall Gazette* described the fog "advancing like a brown wall, covering the whole of the eastern sky. The transition from brilliant sunshine to dense gloom in many districts was instantaneous."[10] Sunday's fog, it continued, was "a strikingly visible embodiment of the blight which public neglect of the smoke nuisance makes one of London's chronic afflictions."[11] Sir Harry Brittain (1873–1974), a leading journalist and Tory MP for Acton, a suburb of London, whose name appeared many times in House of Commons Reports on the passage of smoke abatement legislation, wrote to the editor of *The Times:* "A raid on the Metropolis by King Fog is far more destructive and costly than any two of the Zeppelin raids associated with the Great War. . . . The loss in working hours due to transport delays, the added expense in coal, gas, and electricity . . . Add the accidents (there are always some to deplore), add the injury to the public health, the aggravation of pulmonary troubles, . . . it will be seen that the demands of King Fog are exorbitant."[12] The following November a dense fog hit not only London but the rest of Europe as far as Germany. In London it was compounded by smoke pollution and turned the usual yellow colour. Newspapers in 1922 also noted under "Burglaries in the Fog" that criminals were "no doubt taking advantage of the dense fog which prevailed in London last night."[13] Deaths had also occurred. At Croydon Station the body of a woman was "found by the side of the line at the station with a fractured skull and other severe injuries. Presumably she had fallen from the platform in the dense fog and was struck by a passing train."[14] The caption in *The Times* picture gallery was "When Day Turned to Night."[15]

The fog occurred on the eve of a general election, and the headlines featured "Hundreds of Tons of Fog," as well as "London's November Handicap."[16] The *Pall Mall Gazette* reported the Conservative election victory of 1922 with the apt: "Fog was all around them, but every mind was imbued with a uniform clarity of purpose."[17] *Children of the Fog: A Novel of Southwark,* published in 1927 but set from 1910 to the mid-1920s, described this election night. It was written by a prolific author, playwright, and social activist, Carmel Haden Guest, sometimes referred to as Mrs. L. Haden Guest or Muriel Carmel (1881–1943), whose husband was a candidate in the election. The book opens by establishing a time, location, and weather conditions: "Four o'clock was striking. The fog in South-east London was intense. . . . (It was nearing the end of 1910 and the worst year for unemployment that she could remember.)"[18] The area's poor conditions are made much worse by the fog, but the point is made that the streets already have an "unsavoury odour" which is "swallowed in soot" and that the schoolchildren are "awed into silence by a sense of isolation in the impenetrable darkness."[19] The story follows the life of Joan Crimson, a child at the beginning of the book, whose mother does not love her because she is a physical reminder of a sexual encounter with a stranger in

Figure 7.2 An iceman delivers his wares in spite of the London fog in this photograph from October 1919. All trades had to continue working in spite of the difficult conditions created by the thick London fog. The photographer is not named. Topical Press Agency/Getty Images.

a hotel where her mother was a chambermaid. It is her grandparents who show Joan true love and support; but they die, and she has to survive in her mother's new home with a brute of a stepfather. Joan shows talent as an artist but is denied the chance to pursue her calling until she meets with another artist who initially wants her to model for him but who then realises that she has true artistic ability. They then become lovers. His untimely death and her pregnant state towards the end of the novel seem tragic enough, but she is also attacked by her jealous stepfather, who has until now kept a respectful distance from her. She falls and hits her head on a stone in the street and dies in hospital, seemingly grateful for her release from life, as her nurse perceives: "She was younger than I— and glad to die."[20]

Throughout the book Guest uses fog to amplify her themes. The title itself reflects that fog and poor social conditions are intertwined. London's

Figure 7.3 *Victoria Embankment* (1924), by C. R. W. Nevinson (1889–1946). A celebrated war artist, Nevinson painted this scene from an upper window at the Savoy Hotel, just as Monet had done at the turn of the century. Objects do not disappear behind the fog as in Monet's works, but are more substantial. The delicate pinks and grey tones in the air suggest the haze of the London air. The steam trains puff out white smoke as they go across Hungerford Bridge. © Estate of Christopher Nevinson (BACS) / Museum of London / Bridgeman Images.

young are children of the fog because they grow up in ignorance and poverty. Fog is identified easily with these two social conditions. When Joan's stepfather attacks her at the end of the novel, it is a foggy morning on the embankment, and it enables him to escape to a public house without being seen. Joan's struggle to get away from her stepfather is reminiscent of an earlier incident when as a child on another foggy day, "a drunken man had caught hold of her once when she was returning from school on a foggy afternoon."[21] The cultural world that Joan joins also allows the author to paint the fog in a more artistic manner. A painting by her artist lover illustrates her own area of the city, "an Impressionist painting of Great Charlotte Street on a foggy Christmas Eve, thronged with workers buying their Christmas fare."[22] London may be grey, but this is not described in a negative or hostile manner: "It was a grey evening. Everything was grey—grey rain, grey river, grey wharves, grey barges—a dear misty London grey."[23] A couple of paragraphs later as the young adult Joan describes her imaginary "City Beautiful" that she wants to believe is under the water of the River Thames, her artistic lover adds, "It's a jolly city, well ordered, no fog or smoke."[24]

Haden-Guest's sentimental potboiler links fog to poverty and moral degradation in a familiar way. In *The Waste Land,* the celebrated long modernist poem by T. S. Eliot (1888–1965), fog is linked instead to spiritual deprivation, the dulling of people's sensibility in the routine of the monotonous modern world of clerical drudgery. The poem was written in 1921–1922, mostly in Switzerland, where Eliot was recovering from a nervous breakdown, just as his first wife, Vivien, was also convalescing after a nervous collapse. Tied since the middle of the war to a boring and unfulfilling life as a bank clerk, Eliot reflected on London as an "Unreal City, / Under the brown fog of a winter dawn"—and later referred to "a winter noon," reflecting how fog tended to linger all day.[25] Here, London presents a vision of hell in which people lead spiritually barren lives. The colour brown is chosen above the many colours that Eliot could have picked for fog—black, yellow, white—deliberately because it is a dull colour, matching the dull apparel of the working people walking over London Bridge to work, as if over the River Styx to hell, reflecting the spiritually dead nature of their lives.

II

By the early 1920s it had become possible to measure the density of fog by scientific means. A new body, the Committee for the Investigation of Atmospheric Pollution, which had begun as a private venture in 1912, was now attached to the Meteorological Office. It set up a standard apparatus throughout the country to measure the amount of soot and dust in the air, and concluded that "domestic smoke is responsible for about two-thirds of the smoke problem."[26] The standard gauge for measuring dirt in the air had been designed by Dr. John S. Owens, a consulting engineer in Westminster, who had begun life as a medical doctor and who had calculated that "at noon the impurities" of the fog of Sunday, November 29, 1921, "would give a total weight of 10.8 lb as compared with 3.8 lb in the fog of Saturday."[27] Owens was quoted by the *Pall Mall and Globe* claiming that "at 10.20 to-day there were approximately 340,000 pieces of soot per cubic inch of air, and the diameter of each piece of soot is one twenty-five thousandth part of an inch."[28] The paper exclaimed: "Londoners are breathing and eating absolute soot."[29] Lawrence Chubb, secretary of the Coal Smoke Abatement Society, which was still in existence after the war, suggested that the same fog cost £100,000 in time wasted getting into work on the Monday, as well as the extra cost of damage to health, clothing, buildings, and other property.[30] Together with the meteorologist Sir Napier Shaw (1854–1945), Owens wrote up his findings in a book published in 1925 called *The Smoke Problem of Great Cities*.[31]

But scientific knowledge did not translate into political action. Fog continued to plague London for the rest of the 1920s; indeed it seemed if anything to be getting worse. On December 3, 1924, *The Times* pictured how day turned to night in the Strand at 1:30 P.M.[32] "The whole of London seemed subdued in its premature darkness."[33] This was the result of a peculiar phenomenon that was increasing in frequency in the late nineteenth and early twentieth centuries, when a canopy of smoke hung over the city so densely that it seemed like night-time, even though visibility at ground level was still good, and electric lights could be seen from miles away. London was also fogbound from December 9 to 11, 1924: "In the London area the fog took on a darker hue and a quality more nearly opaque than heretofore."[34] There was a return to the linkboys of Victorian days, now in the era of the motor car, reported the press, as men were once more employed with flares on the streets of the West End.[35] *The Times* summed it up: "Fog has clung about London . . . for three days and nights. It has varied here and there in density, taste and colour; has drifted slowly in banks, and now and then risen from the surface of the streets of the metropolis, but only to gather or to sink again; surely the most reluctant fog that has been known for many years. . . . The moistness of the fog soaked into clothes, and the soot in it irritated eyes and throats."[36] the *Illustrated London News* also carried a full-page spread of pictures of London illustrating different kinds of fog that had occurred on December 2 and 10. It concluded that the fog that began on December 9 was "a real 'London particular,' of the 'pea-soup' variety."[37]

The year 1925 began with a dense fog on January 10 that lasted until January 13 and then returned on January 15. *The Times* headed its news article "Dismal London" and described how it was "said to be one of the densest that has occurred for some years. It was, however, decidedly 'patchy.' In some districts it was impossible to see five yards ahead; in others, lamp posts and houses 50 yards distant were plainly visible."[38] An F.A. Cup match between Arsenal and West Ham had to be postponed, as did many other sporting events. The fog caused fires to break out in many electric tramcars because of the need to run long distances at a very slow speed and with continual stoppages. The spread of the fog was vast. At one point the entire area within a radius of approximately forty miles in every direction from Charing Cross was fogbound. Acetylene flares were requisitioned to guide traffic and pedestrians in the Strand, Trafalgar Square, Whitehall, and Hyde Park Corner.[39] An editorial in the same newspaper reflected: "The natural lie of London, especially after heavy rains, must be responsible for part of the darkness. . . . Nevertheless," it concluded, "it should be every householder's duty to consider carefully how far it lies within his power to prevent an avoidable defilement of the atmosphere."[40] The blame was now being put almost wholly on the household and not on industry, a significant change from the nineteenth century.

Later, in 1925 the usual winter fog in London arrived early, on October 1.[41] Two months later December 4, 1925, was described as a "day of darkest night."[42] The *Evening Standard* headed a story "Midnight at Noon" and described how "utter midnight blackness cloaked London at mid-day. There was no difference to the visibility if one looked to heaven or towards the ground."[43] A collision between a No. 3 bus and a taxicab injured Gertrude, Lady Decies, a prominent member of London "society" who had won the French equivalent of the Victoria Cross for her service as a nurse in France during the war, and another accident caused injuries to the Liberal politician Herbert, Viscount Gladstone, and his wife. The London bus driver was not to be envied, "sitting in the acrid unpleasantness of a London fog holding a steering-wheel and the lives of men and women." "He has, I think," as one writer commented, "developed a sixth sense. His whole being seems acutely conscious of inches."[44] The theatrical world of 1925 mourned "Plays Killed by Fog": "Fog, always a deadly enemy to theatrical prosperity, has

Figure 7.4 The Moscow Dynamo goalkeeper Alexei Khomich peers into the foggy gloom on November 21, 1945, during a match at White Hart Lane, captured by a *Daily Herald* photographer. There was a 54,000-strong crowd, some of whom claimed that Dynamo had twelve men on the pitch at one point. The referee had been chosen by the Russian team and refused to stop the match. The Dynamos won 4–3. A similar fog caused the abandonment of an F. A. Cup match between Arsenal and West Ham in 1925. © Daily Herald Archive / Science & Society Picture Library.

helped last week's national mourning to deal a death-blow to such plays as were hovering between success and failure."[45]

London continued, therefore, to experience numerous fogs after the end of the Great War. The roaring twenties were also the foggy twenties. Writers who devoted their attention to the city could not avoid dealing with its polluted atmosphere. Perhaps the best known of these was Henry Vollam Morton (1892–1979), who earlier had made his name as a travel writer, providing a scoop for *The Times* in 1923 with a report of the opening of Tutankhamen's tomb by Howard Carter. In 1925 he published the first of his many books, called *The Heart of London,* based on his column in the *Daily Express.* The book was obviously enormously popular, since four separate editions appeared within the first year of publication, and twenty editions had appeared by 1941.[46] Its approach is light-hearted. In one chapter, "Ghosts of the Fog," Morton highlights the impact the fog has not only on sight but also on taste: "The fog has a flavour. Many flavours. At Marble Arch I meet a delicate after-taste like melon; at Ludgate Hill I taste coke."[47] He plays around with the usual ways fog is described, so men who sell things "never arrive normally; they loom; they appear, delightfully freezing the blood, howling their wares like the lonely wolf in a picture book."[48] The fog changes people and things into ghosts: "Two motor cars locked together. Fifty grim, muffled ghosts stand round watching and blowing their noses. . . . It is a struggle of prehistoric monsters in a death-grip. So must two clumsy, effete beasts of the Ice Age have fought locked in each other's scaly arms."[49] The fog reduces everything: "Men are like flat figures cut in black paper. All things become two-dimensional. Carts, motor-cars, omnibuses are shadows that nose their way painfully like blind beasts."[50] The effects of the pea-souper on perception are here given an original, humorous twist; reality vanishes under its canopy, London becomes an unreal city, people become like dead things, ghosts, as in *The Waste Land,* or the townscape reverts to prehistoric times, as in *Bleak House.*

Morton wrote about fog in November as if it were an annual event like the opening of Parliament, including it in his book-length descriptive calendar *A London Year.* He describes waking up in the morning "to a melon-tinted gloom. . . . London becomes a city of the dead. The great pulse of traffic ceases to beat; lost stragglers wander through silent, shrouded avenues alive with eerie, cloudlike banks in the red hue of the street lamps."[51] The fog "is eerie, mysterious. The stranger in his first fog finds thrills innumerable; the Londoner, hate it as he does, cannot deny that there is a childlike joy in the sudden dislocation of routine, the astonishing realization that the other side of the road is an adventure and a peril."[52] The variable quality of the fog, noted by many others at various periods, was one of its most notable aspects: "It is a fog of changing, drifting patches. A hundred yards of baffling mystery, twenty yards of semi-clarity—just sufficient to give a man his bearings—and then a long tunnel of pitch-black misery in which people run together in collision."[53]

Morton's tone was not merely facetious; it was also almost affectionate. Indeed a new note was struck by a number of commentators on fog in the 1920s: a note of pride. What would London be without fog? In 1923 *Punch* published a poem called "In Defence of Fog" that began with a sigh of despair because fog would never be defeated:

Figure 7.5 A photograph of Ludgate Circus in the City of London in the fog of November 1, 1922. The patchy nature of the fog, thick in some places and clearer in others, is evident from this picture, taken by James Jarché (1891–1965), a well-known photographer. Topical Press Agency/Getty Images.

Vulgarian, soupy and yellow,
Gone, gone is the hope that relies
On Science to raise up a fellow
Who will one day effect your demise.
He may purge you as white as a Primate,
But nature insists on her own;
For you're part, so it seems, of our climate,
And bred in the bone.[54]

The following year *The Times* repeated this sentiment in more prosaic terms, commenting on the dense fogs of early December 1924 and noting the pride with which Londoners greeted the phenomenon as well as the entertainment that the paper claimed was afforded by it:

The "London particular" is the true London Pride. It is unique, no less than is London gin or London wit. Other places . . . may be able to show a mist or so. Only London has fog. And Londoners are secretly proud of it. . . . Only the larger shareholders in gas and electric light companies; the launderers, and perhaps the soap and face-cream trades, dare to confess their joy in a thorough London fog; but every Londoner feels, on such a day as yesterday, the distinction of being a citizen of so singular a town. . . . Fog breaks the monotony of life; it shows us our familiar surroundings in a new (and an artificial) light. It gives us something to talk about. . . . And those of us who live to see the sensible thing done at last, and the "London particular" deprived of its artificial foulness, will find ourselves sighing for the good old days.[55]

As for the attack on coal fires mounted by the Coal Smoke Abatement Society, this was still seen in many quarters as an assault on the hearth, the true centre of the English home. An article in 1925, written by the playwright and journalist Basil MacDonald Hastings (1881–1928), author of *The Angel in the House* (1915), after a few days of a nasty black fog, defended the open fire under the heading "Fire and Fog."[56] The article was cast in the form of a dialogue between a householder and a coal fire. It opened accusingly: "So it is the coal fire that makes the fog, is it? . . . Let's have it out with him. . . . People . . . are prating of the superiority of electric light, of gas, even of hot water. . . . They are just utterly tired of wandering through soot-steeped streets, rubbing aching eyes, and coughing clear their sore and parching throats. They admit that you are, like the stage coach, exceedingly picturesque, but declare that you are just as out-of-date."[57] The coal fire replied by pointing out that there was a natural problem of sea fogs but also highlighted the psychological benefits of an open fire for the tired businessman or worker: "How often have I seen you baffled, worried, tired, and yet unable to sleep. You sit by me, and gradually I put my arms round you. Gently I press your head back. Soon you are asleep."[58] In view of such objections, progress on smoke control was clearly going to be difficult to achieve.

III

Perhaps the most sustained literary exploitation of London fog through the early decades of the twentieth century was in John Galsworthy's popular series of novels *The Forsyte Saga,* published in six volumes between 1906 and 1921. In *The Man of Property* (1906), the first book of the saga, the young, impoverished architect Philip Bosinney, Irene Forsyte's lover, is killed in a fog. His death is of great importance since Irene is just about to leave her husband, Soames Forsyte, in order to start a new life with him. Soames has just won a court case against his wife's lover. As a result Bosinney will be bankrupted. His emotional state is heightened by the fact that Irene has told him that Soames has raped her. Initially Galsworthy had planned to have Bosinney commit suicide, but was dissuaded by his friend, the critic Edward Garnett: "B.'s suicide is like a chink of light in the photographer's dark room, weakening the negative. . . . When I read it, I said 'incredible,' not in character."[59] It was Garnett who suggested that Bosinney die in the fog, quoting it as one of two alternatives: "The first, and the easiest is—to make Bosinney meet with an accident in the fog—so that you can preserve your psychological analysis of the Forsytes' attitude. In a sense this is cheap, at first sight—but it *might be* artistically perfect."[60] Galsworthy was initially reluctant but then decided: "Bosinney's suicide. I think it is very likely I have made a mistake in *time* over this; the suicide would most probably have come about under the wheels of a 'bus in the fog; instead of the following afternoon. I can alter this, with but little change; and if you like I can leave it in the minds of the reader, as it would be on the minds of the Jury, doubtful whether it were suicide or no."[61]

The chapter describing Bosinney's death is titled "Voyage into the Inferno." Like so many later representations of London fog it is set in the late 1880s. Soames breakfasts alone "after a certain night on which [he] at last asserted his rights and acted like a man": "He breakfasted by gaslight, the fog of late November wrapping the town as in some monstrous blanket till the trees of the Square even were barely visible from the dining-room window." The fog mirrors his mood. He is "haunted by the recollection of her face" and "of her terrible smothered sobbing."[62] Later, when he returns home from his office, the fog has worsened: "through the still, thick blur, men groped in and out; women, very few, grasped their reticules to their bosoms and handkerchiefs to their mouths."[63] The foggy weather discourages women from going out, and one of the reasons for this is in the way they grasp their handbags to stop them being snatched. This sense of fear is reinforced when Soames arrives back home, and is disconcerted to discover that Irene has gone out: "Out at such a time of

night, into this terrible fog! What was the meaning of that?" Soames
has asserted his rights over her, as his property, but she has asserted her
independence: "the incident of the night before had long lost its importance under stress of anxiety at her strange sortie into the fog."[64] He is
only too happy to excuse his behaviour out of concern for her safety. When
she does return, after having told Bosinney of the rape, it is only to go to
her bedroom and eat alone. Soames now finds comfort in looking at his
paintings, significantly one in particular by J. M. W. Turner—an artist
known for his atmospheric paintings and one generally associated with
foggy or misty conditions.

Before Soames has returned from work, Galsworthy describes the way
the fog distorts: "crowned with the weird excrescence of the driver, ha-
loed by a vague glow of lamplight that seemed to drown in vapour before it reached the pavement, cabs loomed dim-shaped ever and again, and
discharged citizens bolting like rabbits to their burrows."[65] Here again,
as in earlier literature, we find the idea of fog creating a subterranean
world. Indeed people, Galsworthy says, actually preferred to travel below
the surface rather than risk the dangers of travelling above ground:
"everyone to-day went Underground."[66] On the same day George Forsyte,
Soames's cousin, is also out. George catches sight of Bosinney leaving his
carriage at Charing Cross station. He suspects that Bosinney is Irene's
lover. George initially thinks that Bosinney is drunk (a common suspicion of men's behaviour in the fog, as we have seen) and begins to follow
him for fun; but then he realises that he is not under the influence of alcohol "but acting under the stress of violent emotion." The reader knows
what George cannot at this stage, that Irene has informed Bosinney of
Soames's rape. The foggy night is described as "a vast muffled blackness,
where a man could not see six paces before him; where, all around, voices
or whistles mocked the sense of direction; and sudden shapes came rolling
slow upon them; and now and then a light showed like a dim island in
an infinite dark sea." The fog mirrors Bosinney's feelings of anxiety and
despair, his sense of not knowing where to go or what to do. Just as the
"voices and whistles" mock any sense of direction, Bosinney realises that
he has no power over Soames's treatment of his wife. He is described as
a "hunted creature . . . not groping as other men were groping in that
gloom, but driven forward as though the faithful George behind wielded

a knout." George suddenly understands what has happened when he hears Bosinney muttering in the fog. He realises that Soames had exercised his "marital rights" over an estranged and unwilling wife in "the greatest—the supreme act of property."[67]

George continues to watch over Bosinney, fearing that he might "put his 'twopenny' under a bus." George wants to share with the passersby his knowledge of the man he watches: "Then even in his compassion George's Quilpish humour broke forth and in a sudden longing to pluck these spectres by the sleeve"—Quilp, as we saw in Chapter 2, is the Dickensian character perhaps most personally associated with fog. George begins to imagine that a passerby might discover the exact reason for Bosinney's pain and be so troubled as to widen his mouth in horror with "the fog going down and down." The swallowing of fog was of course a common nuisance and often led to the spitting out of the black, gritty contents in order to prevent choking. Here George's imagination just conjures the horror of the fog forcing itself down into the mouth of the passerby—as if the London fog replays a form of Soames's violent coercion.[68]

Bosinney rests for a while in Trafalgar Square "under one of the lions, . . . a monster sphynx astray like themselves in that gulf of darkness." He clearly despairs of being able to solve the riddle of Soames's relationship with Irene. The situation might not have concerned George under ordinary circumstances, "but in this fog, where all was gloomy and unreal, where nothing had that matter-of-fact value associated by Forsytes with earth, he [George] was a victim to strange qualms." When Bosinney sets off again through the fog, George continues in pursuit, realising significantly that "it's God's own miracle he's not been run over already." George has to leap aside to avoid a passing cab and realises that he has lost his quarry. He "felt his heart clutched by a sickening fear, the dark fear that lives in the wings of the fog." The reader has been informed earlier that the Forsytes have "conquered London," yet London in the fog eludes them. Later, when George looks out at the still-foggy night, he wonders if Bosinney is still "wandering out there now in that fog. If he's not a corpse."[69] In "Bosinney's Departure," four chapters later, we are informed that Bosinney is dead, "run over in the fog and killed."[70] His possibly self-inflicted death echoes the feelings of suicidal depression recorded by a number of foreign visitors in a London fog.[71] His emotional turmoil, mingling his despair and outrage at Soames's treatment of Irene with his feeling of becoming trapped in a situation, personal and financial, from which there is no way out, is perfectly mirrored in Galsworthy's descriptions of the fog.

Fog recurs in the sequel to *The Forsyte Saga, A Modern Comedy* (1924–28). In the second book, *The Silver Spoon* (1926), Soames's reformist Tory son-in-law Michael Mont is returning from an important dinner with members of the Royal family in a thick fog, accompanied by his loyal wife, Fleur Forsyte. Their cab crawls along slowly in the fog, and their discussion of the dinner leads Mont to comment on how things move quickly in other worlds "except in politics and fog." The cab driver loses his sense of direction in the fog and has to admit that he is lost. "The black vapour, acrid and cold, surged into Michael's lungs," and later the fog tastes of filth. Michael has to get out of the cab to help lead the driver forward while feeling his way with his foot on the kerb. The hope is to use the river or find a policeman to direct them. Michael asks a man with a "refined" voice, who is described as "invisible" in the fog, where they are. The man retorts, ironically, that they are "in the twentieth century, and the heart of civilization." Once again fog is seen as a regression to the primitive world.[72]

Michael becomes disoriented and, losing his sense of direction after stumbling on the kerb, falls down. He fears for Fleur, who would be anxious left alone in the cab—another woman helpless in the fog, or so he sees the situation. He calls out into the void, and another London voice calls out: "Don't cher know where y'are?" When Michael admits to having lost his cab with his wife in it, the voice seems to enjoy it as a joke: "'Lawd! You won't get 'er back tonight.' A hoarse laugh, ghostly and obscene, floated by." Michael is at the mercy of the lower classes, as if he were in the dockworkers' riots in the fog of 1886. But a patriotic fellow-feeling engendered in Londoners by the war comes to his aid. He is helped back to the cab by an ex-serviceman from the First World War who describes conditions as "like no-man's-land in a smoke barrage!" Feeling optimistic, Michael exclaims, "Fog's our sheet-anchor, after all. So long as we have fog, England will survive." Yet on the following page the coachman comments: "These fogs ain't fit for 'uman bein's. They ought to do somethin' about 'em in Parliament."[73] The parliamentarian Michael Mont may signal his polite agreement with the coachman, but this has to be taken in context with his seeming support of London fogs as a part of the Englishman's constitution. This contradiction, seeing fog as a necessary part of London life and also wanting it to be legally removed, was to be part of the continuing debate on its removal. Michael can afford to dismiss it from his mind when he returns to his own living room "with this pretty glowing woman": "why think of its tangle, lost shapes, and straying cries?"[74]

IV

The scene depicting Michael Mont's confusion in the London fog is set in the mid-1920s, when Parliament was in the midst of debating measures to tackle the fog.[75] The earlier foggy day in the 1880s is both metaphorical and a plot device, but in the later incident Galsworthy uses fog to make the point that something should be done politically to abolish these London fogs and perhaps to explain Parliament's inaction. He had been following events in Parliament and the many letters in The Times regarding how to make it safer for cars to find their way in the fog. One letter, typical of many, suggested that telegraph poles should have "white porcelain insulators, for they are guiding angels during foggy weather, and, moreover, the base should also be painted white. These good telegraph poles save many a motorist from the ditch."[76] A later suggestion was to paint kerbstones white.[77] For the time being, none of these proposals was put into action. But efforts to introduce fresh legislation began in earnest once more after the first fogs of the postwar era brought the problem to the attention of the political elite as the campaign for smoke abatement got under way, following the lull experienced during the war.

The debate began with an intervention from a well-known architect. Ernest Newton (1856–1922), former President of the Royal Institute of British Architects, found himself irritated by the novel tendency in the press to regard fog as an indispensable part of London life: "Constant reference to Dickens and his supposed delight in a real 'London particular,' and to other novelists who write with affection of 'dear smoky London,' creates an impression that London's smoke is one of its traditional glories, and that to agitate for its abolition is almost as bad as to speak disrespectfully of Gog and Magog and other established institutions."[78] This was, however, he objected, by no means the case. Such agitation was absolutely necessary. Newton was a proponent of the Arts and Crafts movement, mainly known for his work on domestic houses. Earlier in the year he had written another letter on the subject of "pollution by coal smoke." He described the need "to get rid of coal smoke. . . . It is the one great blight on every effort for improvement." He listed the damaging effects of "this distressing atmosphere" on "our tempers, our lungs, our clothes, and our buildings." He also suggested that as "London [was] perhaps too large to grasp as a whole, . . . boroughs might well compete with each other to be the cleanest, best lighted and best administered"— an idea that was later developed into smokeless zones.[79]

Ernest Newton was not to live to see his suggestions taken up. But his namesake Thomas Wodehouse Legh, Lord Newton (1857–1942), former Paymaster-General in the coalition government during the First World War, had already won a high profile as the most persistent campaigner of the age when it came to clean air and the ending of London fog. For Newton the purity of the air was as important as the purity of water and food: "There have been innumerable conferences on the subject," he said, "and the general ill effect upon the health and comfort of the community is not disputed. It is not disputed either that, unfortunately, England suffers more than any other country."[80] He focused on two main areas of the country. One was London: "London under present conditions receives only about one-third of the winter sunshine as compared with places in the immediate neighbourhood. The annual sootfall in London is no less an amount than 70,000 tons, which, I believe, formed in the shape of a pyramid would occupy more space than the Victoria Tower."[81] March 24, 1914, had seen the Second Reading of his Smoke Abatement Bill in the House of Lords. An earlier attempt to introduce a Bill in the House of Commons in April 1913 had actually been drafted by the Coal Smoke Abatement Society. Gordon Harvey, MP for Rochdale, had proposed it, however, without the remotest hope of it getting through the House of Commons. Newton used his Bill to encourage setting up a committee to investigate the matter thoroughly. He acknowledged that with the good work done by organizations such as the Coal Smoke Abatement Society, public opinion was changing and demanding cleaner air. It was agreed that

Figure 7.6 "The Cenotaph" (1921), taken by the photographer Fred Judge (1872–1950), who established a very successful postcard business using his own photographs. This may be part of a continuing London series of cards that included the earlier "The Charm of a London Fog" (1909). © RPX / Royal Photographic Society / Science & Society Picture Library.

a committee of inquiry would be set up, and Newton was asked to sit on it. At this point Lord Newton withdrew the Bill, and the issue disappeared beneath the greater fog of war.[82]

After the war, the committee set to work under its chairman, Lord Newton. It held nearly fifty meetings and examined 150 witnesses, and its report was published in 1921.[83] By November 29, 1922, the newly elected Conservative government was being tackled on the future of the Smoke Abatement Bill. Sir Harry Brittain asked if the government knew "the financial loss suffered by the Metropolis, in addition to the effect on the health of its citizens, by the series of fogs during the last fortnight; and what steps it is proposed to take to mitigate this evil?"[84] He did not receive a satisfactory answer.[85] Indeed there was no great faith that the government of the day would follow through with effective legislation. "No Government," Newton complained, "has for many years taken any action with the exception of appointing committees whose labours had little or no result."[86] It was his belief that "half the smoke, or approximately half, with which we are afflicted in this country is produced by domestic houses and chimneys; and there is no legislation which touches the question of domestic smoke at all."[87] His committee had even recommended withholding permission to build new homes if new standards were not going to be met. With the building of many new homes after the war, it was an ideal opportunity to change a very wasteful and polluting method of heating and cooking by coal. However, the only action that the government had undertaken to promote this recommendation was "an emasculated and abbreviated report of our Interim Report," in what Newton describes as a "dismal" and "particularly unattractive" journal called *Housing*, which, he says, "I should think nobody takes any interest in and which finds its way into the waste-paper basket."[88]

The push to bring in a Bill to abate smoke continued after the final report of the Newton committee. A deputation organized by the Coal Abatement Society met with the then Minister of Health, Sir Alfred Mond (1868–1930), who had been first Commissioner of Works earlier in the decade, on March 20, 1922, to urge the government to take action on the lines recommended by Newton's committee. Questions were repeatedly asked in Parliament to keep up the pressure.[89] Mond was an industrialist whose fortune was founded on metals and chemicals. He had a professional interest in the issue of pollution as well as a material interest in pinning the blame on domestic fires. Newton expressed his appreciation of Mond: "He is, so far as I am aware, the first Minister who has taken the smallest interest in this question, and I really believe that if he is allowed by his colleagues to do so he is anxious to identify himself with a reform of this nature. All I have to say, in conclusion, is that if Sir Alfred Mond is successful in introducing a Bill and getting it through Parliament, he will be more deserving of a monument than many heroes of the past, whose effigies decorate or disfigure the squares and streets of the Metropolis."[90] There was only "one slight inconsistency," as the historians Eric Ashby and Mary Anderson noted, during the meeting with Mond, "at his back throughout the interview there burned a blazing coal fire!"[91]

On July 24, 1922, the Second Reading of a Bill based upon the recommendations of the Newton committee came before the Lords, but it left out government buildings, notoriously some of the worst offenders in terms of smoke pollution.[92] In Westminster, for instance, there were complaints about the Ministry of Works itself, whose emissions of black smoke "cannot be without a deleterious effect upon the pictures in the National Gallery and the National Portrait Gallery, the buildings of which are within some thirty yards of the chimney."[93] Later in the decade the matter of volumes of black smoke issuing from the smokestack of the Palace of Westminster itself between the hours of ten and eleven A.M. was referred to Parliament.[94]

Newton was aghast at the government's willingness to exempt its own departments from the Bill, pointing out that in Germany government departments had taken the lead in addressing the smoke problem. He now realised that governments did not see a Smoke Abatement Act as a way to win votes. More delays followed. Newton was by now exasperated with what he saw as government procrastination: "I have waited for five months this year. I waited the whole of last year, and I personally inquired about this question for two years myself. Really, it cannot be necessary for a Government Department to take all this time to consider when they should bring in a Bill."[95] Perhaps prompted by this diatribe, the Earl of Onslow, Parliamentary Secretary of the Board of Education, introduced a Bill in the Lords on July 26, 1923.[96] It too disappeared from view. On May 27, 1924, Onslow asked about its whereabouts.[97] Finally on the July 16, 1924, the Second Reading of the Public Health (Smoke Abatement) Bill was introduced by Earl De La Warr, a Bill which in all major essentials had been given a Second Reading twice before.[98]

On August 1 the Bill went to the committee stage. Its additions to the 1875 Act involved again the exemption of iron and steel processes for at least five years, and in relation to the Public Health (London) Act 1891, fines for non-consumption of smoke by furnaces and steam vessels were reduced to £5 and £10 from £25 and £50. An amendment to give other industries a chance to opt out of the law was also discussed. A further amendment was suggested by Lord Kylsant (1863–1937), a shipping magnate with a reputation for acting without consultation, to include exemptions for shipping. Lord Newton, who had been reluctantly agreeable to other exemptions, now exploded:

> For two years I sat with a number of other gentlemen on an inter-Departmental Committee, and not a single representative of the shipping interest appeared before us during the whole of that time, nor was

any representation made to us with regard to that particular industry. Now, at the eleventh hour, the noble Lord comes and wants his own particular industry to be excluded. . . . I do not think that the modest proposals in this Bill are likely prejudicially to affect the shipping interest to any important extent, and I am fortified in this view by the fact that recently I saw a notice that a shipowner had died leaving over £3,500,000. That does not look as if the shipping industry was in a bad way.[99]

As it happened, Kylsant was himself in a bad way. Although he became chairman of the shipbuilding firm Harland and Wolff in 1924, his other businesses were getting into difficulties, and he began moving money around to conceal their debts. In 1928 he was accused of false accounting, and three years later he was imprisoned for fraud.

Meanwhile Newton continued to insist that government buildings be included within the Bill: "I do not like to be disrespectful of a Government measure, but it does seem to me a piece of monumental impudence to bring in a Bill dealing with a social evil and to exempt all Government establishments from the proposed penalties. It is almost as if you were to suggest that no person in Government employ should be prosecuted if he got drunk."[100] Not only were government buildings to be exempted, however, but there were also objections to a provision that newly built private dwellings should be required to install heating which would emit very little smoke. Lord Banbury of Southam (1850–1936), a stockbroker, a Liberal, and chairman of the Great Northern Railway until it was merged with other companies in 1923, suggested that this was the beginning of the end for the liberty of the individual: "The noble Lord says that he does not want a housemaid to carry a coal scuttle up three or four floors. He says there should be a gas fire. I have always believed that this was a free country, and if I want to have a coal fire there is no reason why the noble Lord should come and tell me that I must have a gas fire simply because he likes a gas fire. We are going back to the days when nobody could do anything at all without the consent of some official."[101] Questions in the House of Commons gathered pace, however, and began to push the government forward. The Secretary of the British Medical Association commented wryly: "If three cabinet ministers died on one day and their death was attributed to fog the Government would then act in this matter of Smoke Abatement."[102] Although this was unlikely to happen, however, events in Parliament were now at last coming to a head, boosted by the occurrence of another severe fog. On December 10, 1925, Neville Chamberlain (1869–1940), Minister of Health (and later Prime Minister) was asked in the House of Commons if he was "aware that it has been calculated that at least 1,000,000 bushels of soot fell over London on the two days preceding last week's black fog; and will he take steps to bring in a smoke abatement Bill at the earliest possible date, in view of the damage to health, property, and industry which smoke and fogs create?"[103] Further questions increased the pressure. On March 23, 1926, the Bill had its Second Reading in the House of Lords for the fourth time.[104]

The Bill went to committee on April 22, 1926, and the usual amendments were put forward on whether new housing, sailing vessels, and government buildings should be exempted. A very lively discussion ensued, with Lord Newton taking the lead again.[105] The Bill finally passed the House of Lords on May 10, 1926. But now of course, since it had been introduced in the upper chamber, it had to pass through the House of Commons. It was debated in Second Reading on June 22, 1926. And it received the backing of the government. As Minister of Health, Neville Chamberlain rose to speak in its favour. He outlined the benefits of a cleaner atmosphere especially in relation to "the revelation of the healing and vitalising character of sunlight": "Even now, however, I doubt whether those who habitually dwell in towns fully realise the extent to which we are deprived of this essential factor by the condition of our atmosphere. It was estimated by Lord Newton's Committee that those who live in the country get 20 per cent. more sunlight than those who live in towns, and it is a matter of common knowledge that the occurrence of smoke fogs in towns is immediately followed by a rise in the death rate from respiratory diseases."[106] Chamberlain extended the definition of smoke from black to include other colours as well and to include the emission of grit and ash and substances emitted not just by chimneys but by other sources of pollution too. Fines were also increased, but exemptions were extended to certain industries for at least five years. In cases where manufacturers planned to install expensive equipment to reduce their smoke output but had not yet done so, they were to be allowed extra time to finance this.

The most controversial problem, as Chamberlain realised, was the omission of any provision to oblige new homes to be built with smoke-

Figure 7.7 A woman leads a car through Regent's Park using a large white scarf to show the driver the way in a fog on October 25, 1938. With visibility reduced to a few yards, it was necessary to lead cars to avoid accidents. The photograph was taken by William Vanderson, a celebrated Fleet Street photographer. William Vanderson/Getty Images.

free heating and cooking facilities. He defended this omission by pointing out that 75 percent of new homes being erected had gas stoves installed rather than open ranges. The real answer lay in making gas and electricity cheaper and more available. In this way smoke abatement could come about by stealth. This explains why a hard-fought provision on restraining domestic smoke was dropped from the Bill at an earlier stage on the personal ruling of Chamberlain.[107]

Shipping was also excluded because the Bill would have had to include foreign ships being brought into port, and retaliatory measures were feared from other countries; and there was the usual exemption of Crown property on the basis that any infringement would have to be brought to Parliament for it to be dealt with. Chamberlain summed up, presenting the Bill as a sensible measure mainly implementing existing regulations or making them more effective: "This is not a revolutionary Bill. It is an attempt to carry out the recommendations of the Newton Committee, to strengthen the administration of the existing provisions, to strengthen the law where it is found to be weak and, at the same time, to see that no undue hardship or injury is imposed upon manufacturers in carrying out the provisions of the Bill as enforced by local authorities."[108] Thomas Shaw (1872–1938), a trade unionist and Labour MP who had served in the minority Labour administration of 1924, supported the Bill. He was a realist where the domestic fire was concerned: "We have to recognise that the open fire in this country is an institution and also a sentiment. There is no workingman who does not like to sit by a cheery open fire."[109] Shaw castigated the industrialist who "is content to let people live in the smoke and grime, though he often takes the opportunity of getting out of it."[110]

And indeed the National Union of Manufacturers was "unanimously of the opinion that in the present state of industry it is most undesirable to pass into law a Bill of this nature, which may result in materially increasing the expenses of manufacturers."[111] Their anxieties were scotched by Sir Alfred Mond, the former Minister of Health, who was that very year amalgamating four separate companies to form Imperial Chemical Industries (ICI), one of the world's largest corporations, of which he was to become the first chairman: "I have been for many years now connected with factories burning something like a thousand tons of coal, with practically no smoke at all," he said. "That improvement was not brought about merely to make life more pleasant or to preserve the amenities, but to save an enormous waste of fuel. . . . This offensive smoke is not really a necessity, and if this Bill has one fault it is that it safeguards a little too much, and is a little too much in favour of what I would call the reactionary manufacturer."[112] It was, as Lieutenant-Commander Astbury, Conservative MP for Salford West, asserted, the smaller manufacturers who would suffer: "They started their works years ago, they have no room to expand. Undoubtedly they are emitting more smoke than they ought to, but when they cannot expand their boiler power and cannot extend their chimneys then, if these Regulations are to be carried out, there is only one thing to be done—the place has got to be closed down."[113] In the end the debate took over two hours, and the Bill was then committed to a Standing Committee. By a lucky chance for the reformers this coincided with the first fog of the season. London suffered two days of relatively bad fogs from November 24 to 26, 1926.[114] Richard Barnett, a member of the Standing Committee, complained on behalf of "those of us who have been compelled to breathe the air of the Metropolis during the past two days."[115] On December 15, 1926, the Bill was granted the Royal Assent—a Bill, now an Act, whose groundwork had been laid before the beginning of the First World War.

V

During the progress of the Bill through Parliament, it had been amended so many times that in the end it was not much of an advance on the Act of 1875. It provided for stiffer penalties for pollution, and it gave more powers to local authorities. It no longer required polluting smoke to be black before action could be taken against it. But crucially it contained no measures against domestic coal-fire smoke. Several MPs defended the Englishman's right to a coal fire blazing in his own hearth. Suspicion of gas was still widespread. Richard Storry Deans, a Tory MP, spoke for many when he declared: "although I may be told that the smoke from my coal fire assists in poisoning the people outside, I prefer that very much to being poisoned by a gas fire within my own house."[116] Local authorities were slow to use the powers granted to them under the Act. By 1932 local standards of smoke emission had been fixed by a mere 155 councils, but they applied only to black smoke. The vast majority had done nothing.[117]

The situation was made worse, if anything, by continually poor labour relations in the coal industry, which culminated in the General Strike of 1926. In this situation the coal industry, its profits in danger, fought hard against the smoke abatement movement, stressing the virtues of coal fires and accusing the campaigners of being financed by the gas and electricity industries. By the 1930s it was actually advertising the virtues of the "traditional coal fire." However, the case for greater smoke control was actually strengthened by miners' strikes and the consequent shortages of coal supplies. In 1921, during a major strike, Sir Napier Shaw claimed that the dirt in the air was about two-thirds less than it was in May 1920, when there had been no coal strike.[118] A month after the strike, Walter Trevelyan Thomson (1875–1925), a prominent steel merchant, directed Sir Alfred Mond's attention "to the appreciable improvement in the health of urban populations at the present time, attributable by many medical authorities to the purer condition of the atmosphere due to reduced coal consumption."[119]

Underlining the feebleness of the new Act's provisions, fogs continued to visit the metropolis for the rest of the 1920s. A thick fog descended on October 5, 1927, which was only short-lived, but on November 24, 1927, it was reported: "An almost unprecedented darkness brooded over London during nearly the whole of yesterday, and in the darkest hours, and in the darkest places it was very dark indeed. So dark in fact was it that the sky at noon looked exactly like the sky at night. . . . It was as if the sun had never risen."[120] The darkness was caused by an accumulation of smoke in the atmosphere above which was held there by a marked temperature inversion.[121] As the smoke fell to the ground, there was a spell of fog that began on Saturday, November 26, 1927, and continued for several days. Even more worryingly, yet another day of total darkness occurred without any fog on the following Tuesday, November 29. At ten o'clock that morning, pedestrians walking across Blackfriars Bridge found themselves moving from light into darkness halfway across: "The effect was weird, as looking backward everything was normal, but on the City side of the bridge lamps were alight and darkness made it like midnight."[122] "Oh, to be out of London now November's here!" one correspondent wrote. "During the past week we have been dragging out a depressed existence amid a sort of bilious gloom, the long hours of artificial light inducing a dissipated, up-all-night sort of feeling, without the pleasure of having earned it."[123] The following year another dense fog marred the spectacle of the opening of Parliament.[124]

As if to announce that more needed to be done, the National Smoke Abatement Society, formed in 1929 by an amalgamation of all the previously existing pressure groups, published a new edition of John Evelyn's *Fumifugium* in 1933, with an introduction by the writer and journalist Rose Macaulay: "Still we find soot in our chambers, and hear such snuffing, barking and coughing in London churches and assemblies as is not (for all we or Mr. Evelyn know) to be found elsewhere under heaven."[125] Macaulay was at the height of her fame after the publication of *They Were Defeated* (1932), an amalgam of fiction and biography exploring a female writer and her family in seventeenth-century England. This had most likely prompted the publisher to commission her introduction.[126] Henry

Des Voeux, the President of the National Smoke Abatement Society, also underlined the limitations of the 1926 Act with a letter to *The Times* in 1934, pleading that "surely the time has come now for the raising of a cry for air cleanliness, which is as essential a need as water cleanliness."[127] Gradually, indeed, fogs began to decline once more, not because people were using smokeless fuel, which hardly existed in a commercial form at this time, but because they were converting to gas. By 1938 60 percent of the national output of gas was being used for domestic purposes, and less than half of domestic energy consumption was fuelled by coal.[128]

Nevertheless, the decline was slow. From a peak of more than seventy days of fog a year recorded by the Greenwich Observatory in the early 1920s, the incidence fell to around forty to fifty in the 1930s, reaching a low point of only twenty-eight foggy days in 1938.[129] And there were still major outbreaks of dense and prolonged fog from time to time. At the beginning of 1930 a thick and persistent London fog impeded the progress of King George V to the House of Lords to open an important Five-Power Naval Conference. His car had to be guided by policemen.[130] November and December of the same year had significantly foggy days that enveloped London and allowed *The Times* staff photographer to produce a photographic "fog study" of the conditions.[131] December 17, 1930, was another foggy day that year, and it produced a "day of darkness"; it was followed by further foggy days under a week later that threatened to disrupt Christmas.[132] No doubt the fog continued to reduce audiences in London's theatres, but it also provided the inspiration for the famous playwright Ben Travers. As he recalled in his autobiography, his production "*A Night Like This* was an elaborate affair with a large cast and six sets. One of these represented a London exterior in a thick fog which was well suggested by means of a gauze curtain and skilful lighting. An old-fashioned growler with a real cab-horse was discovered."[133]

Late October and early December the following year were blighted by another few days of fog, which made polling in the General Election difficult (but still led to a Labour defeat and victory for the National Government). It also allowed the staff photographer of *The Times* to produce yet another "study," this time of Westminster.[134] The decade continued with fogs in London reported in January 1933 and 1934 and November 1934. Eric Hobsbawm (1917–2012), later to become a famous historian, who had been living in Berlin with his uncle and aunt following the death of his parents, arrived in London in March 1933 after the failure of one of his uncle's business ventures. He used the fog of November 1934 in his diary, which he still wrote in German, as a platform to hone his writing skills: "The fog was thick. Lay over everything. One is isolated. Here am I, in my world, ten metres' circumference. Beyond that, whiteness that sucks everything up. One is thrown back onto oneself and one's impressionability enlarges and deepens itself.—I walk through Hyde Park, e.g., All the trees are motionless, turned to stone like Niobe, stretching out their branches. Ghosts. The fog drives past my feet in little shreds, the breathy exhalation of the asphalt, cigar-smoke." As with so many other new arrivals in London, Hobsbawm perceived the fog as isolating, diminishing, and ghost-like.[135] Perhaps it was this fog that also caught the attention of Noel Gay (1898–1954), who wrote "A thick thick fog in London." A recording of it was made by Jack Payne and his band in 1935.[136] This comic song tells the story of a man sent out by his wife late on a foggy night to walk the dog. He loses the dog and knows he cannot return without it. He then gets lost and falls into a moat by the Tower of London. A policeman who pulls him out believes him to be drunk (a common mistake). When he finally gets home, the dog is, of course, sleeping comfortably beside the bed. Gay was known for London ditties, most famously "The Lambeth Walk," which he wrote for the musical "Me and My Girl." The year 1937 heralded another popular song on the subject of London fog. "A Foggy Day in London Town" was written by George and Ira Gershwin and introduced by Fred Astaire in the 1937 film "Damsel in Distress." It is about a stranger arriving in London and feeling further isolated by the fog: "It had me low and it had me down." However in this song it proves to be fortunate as the hero meets the love of his life "and through foggy London Town/The Sun was shining everywhere."[137] Celebrated in song on both sides of the Atlantic, London's fogs had achieved worldwide celebrity. They recurred in December 1935 and again in February 1936. September 1936 saw the use of loudspeakers from police cars to guide pedestrians and cars through the fog. In October 1938 and January 1939 Ludgate Circus suffered a "blackout" through an overhanging fog.[138] There seemed to be no end in sight.

Figure 7.8 "Fog Flares in Whitehall," a photograph taken on December 23, 1935, by Edward George Malindine (1906–1970), who was an official photographer for the War Office during the Second World War. Flares such as this one were often set up to warn drivers of junctions and other hazards lost to view in the fog. © Daily Herald Archive / Science & Society Picture Library.

In all of this Londoners maintained a phlegmatic attitude that not only treated fogs as an inevitable part of city life but even seemed to glory in the sangfroid with which they behaved as darkness descended upon the land. Here was a foretaste of the "Blitz spirit," when plucky Londoners carried on calmly and stoically as German bombs rained down on them in 1940–1941; perhaps the experience of fogs even inured them to hardship and prepared them for the conditions of siege under which they had to live during the early part of the war. As *The Times* remarked in November 1934:

> The behaviour . . . of Londoners in particular, in these annual visitations of fog is one of the most remarkable things to which a psychologist could devote his attention. For about a dozen days in winter Londoners share the Lapps' prerogative of never seeing the sun during all the twenty-four hours. They understand what was so graphically described as "palpable

darkness," a darkness that can be felt. They grope about the streets in pathetic endeavours to reach their accustomed haunts, and sit for hours in
trains which dare not break forth from their platform moorings. Breathing
becomes painful, clothes and body clammy. Yet the victims of nature's
playfulness, as it is imagined, take this all in good part. They see something quite humorous in omnibuses being guided home by their conductors, and, if the truth must be told, the Londoner would not like to be
parted from his fog. It has become an essential element of his existence,
and he glories in his shame."[139]

As the prospect of war became more likely, fog was even seen ironically
as a possible part of air defence from hostile attack: "Surely thickly-diffused
fog and smoke generators in the charge of voluntary organizations could,
with half an hour's warning, make and maintain an effective shroud over
London. . . . In fact, the countless chimney pots of our cities could provide an artillery that no aircraft could face or overcome."[140]

Londoners' stoicism in the face of such adversity was also observed
by a foreign visitor, the Chinese artist and travel writer Chiang Yee (1903–
1977), who arrived in London in 1933 and subsequently found employment
designing ballet sets. At first he did not like the city: "Most of the time
working under electric light and walking in a smoky and foggy atmosphere, I could not help feeling a growing distaste for this environment,
and I suppose most Londoners have a similar experience."[141] Upon arrival
in the Lake District, he breathed a sigh of relief, after he "had endured
London fogs for so long."[142] In *The Silent Traveller in London*, first published
in 1938, however, he devoted a whole chapter to the topic, because "London
fog is such a phenomenon."[143] The Chinese, he wrote, loved their own
mists and fogs, and many had heard of London fog; one friend even wrote
from China "asking whether the London fog really was as thick as pea-
soup or able to be cut by a knife."[144] It might not have been as thick as
this, but, he confessed, making his way through it was difficult: "I felt I
had to walk on the way more strongly and heavily than usual, as if I
had to push something which was pouring around my body."[145] He
found the reality very different from what he had anticipated. It was
the difference in colours that intrigued him: "The fog here is not the
pure white colour I used to know, but yellowish grey and sometimes
blackish. The particles of it do not strike the face with coolness and

refreshment, but my nostrils detect in it the presence of smoke and a very oppressive air."[146]

Yet Chiang found the variable hues of fog startlingly beautiful, like other artists before him: "The morning and evening mists in spring and summer give a greenish colour under their veil. . . . In autumn the mist changes into a yellowish and reddish colour, but in winter it becomes grey or blackish. As its colour is always changing, it supplies an inexhaustible sight for me to look at."[147] Unfortunately Londoners did not seem to appreciate it. They had no imagination, "so that is why they only see London fog as a foe or a matter of rage": "To be sure, a part of all human action should be hidden under a cover such as fog, so that it might be visible and invisible at once, and I think that is why London has a particular beauty, perhaps more than any other city in the world."[148] In fact this fog reported in *The Times* the following day was noted for the cheerfulness of spirits displayed by people having to walk home: "Large numbers of people decided that for anything up to five or six miles the quickest and warmest way home was on foot, and many reasonably cheerful walking parties were made up among employees of big business houses."[149] Chiang liked to imagine what people were doing under the fog and "to picture the attractive movements of humans": "As they appeared to me in the fog, they were all lovely creatures, with nice-looking faces. . . . Neither rich nor poor, carrying on their duties as they should be, without class or difference in age."[150] He made his way up to the top of Westminster Cathedral, although he was advised not to because it was a foggy day; he was the only one at the top: "As I walked round all four sides of the tower I thought I was living in heaven. I could not see the near-by chimney-pots underneath my feet and really had the feeling of having got away from London's noisy traffic for a while, although it was quite near me still. Through the vast white mist in front of me I could even imagine far, far away, my remote home!"[151]

Another visitor from East Asia, Shigeru Yoshida (1878–1967) became ambassador to London in 1936. His wife, Yukiko—or as she was generally known, Yuki (meaning snow)—was a cultured, sensitive, and artistic woman who had been to London before and formed an attachment to it. She wrote a memoir of her time in London called *Whispering Leaves in Grosvenor Square*. Like Chiang, she recognized the aesthetic appeal of

Figure 7.9 "Fog Scenes in Central London at Night" (1934), a photograph taken by James Jarché. The headlines on the newspapers reveal the disruption to rail transport caused by the fog. © Daily Herald Archive / Science & Society Picture Library.

London fog, echoing Victorian writers in their descriptions of the fairy-tale world into which it transformed the metropolis: "I think the fog is the veil of an artist, making the stately stone buildings look even romantic, and when the streets are lit the fog transforms the scene into a fairy city."[152] Yet it could also mirror feelings of gloom and despondency, not merely individually but also collectively. It was a foggy day when Edward VIII announced that he was giving up the throne in order to marry the twice-divorced American Wallis Simpson, against whom the social and political elites had closed ranks in opposition. For Yuki Yoshida, the weather captured the mood of the nation precisely: "On the morning of the 11th December I heard the sad news of the Abdication. The fog closed in the windows of my room and only the subdued noise of the traffic reached me through the gloom."[153]

As the murk closed in, enterprising retailers saw an opportunity. Selfridges department store offered to provide light and enjoyment after Sir William Arbuthnot-Lane (1856–1943), a renowned surgeon and President of the New Health Society, had suggested "that the chief danger of a fog was that its darkness depressed our spirits."[154] In 1934 the store's copywriter maintained: "Those of us who live in London have already this year had some hint that, although the old pea-soup-and-pepper fogs may have gone, there are still within the resources of the weather fogs sufficient to turn a rail journey of half an hour into one of two hours."[155] Nevertheless, he promised, the journey to Selfridges was still well worthwhile. Not even the prospect of an afternoon at Selfridges, however, could lift the spirits of the young poet George Barker (1913–1991). For Barker in 1940, November meant fog: "The horses cough their white blooms in the street, / Dogs shiver and boys run; the barges on the Thames / Lie like leviathans in the fog" (once more a prehistoric allusion to fog's regression of time to the era of the Megalosaurus, reminiscent of the opening page of Dickens's *Bleak House*).[156] Barker recorded his disappointment with life: "as I loiter in the haze / Where fog and sorrow cross my April days."[157] For Barker, as for many others, notably the exiles and émigrés living in the capital during the nineteenth century, fog became a symbol for "failure and distress" which, like lights through a fog, "can / Paralyse will and deter determination."[158] He was soon to emigrate to Japan, and thence to America, to try and find his fortune in clearer climes.

VI

Fog appeared more commonly in novels than in poetry. A notable example at this time was *Party Going* (1939) by Henry Green, the nom de plume of Henry Vincent Yorke (1905–1973), who came from a wealthy family of industrialists and began writing modernist novels in the late 1920s. Here the foggy weather not only determines the way the characters behave; it also brings out their personality traits and the class divisions within society. The writer John Updike beautifully summed up the story as "the anxieties and erotic manoeuvring of a few conspicuously spoiled, silly young rich waiting for a train." But Updike says that beyond this it is "a

Figure 7.10 Fog at Liverpool Street Railway Station on January 29, 1959. Most rail services were severely delayed or cancelled during fogs. There were also many serious accidents. Fog detonators were used to warn drivers to stop the train because men were working ahead, because there was an obstruction on the line, or because the fog was so thick that signals could not be easily seen. They were invented by Edward Alfred Cowper (1819–1893) in 1841. Edward Miller/Getty Images.

paradigm of life, life surrounded by a fog of death and threatened Departures."[159] The story centres on a group of young people, dubbed "bright, young things," who are meeting at a London railway station in order to go away to a party on the Continent.[160] However, the journey is impeded by a fog that descends on London, and it not only delays the people meeting at the station but also prevents the trains from leaving. They remove themselves to the station hotel, which is where the action takes place. Other people of different classes are also unable to leave the station, and the crowds build up inside, creating a situation of mounting panic.

Green's writing style is experimental. Among other things he often excludes the definite and indefinite article, which has the effect of making his descriptions stark and immediate. The book opens in this characteristic style: "FOG was so dense, bird that had been disturbed went flat into a balustrade and slowly fell, dead, at her feet."[161] The rhythm of these lines resembles poetry, with an emphasis on monosyllables such as "fog," "bird," "flat," and "dead." The hard *d* sound dominates the line. The prose continues: "There it lay and Miss Fellowes looked up to where that pall of fog was twenty foot above. . . . She bent down and took a wing then entered a tunnel in front of her, and this had DEPARTURES lit up over it, carrying her dead pigeon." It appears to indicate an entry into the land of the dead: "No one paid attention, all were intent and everyone hurried, nobody looked back."[162] As in *The Waste Land* or *The Forsyte Saga,* fog has created a world of ghosts—a recurring feature of its use in the literature of the interwar period, when so many millions of ghosts of men killed in the war inhabited people's imaginations.

Green echoes Eliot's description of working people moving through the office district of London around the station (in this case going home from work rather than making their way towards it): "Now they came out in ones and threes and now a flood was coming out. . . . As pavements swelled out under this dark flood so that if you had been ensconced in that pall of fog looking down below at twenty foot deep of night illuminated by street lamps, these crowded pavements would have looked to you as if for all the world they might have been conduits."[163] Pedestrians are able to move forward, but "the traffic was motionless for long and then longer periods."[164] One of the party, Julia Wray, decides to walk to the station, realising that she will probably get there before her luggage does. She loses her identity when she leaves her "warm rooms with bells and servants and her uncle, . . . a rich important man—she lost her name and was all at once anonymous." Like women walking alone in the fog in Victorian times, she is courting danger. People "were divided by this gloom and were nervous."[165] Julia begins to feel afraid. The air she breathes is harsh, and "where there were no lamps or what few there were shone at greater distances, it was like night with fog as a ceiling shutting out the sky, lying below tops of trees."[166]

But as the fog shuts out the sky, Julia fears that it will suddenly drop down to the ground and "she would be lost." It is still only half-past four in the afternoon. Another character, Alexander, also going to the party, describes the sensation from the relative comfort of a taxicab: "He did not know where he was, it was impossible to recognize streets, fog at moments collapsed on traffic from its ceiling. One moment you were in dirty cotton wool saturated with iced water and then out of it into ravines of cold sweating granite with cave-dweller's windows and entrances."[167] The image of fog returning London to a prehistoric state seemed too obvious for a writer to ignore, as did the effect of fog in blurring perceptions and altering reality, when "the station master came out under that huge vault of green he called his roof, smelled fog which disabled all his trains, looked about at fog-coloured people, his travellers who scurried though now and again they stood swaying and he thought that the air, his atmosphere, was wonderfully clear considering, although everyone did seem smudged by fog."[168]

Both Julia and another character, Amabel, hope to accompany the organizer of the party, Max, to the event, and this triangular relationship introduces a further element of tension into the story. Amabel feels that she has become ill under the stress and has been advised by her doctor "to go away to the sun out of this frightful fog."[169] Other members of the group arrive at the station by car. Mr. and Mrs. Hignam crawl along, "continually in traffic blocks," whereas Alexander "was on his way, bowling along in his taxi the length of cricket pitches at a time, from block to block, one red light to another, or shimmering policeman dressed in rubber."[170] Alex's image of his journey, likened to the gentlemanly game of cricket, quickly dissolves into the more hallucinatory aspects of the atmosphere: "Humming, he likened what he saw to being dead and thought of himself as a ghost driving through streets of the living, this darkness or that veil between him and what he saw a difference between being alive and death."[171] In a later scene Julia and Max look down from the station hotel window on the crowds of people who have been forced to congregate there due to the fog and the delay to the trains' departures. Julia and Max cough "as fog caught their two throats," or possibly it is another kind of smoke "from those below who had put on cigarettes or pipes, because tobacco smoke was coming up in drifts."[172]

Green's modernist sensibility mingles classic metaphors of fog with both a political reading, that of the young spoilt rich against the hardworking masses, and a knowing sense that all is about to change when war breaks out. Although he came from a wealthy family, Green enjoyed working on the industrial floor of his own factory. He was, as Frank

Kermode points out, "an old Etonian and a Communist sympathizer."[173] Kermode goes on to write that "Green was always interested in the narrative effect of sensory failure. His first, undergraduate novel, *Blindness,* has a hero who must confront the world after losing his sight in an accident. In *Loving* there is a marvelous game of blindman's buff."[174] In *Party Going* Green employs a standard symbol of sensory failure by using London fog, which blinds, distorts, and deafens. Kermode says of "sensory failure," that it is "an interruption in the conventional processing of information, in our knowing dully, for the sake of convenience, where and what we are, may make for a momentary strangeness in the world or in the book."[175]

In the Victorian era London fog had been linked to crime, immorality, transgression, and despair, but the association of fog with death in the minds of so many writers in the interwar years is notable. For Morton the fogbound townscape turns people into ghosts; Eliot sees them flowing through the streets like the endless procession of souls crossing the River Styx into the underworld; Galsworthy's fog echoes with ghostly laughter. Like Eliot, Chiang Yee sees Londoners in a fog as unthinking, unfeeling creatures, lacking all awareness of their surroundings; George Barker thinks fog paralyses the human will; Henry Green's character considers himself a ghost as he drives through the fog, echoing Eliot's description of the unthinking masses flowing through the streets. Looming over all this is the collective memory of the First World War, when, as one veteran remarked, walking through no-man's-land was like walking through a fog. In some ways the experience of the war had narrowed the imagination; fog could no longer be used metaphorically in the myriad ways in which it had been employed by so many writers before 1914. The new war that broke out in 1939 was a very different kind of war, one that seemed far less futile than the Great War of 1914–1918. If writing about that war stressed above all the monotony and pointlessness of life in the trenches, the literature of the Second World War and the period that followed it was far more varied and diverse, opening up fresh possibilities of viewing London fog as a creative source—at least as long as it continued to plague the streets of London in the winter months, as it had through the 1930s despite all that campaigners did to try and diminish it.

CHAPTER EIGHT

The Last Gasp

I

The typical image of London during the war is of a city wreathed not in a traditional fog but in the smoke and flames of the Blitz. There was a widespread feeling that the great London fogs were things of the past. In *Put Out More Flags,* a novel by Evelyn Waugh written after he was evacuated from Crete in May 1941, the decline of fog is used as a symbol of the decline of Britain. The shambles of the British expedition to Crete had left Waugh feeling deflated, and he used his time on a slow ship home to write a story concerning characters he had already used in *Black Mischief* (1932). *Put Out More Flags* is set during the phoney war of 1939–1940. Ambrose Silk, an aesthete who cultivates an image as a reincarnation of Oscar Wilde, feels happier in the past than he does in the present, and his views on coal fires are meant to reflect this. He expatiates on the decline of England, which, he declares, "dates from the day we abandoned coal fuel. . . . We used to live in a fog, the splendid, luminous, tawny fogs of our early childhood. The golden aura of the Golden Age. . . . We designed a city which was meant to be seen in fog. We had a foggy habit of life, and a rich, obscure, choking literature. The great catch in the throat of English lyric poetry is just fog, my dear, on the vocal chords. . . . Then some busybody invents electricity or oil fuel or whatever it is they use nowadays. The fog lifts, the world sees us as we are, and worse still, we see ourselves as we are."[1] Here is another positive, if ironically, expressed view of London fog to match those which were expressed by a variety of authors in the interwar years. Ambrose Silk's Wildean paradoxes floated on a sea of nostalgic lament about the decline of artifice and pretence.

Yet for all the impression of fog as a thing of the past, public debate about the continuing need for smoke abatement did not die down, despite the priorities of the war. Neither did the war mean that there were no fogs in London. In October 1943 a typical London fog threatened to spoil the leave of several hundred American sailors who had to be shepherded around by volunteers from the American Red Cross. Meanwhile Major Frank Markham MP (1897–1975) dared to introduce the subject whilst the House of Commons was examining the activities of the Ministry of Air in the middle of the war.[2] He wanted an agreement that meteorologists would expand their role into measuring air pollution, especially the amount of sunshine lost through the dirty air, because "it can be shown that Victoria Street, Westminster, just outside here, loses over 60 per cent of ultra-violet radiation every year": "I suggest that we are losing in this country one of the greatest assets God has given us—that is, unpolluted sunshine—because no Minister has taken the responsibility of keeping our air clean, and I suggest that the Secretary of State for Air should extend his functions and become the guardian of the air, and give us back that sunshine which since the industrial revolution we have lost. This pollution has been greatly increased recently by the action of the Ministry in encouraging smoke production, rather than its abatement."[3] Unfortunately Markham was ruled out of order by the Deputy Speaker.

However, others also raised the matter, largely in connection with proposed new building in a postwar country. The Conservative MP Edward Keeling (1888–1954) demanded that smoke abatement legislation should be agreed upon before building of new houses began.[4] An editorial in a London paper outlined the dilemma. A recent selection of interviews had shown only 34 percent of the population in favour of central heating, with 44 percent neutral and 21 percent opposed. The paper blamed the housewife for being too much in love with her open fire and not appreciating the virtues of central heating. The article concluded that "no amount of vocal prejudice should dissuade those responsible for planning and building new houses" from installing central heating. It continued: "Outside the home, the damage done to health, buildings and agriculture by atmospheric coal pollution is estimated at not less than £50 millions a year. It is not presumptuous to assert that on this topic the average housewife is less than usually well-informed, either as to her own or the public interest. Try it, madam, and see!"[5] Both Markham and Keeling continued to promote smoke abatement, the latter through installation of cleaner grates and the former by endeavouring to get the government to devote more attention to the issue.

In March 1945, just before the end of the war, Markham attempted to get the new Ministry of Fuel and Power to take responsibility for the abatement of smoke even though he acknowledged that there were already four ministries doing the same thing: the Ministry of Health, which he dismissed as ineffectual as it was committed to using "methods of persuasion" rather than compulsion; the Department of the Lord President of the Council, responsible for scientific research; the Air Ministry, responsible for purity of air and meteorological investigation; and finally the Ministry of Fuel, whose concern was with the "origin of all these nuisances": "In short, I put my argument in this way. In the past four great Departments have been playing about with smoke abatement and very little has been done. The time has come for a single Department to be responsible, root, stock and branch, and for making sure that there is some progress."[6] But he got nowhere. The amendment was withdrawn in spite of the fact that London had endured another spell of fog in January 1945.[7]

The end of the war was followed by a fog in London in 1946. *Time* magazine reported, "Street lights swung suspended in midair like furry halos. Snub-nosed busses, bunched in convoys, crawled in low gear behind inspectors pacing ahead with lanterns. Three passengers were killed in a suburban train crash."[8] Admiring Londoners' stoicism, the article continued: "Londoners had long since come to regard a Big Fog as a kind of picnic. Under the cloak of pea-soup anonymity, whistling as they felt their way, strangers walked and talked with strangers in a manner unthinkable in bright daylight."[9] Another major fog occurred towards the end of November 1948. *The Times* greeted "the first fog" as "not an honest enemy. . . . There is something horribly stealthy about its approach; it settles down with 'the inevitability of gradualness.' . . . It is in this matter of journeys that the fog demon displays his true malignancy. He will insist on spreading his murky empire at the beginning and at the close of day, just when poor daily-breading mortals could most gladly dispense with it."[10] The same article compared the countryman's experience in the fog when he decides to leave the comfort of his home. Being out in a country fog calls to mind the pattering of the Hound of the Baskervilles and other creatures of the romantic imagination. However, "his urban brother, sitting in his office with the lights on, with a prospect of a homeward journey punctuated by fog signals," is less romantic.[11]

Figure 8.1 Two policemen try to see the sixty-four-foot Christmas tree, an annual gift from Norway, in Trafalgar Square on the foggy day of December 1, 1948. Warburton/Getty Images.

According to the *Evening Standard*, November 1948 experienced "London's longest-ever fog": "By 5 P.M. this evening it had lasted 92 hours—five hours longer than the previous record, set at Christmas 1944."[12] As usual, it affected sporting fixtures and transport. The cruise liner *Queen*

Elizabeth was unable to depart for several days, and shipping was at a standstill in the Thames, with "hundreds of ships . . . anchored between Gravesend and Southend."[13] Thirty-one ships were left waiting to sail from London docks, some carrying perishable foodstuffs. About sixty-five colliers, carrying about 120,000 tons of coal, were also held up in the Thames. When the fog finally began to lift on December 1, the movement of the massed ships was likened to the convoys gathering before D-Day.[14] With visibility described as "almost nil," fog services were being run from all London's stations, and bus "conductors were having to walk in front of their buses in East and South-east London."[15] One traveller at least wrote of her "admiration for and gratitude to the bus crews, and especially the drivers": "In the long fog we have just endured [they] carried on under almost impossible atmospheric conditions and helped us to go about our business and to get home."[16]

Many actors and personalities were unable to arrive in time for the Royal Command Film Performance that year. Phyllis Calvert had to be diverted to Bologna, Italy, and the following day spent an hour and three-quarters circling over Northolt before landing. The ornithologist and artist Peter Scott was less lucky: his plane from New York would not take off until London's fog cleared. He touched down too late for the showing of the John Mills epic about his father, *Scott of the Antarctic*.[17] West End theatres, in what they called a "fog slide," reported a 10 to 20 percent drop in attendance over the foggy period, hitting mainly the cheaper seats, perhaps revealing that many of these seats were purchased on the night.[18] A number of accidents occurred and of course a number of robberies.[19] The *Evening Standard* described the situation: "Filth and grime blanket London. The stagnant foggy air, polluted and thickened by the dust and smoke from a million chimneys, smears and sullies the whole city and all who live there."[20] The newspaper criticised the government, describing its response to the problem as "lackadaisical," and referred to *The Simon Report on Domestic Fuel Policy,* published three years previously, which had made "35 practical recommendations to rid Britain of the smoke nuisance." But what had happened to this report? the paper asked: "Has it been lost in that particularly dense fog which hovers permanently over Whitehall? It is time the Government acted to clear Britain's lungs."[21] The British Gas Council saw the fog as a means to promote its own source of energy in an advertisement that appeared in December 1948: "Those who use gas and coke help to keep the air clean and minimise the loss caused by fogs; they help, too, to save a part of the nation's wealth."[22]

There was some attempt to raise the issue of smoke abatement in Parliament on the back of these fogs; but the debate was frequently combined with legislation about the need for new housing, following the Blitz, and whether builders should be forced to introduce cleaner methods of heating and cooking. Questions on the general subject of smoke abatement legislation continued to be raised in early 1948. The Labour MP Ellis Smith (1896–1969) asked the Minister of Health, Aneurin Bevan (1897–1960), when "a modern policy of smoke abatement" was going to be applied.[23] But it was only after the December fog of that year that demands for smoke abatement became more urgent. On December 9, 1948, Leah Manning (1886–1977), who represented Epping, which was sometimes affected by London fog despite its rural location, asked the Lord President of the Scientific Research Council, Herbert Morrison (1888–1965), "what steps are being taken by the Scientific Research Council in respect of Smoke Abatement, in view of the menace to health, and the serious results to industry, commerce and transport caused by fogs such as this country recently suffered?"[24] Morrison replied rather evasively that "the reduction of smoke in the air will not prevent fogs, but it should reduce their intensity and frequency."[25]

It is surprising that Morrison was not more supportive of smoke-abatement ambitions as he had created the Metropolitan Green Belt in the 1930s and was a staunch Londoner, born in Stockwell and dying in Peckham. He was perhaps reticent because he had supported the recent nationalization of the coal industry, and there was some suspicion among smoke-abatement activists that the coal now used was of a lower quality and, containing more dirt and stones, produced more smoke than the coal used when the industry was private. In addition much of the higher-quality coal was being exported overseas, and this provided income to the country that was desperately needed at this time. The following year Fred Longden (1889–1952; representing Birmingham Deritend) asked Aneurin Bevan whether he felt that the 1936 Smoke Abatement Act provided adequate powers to deal with the nuisance.[26] Arthur Skeffington

(1909–1971; representing Lewisham West) followed up with a similar question, to which Bevan replied, like Morrison somewhat evasively, that "in the main the legal powers are adequate. The chief difficulties are the practical ones."[27] "I have no power to make regulations governing the arrangements which factories must make to control emission of smoke," he said on another occasion. Local authorities had powers under the Public Health Act 1936 to deal with noxious emissions. "I have no reason," he declared, "to suppose that these powers are inadequate to deal with any smoke nuisances."[28]

Yet London fog, Fred Longden declared, was clearly not being dealt with. He followed up his earlier question a year later with one that placed an even greater emphasis on the urgency of the need for change: "We all know what smoke fog does to our eyes, how it robs us of sighting and daylight. . . . There is also an adverse effect on plant life in the vicinity of such emissions from factories and workshops through the impurities discharged, where we see stunted growth, little green and no green at all and contaminated herbs which cattle eat—and we eat the cattle. Further, our buildings are corroded on the outside; they are dirty, even filthy. As a result overall costs are enormous to our people and country."[29] He called for an urgent investigation into how to reduce smoke and improve the health of the nation. Arthur Blenkinsop (1911–1979), the Parliamentary Secretary to the Ministry of Health, again fudged the issue. Dividing the problem into two categories, industrial and domestic, he acknowledged that with the greater need to increase industrial productivity after the war and the fact that often older machinery was being used, it was not a good time to reduce smoke. He pointed to the establishment of smokeless zones in some areas through Private Member's Bills as a way forward. He mentioned the argument that domestic fires caused fogs but observed: "My wife, who is a staunch believer in at least one coal fire, would certainly disagree, as doubtless would many other people."[30] He acknowledged that local authorities were now obliged to install grates approved by the Ministry of Fuel and Power but admitted progress was slow. Mrs. Blenkinsop was not the only one in love with her coal fire; George Orwell, a few years earlier in the *Evening Standard,* complained of a "noisy minority [who] will want to do away with the old-fashioned coal fire" and later added that "the first great virtue of a coal fire is that just because it warms one end of the room, it forces people to group themselves in a sociable way"[31]—a senti-ment that Charles Dickens had shared in the previous century.

Circumstances—the need for the rapid construction of cheap new housing, the revival of industry after the war, a continued nostalgia for the virtues of the old-fashioned coal fire, the low legislative priority of is-sues other than those related to postwar reconstruction—seemed to be conspiring to frustrate the campaign for smoke abatement. Many people continued, despite the evidence of their own eyes, to feel that the great London fogs were a thing of the past.

In the book *In Search of London,* first published in 1951, Henry Vollam Morton recalled being caught in a "thick pea-souper which tastes like iron filings at the back of your throat," turning "every lamp into a downward V of haze." It gave "to every encounter a nightmare quality almost of terror, of one of the most exciting acts of God."[32] Deploying a familiar trope, he noted how "two taxis in collision look in the gloom like a couple of prehistoric monsters locked in clumsy conflict." And indeed, during one such fog, walking along the Haymarket in the West End, he heard "an odd shuffling sound," made by "something tall and moving." As it passed "into a thin funnel of light from one of the lamps," he recognized it as the "hindquarters of an elephant." "Once I knew what it was, it seemed quite in keeping with the general fantasy of a London pea-souper." The man leading the elephant through the gloom was trying to get it to a Christmas circus being held at Olympia and had got lost. Morton offered to hold the elephant while the man telephoned from a public call box to say he was on his way. "I wonder," Morton asked, "how many people can claim to have held an elephant in the Haymarket?"[33] Now living in South Africa, Morton felt nostalgic about his London years. "Sometimes," he wrote wistfully, "I have found myself longing quite absurdly for the first fog. . . . When I no longer feel any excitement for these things, I shall know that I am getting old."[34] His wish was soon to be fulfilled more dra-matically than he could have imagined.

II

On December 4, 1952, the usual winter fog descended upon the capital. Although no one knew at the time, it was to be not only one of the greatest of the London fogs but also one of the last. As was usual with the worst fogs, a cold front had moved in across London. The air was unusually still, and many householders lit fires in their household grates to keep themselves warm. In these cold, damp conditions many people would have kept their fires going throughout the night by banking them up with "slack," consisting of tiny bits of coal and coal dust. Fumes discharged from chimneys lingered in the still air outside. Soon the capital was smothered in a thick yellow fog. It lasted for almost a week, until it abated with a change in the weather on December 9. One Londoner commented, "You was always used to a fog, I mean, come winter you always knew you were going to get a fog. But that particular one, it was so thick and yellowy that it was just different from all the others and that one did jolt the government."[35] Joan Matthews remembered being "in the last great smog": "I went up to work that day and by two o'clock in the afternoon you couldn't see across the corridor. It was thick, yellow, and somebody knocked on the door of my office and said, 'Go home, we're closing.' . . . I'll never forget it because the smog was so thick you really felt like you were walking into a war. Extraordinary."[36]

The fog belt, reported *The Times,* extended for about twenty miles from the centre of London in all directions, "from Wood Green to Highgate, Harringay, Enfield, Epping, Holloway, and Palmers Green. Conditions were almost as bad in parts of south-east London, including the Blackwall Tunnel, Plumstead, Abbey Wood, Belvedere, Erith, and Bexhill."[37] It was no great surprise that the first electric power cuts of the winter were announced in the same issue because of hugely increased demand on electricity supplies, prompting even more people to turn to their coal fires to create heat and light.[38]

There was no escape. Entertainments were curtailed. A performance of *La Traviata* at Sadler's Wells had to be stopped after the first act because the audience could no longer see the stage. Tickets were refunded.[39] A concert at the Wigmore Hall had to be suspended for the same reason.[40] In the era of live television the BBC had to make several last-minute programme changes because "artists were unable to reach the studios."[41] Parliamentarians reported fog seeping into the chamber of the House of Commons, and some even felt the need to hurry up debates in order to catch earlier trains.[42] Almost all sporting fixtures in London were cancelled, including rugby and football matches, as well as horse racing. People had to bathe and change clothes when they reached home after travelling through the fog. The results confirmed just how many sooty particles were in the outside air: "I went and had a bath and I couldn't believe it. When I got out there was about an inch of grime round the edge of the bath and all my clothes were filthy."[43]

Transport of all kinds was seriously affected. *The Times* reported that the fog had caused "widespread interruption of road, rail, and air services, and brought shipping in the Thames to a standstill."[44] A lucky few air travellers could fly out from Bournemouth, instead of from London Airport, but many others simply had to wait for the fog to clear.[45] The authorities were not going to take any chances under these circumstances as an aeroplane on a scheduled flight from Paris to London had crashed on October 31, 1950, trying to land in thick fog at London Airport. Twenty-eight passengers out of a total of thirty had been killed.[46]

Local journeys were also severely disrupted: "By 10 P.M. all bus and trolleybus services in the London Transport area, except for three routes, had been withdrawn," and British Railways were running "a special fog service . . . in the London area." Drivers whose cars broke down on the roads were unable to get help, as "the crews of the Automobile Association's radio-controlled breakdown vans found it almost impossible to locate members who telephoned for help."[47] The same article reported that "there was hardly half a mile of road in the centre of London where visibility was more than five yards."[48] Ambulance workers and firefighters had to walk in front of their vehicles.[49] As night fell on Saturday, visibility grew worse, and London, cleared of most of its traffic, was eerily silent "apart from an occasional convoy of buses crawling nose-to-tail back to their depôts."[50] *The Times* reported many "burglaries, attacks, and robberies under cover of fog."[51] One burglar climbed a drainpipe and gained access to three flats in the same building in Princes Gate unobserved; one of the victims was the actor Kenneth More. Another burglary was committed by thieves who boldly propped a ladder up to a balcony in Cheyne Place, Chelsea.[52] Nobody noticed because it was barely visible, and there were hardly any pedestrians passing by.

Londoners who lived through this fog recalled the problems of getting about. Most were just determined to get on with their lives. Carol

Handley, who lived in Cartwright Gardens, Bloomsbury, remembered, "I had to catch a bus to work from the Euston Road and you could not see a bus with all its lights on inside and out approaching until it almost reached you. It was weird walking anywhere—one tried to avoid it—because you could only see a few feet in front of you and all familiar landmarks had disappeared. At times conductors (buses had them then) would get out to guide the driver across a junction and buses could not travel at more than walking pace. But they kept going."[53] As in 1873, so in 1952, the fog coincided with preparations for the annual Smithfield show, now held at Earl's Court. The animals' journey to the show was delayed. It was reported that "some entries from Cornwall" took "seven hours to travel from Paddington station to Earls Court by lorry."[54] By the time the show officially opened on Monday, December 8, an Aberdeen Angus had died, and twelve other animals had had to be slaughtered. Many other animals were suffering from breathing difficulties and had to be given oxygen. Basil O. E. Walpole, Veterinary Officer to the Smithfield Club, noted, however, that "the sheep and pig exhibits escaped ill-effects from the fog." This he attributed "to the fact that these animals were on the first floor, where the atmosphere was much less contaminated. . . . Furthermore, sheep and pigs lay with their heads nearer to the floor, thus having the advantage of the straw acting as a filter."[55] Another explanation, oddly, was dung. The prize cattle's bedding was changed more often than that of the sheep and pigs, whose dung thus produced more ammonia gas, an alkali that proved beneficial when it mixed with the air they breathed. The Atmospheric Pollution Section in St. Bartholomew's Hospital began experimentally issuing ammonia bottles to patients suffering from the effects of air pollution.[56]

Other animals too suffered in the London fog. An article on "smoke and the zoo" appeared in 1936 detailing how a great many animals had "very dirty coats. . . . Polar bears and birds with soft white plumage, such as Spoonbills and White Peafowl, become extremely dirty." This was bad enough, as the condition of the coat could affect the general health of the animals, but also the lungs of the animals and birds were damaged; specifically, "many Felines in the Lion house die from chronic bronchitis, fibrosis and gangrene of the lungs associated with blackening of the lungs by dust deposit." Animals too suffered from the depressing effects of fog, and this was noted by the superintendent of the Regent's Park Gardens:

LONDON, DECEMBER 1952. *A prize bull at the Smithfield Show at Earl's Court protected from the fog by a sacking mask soaked in whisky and water. Sixty cattle had to be given intravenous injections, nine had to be slaughtered and five died.*

Figure 8.2 This prize bull at the Smithfield Show in 1952 had to be protected from the fog by a sacking mask soaked in whisky and water. (*Picture Post,* 31 October 1953). Reproduced by kind permission of the Syndics of Cambridge University Library.

"Such depression and loss of vitality naturally tends to affect physical health." Similarly, the article concluded, the London fog must also affect the health and well-being of domestic pets, as well as having an impact on the economic value of poultry and livestock for smallholdings.[57]

The 1952 fog was particularly ferocious. It quickly became known as the "Great Killer Fog" of 1952.[58] Tom Driberg (1905–1976), a Labour parliamentarian representing Maldon, raised the issue of the extra number of deaths in the Greater London area as early as December 16. The Minister of Health, Iain Macleod, had to admit that deaths from all causes during the week ending December 6, compared with the same week the previous year, showed an increase of 519. The following week the number had increased still further. "Deaths from all causes in Greater London during the week ending December 13," it was reported in the House of Commons, "were 4,703, compared with 1,852 in the corresponding week of 1951."[59] The mortuaries quickly filled up. During the first three months of 1953 there were 8,625 more deaths than expected. The government confirmed the extra deaths after December 20 but attributed many of them to an influenza outbreak, although an official report listed 2,970 as unexplained. Even as late as March 1953 the *Daily Express* questioned the extent to which the fog had contributed to later illnesses and deaths. Scientists have argued convincingly, however, that these "excess deaths could be attributable to air pollution through a delayed effect from the smog itself."[60] It was reported that "only on four occasions had the number of weekly deaths in . . . London exceeded those in the week that followed the recent fog."[61] Air-pollution levels remained high through January 1953.[62] "If excess deaths in these months were related to air pollution, the mortality arising from the smog of 1952 could have been as high as 12,000 deaths rather than the 3,000–4,000 generally reported."[63]

Dr. Somerville Hastings (1878–1967), MP for Barking, stated that patients admitted to hospital during the heavy fog in December were still there. "If we are to continue to live in London in health," he said, "something must be done to prevent these serious epidemics of fog, and the continuous descent of a certain amount of sulphur dioxide into the atmosphere."[64] There were many individual stories of the effects of fog on health. A businessman from Harpenden, Hertfordshire. described a dinner held on December 5 in London: "Fog and fumes penetrated the large dining hall in the hotel that night. Still I did not worry but put it down largely to the big company . . . and the smoking of pipes, cigars, etc."[65] His journey home was unsurprisingly delayed by the fog, but by December 7, he said, "the fog had me in its grip, and I perforce had to stay in bed for the next fortnight with a bad attack of bronchitis."[66] He admitted that it was not until three months later that he felt fully fit again.

The economic health of the nation was also affected, especially as the fog had occurred during the run-up to Christmas. The journal for the Smoke Abatement Society, *Smokeless Air*, quoted "one firm of multiple shops [which] estimated that its turnover was down by 34 per cent. compared with the previous year." Other retailers complained of the soiling and damage to their stock, especially stock that had been on display in their windows: "Dresses were also badly affected and markdowns will be very considerable. . . . Also the exterior of our building, which had been cleaned a few weeks ago for the Coronation, has lost its freshness."[67]

III

It was above all the great fog of 1952 that left its traces on literature. But conditions for the literary uses of London fog had changed. During the Second World War, as in the First, noxious vapours and deadly gases had come to public attention, but this time they were applied silently, away from the war zones, and in a form not visible to the naked eye: in the extermination camps at Auschwitz, Treblinka, and elsewhere in Nazi-held central Europe. There was little discussion of the mass extermination of Europe's Jews in the 1940s and 1950s, and by the time it came to haunt the European memory, London fog was gone. More immediately as far as Londoners were concerned was the fact that millions of gas masks had been distributed to them during the war. Every household had its supply, to be used for protection against gas attacks from the air. But these never materialized; Hitler, like Churchill, refrained from using gas weapons for fear of what the other side would do in return. Mass gassing in the Second World War did not enter contemporary consciousness. Apocalyptic scenarios had in any case disappeared in the real apocalypse of World War I, when the use of mustard gas on the battlefront outdid anything that London fog could do in threatening life and health. If London fog was going to re-emerge as a literary metaphor, it was only in a strictly personal, individual form, describing the state of mind and being of the individual, not of society as a whole.

Figure 8.3 *London Fog,* by Stella Rankin (1915–2009). Rankin taught at St. Martin's School of Art, London, in 1958–1959, then at Goldsmiths' College, also in London, in 1959–1961. This 1959 painting presents a more modern view of London fog. The fog makes the trees seem to move. Reproduced by kind permission of Chelmsford City Museums.

Unlike so many novels of the early decades of the twentieth century, postwar fiction did not look back to the high point of London fog in the 1880s; too much had happened in between; too great a temporal and cultural distance now lay behind; too many serious contemporary social issues were raising their heads in the difficult period of social and moral readjustment that followed the end of the war. The "angry young men" of the literary 1950s and the "kitchen-sink dramas" of the 1960s addressed current problems of life in a modern urban setting. One of the most popular novels of 1960, *The L-Shaped Room* (1960) by Lynne Reid Banks (1929–), used a great London fog—undated but drawing on the experience of 1952—as a central metaphor. The book's main character, Jane, single, pregnant, and poor, is forced to rent a dingy apartment in a poor part of the city. She has been talking to a prostitute in the basement flat of her house in Fulham. There is a thick fog outside. "What a lousy night!" says the prostitute as she goes out the front door: "I hate this bloody mist, it gets into everything and makes your hair straight." The fog made her eyeliner go runny, and "her hair was hanging in strands from under her hat." As Jane looks at the receding figure of the prostitute, she sees her "reach up and tuck a strand of hair into place before the dark mist swallowed her up."[68]

A craving for Indian curry—a consequence of pregnancy—leads Jane too out into the foggy night; and after a huge meal by herself, she has to make her way home in the fog, which "had got considerably thicker" and "very cold": "the temperature seemed to have gone down, and I was shivering even while I sweated from the furnace-like emanations of the curry." Her bus reaches (significantly) World's End, but at this point "the streets were darker, the fog seemed to close in and the bus was forced to nose its way cautiously along in first gear." A car had crashed into a bus two nights previously, so the driver shows extra caution. It is even more frightening for the young woman when she gets off the bus, not even sure that this is her stop: "I felt my way along, a few steps at a time, and every time I heard a voice or a footstep I stopped dead, clinging to whatever bit of masonry was under my hand and almost cowing with fright." Turning into the street where she hopes her house lies, she is even more frightened by the eerie silence: "Far, far away I could hear the slow, grinding sounds of traffic—but muffled, as if I were wearing ear-plugs." The city takes on the aspects both of the supernatural world and of the jungle: "I moved like a ghost from lamp to lamp, tiptoeing for some reason, as if I were in a jungle in dread of attracting the attention of wild animals prowling near me. I couldn't decide whether I felt safer near the lamps, or in the dark stretches between." A combination of the heavy meal, her pregnancy, and the cold makes Jane feel unwell, and although she takes hold of a lamp-post to steady herself, she slides downwards and strikes the ground: "and I smelt a very strong smell of dog."[69]

This is Jane's lowest point—she has been contemplating an abortion, the man she slept with the previous night has disappeared, she has been called a whore by her friend Johnny, and now her huge curry meal appears to have brought on a miscarriage. Her saviour ironically is the prostitute she had talked to earlier, who finds her and leads her back to the house. Ungratefully, Jane wants to hide her condition from the prostitute and leaves her outside the front door. She has reached rock bottom, brought low in a condition where she is unable to see anything clearly any more. London fog is a symbol of the moral decline and fall of Jane Graham (as she perceives it in her own mind). She has lost her way in life, just as she loses it in the fog. Moral blackness has swallowed her up, just as it swallowed up the prostitute. The use of fog as a metaphorical way of representing Jane's moral uncertainties and mistakes may well have occurred to the author when, in her capacity as a journalist for London Television, she had interviewed Sir Ernest Smith, President of the National Smoke Abatement Society, during the society's annual conference, held in Bournemouth in 1955, questioning him about the society's campaigns that had emerged out of the great fog of 1952.[70] Perhaps this, more than anything, brought her attention to the idea of making smoky London part of her novel's structure.

If *The L-Shaped Room* addressed with unprecedented openness and honesty the problems of sexual morality concealed in most previous literature by euphemisms and circumlocutions, a novel by the Afro-Caribbean writer Samuel Selvon (1923–1994), published in 1956 but set, like Banks's story, in the great fog of 1952, addressed another emerging social concern: the place of immigrants who had come over from the West Indies in growing numbers after the war to seek employment in London. On their arrival they found widespread racism and rejection. They became, in the words of the novel's title, "the lonely Londoners." Selvon himself, born in Trinidad, came to London in 1950 and soon earned with his stories, written in a West Indian vernacular, the title of the "father of black writing" in Britain.

The novel's opening lines conjure up a picture, familiar from a wide variety of previous representations of London fog, of a "grim winter evening, when it had a kind of unrealness about London, with a fog sleeping restlessly over the city and the light showing in the blur as if it is not London at all but some strange place on another planet."[71] And indeed the West Indian immigrants are living in a strange place, symbolized by the alienating fog. The main character in the novel, Moses, has been in London for a decade and, as his name implies, acts as a guide for new ar-

rivals. At the beginning of the novel Moses is on his way to meet yet another new immigrant, who has been told that Moses will meet him and
acquaint him with life in the great metropolis. Moses does not know
the person and is already in a bad mood at having to leave his warm
bed to go through the damp, cold, and unhealthy streets to the railway
station at Waterloo, where the trains come in from the transatlantic
harbour town of Southampton. The fog of the opening scene reflects
his grim mood, and it also has the practical effect of making the journey
much slower than it usually is: "He sigh; the damn bus crawling in the
fog, and the evening so melancholy that he wish he was back in bed."[72]

The fog is not the only factor in making Moses melancholy. Waterloo was the station of his own arrival and will possibly also be that of
his departure, should he ever be able to leave England. It is a reminder
of the homeland he has left behind, especially when the newly arrived
immigrants disembark: "Perhaps he was thinking is time to go back to
the tropics, that's why he feeling sort of lonely and miserable."[73] When
Henry Oliver, the man Moses has been asked to meet, leaves the train,
"Moses watch Henry coming up the platform, and he have a feeling
that this couldn't be the fellar that he come to meet, for the test have on
a old grey tropical suit and a pair of watchekong and no overcoat or muf-
fler or gloves or anything for the cold, so Moses sure is some test who
living in London a long, long time and accustom to the beast winter.
Even so, he really had to feel the fellar, for as the evening advancing it
getting colder and colder and Moses stamping he foot as he stand up
there."[74]

Henry is quickly nicknamed "Sir Galahad" by Moses. Galahad's
natural points of reference, such as the sun or the sky, common to all inhabitants of the planet, also appear strange, even manufactured: "On top
of that, is one of those winter mornings when a kind of fog hovering
around. The sun shining, but Galahad never see the sun look like how it
looking now. No heat from it, it just there in the sky like a force-ripe orange. When he look up, the colour of the sky so desolate it make him more
frighten."[75]

The image of the force-grown orange is a reminder of home. Galahad
too is like the artificially produced orange-sun: he has been taken out of
his own natural environment to develop in the artificial circumstances of

the city. The strangeness of his new surroundings is accentuated for the West Indians when they go home and light a fire: "Tanty put more coal on the fire. 'Your only causing smog,' Tolroy say. 'Smog? What is that?' 'You don't read the papers?' Tolroy say. 'All that nasty fog it have outside today, and you pushing more smoke up the chimney. You killing people.' 'So how else to keep warm?' Tanty say."[76] Standard English is employed only when Selvon is describing London through accepted clichés of place, such as fog. "In the grimness of the winter, with your hand plying space like a blind man's stick in the yellow fog, with ice on the ground and a coldness defying all effort to keep warm, the boys coming and going, working, eating, sleeping, going about the vast metropolis like veteran Londoners."[77] The standard English employed reveals that the "boys" are becoming assimilated even through the language which had shown them to be different. As with Tanty piling her fire up with coal to keep out the cold, the only recourse is to follow the language and habits of the native Londoners. And it is not the Londoners of the working classes, those people amongst whom the immigrants tend to live, but the language of the educated middle classes.

As a new writer creating a new type of literature, Selvon uses the established image of fog to convey London's dirty reality but also to convey the confusion felt by those who had entered the country expecting to be welcomed as British citizens and finding that they have been demonized. As well as providing an established literary image through which London is known, fog is also used as a metaphor for contamination and racism. Moses blows his nose: "The handkerchief turn black and Moses watch it and curse the fog. He wasn't in a good mood and the fog wasn't doing anything to help the situation."[78] Just as the fog causes Moses to turn the handkerchief black, so he realises that the white majority population fears that the immigrants will somehow contaminate them too.[79]

Selvon's use of fog as a metaphor is unusually complex and subtle. Its possibilities were not lost on the writers of genre fiction either. Perhaps inevitably, it features in detective fiction set in that time, notably in Christianna Brand's (1907–1988) *London Particular*. This novel was published in 1952 but in March of that year, so it could not have been informed by the great fog of December. It illustrates how past fogs, even of a lesser magnitude, could provide a creative stimulus especially in detective fiction. This story involves a recurring character in Brand's work, Inspector Cockrill, perhaps best known now as the Inspector played by Alistair Sim in the 1946 film *Green for Danger,* based on Brand's novel of 1944. Brand (1907–1988) was born in Malaya and brought up in India but came to England for a convent education. After her father lost all his money when she was seventeen years old, she was forced to earn her living in various jobs such as model, dancer, nursery governess, and shop assistant. It was in the latter job that she first started to write crime fiction, turning her private fantasy of killing a co-worker into the basis of her first book. She wrote many crime novels, including seven in which Inspector Cockrill appears. She also wrote children's fiction, and her series of stories *Nurse Matilda* became the basis of Emma Thompson's film *Nanny McPhee* (2005).

Brand's crime novel *London Particular* was retitled *Fog of Doubt* for the U.S. market, indicating that the publisher doubted that her American readership would know what a London particular was and wanted to point more forcibly to the thematic use of the London fog as background to the crime. In the introduction to the reissue of the novel in 1988, P. D. James writes that "Brand has written that this is her favourite among her novels."[80] From this later perspective, James feels the need to describe a London particular: "And if any younger readers wonder whether the *London Particular* was as impenetrable as here depicted I can assure them from personal experience that it was. To be out in a London pea-souper was to stifle in an evil-smelling, disorientating blanket in which time, direction and distance no longer had meaning."[81] The novel opens immediately describing the fog: "The dank grey fog was like an army blanket, held pressed against the windows of the car."[82] The image of the blanket is a conventional one, but the fact that it is an army blanket suggests the proximity of the Second World War. A driver and his passenger are lost in the fog and watch as others try to find their way: "A bus crept by, a ghost bus, a-glimmer with eerie lights, with more lights making pin-points in the leaden dark where a line of lesser vehicles crawled in its broad wake."[83] For many drivers lost in the fog following a bus was their only hope of finding where they were. Brand seems to be enjoying flexing her creative muscles in describing the fog as she continues with "the little car

Figure 8.4 An advertisement for a new play, *Wanted for Murder*, on a foggy street, January 1, 1936. It could be extremely dangerous to walk through London on a foggy night. Lacey/Getty Images.

stealing through the muffled murmur of the fog-blanketed city like a marauding cat—creeping along on its belly, grey body melting into the grey, only its two bright eyes round and agleam in the night."[84]

The fog provides the background to the murder of Raoul Vernet, who has come from Geneva to see his friend Matilda, sister-in-law to Rosie, who is young, flirtatious, single, and pregnant. Raoul may be the father of the unborn child. Rosie is adored by her brother, Thomas, Matilda's husband, and by Tedward, a middle-aged friend of the family. The detective, Cockrill, is called in as a friend of the family, his intrusion welcomed by the Inspector already on the job. The killer is, in fact, Tedward, who is in love with Rosie and knows she is pregnant, as she has asked him as a doctor and a friend to help her get rid of the child. He has been led to believe that Raoul was the father and has killed him out of his love for Rosie. His alibi has been established in the opening pages of the book when he is driving through the fog with Rosie. He stops the car and gets out with the excuse of trying to find out where they are, returning

"These white lines are an absolute godsend in the fog."

Figure 8.5 This sketch by David Langdon actually appeared before the great smog of 1952 but forecast the disruption to traffic during that time. White lines were introduced in 1940. In a later issue *Punch* commented, "Londoners are saying that during the great fog their tubes were even more congested than usual at this time of the year." (*Punch,* 26 November 1952, p. 643; *Punch,* 17 December 1952, p. 725). Reproduced by kind permission of *Punch* © Punch Limited.

later than expected, blaming the fog for his delay. In fact he has just walked to the house where Raoul was staying and murdered him. Interestingly Tedward calls himself "The Avenger"—the name of the serial murderer in Marie Belloc Lowndes's *The Lodger,* referred to in Chapter 4—a man who kills women who he considers are too free with their sexual favours, an accusation justly levelled at Rosie, especially as there is a great deal of uncertainty over who the father of her child is. She is unworthy of this act of vengeance, and indeed she commits suicide before the end of the book. Here is fog as a plot device but also a symbol of obscured morality, of a world of murder, sexual promiscuity, abortion, and suicide.

Gideon's Fog, another detective novel, appeared some years later. It was one in a series of novels featuring Inspector Gideon, written by "J. J. Marric," a pen name adopted by the prolific and best-selling thriller writer John Creasey (1908–1973). The book was published in 1974 but is set in the

1950s, perhaps towards the end of the decade (though the exact date remains unspecified). It opens in the middle of a great fog as Gideon stops his car because he sees a boy carrying a candle "inside a jam jar suspended by a piece of string tied about the rim."[85] This reminds him of his own childhood, around four decades before, when "a dozen other lads of his age would do the same thing, enjoying the adventure, the sense of superiority over an adult, the sense of earning money. The fogs really had been fogs in those days!"[86] Ordinary electric torches are available, we are told, and other people use them to get about; but the use of the old-fashioned candle in a jar harks back to an earlier era. The candle-holders were the modern equivalent of the Victorian linklighters in more ways than one. Just as the linklighters were often associated with criminal elements, so too the boys holding candles in Gideon's Fog are being used by three older men to draw innocent people, stumbling about, bewildered, and lost in the fog, into a deserted side street so that they can be robbed. The author, in spite of beginning with crimes that could only have occurred in a fog, reports: "In a bad fog the real professionals stayed at home. A few small-time criminals burgled houses near their own homes."[87] In fact, according to this work of fiction, the fog is almost a hindrance to the professional criminal, as those planning "to leave the country by air, with stolen jewels or currency in their baggage, had to sweat it out at the airports."[88] Yet the story centres on a serial killer who waits for the cover of fog in order to murder his female victims. The fog that opens the story also sets off the various narrative links in the story, including the kidnapping of the Deputy Commander of Police. However, after the opening, the fog does not figure again except as a metaphor of Gideon's frustration in not solving the case of his commander's disappearance: "I feel as if I'm in a fog, and can't see a damned thing clearly."[89]

Filmmakers of the 1950s used fog similarly as a cloak for crime. A notable example is Val Guest's The Runaway Bus (1954), which marked the screen debut for Frankie Howerd (1917–1992), who was until then famous in Britain as a comic on stage and radio. Guest had suggested that Howerd might appear in a film. He agreed, as long as it was a comedy thriller, so that if the comedy did not work, then the thriller aspect might; that his name did not appear first above the titles; and that his favourite comedy actress, Margaret Rutherford, was asked to appear in it. As the film begins, fog descends, and aeroplanes are unable to leave from London Airport. The outspoken Cynthia Beeston (Rutherford), a forceful proponent of "Positive Thought," insists on being taken to Blackbushe Airport, where she might be able to fly to Dublin. The reserve driver Percy Lamb (Howerd) is told to take her and a number of other passengers to the other airport. Howerd's character does not inspire confidence, as he cannot even find his way to the bus through the fog for the first fifteen minutes of the film. The plot is further complicated by the fact that robbers have stowed gold bullion in the back of the coach in order to get it out of the airport under the police force's nose. The criminal's leader is none other than Cynthia Beeston, which explains why she is so insistent on leaving the airport. Lamb is unable to find his way to the other airport, and one of the passengers eventually has to get out to lead the coach so that it does not end up in the ditch. The film was made at Southall Studios in London on so low a budget that it could not afford scenery; instead, a fog generator was used so that little was visible behind the action. According to Howerd, "even the fields were studio backcloths, their patent phoniness wreathed in fog."[90] Fog may have had this practical and financial use for the movie-makers, and it certainly sped up production to help get Howerd onto the screen while his popularity was riding high; but it was no doubt London's experience in 1952 that brought it so readily to Guest's mind. The artificial fog machine had an unfortunate side effect as it made cast and crew ill. The technicians tried different chemical mixtures, but the impact was the same. "They were advised to drink milk before the day's shooting to reduce the feeling of sickness, but this made them even worse."[91] In the end the crew were allowed to wear masks but, of course, this was denied to the actors.

A Doris Day film, *Midnight Lace,* that came out in 1960, centres on a newly wed American's claims to be a victim of a stalker. The opening shot of the film begins in "a real London fog," as a man from the American embassy calls it, but also with the reassuring figure of a London police constable. The feistiness of Day's character is shown by her rejection of the offer of a taxicab being called for her. She is confident enough to walk from the American embassy through Grosvenor Square to her own home. The thickness of the fog is emphasised by a mother telling her young son to hold tightly onto her, as he has already been lost in the fog, and by the

Figure 8.6 Engineers produce artificial fog at Elstree Studios—a necessary function for films requiring foggy scenes. © Daily Herald Archive / Science & Society Picture Library.

appearance of a blind man, heralded by the sound of a stick tapping on the ground, the only one able to see in a blind world. It is at this point that Day's character hears a voice threatening her, so close that he can touch her coat, but she of course cannot see him. The threat is made more frightening in the fog and highlights her isolation. Her husband, played by Rex Harrison, dismisses the incident as the kind of practical joke often played in a "pea-souper." Whenever there is a thick fog in London, a real pea-souper, he tells her, the practical jokers crawl out of the woodwork; he even suggests that some wag might have placed a bedpan on the top of Nelson's Column during the fog. He describes how he lost his hat in the fog: someone took it from his head as he put his head out of a taxi to see where they were, and it was stolen in conditions "as black as ink." Other threats follow, now mainly on the phone, but Day's character only hears them when no one else is around. Her sanity comes into question through repeated threats to her life that she cannot prove.

Finally it is discovered that it is her husband who is the instigator of these threats and planning to kill her because he is after her fortune. The film (screenplay by Ivan Goff and Ben Roberts) is based on the play *Matilda Shouted Fire,* by Janet Green (1908–1983), a writer who is mainly known for the controversial Dirk Bogarde film *Victim* (1961), which tackled the issue of homosexuality when it was still illegal, and the earlier, equally controversial, but lesser-known work *Sapphire* (1959), which dealt with racism against Afro-Caribbean immigrants to Great Britain in the late 1950s. Fog was used here again to portray a woman under threat.

Gideon's Fog, The Runaway Bus, and *Midnight Lace* are works of pulp fiction that use London fog in a familiar manner as a plot device, as a cloak under which villains could go about their nefarious business. There is not much complexity or subtlety in its deployment or representation; it is just fog. For Lynne Reid Banks and Samuel Selvon, by contrast, fog offered thematic possibilities, denoting the individual subject's state of mind, moral position, emotions, and feelings. This was the last time, however, that London fog was to be used by serious writers addressing contemporary problems—even such an obvious and basic one as crime. For the events of 1952 galvanized public opinion to such a degree that serious efforts were now resumed to bring an end to the traditional London particular—and this time, unlike in the 1920s, 1930s, and 1940s, with a real chance of success.

IV

Questions began to be raised in Parliament before the last wisps of the 1952 great smog had blown away. Tom Driberg MP asked for "an inter-Departmental committee to inquire into the causes and cure of London fog."[92] He was informed that a committee already existed for this purpose under the Fuel Research Board. The following month the Conservative Minister of Health, Iain Macleod, had to admit that the Ministry of Health was not represented on this committee, defending this omission by suggesting that the committee's remit was restricted to causes, whereas his department's concern was more with effects.[93] Sir Edward Keeling stated in the same debate that in Westminster alone deaths from heart diseases had nearly doubled during the fog, and those from lung diseases had been almost five times greater.[94] A call to grant an official subsidy to the Smoke Abatement Society was rejected.[95] However, the "Great Killer Fog" of 1952 caused a major outcry in Fleet Street, the London headquarters of Britain's national press.[96] The *Daily Mirror,* on September 28, 1953, demanded smoke abatement legislation before the next fog season. The *Daily Express* printed an article on the subject with the headline "Murder."[97] *Picture Post* ran two double-page spreads over two issues on the "smog" issue.[98] The executive committee of the National Smoke Abatement Society renewed its campaign for an investigation "in view of the abnormal concentration of pollution in the atmosphere during the fog period and its exceptionally serious consequences."[99]

During January 1953 the matter was raised again in Parliament, this time directed towards Harold Macmillan, the Conservative Minister of Housing. He was asked by Norman Dodds (1903–1965; MP for Dartford) whether an interdepartmental committee had inquired into the causes and effects of fog.[100] On further questions being raised, Macmillan rejected the need for further general legislation as demanded by MPs such as Barnett Janner (1892–1982; Labour MP for Leicester and previously for Whitechapel, in London's East End). Lieutenant-Colonel Marcus Lipton (1900–1978; Conservative MP for Lambeth and Brixton, two of the areas worst affected by fog) was clearly exasperated and asked what was being done "as a result of 6,000 deaths that took place in the Greater London area in December as a result of the fog." He was dismayed by Macmillan's "complacency in dealing with this problem."[101] Dodds also noted "the amazing display of apathy."[102] *Smokeless Air* highlighted one of the major problems for those who supported clean air: "One of the most sinister features of smoke-fog is this very way in which it induces an attitude of apathetic acceptance. If, as with other plagues, it was followed by its own distinctive disease, it would be very different, but when John Smith dies of bronchitis three days after the fog, . . . well, he *might* have died soon of bronchitis anyhow."[103] The parliamentarians, the press, and the pressure groups were clearly not going to let go of the issue. The impact of the 1952 fog had simply been too great.

"For some reason or another," complained Macmillan in a confidential memo, "'smog' has captured the imagination of the press and the people. All yesterday my Public Relations Officer was rung up with this question, 'What is the Government going to do about the "smog"?' "[104] The creation of the welfare state by the Labour government immediately after the war had, he complained, created the expectation that any and all problems affecting the population should be solved by the government of the day.[105] Pending anything more dramatic, the National Health Service, itself the creation of the postwar Labour government, announced that doctors would be allowed to prescribe masks for those people "who suffer from disease of the heart or lungs and who live or work in an area where smoke-polluted fog is likely to occur."[106] These masks were offered in two forms—one a semi-rigid frame capable of being moulded to the face, and the other a more flimsy version to be fastened by tapes, similar to those worn by surgeons. The semi-rigid type was more expensive, at 3s 6d (about £4.40 in today's money), whilst the simpler version would cost the service 1s 11d (about £2.40). Both would incorporate removable pads of thin gauze and cotton tissue to filter out grits and soot. All would be provided free of charge as long as a doctor had prescribed them. The flimsier type of mask was pictured being fitted in a chemist's shop in Charing Cross on the same day as the recommendation came into force—November 17, 1953. Chris Prior, a London schoolboy, recalled walking to school in Harringay: "My mum made me a smog mask, which was layers of muslin and cotton wool, and you tied it over your ears and you'd walk to school. As soon as you got to school they took you inside and closed the doors quickly, and when you took the mask off it was all brown inside, like marmite. You'd have a fresh one to come home with."[107] Other do-it-yourself masks were shown in the *Illustrated London News*.[108] One American tobacco firm, seeing an ideal opportunity for advertising, had offered to provide masks free of charge but with its brand stamped on them.[109] The irony of providing masks to protect people from the effects of the polluted atmosphere while encouraging them to damage their lungs through inhaling tobacco smoke is probably much more appreciated now than it was then. Nevertheless, the company's offer was rejected. *Punch* saw the funny side of the offer of masks as well as their inadequacy in dealing properly with the problem: "Smoke and fog / Mean smog. / Ask / For a smask. / (We're in a huddle / About the smuddle.)."[110] The impoverished aristocratic milliner Denisa, Lady Newborough (1913–1987), saw a way of making some money by offering a more fashionable alternative to the National Health fog mask. In Hugh Massingberd's celebration of eccentric lives she is described as "many things: wire-walker, nightclub girl, nude dancer, air pilot. She only refused to be two things—a whore and a spy."[111] She also designed extravagant hats, her most famous being ironically one called "The Nicotine Hat," a design based around cigarettes. Her smog mask was incorporated into the design of a hat and attached to the back of it when not required. It could then be deployed at a moment's notice should a fog suddenly materialise. It would, needless to say, have been useless in combatting the effects of the polluted air on the larynx and lungs. Another designer, Gina Davis, produced a more down-market version in 1959, a simple crocheted hat with an anti-smog mask attached. A British Pathé newsreel, *Masks Beat Smog* (1959), shown in cinemas at the time, also reported on a new smog mask from Paris. Looking much like a spaceman's helmet, it had an extra accessory that could supply filtered air through a pack carried on one's back, but it was severely impractical; drink could only be consumed through a straw, and eating was impossible.

To Macmillan the masks provided by the National Health Service were simply a means of meeting people's evident need to see something being done: "There are some short-term things which we have done, and can do. We can gain popularity by doing them well—the masks, the warning signals, etc," he wrote cynically.[112] The Minister of Health, Iain Macleod, acknowledged the need for these masks during a really thick, yellow killer fog, but stressed reassuringly: "It is, however, important not to confuse it with the more normal fogs with which we have long been familiar, or to exaggerate its effect on normal healthy people."[113] But playing down the danger was not enough, so thoroughly roused was public opinion, and few were going to be satisfied with a merely palliative measure such as the prescription of masks. The problem, it was now very widely felt, had to be tackled at its root.

Norman Dodds MP had promised in his previous debate to raise the matter again and did so three months later when he demanded to know why there had not been a government inquiry into the death toll resulting from the great fog of 1952.[114] In addition to the deaths he also highlighted the number of people who were made ill by the fog, noting that an extra 25,000 people had claimed sickness benefit after the fog. He quoted the estimated cost of the fog to London alone as "about £10 million in expenses, depreciation and loss of time. That was in just four days."[115] Again the government was accused of apathy. Macleod was reported as saying at a dinner that "he seemed to get nothing but questions about the fog and its effects on people's health. 'Really, you know,' he said, 'anyone would think fog had only started in London since I became Minister.' "[116] Dodds also related that many people were worried that the London fog might have been saturated by atomic-pile pollution from Harwell, a nuclear plant only fifty miles from London. He compared the government's attitude to the higher number of deaths in London to the reaction of the U.S. government, which had immediately set up an exhaustive investigation into the great smog disaster in Donora, Pennsylvania, in 1948, even though it had only caused twenty deaths.

Ernest Marples (1907–1978; Conservative MP for Wallasey), Parliamentary Secretary to the Ministry of Housing and Local Government, complained at the lack of time left to him to answer the questions that Dodds had raised effectively. He did not dispute the number of deaths quoted but added, "Whether his diagnosis as to why they died is correct is another matter. I do not know, but I should have thought not."[117] Marples, backed into a corner, suggested what many other government officials had suggested in the past, the setting up of a committee: "Progress is no simple matter, and it is futile to think that air pollution can be abolished overnight, but the Hon. Gentleman has not given me time in which to reply as fully as I would like. He asked me what are we going to do about it, and I would reply that the Government have decided to appoint a committee under an independent chairman, to undertake a comprehensive review of the causes and effects of air pollution, and to consider what further preventive measures are practicable. My right hon. Friend hopes to make a further announcement shortly on the membership and terms of reference of this committee."[118] This statement reflected among other things the view of Harold Macmillan, who had been casting about for a decision that might have the appearance of action without actually requiring anything dramatic: "Ridiculous as it appears at first sight, I would suggest that we form a Committee. Committees are the oriflamme of democracy."[119] The committee duly came into being. It was instructed "to examine the nature, causes and effects of air pollution, and the efficacy of present preventive measures; to consider what further preventive measures are practicable; and to make recommendations."[120] The Chairman was Sir Hugh Beaver, a scientist and managing director of A. Guinness, Son & Co. Ltd. He had considerable experience in working on committees. The Deputy Chairman was Sir Roger Duncalfe, who was connected with the glue and chemicals industry.[121] Not surprisingly, the setting up of yet another committee was greeted with scepticism. There was a feeling of having been here before, especially within the pages of *Smokeless Air*, when it quoted the words of the Newton report: "No Government has, for many years, taken any action with the exception of appointing committees, whose labours have had little or no result," even though three of the National Smoke Abatement Society's leading members were represented on the committee, and another member, Dr. Foxwell, a fuel technologist, had written many articles for *Smokeless Air*.[122]

Macmillan was keen to be seen to act before the committee's report was published: "We cannot do very much, but we can seem to be very busy—and that is half the battle nowadays."[123] The idea was to co-ordinate the efforts of different government departments to deal with the problem of air pollution in the capital: "The Government," it was minuted, "might gain credit by making it clear that the activities of the several Departments concerned were under strong central control and direction."[124] Thus another committee was set up to rival the Beaver Committee. David Maxwell Fyfe, the Home Secretary, was put in as Chairman, as according to Macmillan's own notes, "he commands universal confidence."[125] The report of the Beaver Committee was to be delayed until the Ministerial Committee had met and made its recommendations, thereby showing that government was taking a lead. Fyfe was inclined to support at least some action as he wrote in a private memorandum to the Cabinet: "We cannot rest for so long on the statement which it is proposed to make to-morrow on behalf of Her Majesty's Government and people will expect, with some justification, that the Government should announce some further activity (what one might call a middle-term policy) before a year is up."[126] The lack of genuine commitment to legislation was palpable.

Before the Beaver Committee made its report, the subject came up in the House of Lords, presented by Basil Mackenzie, Lord Amulree (1900–

1987), a physician at University College Hospital in Bloomsbury, who wished to draw attention to the danger caused by the fog to the health of the people of London and to ask whether much progress had been made in supplying an adequate amount of smokeless fuel for domestic use.[127] In a long and impassioned speech Lord Amulree covered the impact that the December 1952 fog had had on people's health, as well as its impact on animals at the Smithfield show and its effect on plants: "there were fine displays of winter-flowering plants in the gardens at Kew which were completely destroyed."[128] He recommended the use of smokeless fuel and the implementation of smokeless zones, mentioning that one was to be set up in the Borough of St. Pancras. He also mentioned a new factor in the debate, that of the introduction of power stations in the London area. There were nine at this time, and although they had customarily washed their fumes before the war, this practice was stopped during the war because it made the fumes luminous, contravening the blackout policy; the practice was not taken up again as reintroduction cost money. This highlighted a dilemma that smoke in fog could at least be seen and was rightly viewed as a major problem; but with new scientific advances the content of the air could now be analysed, and the less visible factor of sulphur was beginning to be seen as another major problem and equally dangerous to breathe. In this case the face masks offered would be useless as a protection. Earl Jowitt (1885–1957), Labour Lord Chancellor under Attlee, rose to ask, among other things, why it had taken the government so long to set up a committee of inquiry: "Why on earth, after the experience which they had had in the first week of December, did they wait until July to appoint a Committee, if they realised how grave this matter was?"[129]

As it turned out, and to the surprise of some people in government itself, the Beaver Committee was no mere window dressing. With its subcommittees it held a total of 133 meetings as well as visiting many interested organisations. It presented an interim report to Parliament on December 2, 1953. Its draft recommendations were forwarded both to Macmillan as Minister for Housing and, on the subject of smokeless coal, to Geoffrey Lloyd as Minister of Fuel and Power. In addition to Macmillan's cynicism and his disbelief in the efficacy of government action on the issue, the danger of piling extra costs on industry by enforcing smoke controls weighed heavily with him. "We do what we can," he wearily replied to one parliamentary critic, "but of course, the Hon. Gentleman must realise the enormous number of broad economic considerations which have to be taken into account and which it would be foolish altogether to disregard."[130] Clearly the government could not be relied on to take decisive action. It was more concerned with appearances than with realities and was obviously dragging its feet. Macmillan's statement on the report stressed that the government had already taken action in several areas; it had already increased the domestic allocation of smokeless fuel; statutory powers had also been given to several local councils to establish smokeless zones; and improved heating appliances had been put into new local-authority housing since 1948.[131] "It must be accepted that the complete cure of pollution, if indeed it ever be attainable, is bound to take many years. The Committee are now embarking on a detailed examination of the many practical difficulties involved in further measures."[132]

While the ministers and the committee were considering and amending the Beaver Committee's interim report, the government issued official advice to householders during persistent foggy weather in London, in the following terms:

1. Coal fires should not be banked up at night.
2. Those who can use smokeless fuels should confine themselves to those fuels during periods of fog.
3. Rubbish should not be burnt nor bonfires lit while the fog lasts.
4. Elderly people and those suffering from chronic heart or lung conditions might be helped by wearing a mask or scarf wrapped round the mouth and nose if they have to go out in the fog.
5. The general public should refrain from bringing motor vehicles into densely-populated areas.[133]

Almost a year later Arthur Blenkinsop was still asking for the final report of the Beaver Committee.[134] A week later Duncan Sandys (1908–1987), the Tory Minister of Housing and Local Government, was able to inform members of the House of Commons that he had received the final report of the Beaver Committee the previous week and had arranged to have it published.[135] It was finally presented to the world on November 25, 1954. Norman Dodds again raised the issue as to what the government proposed doing based on the report.[136] There seemed to be no urgency to implement its recommendations, even though later commentators described it as "not particularly innovative."[137] Earl Jowitt, in addition, in the House of Lords, supported any recommendations that might be pursued from the report: "If the Government could, as that Report states, introduce a scheme whereby, in the next eight or ten years, something like 80 per cent. of the smoke which befouls our atmosphere could be eliminated, then I believe that the health and happiness of the dwellers in our cities would be enormously increased."[138] A week later further pressure was put on the government to act, but Sandys's reply was still evasive: "it is just as well to study this important Report before rushing into legislation."[139]

V

Things did not look as if they were moving forward with any sense of urgency. Everyone, especially in government, was delaying and procrastinating. Legislation still seemed a long way off. Yet most major fogs brought forth a prominent campaigner to speak against the foul state of the air, whether the person in question wanted to exploit it for his own reputation as an issue of public concern, especially amongst Londoners, or whether he was acting out of a genuine desire to make a difference or both. In the 1950s such a champion emerged in the unlikely figure of Sir Gerald Nabarro (1913–1973), Conservative MP for Kidderminster. Known for his booming voice and large handlebar moustache, Nabarro cultivated an upper-class image but came in fact from a humble Jewish background. He was the son of a shopkeeper, had been educated at state schools, and had served in the ranks in the army before starting work in a factory and eventually founding his own business. His flamboyantly expressed opinions included the retention of capital punishment, opposition to the European Community (as it then was), and strongly racist views which were on one occasion censored by the BBC. Nevertheless, Nabarro became a vociferous advocate of air-purification legislation and also wrote many letters to the press. In response to a series of articles on smoke in *Picture Post,* he advanced "a 10-point Plan" in which number ten was, "Lay a White Paper before Parliament setting out causes, effects and cures for the present

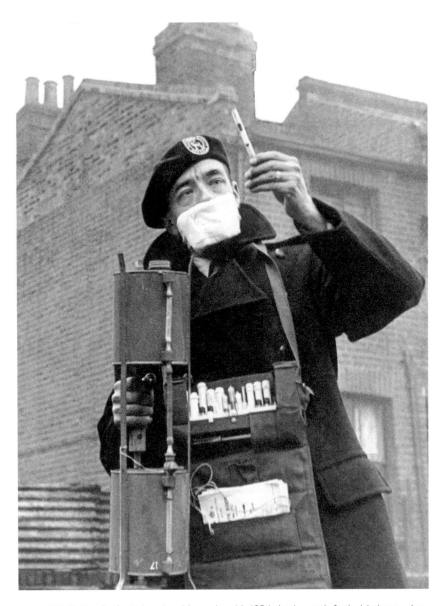

Figure 8.7 Testing for fog in London, November 16, 1954. As demands for legislation to clean London's air grew louder, it became important for scientists to gather concrete statistics on the amount of smoke particulants in the air. This collection of information enabled the Beaver Committee to look at the problem on a much more scientific basis. © Daily Herald Archive / Science & Society Picture Library.

killer smogs. Put a 'Smoke Act' on the Statute Book to give legislative effect to the foregoing proposals."[140] His other points included certified training for boilermen; requiring every city and town with more than 25,000 people to follow the "smokeless zone" regulations on the Manchester model; the encouragement of the gas industry to become a two-fuel industry (gas and coke); incentives to replace inefficient grates in households; a ten-year programme of railway electrification, and a national corps of smoke abatement officers armed with full powers. Many of these suggestions were far from new and would have been recognized by nineteenth-century campaigners. Still, they gained added urgency from the recent memory of 1952's "killer fog." And after the Labour government's huge expansion of the welfare state, the public's expectation of state action, as Macmillan had earlier suggested, had become far greater than it had been in Victorian times.

In November 1954 Nabarro won first place in the ballot for Private Members' Bills. He decided to pursue the evidence uncovered by the Beaver Report, which had appeared only days before. Nabarro secured the help and advice of the Smoke Abatement Society and tabled a Bill with the title "Clean Air." Sandys welcomed the measure, a "revolution at the fire-side."[141] He was indeed soon to go on to establish legislation for Green Belts around major towns and cities. However, because a Private Member's Bill could not include financial provisions, he asked Nabarro to withdraw the Bill against his assurance that a Government Clean Air Bill would be brought in that session. Nabarro obliged but did not let up in his campaigning. As *Smokeless Air* pointed out, "The Nabarroean strategy has proved to be most successful. It has provided invaluable publicity. . . . It has accelerated Government consideration and decision."[142] Nabarro even designed his own envelope franking, which read "GERALD NABARRO'S CLEAN AIR (ANTI-SMOG) BILL, 2nd Reading—Friday, 4th February, 1955."[143]

Nabarro's publicity must have been further helped by a frightening darkness caused by a smoke cloud that passed high over London on January 16, 1955, in the early afternoon. "Darkness was intense in places, coming rapidly but lasting only for a short time. . . . The total width was estimated to be at least 20 miles, and at its densest some two miles deep."[144] It provided some sensational headlines, with some people believing that

Figure 8.8 Smog wardens in London in 1955. There had been smoke inspectors since the nineteenth century, but they lacked the scientific evidence and the legislative backing to make a difference. By the middle of the twentieth century, this was no longer the case. © Daily Herald Archive / Science & Society Picture Library.

the end of the world had come. It was described as an "extraordinary and ominous demonstration of the effects of smog. A black cloud of smoke, sulphur and grit hung over the capital smothering in turn each area in a murky blanket of darkness." The journalist waxed lyrical in his description: "It was as if a giant vulture had suddenly obscured the sun, turning noon into midnight."[145] The pocket of sooty air was blown westwards towards the Chiltern Hills, where it piled up into an immense pillar before being blown back over London again. By this time "its smoke content was so high that it made breathing uncomfortable in the West End and City areas."[146] For a short while the city was covered in almost total darkness.[147]

In the event, Parliament was dissolved in the spring of 1955. Such was the progress made on the issue, such was the strength of public feeling, that both Tory and Labour election manifestoes included promises for Clean Air legislation. But since the Tories won the election, it fell to them to implement the promise made to Nabarro. Support for a Clean Air Bill was given impetus by another bad fog between January 3 and 6, 1956. It was concluded that an additional 1,000 deaths occurred in the Greater London area from severe respiratory problems this time.[148] Together with this renewed outbreak of atmospheric pollution, it was generally felt that the London fog of 1952 had "done for the cause of smoke abatement what months and even years of propaganda work could not do."[149] The passage of a new Parliamentary Act seemed inevitable.

On July 5, 1956, the Clean Air Act was finally passed into law. Its major innovation was its focus above all on domestic sources of smoke pollution; it provided a scientifically measureable definition of "dark" rather than the old "black" smoke test using the Ringelmann chart and it gave industry seven years to comply with the relevant provisions. Most importantly, it provided for the creation of smokeless zones in the city.[150] Just as the parks of London were frequently referred to as "the lungs of London," so the smokeless zone was referred to as a "window in the fog." Many smokeless zones had already come into being before the passing of the Act, which reflected the changing attitude of the public and local government determined to clean up the air. As the smokeless zones were based on an idea proposed by Charles Gandy, a Manchester lawyer and smoke-abatement pioneer, as early as 1935, it was appropriate that Manchester became the first city to establish smokeless zones of its own, in 1946. That same year a City of London (Various Powers) Act was passed giving the City (that is, the old core of London, now the financial district) the power to create a smokeless zone. Coventry followed in 1948. There were many problems in setting up a smokeless zone. Objections were often accepted from those who had vested interests, such as industrialists or landlords who did not want the expense of converting grates for smokeless fuels. Other people could not see the point in them—after all, the argument followed that smoke did not acknowledge borders between smokeless zones and areas surrounding them which were not. Tests carried out in Hyde Park, London, showed that on windy days pollution was only 27 percent of that in the surrounding area, but on calm days, with little wind to dissipate the nuisance, pollution in the park was 85 percent.

Thus if an area was ringed with smoke-producing areas, some improvement might be looked for only under windy conditions. Still, the time for smokeless zones seemed apposite since coalite (the most common kind of smokeless fuel, a kind of coke developed in 1904) was no longer rationed, as it had been during and immediately after the war. *Smokeless Air* instituted a special section called "Smokeless Zone News." Attitudes had changed, especially in regard to those vested interests who had stalled change in the past. In 1946, when the City legislated to establish a smokeless zone area, the Associated Owners of City Properties, fearing that this would entail much expense to their members, argued that the passing of the clause should be on condition that the prohibition "should apply only to new and modernized buildings and that it should only operate in regard to other existing buildings as and when they are modernized."[151] Nevertheless, their objections met with no success, and from October 2, 1955, the whole of the City of London became a smokeless zone.

The Lord Mayor of London, Sir Seymour Howard, felt that "it might be wondered why we have done this while similar action has not been taken in adjacent areas. But," he continued in a strong spirit of self-congratulation, "this city has ever been in the van of all wise and beneficent movements, and I hope our neighbours will soon follow our lead."[152] An advisory centre was opened between July 11 and 22 in Cannon Street to assuage the fears of property owners and others and to give support and advice where it was requested. Of course, the City was in many ways an ideal place to begin establishing smokeless zones in London because it was a business district with very limited quantities of private housing (only some 5,000 people lived there), and the many new buildings which were being constructed at the time to replace those damaged in the war could ensure that more up-to-date methods of heating were used. At the same time, the Borough of St. Pancras, just to the northwest of the City, set up a Consultative Committee on Air Pollution in which representatives from the railways, transport, industry, and domestic communities were represented. In spite of ensuring that the railways were on board, St. Pancras (London) Borough Council opened legal proceedings against British Transport (the umbrella body for the state-owned railways at the time) for using engines that were not constructed on the principle of consuming their own smoke. The case was dismissed, and the magistrate described "as 'Gilbertian' a situation in which, if he imposed fines on summonses brought for the public benefit against a nationalized undertaking, the public would have to pay the fine. 'The public are prosecuting the public,' he added. 'It is a ridiculous situation.'"[153] The following year the Borough of St. Pancras prosecuted other state-owned railways for smoke nuisance—one in Chalk Farm and another in King's Cross. The pressure began to have some effect.

Ordinary people also made their feelings known when the Chalk Farm Tenants' and Residents' Association held an "Anti-Smog Week" from July 22 to 28, 1956. This culminated in a public meeting in which the residents demanded that the British Transport Commission take immediate steps to reduce substantially the smoke and grit nuisance caused by the firing of locomotives at Camden depot, by roofing-in the shed and erecting a high chimney with a smoke-washing plant or by removal of the depot to a nonresidential area.[154] The following year the Chalk Farm Tenants' and Residents' Association held a second Clean Air Week. In October of the same year the Borough of St. Marylebone formally opened its Clean Air Campaign. The Deputy Mayor and Councillor, Robert Sharp, announced St. Marylebone's intention to be the first London borough, after the City of London, to take up the cause of clean air. Lambeth seemed likely to be the first borough council in London to create a smoke-control area, around the Oval cricket ground. Holborn Council declared its intention that the whole of the borough should become a smoke-control area at some future date. The race between the boroughs was on.

Soon a White Paper produced by the Minister of Housing and Local Government (CMD 1113) published a summary of the clean-air programmes submitted to him by local authorities for the establishment of smoke-control areas. It showed that the County of London was far in advance of the rest of the country, with all but two of the twenty-eight metropolitan boroughs submitting their programmes. Out of the forty-five regions in the country which gave a date for completion in the 1960s, half were in the Greater London area. Most other areas gave dates for completion in the 1970s. St. Marylebone gave a projected completion date of 1962. Lambeth, despite having declared its intention of becoming a smokeless borough as early as the mid-1950s, gave a completion date of 1980. It was the Metropolitan Borough of Holborn which achieved the

Figure 8.9 November 12, 1954: a woman reads a London Borough of Holborn poster, warning of fog. Holborn was one of the first smokeless boroughs after the City of London introduced local regulations. The great smog of 1952 led many of the London boroughs to issue their own advice on trying to reduce the smoke by using smokeless fuels. Popperfoto/ Getty Images.

distinction of being the first completely smoke-free London authority after the City of London, on December 1, 1962. The City of London had been a special case, using its own Act, but Holborn was first under the provisions of the Clean Air Act of 1956. This was made more remarkable by the fact that the council had decided in 1956 that the whole borough should eventually be smoke-free only by 1968.[155]

The drive to purify the air was backed by an increasingly sophisticated and intensive propaganda campaign. Interested parties such as the Solid Smokeless Fuels Federation, representing the manufacturers of smokeless fuels, such as Coalite, Rexco, Gas Coke, Welsh Dry Steam Coal, and others, arranged an exhibition on "fuel efficiency and smoke abatement" in the entrance hall of the Charing Cross underground station from April 7 to 25, 1953, and demanded in a poster, "Why not a Smokeless Zone in Central London?" Other self-interested groups also actively supported smoke abatement. The British commercial gas industry had produced a film in 1937 called The Smoke Menace (1937). After the Gas Council was fully nationalised in 1948, it sponsored 200 films "for the purpose of making better known the services of the gas industry"; many of these concentrated on air pollution.[156] In 1954 Jack Howells (1913–1990), a well-known documentary maker and later winner of an Academy Award for his film Dylan Thomas (1963), about the Welsh poet, wrote Guilty Chimneys (1954). Made by the Pathé Documentary Unit and directed by Gerard Bryant, it was screened widely by the National Smoke Abatement Society, as well as being promoted within the society's journal.[157] The film may have been suggested by the earlier short film from the gas industry, The Smoke Menace (1937) referred to above. Both films played an important part in promoting national legislation, bringing much greater publicity to the topic of cleaner air and championing the creation of smokeless zones. Guilty Chimneys is centred on the 1952 London fog. An opening rural scene in sunshine is replaced quickly by a montage of terraced London houses with chimneys belching out smoke. An ambulance is seen trying to get through the fog to get its patient to the hospital. A voice-over informs us, "This is not a road-crash victim. Let's be kind and call it manslaughter, or if you like murder. The culprit is known—we created this and the victim will be dead within a week."[158] Examples of alternate smokeless sources of power featured were not restricted to gas but also included coke and nuclear power. This film was followed by *Window to the Sky* (1959) and *Clearing the Air* (1965), devised by Alex Strasser, which concentrated on the Clean Air Act's municipal implementation and the setting up of smoke-control areas. In 1961 the National Coal Board riposted by distributing *The Air We Breathe* (1961), but even here as the title suggests "air quality was the predominant issue."[159]

There is always a lighter side to any story, and London fog provided many comedians with material. Bob Hope (1903–2003) came over in the late 1950s to film *Iron Petticoat,* the first film he worked on outside America and in the country of his birth. While over in the United Kingdom he performed on stage and jested:

> I'm sorry I was late getting here, I was lost in the fog. . . . I wanted to whistle for a cab, but I couldn't find my mouth.
>
> I wondered if anybody would find me out there and rescue me. Suddenly I saw a light in the distance. Slowly it became clearer and clearer and finally I could make it out. . . . It was the end of my cigarette.[160]

It looked as if the war had been won against smoke both in practice and in sentiment; ordinary people and politicians were convinced that this was the right way to go. Public opinion had finally been converted to the belief that domestic coal fires were a major, perhaps even the paramount, cause of London's choking yellow fogs. The health hazards of pea-soupers were now almost universally recognized. Legislation had been brought in that promised an effective reduction in the emissions of sulphurous fumes in the capital. However, the story was not quite finished. London fog was soon to make one last attempt to reassert itself.

The Death of London Fog

In April 1956 the Russian Premier, Marshal Bulganin, on an official visit to London, praised the clear and sunny weather that greeted his arrival. "London fog," he reported, "seems to be a thing of the past."[1] Perhaps he was misled by the fact that his visit took place well after the normal end of the foggy season, for in fact the era of London fog was by no means over. The capital suffered a number of winter fogs in the years immediately following Bulganin's visit, though none of them was particularly serious. Then on December 4, 1962, London and its environs were enveloped in a fog of such density and persistence that people were inescapably reminded of the great fog of 1952, a decade before. Already on the first evening of the fog the *Evening Standard* reported delays to rail, car, and bus journeys, along with many accidents on the roads, including the collision of two London Transport buses in Manor Park, in which many of the passengers were injured.[2] Many ships were held up by the fog, and the London bus service cancelled all its services on December 7.[3]

Sporting events were also affected, some more than others. A boxing match between Vic Andretti and Belarmino Fragoso, champion of Portugal, held at Finsbury Park, had to be refereed by the Secretary of the Board of Control, as the official referee was unable to get there because of the fog (even more bizarrely, it was later discovered that the real Fragoso was still in Portugal, unable to fly to London because of the fog, and Andretti, who won, had beaten an impostor—Fragoso's step-brother, who stood in for him to avoid losing the fee). Fog even found its way into the squash courts for the women's championship at the Landsdowne Club, Mayfair.[4] It prevented the Tottenham Hotspur team from flying out from London Airport for a match against Glasgow Rangers in the second leg of a European Cup Winners' Cup match. The team had to take the train instead. In spite of the footballers' effort to get there, the match was postponed because there was fog in Glasgow too. Many other soccer matches were simply abandoned when it was no longer possible for players to see each other. A concert of Viennese waltzes was affected by the fog, "with traces of fog blurring visibility" in the Festival Hall on London's South Bank.[5] Christmas sales were seriously affected, and discounts were prolonged for an extra week "owing to last week's fog."[6]

On the North Circular road thousands of cars were unable to move on their way into London, and many drivers just abandoned them, making the situation worse. Even the Royal Automobile Club was unable to help, as most of its own vehicles were fogbound.[7] The Duchess of Kent had to abandon an attempt to get to Stansted to fly out of the country, her party reportedly only reaching the outskirts of North London.[8] Yet again the Smithfield Cattle Show was affected by the fog, though only to the extent that the judge of the live section was held up by the weather. This proved most embarrassing as the Prime Minister was visiting the show.[9] He did not make it to a dinner at the Other Club at the Savoy Hotel due to the fog, but Sir Winston Churchill was able to attend, even though he had only been released from hospital in August.[10] Children at a school in Bow, East London, were forced to spend the night camping in their classrooms because they too were unable to get home; a taxi driver who had come to collect one of the children was also forced to spend the night at the school because of the fog. A primary school in West Hendon sent home the children, aged between two and five, wrapped in blankets, on a school bus which took six hours to arrive at its destination in Willesden, only four miles away.[11]

The press reported a plethora of bizarre and tragic incidents. A fireman whose train had broken down during the fog fell to his death from a viaduct when he left his engine in order to lay detonators on the track behind him to warn other trains of the obstacle ahead.[12] Birds got lost in the fog, and it was reported that a Slavonian grebe was found in the middle of Regent Street, having been "unable to see the ground or the stars."[13] A monkey was also reported lost in the fog in Oxford Street.[14] An accident reminiscent of the nineteenth century occurred when a man walked into the Thames with his bicycle at Richmond (fortunately he was able to hang on to the embankment by a chain before being rescued).[15] Even the Christmas tree sent annually from Norway for Trafalgar Square was delayed by the fog.[16] And of course criminal activities also featured heavily in the reporting of the fog, including burglaries and car thefts.[17] In one

Figure C.1 This swan was killed by a car during a thick fog on January 24, 1934. Many birds became lost and exhausted from trying to locate a safe place to roost when visibility was reduced. They were often forced to land on roads. Topical Press Agency/Getty Images.

incident the police were called by a woman who saw a masked man trying to break into her house (it proved to be her husband, who had lost his keys and had used his scarf across his face to protect himself from the dirty atmosphere).[18]

It was not gloom for everyone, however. Hotels were quick to capitalise on the foggy conditions. Many were fully booked because of the Smithfield Cattle Show, but allowed people to sleep in corridors and on sofas overnight, as they were unable to get home.[19] Smog masks sold out, and one of the companies providing them contemplated setting up a temporary shop at Waterloo railway station to sell more, although the fog had passed before it could do so.[20] A scientist from Washington, DC, flew all the way over to London to experience the fog and almost missed it because his aeroplane was diverted to Frankfurt. When he did eventually arrive in London, just in time to experience the final hours of the fog and collect a few samples of the polluted air, he commented: "You people sure don't exaggerate. . . . I've never seen or tasted anything like it and I didn't enjoy it one little bit. It set off a beautiful cough."[21]

The same newspapers ironically reported the arrival in London of the film stars Richard Burton and Elizabeth Taylor, fresh from the set of *Cleopatra* (where they were rumoured, correctly as it turned out, to have started an affair), to begin filming *The VIPs,* about a group of passengers stranded at an airport by fog.[22] The film, written by Terence Rattigan, was actually conceived as he had waited at London Airport in October 1960 when a fog came down "like the curtain at the Queen's Theatre"—a reference to the fate of his most recent play.[23] He described the experience: "As flights began to be delayed, the calm of the room was slowly broken, executives and government officials began to fume. Alternative travel arrangements were discussed, then cancelled then reconsidered. The day wasted away in growing bad temper. The airport remained closed for forty-eight hours."[24] He also incorporated a story confided to him by his neighbours in London, Laurence Olivier and Vivien Leigh, when Leigh had run away from Olivier with the actor Peter Finch in December 1955. Fog had delayed their takeoff, and the waiting period was sufficient "to convince Vivien of what she stood to lose."[25] "'Vivien saw through the ruse,' Rattigan confided to a critic who had questioned the unreality of the film, 'but if Larry did, too, he didn't say anything.'"[26]

The Times reported on the third day of the 1962 fog that the total number of deaths from respiratory failure over the two days was now 55, compared with the usual rate of 6–8 deaths in a two-day period.[27] By the fourth day the death toll had risen to 90 in the Metropolitan Police Area.[28] It was only on the fifth day, December 8, that the weather changed and the fog cleared. Advice continued to be given to wash curtains and windows to remove the dangerous acid products accumulated in the foggy weather, but the most serious effects were on people's health—the final death toll was given as 750.[29]

The press had been accused in the past of failing to register the proper level of concern about London fog, but in reporting the outbreak of fog in 1962 "the position was reversed, and in some London papers," according to *Smokeless Air,* "the smog was given the full sensation treatment."[30] This led to reports in foreign journals that "a choking, chemical-laden smog settled over Greater London for four days this month and created a major medical crisis. . . . The number of persons collapsing and dying in the streets rose to three times the normal rate."[31] In contrast to the reporting

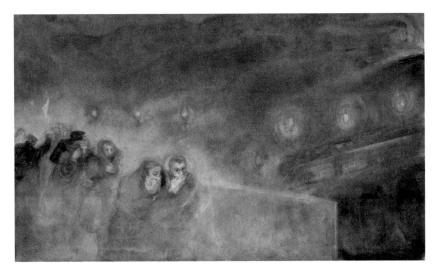

Figure C.2 *Killer Fog,* by Jacqueline Morreau (1929–), commissioned by the London School of Hygiene and Tropical Medicine for the fiftieth anniversary of the 1952 fog. Morreau was brought up in California but settled permanently in London in 1972, so she had both an American and a London perspective. Her painting emphasises the threat posed to health by fog, with people covering their mouths for protection. Reproduced by kind permission of the artist and her husband.

of previous fogs, the focus was not so much on the density of the fog as on the level of the sulphur content within it. The newspapers reminded their readers that both crude oil and coal contained sulphur, and the emissions from these sources led to the formation of sulphur dioxide and eventually sulphuric acid. A press report referred to "smoke and sulphur pollution in London . . . as fog lay over the city."[32]

One correspondent to *The Times* noted, "The severe pollution by smoke of London's atmosphere this week may be slightly less, but that by sulphur is probably more than when the great fog occurred 10 years ago almost to the day."[33] The correspondent was Dr. Rudolph Lessing (1878–1964), a well-known campaigner against smoke. He admitted that this was not a new issue, and indeed he even referred to an article in the same paper from March 21, 1929, and subsequent correspondence, pointing to the same pollutant. He conceded that "the (Beaver) Committee's recommendations were based on a realistic appreciation of what could be achieved in the then state of knowledge in respect of the emission of smoke into the atmosphere."[34] But it was clearly not enough. A consulting chemist and chemical engineer, Lessing was an authority on coal and its treatment and had been President of the National Society for Clean Air from 1956 to 1958. His letter heralded a new campaign. The Clean Air Act of 1956 had done its best and had at least removed the most visible specks of grit from the air, but more was required. The press and the people of London, with Parliament's help, were by this time more than willing to achieve this new goal.

The major enemy was now sulphur dioxide, not the smoke, grit, or dust tackled in the Clean Air Act. A doctor warned in the *British Journal of Diseases of the Chest* that the Central Electricity Generating Board was wrong to site new power stations within large cities because of the emission of sulphur dioxide: "The Battersea and Bankside power stations in London were equipped with plant to remove sulphur dioxide. For a variety of reasons this is not planned for future stations and all the sulphur dioxide produced will be discharged into the atmosphere."[35] The Electricity Board, in a response not dissimilar to William Frend's suggestion in the nineteenth century, was that its policy was to use a tall chimney that "disperses the gases in the atmosphere."[36] The National Society for Clean Air weighed in with a view that many of the press and radio comments on the 1962 fog had been "hysterical, hasty and ill-considered."[37] The *Evening Standard* headline announced, "It's a Killer: 32 Dead in Two Days" and as a subheading "Smog Is as Bad as in 1952, Red Warning to Hospitals."[38] The Society especially deplored a leader in *The Times* claiming that smokeless zones were "confidence tricks" because they did not reduce sulphur dioxide, now regarded as "the lethal agent."[39] It also criticised the BBC television news magazine *Tonight,* shown on December 8, 1962, in which the Clean Air Act had been called "something of a swindle" by an anonymous physician and "largely eyewash" by the show's presenter, the bearded Scottish reporter Fyfe Robertson.[40] *Clean Air* magazine, in contrast, still felt that the Act "was doing more to reduce low level sulphur emissions than any other measure in being or proposed."[41] Other parties with vested interests weighed in. The Central Electricity Generating Board quoted figures drawn up by the Medical Research Council that showed the increase of sulphur dioxide in this latest fog outbreak as 190 parts in 100 million, whereas in 1952 it was gauged as 134 parts in 100 million. But the mortality rate was distinctly lower in 1962: 400 deaths recorded as

Figure C.3 A policeman in a fog mask on January 1, 1962, during the last great London fog of the twentieth century. This mask may look more complex than the usual cloth ones, but it probably only filtered out the large particles and would not have protected from the hydrocarbons now becoming increasingly problematic in London's air from vehicle exhaust fumes. Keystone/Getty Images.

against the conservative 1952 figure of 4,000.[42] Thus, the Board concluded, sulphur dioxide was not as dangerous as other components of the fog.

Nevertheless, public alarm at the occurrence of a major fog six years after the Clean Air Act had been thought to have brought an end to the problem prompted pressure for the tightening and extension of its provisions. In 1965 the trade unionist and Labour MP Bob Edwards (1905–1990) attempted to introduce a Clean Air (Further Provisions) Bill which had been prepared in light of the experience of the 1956 Clean Air Act. But as with many other similar measures in the past, it could not be passed owing to lack of parliamentary time. There the matter rested. By the mid-1960s, in any case, it was clear that the 1956 Clean Air Act was finally having an impact. The year 1962 proved to be the last serious London fog. London smoke-control orders were quickly extended, and by 1968 they covered 65 percent of premises in the city. London fogs were finally a thing of the past. Born in the early Victorian era, the pea-souper died 120 years later, in the 1960s.

Of course foggy days continued to occur, but for the most part these were white fogs and not the traditional, familiar, dirty yellow-brown ones. There was a coda to the story when, in 1968, the last in the long line of unlikely advocates of cleaner air, the flamboyant publishing magnate Robert Maxwell (1923–1991; MP for Buckingham), introduced a similar Bill to that proposed three years previously by his Labour colleague Bob Edwards. Maxwell justified his Bill with reference to the growing population of London and in the light of recent scientific announcements that "oxygen would quickly disappear from the atmosphere if all the green plants should be killed." He gave a history of air pollution in the nineteenth century and advertised his literary credentials by mentioning *Bleak House* and *The Forsyte Saga*.[43] The Bill's provisions tightened the law on grit emissions and heights of chimneys and gave the Minister power to direct local authorities to submit programmes of smoke control and require them to carry them out. This final aim proved the most contentious. However, the Bill passed into law in 1968.

This was not quite the end of the story. Two years later, in 1970, David Watkins (1925–2013), a trade unionist and Labour politician who represented the steelmaking constituency of Consett, raised the issue again. Watkins was not a very prominent parliamentarian (his memoirs were titled *Seventeen Years in Obscurity*), but he was one of the first politicians to take cognisance of the new threat to London's air quality posed by the ever-increasing number of motor vehicles on the capital's roads.[44] In February 1970 he raised the issue in a debate in the House of Commons: "While recognising that enormous improvements have been made in London, I think that hon. Members on both sides of the House who spoke about these were being a little over-optimistic in saying that the sun now shines as brightly in London as in the country areas. The fact is that, notwithstanding the smokeless zones—and, certainly, the terrible smogs of bygone days will never occur again in London—there is still a considerable amount of pollution in London, and this is the measure of the further progress which now needs to be made."[45] Little was done immediately, however, to limit the rising levels of hydrocarbon pollution from motor-vehicle exhausts. In December 1991, indeed, 160 Londoners were said to have died because of a week-long period of high air pollution.[46] Another shorter period of high pollution levels occurred in early August 2003, when people with respiratory illnesses were warned to increase the dosage of their medication and avoid exercising outside.

Unlike the fogs of the past, which occurred in wintertime, the new London smog was caused by hot weather and still conditions, in which "the ozone, a volatile gas formed by sunlight acting on pollutants" such as car exhausts and industrial pollutants, failed to disperse. This was "very different from the old pea-soupers—acrid, clingy smogs caused by factories and fossil fuels."[47] The introduction of a low-emission zone in London, where vehicle exhaust emissions were subject to a charge, and the increasing use of catalytic converters and similar devices to control and reduce exhaust fumes have had some effect, but the dangers to health from hydrocarbon smogs continue. This is, however, no longer a "London particular" but a phenomenon of far wider dimensions.

Air pollution continues to be a worldwide problem, especially in countries that are experiencing their own industrial revolution. In 2013 China experienced the worst air pollution for decades, and cities had to take emergency measures to combat the smog by grounding flights and shutting schools. According to the *Guardian:* "Beijing spent more than half of the year shrouded in a pea-soup haze." The authorities in China's capital city promised to allocate £75.8 billion towards reducing the air pollution and to tighten restrictions on coal burning and vehicle emissions.[48] A documentary about air pollution in China "notched up some 100m views on major Chinese video portals" within four days of the programme being aired in China.[49] But Londoners cannot be complacent. A recent report by scientists at King's College London on emissions research "found nitrogen dioxide concentrations on Oxford Street to be worse than they are anywhere else on Earth."[50] According to the head of the research group, David Carslaw: "That's higher than Beijing and Dhaka, higher than anywhere where face masks are the norm, . . . and more than 11 times the norm."[51] Air pollution nowadays comes mainly from diesel engines and is "produced by sunlight reacting with nitrogen oxides and volatile organic compounds and the result is ground-level ozone or smog."[52] According to recent statistics 29,000 people die prematurely each year in Britain from man-made pollution, mostly from motor vehicles. Following the same economic line of arguments employed in the nineteenth century, it is noted that air pollution costs Britain £6–18 billion a year with much of

Figure C.4 Canned London fog, shown in an American newspaper as "a souvenir of this tight little island." The article goes on: "There is also a testimonial from a charming gentleman called Sir Foggy-Fogget, who declares: 'For that delightful feeling after a hot, sunny day, I always use Fresh London Fog'" (*Eagle*, 15 April 1961, p. 9). Photo: Etsy sale listing by Quinn, TheeLetterQ shop.

the cost coming from treating respiratory diseases and heart attacks.[53] ClientEarth, a campaign group made up of scientists, lawyers, and policy experts, has recently won a five-year battle in the UK Supreme Court to force the UK government to take action. The judges ruled in no uncertain terms that "the new Government, whatever its political complexion, should be left in no doubt as to the need for immediate action to address this issue."[54] Yet because hydrocarbon pollution makes itself visible more as a haze than as a dramatically coloured, impenetrable blanket of yellow-brown fog, and because it is now a universal urban phenomenon rather than a characteristic of one particular city above all, it has failed to capture the imagination of writers and artists in the same way as the traditional pea-souper.

London fog is dead. For some time, however, the rest of the world refused to recognise its demise. So inextricably had thick yellow fog become linked with the identity of the city that for years after it had vanished, visitors came to London expecting to find "foggy London town," as George Gershwin's ever-popular song of that title described it. But they could only come across it in souvenir shops that sold tin cans labelled "Genuine London Fog." Yet the belief was hard to eradicate. In 1972 the writer of "*The Times* Diary" reported: "London does not have fogs any more. I know because I have been in numerous audiences in America when British ministers, officials and other propagandists have delivered the breathtaking news to amazed locals."[55] The same year Foreign Secretary Sir Alec Douglas-Home had to go to some lengths to persuade the Chinese Foreign Minister, Chi Peng-fei, that the British capital was no longer permanently wreathed in yellow fog.[56] In 1973 the Chairman of the London Tourist Board, Sir Anthony Milward, announced a major attempt to persuade people to holiday in London during the winter months. However, he had to admit: "People in Europe really do think that there is still such a thing as London fog which descends over us as soon as winter comes."[57] In 1982 a rather sniffy review of a book titled *Onyx* by Tony Chiu (a thriller set in 1970s London), commented on the author: "As an American who presumably wants his books to sell in England, he had better learn that we no longer have pea-souper fogs in London."[58] Americans' association of London with fog has been hard to shake, however, not least because of an enduring brand name. In 1954 the Londontown clothing company, an entirely American firm, introduced its famous London Fog raincoats, which went on to dominate the U.S. market for raincoats and eventually lent their name to the whole company, known since 1994 as London Fog Industries. The *New York Times* referred to the name when the coats first appeared in 1954, presumably thinking of claims that the coat combined style with an ability to withstand the worst climactic conditions: "Every once in a while a name comes along for a product that is exactly right. It describes the product exactly and does a selling job that even the legendary 10,000 words cannot do. Such a one is London Fog."[59]

A recent "counterfactual" novel by C. J. Sansom, *Dominion,* is set in a Britain that has surrendered to Nazi Germany. The British people live under German occupation, with the resistance movement led by Winston

Churchill trying to keep the fight going against the country's new Nazi rulers.[60] Sansom sets the action in London in 1952 in the month of the great killer fog, which still occurs despite Sansom's alteration of the historical context, following the *ceteris paribus* rule of alternate history, requiring only a single change in the time line from which others changes flow, in order to render the sequence of events plausible.[61] The fog adds to the mystery and tension of the counterfactual action. Of course, given the Nazis' record of ruthlessly plundering the economies of the other countries they occupied, from France to Poland, it is probable that industrial emissions in London would have fallen sharply between 1940 and 1952, and an impoverished population would not have been able to keep the home fires burning since most of the coal would have been carried off to Germany. Yet Sansom's novel does show that it is almost impossible to separate London from its fogs when writing about the 1950s.

Natural fogs still occur in London from time to time and will always return when the atmospheric conditions are right. In December 2013 a thick fog descended upon the capital, disrupting air traffic and causing chaos on the roads. But it was white, with no visible sign of pollution—no different from fogs in the valleys of Dartmoor or on the low-lying fields of the East Anglian fens.[62] Gradually the recognition dawned that London was no longer subject to dense yellow or brown fogs of the traditional kind. London fog began to establish itself in the collective imagination as a characteristic of the Victorian era. By the 1980s it was beginning to appear on films, on television, and in books as a quick and easy way of denoting London in the decades when it was at its height, in the 1880s and 1890s. If a television drama opens with a foggy street, with gas lamps casting their feeble light onto the pavement, we now know immediately that we are in Victorian London, even though, whether through a failure of the imagination or a deficiency of technology or a need for the viewers to be able to see the characters who are about to enter the scene, the fog is never impenetrable and is usually white instead of yellow or brown.

We also know, however, that the appearance of an image of a foggy London street, dimly lit by gas lamps, is a warning that something dreadful is about to happen. One only has to look at the recent television drama series titled *Penny Dreadful* to see how often the streets are overhung with a slight mist, if not a fog.[63] Here the fog indicates the presence of the supernatural and the criminal. The oft-used trope of London fog as a veil to conceal London crime and a mystery to be solved by a clever detective is often reduced to a simple signifier of a crime drama set in the Victorian era. This applies above all, perhaps, to the two best-known Victorian criminal narratives, those of Sherlock Holmes and Jack the Ripper. If the exploits of any fictional character are associated with London fog, it is surely those of Sir Arthur Conan Doyle's consulting detective and the anonymous murderer who terrorized women in the East End in 1888. The use of fog as a simple signifier for Holmes's detective exploits has indeed a long history. Gavin Brend claimed in 1951 that Sherlock Holmes will always be connected with "the greasy, brown, swirling fog."[64] But it was really only after the end of London fogs in the early 1960s that the use of fog to signify nineteenth-century London took off. A French biographer of Conan Doyle noted in 1964 the connection between the stories of Sherlock Holmes and fog: "In spite of the variable weather, Conan Doyle likes best to show us Baker Street in the morning dimness of all-pervading, mysterious fog."[65] In 1965 the British film *A Study in Terror* was released. It has Holmes investigating the Jack the Ripper murders. According to Gary Coville and Patrick Lucanio "some sources assert that the script was adapted from an original treatment by Adrian Conan Doyle [Arthur Conan Doyle's son] titled *Fog*."[66] Although Adrian Conan Doyle's original input is disputed, nevertheless in the movie the opening title credits form themselves into shapes out of the fog. The reviewer of a 1974 theatre production of a play based on two Sherlock Holmes stories, "A Scandal in Bohemia" and "The Final Problem," welcomed the production: "what pleasure to creep under a blanket of real old-fashioned London fog."[67] Vincent Starrett (1886–1974), a noted "Holmesian" and writer of a Sherlock Holmes pastiche, wrote in a similar vein: "I've always wanted to do a synthetic Sherlock. . . . The reason would be to produce a Holmes adventure that I could completely admire, and which would contain everything I like—the opening at the breakfast table, with a page or two of deduction; the appearance of Mrs Hudson, followed instantly by the troubled client, who would fall over the threshold in a faint; the hansom in the fog, and so on."[68] Christopher Frayling referred in 1996 to "the foggy surroundings of Baker Street."[69] As recently as 2004 the *Radio Times* announced a new Sherlock Holmes story by describing the setting in

Figure C.5 *The Avengers*, a spy adventure series shown on British commercial television, ran from 1961 to 1969. This still is from one of the later episodes, "Fog" (season 7, episode 24, first aired 12 March 1969 in the UK). It was described by many viewers as atmospheric, with fog being a main component of the mystery, which involved a modern-day Jack the Ripper. Associated British Corporation / CANAL+Image UK Ltd.

"London 1902: A pea-souper swirls, another debutante has been murdered."[70] In 2005, as a history of the detective story puts it: "There are many who read, or reread, the Holmes stories for their evocation of the humdrum background—the fogs and hansom cabs and domestic interiors—of gaslit Victorian London."[71]

In the introduction to *The Sign of Four,* Peter Ackroyd comments: "In fact, the urban fog has become part of the mystery of the Holmes adventure; it represents the impenetrability of the city, its viscous materiality as well as its pallid obscurity. These in turn become the metaphors for those opaque and clandestine elements which Holmes in the course of his activities, manages thoroughly to disperse."[72] Yet London fog actually appears very seldom in the Sherlock Holmes stories. The most obvious use of fog, and one which is very much integral to the plot's creation of suspense, is in *The Hound of the Baskervilles;* however, this is not a London fog but a country mist. Actual London fog is described at some length in "The Adventure of the Bruce-Partington Plans" and *The Sign of Four,* in a more cursory way in "The Red Circle," and even more briefly in "The Dying Detective" and "The Copper Beeches." Of the two Holmsean stories in which fog is described in depth, "The Bruce-Partington Plans" describes a thick yellow London fog in all its greasy and oily viscosity and accords it a central role in the plot. In *The Sign of Four* Conan Doyle extends his description of the fog to convey a sense of the imprisoning nature of London life. In "The Abbey Grange" (1904) Conan Doyle even harks back to his Scottish roots and refers to the fog as "the opalescent London reek"—thus recalling the nickname of Edinburgh: "auld reekie."[73] Yet this is all. In the overwhelming majority of Sherlock Holmes mysteries, the air is clear. The close association of London fogs with Sherlock Holmes described by Peter Ackroyd is purely a phenomenon of the late twentieth and early twenty-first centuries.

The case of Jack the Ripper is even more striking. The Ripper murders have long been portrayed by commentators as having taken place in foggy Victorian London, and indeed they were actually committed at the very height of London fog's density and frequency, in the late 1880s. As we have seen, the first fiction centred on a Jack the Ripper–style murderer, by Marie Belloc Lowndes, used London fog throughout. A 1935 French novel further captured this feeling when its first page recorded of Jack the Ripper: "The mere syllables of his name evoke the special atmosphere of sordid alleyways teeming with people, foggy evenings, and a phantom that looms up from nowhere. . . . Blood, filth and fog—those are the three essential elements of Jack the Ripper's world."[74] Here again the association only really became indelible from the 1960s onwards, as London fogs ceased to be a problem of the contemporary city. In a similar vein twentieth-century television dramas based around the Whitechapel murders almost invariably insist on the fog being an important part of events, including a 1969 episode of the ABC television series *The Avengers,* titled "Fog," in which the murderer is called the Gaslight Ghoul (Figure C.5).[75] Even the science-fiction series *Star Trek* had an episode, written by Robert Bloch (the author of Alfred Hitchcock's movie *Psycho,* 1960) and first aired in 1967, in which a timeless force of inhumanity, known as Jack the Ripper on earth, inhabits the foggy side of an alien planet (Figure C.6).[76] The authors of a survey of Ripper literature claimed in 2002 that the murders by Jack the Ripper "represent a real-life mystery from the era of Sherlock Holmes—the bygone romantic era of high Victorian society, gaslights and swirling London fog."[77] As the Ripperologists Gary Coville and Patrick Lucanio maintain: "Like a potent witch's brew, a writer or director merely needs to add a soupçon of fog, a dram of yellow gaslight, a hint of echoing footsteps, a modest dose of darkness. . . . The result screams 'Jack the Ripper.'"[78] For those unfamiliar with modern London, the effect lingered on: as one of the characters in the 1972 film *Frenzy,* directed by Alfred Hitchcock, says: "Foreigners somehow expect the squares of London to be fog wreathed, full of hansom cabs, and littered with ripped whores—don't you think?"[79] Yet each of the Ripper's crimes was actually committed on a night without fog. On only one of the nights was it even raining. Otherwise the skies were clear.[80] The signifier has completely obliterated the history. Indeed viewers would now probably not find a television depiction of the Ripper murders without fog in the background credible.

London's pea-soupers thus live on in the public imagination, now associated with only one short phase in their long career, a career that in all stretches over nearly a century and a half, from the 1830s to the 1960s. During that period London fogs inspired novelists of genius, from Charles Dickens to Robert Louis Stevenson, Henry James to Joseph Conrad, to

Figure C.6 The original *Star Trek* science fiction series on NBC television had a Jack the Ripper theme in which an eternal entity, referred to as "Redjac" (Red Jack), feeds on fear and has committed a string of murders throughout the galaxy, including those attributed to Jack the Ripper, as a means of sustaining itself. This still is from "Wolf in the Fold" (season 2, episode 14, first aired 22 December 1967). The original series ran for three seasons only, from 1966 to 1969. A Desilu Studios Production; CBS Television Studios / Paramount Pictures.

create some of their most powerful and imaginative writings; fogs prompted cheap, pulp-fiction fantasies of death and destruction; fogs went hand in hand with the rise of crime and detective novels; and London fogs were immortalized by some of the greatest artists of the age, above all by Claude Monet and James McNeill Whistler, as well as being depicted by many lesser ones. London fogs lent themselves to the most sophisticated and complex kinds of literary representation as well as to the cruder and simpler uses as a symbol of mystery and obfuscation favoured by writers of crime and detective stories. Their longevity owed something to legislative inertia and scientific uncertainty and more than a little to a feeling among Londoners that London would not be London without them, but most of all they persisted because of the refusal of industrialists and those who represented them to bear the costs of bringing under control the sulphurous smoke emissions that caused the fogs, and because of ordinary citizens' attachment to domestic coal fires and the reluctance of politicians to invade the home and interfere with the coal-fire hearth, that potent and popular symbol of cosy domesticity.

Gradually, however, British politicians began to grapple with the problem of smoke pollution and London fog. Scientists came to learn more about the causes of fog, smoke-abatement pressure groups became more vocal and more insistent, and health became a greater priority for the nation, above all with the creation of the National Health Service after the Second World War, which gave everyone a feeling of responsibility for the health of all and imposed new financial burdens on the government and the taxpayer for disease prevention. As peacetime mortality rates fell and the memory of the mass slaughter of the World Wars faded, so life became more precious, and the easily preventable death of thousands of Londoners from asthma, bronchitis, and other lung conditions, turned fatal by fog, came to be regarded as an outrage in the mid-twentieth century as it had not in the mid-nineteenth. Foggy London town is no more, and the pea-souper has, both in reality and in fiction, been consigned definitively to the past.

Notes

Acknowledgements

Index

Notes

1. The Birth of London Fog

1 Peter Brimblecombe, *The Big Smoke: A History of Air Pollution in London since Medieval Times* (London: Methuen, 1987), p. 8. Old Seacoal Lane is near Ludgate Hill and off Limeburner Lane.

2 Ibid., p. 30. For more detail of attitudes to smoke pollution even earlier than Tudor times, see Peter Brimblecombe, "Writing on Smoke," in *Dirty Words: Writings on the History and Culture of Pollution,* ed. Hannah Bradby (London: Earthscan, 1990), pp. 93–113.

3 All quoted in Emily Cockayne, *Hubbub: Filth, Noise and Stench in England, 1600–1770* (New Haven, CT: Yale University Press, 2007), pp. 208–9.

4 John Evelyn, *A Character of England: As it was lately presented in a Letter, to a Noble Man of France* (London: John Crooke, 1659), p. 27.

5 John Evelyn, *Fumifugium; or, The Inconvenience of the Aer and Smoake of London Dissipated* (1661; repr., London: National Society for Clean Air, 1961), pp. 12, 11.

6 For more on Sir Kenelm Digby and Margaret Cavendish, see Brimblecombe, *Big Smoke,* pp. 43–47.

7 Evelyn, *Fumifugium,* p. 18.

8 John Evelyn, *The Diary of John Evelyn,* ed. E. S. De Beer, vol. 3 (Oxford: Oxford University Press, 2000), p. 296 (13 September 1666).

9 Ibid., p. 310.

10 Evelyn, *Fumifugium,* p. 16.

11 Ibid., p. 23.

12 Ibid., p. 17.

13 Ibid., p. 18.

14 Ibid., p. 20.

15 Samuel Pegge, preface to *Fumifugium; or, The Inconvenience of the Aer and Smoake of London Dissipated, Together with Some Remedies Humbly Proposed,* by John Evelyn (London: B. White, 1772), p. iii.

16 Pehr Kalm, *Kalm's Account of His Visit to England on His Way to America in 1748,* trans. Joseph Lucas (London: Macmillan, 1892), p. 26.

17 Pierre-Jean Grosley, *A Tour to London; or, New Observations on England, and Its Inhabitants,* trans. Thomas Nugent, vol. 1 (London: Lockyer Davis, 1772), pp. 43–45.

18 J. Cuthbert Hadden, *Haydn* (1902; repr., Cambridge: Cambridge Scholars Press, 2002), p. 67. See also Cockayne, *Hubbub,* p. 146.

19 Hadden, *Haydn*, p. 52.

20 Eric Gustaf Geijer, *Impressions of England, 1809–1810,* trans. Elizabeth Sprigge and Claude Napier (London: Jonathan Cape, 1932), pp. 82–83.

21 Ibid., pp. 84, 113.

22 Quoted in Roy Porter, *London: A Social History* (London: Hamish Hamilton, 1994), p. 97.

23 Pegge, preface to *Fumifugium*, p. v.

24 HC Deb 08 June 1819 vol 40 c976.

25 "Analysis of Scientific Books," *Quarterly Journal of Science, Literature, and the Arts* 12 (1822): p. 344.

26 Ibid.

27 Ibid., p. 345.

28 Quoted in Eric Ashby and Mary Anderson, "Studies in the Politics of Environmental Protection: The Historical Roots of the British Clean Air Act, 1956, I: The Awakening of Public Opinion over Industrial Smoke, 1843–1853," *Interdisciplinary Science Reviews* 1, no. 4 (1976): p. 279.

29 John Hotten, *The Slang Dictionary: Etymological, Historical, and Anecdotal* (London: Chatto and Windus, 1874), p. 298. Earlier editions date from 1859 and 1860.

30 Evelyn's tract was reprinted several times in the twentieth century, twice in 1930, one of these being a reaction to a request from *The Times* when it was printed as part of a debate regarding the site of the Chelsea power station in 1930. *The Times,* 29 November 1929, p. 20, col. D; also see 10 April 1929, p. 13, col. A. Five further printings were produced, and it became a standard reference for the National Smoke Abatement Society, which reprinted it in 1933. The later edition, published in 1961 by the Society's successor body, the National Society for Clean Air, came with an introduction by Arnold Marsh, the secretary of the National Smoke Abatement Society. The National Smoke Abatement Society became the National Society for Clean Air in 1958. John Evelyn's portrait adorns the Society's magazine.

31 "Analysis of Scientific Books," p. 353.

32 HC Deb 07 May 1821 vol 5 cc535–8.

33 Brimblecombe, *Big Smoke*, p. 109.

34 "Analysis of Scientific Books," p. 353.

35 *The Times,* 6 November 1805, p. 2, col. C; and 6 November 1806, p. 2, col. C.

36 *The Times,* 11 January 1812, p. 3, col. C.

37 Quoted in Brimblecombe, *Big Smoke*, p. 113.

38 *The Times,* 29 December 1813, p. 3, col. C.

39 Ibid.

40 Johann Georg Kohl, *England and Wales* (1844; repr., London: Frank Cass, 1968), p. 177.

41 *Magazine of the Friends of Kensal Green Cemetery,* April 1997.

42 *The Times,* 2 January 1818, p. 2, col. E. See also references to other fogs in *The Times,* 1 January 1818, p. 2, col. C; 23 December 1818, p. 3, col. C.

43 *The Times,* 31 October 1821, p. 3, col. D; 12 December 1822, p. 2, col. C; 13 November 1828, p. 2, col. C; 21 November 1829, p. 2, col. C; for fogs in 1820, 1826, and 1828 see Luke Howard, *The Climate of London Deduced from Meteorological Observations, Made in the Metropolis, and at Various Places around It,* vol. 3 (London: Harvey and Darton, 1833), pp. 36–37, 207, 303.

44 Lord George Byron, *Don Juan,* ed. T. G. Steffan, E. Steffan and W. W. Pratt (New Haven, CT: Yale University Press, 1982), 10.82, p. 395.

45 Ibid., 4.104, p. 215. Earlier in the poem Byron describes "A little cupola" where "Dante's bones are laid."

46 Thomas Carlyle to Alexander Carlyle, 14 December 1824, in *The Collected Letters of Thomas and Jane Welsh Carlyle,* ed. Charles Sanders, vol. 3 (Durham, NC: Duke University Press, 1970), p. 219.

47 Howard, *Climate of London,* p. 207.

48 Ibid., p. 303.

49 *The Times,* 21 November 1829, p. 2, col. E.

50 *The Times,* 15 December 1829, p. 2, col. C.

51 Brimblecombe, *Big Smoke,* p. 111.

52 Nathaniel Parker Willis, *Pencillings by the Way* (1835; repr., London: T. Werner Laurie, 1942), p. 401.

53 Quoted in Nicholas Reed, *Monet and the Thames* (London: Lilburne, 1998), p. 7.

54 *The Times,* 30 November 1840, p. 7, col. B; 1 December 1840, p. 3, col. C; 21 January 1842, p. 5, col. B; 22 February 1842, p. 6, col. C; 8 November 1842, p. 5, col. F; 7 December 1842, p. 3, col. C; 14 November 1843, p. 3, col. C; 14 December 1843, p. 3, col. B; 6 November 1844, p. 6, col. E; 22 November 1844, p. 5, col. G; 30 December 1844, p. 7, col. F.

55 Peter Styles, *The Bachelor's Walk in a Fog* (London: Sherwood, Gilbert and Piper, 1840), verse 22, p. 8.

56 Michael Ball and David Sunderland, *An Economic History of London, 1800–1914* (London: Routledge, 2001), p. 42.

57 Ibid., p. 75.

58 Stephen Inwood, *A History of London* (London: Macmillan, 1998), pp. 411–44.

59 Both quoted in Brimblecombe, *Big Smoke,* pp. 117, 125–26.

60 Max Schlesinger, *Saunterings in and about London,* trans. Otto Wenckstern (London: Nathaniel Cooke, 1853), p. 84.

61 *Morning Leader,* 22 October 1901, quoted in Henry T. Bernstein, "The Mysterious Disappearance of Edwardian London Fog," *London Journal* 11, no. 2 (1975): p. 194.

62 Joseph Ashby-Sterry, "November," *The Lazy Minstrel* (London: T. Fisher Unwin, 1886), p. 141.

63 J. B. Cohen, *The Air of Towns* (Washington, DC: U.S. Government Printing Office, 1896), p. 23.

64 William Makepeace Thackeray, *The History of Pendennis* (1850; repr., London: Penguin, 1986), p. 310.

65 Schlesinger, *Saunterings*, p. 154.

66 John Kersey, *The New English Dictionary* (1702; repr., Menston, UK: Scolar, 1969), s.vv. "fog," "mist," "smoke."

67 Francis Grose, *A Classical Dictionary of the Vulgar Tongue* (London: S. Hooper, 1788), s.v. "fog."

68 Humphrey Tristram Potter, *A New Dictionary of All the Cant and Flash Language* (London: J. Downes, 1795), s.v. "fog."

69 William Frend, *Is It Impossible to Free the Atmosphere of London, in a Very Considerable Degree, from the Smoke and Deleterious Vapours with Which It Is Hourly Impregnated?* (London: Charles Wood, 1819), p. 62.

70 "Abstract of Evidence and Reports Made by a Select Committee of the House of Commons, on Steam Engines and Furnaces," in *An Historical and Descriptive Account of the Steam Engine . . . with an Appendix of Patents and Parliamentary Papers Connected with the Subject,* by Charles Frederick Partington (London: J. Taylor, 1822), p. 48 (of appendix).

71 *The Oxford English Dictionary,* ed. J. A. Simpson and E. S. C. Weiner, 2nd ed. (Oxford, UK: Clarendon, 1989), s.v. "pea-soup."

72 Herman Melville, *Journal of a Visit to London and the Continent, 1849–1850,* ed. Eleanor Melville Metcalf (Cambridge, MA: Harvard University Press, 1948), pp. 45–46.

73 Quoted in Fred Kaplan, *Henry James: The Imagination of Genius, a Biography* (London: Hodder and Stoughton, 1992), p. 177.

74 *New York Times,* 2 April 1871, p. 3.

75 *New York Times,* 29 December 1889. Quoted in David Stradling and Peter Thorsheim, "The Smoke of Great Cities: British and American Efforts to Control Air Pollution, 1860–1914," *Environmental History* 4, no. 1 (1999): p. 12.

76 *A New English Dictionary on Historical Principles,* ed. James A. H. Murray (Oxford, UK: Clarendon, 1905), s.v. "pea-soup," quoting *Good Words* (London: Isbister, 1883).

77 Ibid.

78 *The Times,* 12 August 1937 and 19 August 1937. After these two appearances the advertisement was dropped.

79 *The Times,* 25 March 1950, p. 5, col. C.

80 *The Oxford English Dictionary,* 2nd ed., s.v. "pea-soup."

81 C. I. Johnstone, *Cook and Housewife's Manual* (Edinburgh, UK: Oliver and Boyd, 1827), p. 144.

82 Commissariat Relief Office, *Means of Providing Cheap Food* (Dublin: Her Majesty's Stationery Office, 1846), pp. 3, 6.

83 Thomas Hardy, *Tess of the d'Urbervilles: A Pure Woman* (1891; repr., London: Penguin, 1978), p. 80.

84 James Payn, *Notes from the "News"* (London: Chatto and Windus, 1890), p. 8.

85 Thomas Carlyle to John Stuart Mill, 12 January 1833, in *The Collected Letters of Thomas and Jane Welsh Carlyle,* ed. Charles Richard Sanders, vol. 6 (Durham, NC: Duke University Press, 1977), pp. 300–301.

86 *Punch's Almanack for 1851,* included with *Punch* 19 (1850) in unnumbered pages at the beginning.

87 Thomas Miller, *Picturesque Sketches of London: Past and Present* (London: Office of the National Illustrated Library, 1852), p. 243.

88 Both quoted in Cockayne, *Hubbub,* p. 208.

89 R. J. Morris, *Cholera 1832: The Social Response to an Epidemic* (London: Croom Helm, 1976), pp. 159–96; Michael Durey, *The Return of the Plague: British Society and the Cholera, 1831–2* (Dublin: Gill and Macmillan, 1979), pp. 50–76, 101–34.

90 Sara Jeannette Duncan, *An American Girl in London* (London: Chatto and Windus, 1891), p. 30.

91 Inez Haynes Irwin, "The Californiacs," 1919. See http://www.gutenberg.org /files/3311/3311-h/3311-h.htm.

92 Bob Hope, *I Owe Russia $1200* (London: Robert Hale, 1963), p. 31.

93 Charles Dickens, *Bleak House* (1853; repr., London: Penguin, 1974), p. 179.

94 *The Oxford English Dictionary,* 2nd ed., s.v. "London."

95 *The Routledge Dictionary of Historical Slang,* ed. Eric Partridge and Jacqueline Simpson (London: Routledge and Kegan Paul, 1973), s.v. "London ivy."

96 Charles Dickens and W. H. Wills, "Spitalfields," *Household Words,* 5 April 1851, in *The Uncollected Writings of Charles Dickens,* ed. Harry Stone, vol. 1 (London: Allen Lane, Penguin, 1968), p. 231.

97 Dickens, *Bleak House,* p. 76.

98 *Slang and Its Analogues, Past and Present: A Dictionary Historical and Comparative of the Heterodox Speech of All Classes of Society for More than Three Hundred Years,* ed. John S. Farmer and W. E. Henley, vol. 5 (London, 1902), s.v. "London Particular (or London Ivy)."

99 Mark Staniforth, *Material Culture and Consumer Society: Dependent Colonies in Colonial Australia* (New York: Kluwer Academic/Plenum, 2003), p. 82.

100 *New York Times,* 2 April 1855, p. 1.

101 John Ruskin, "The Storm-Cloud of the Nineteenth Century," a lecture delivered on 4 February 1884 in *The Complete Works of John Ruskin,* ed. E. T. Cook and Alexander Wedderburn, vol. 34 (London: George Allen, 1908), pp. 14–15.

102 *Farmhouse Cookery: Recipes from the Country Kitchen* (London: Reader's Digest, 1980), p. 21.

103 Dickens, *Bleak House,* p. 510.

104 *The Times,* 27 December 1904, p. 11, col. A.

105 Alison Lurie, *The Nowhere City* (1965; repr., London: Penguin, 1977).

106 *The Times,* 11 November 1953, p. 9, col. D.

107 *The Times,* 13 November 1953, p. 9, col. D.

108 J. B. Sanderson, "The National Smoke Abatement Society and the Clean Air Act" (1956), in *Campaigning for the Environment,* ed. Richard Kimber and J. J. Richardson (London: Routledge, 1974), p. 36.

109 Elizabeth Gaskell, *North and South* (1855; repr., London: Penguin, 1986), p. 96.

110 Ibid., p. 532n1.

111 *The Times,* 7 December 1842, p. 3, col. E; 30 December 1844, p. 7, col. G.

112 Judith Flanders, *The Victorian City: Everyday Life in Dickens' London* (London: Atlantic Books, 2012), p. 53.

113 Anthony S. Wohl, *Endangered Lives: Public Health in Victorian Britain* (London: Dent, 1983).

114 Ibid., p. 212.

115 Charles Manby Smith, *Curiosities of London Life; or, Phases, Physiological and Social, of the Great Metropolis* (London: William and Frederick, 1853), p. 80.

116 *Punch* 17 (1849): p. 194.

117 See the *Graphic,* 9 November 1872, p. 431.

118 HC Deb 27 June 1843 vol 70 cc445–6.

119 Parl. Pp. *(H.C.)* 1843 (583) Report from the Select Committee on Smoke Prevention (Mackinnon Report), pp. 79–80.

120 Ibid., p. 86.

121 Ibid., pp. 79–80.

122 Quoted in Ashby and Anderson, "Studies in the Politics of Environmental Protection," p. 282.

123 William Cooke Taylor, *Notes of a Tour in the Manufacturing Districts of Lancashire* (London: Duncan and Malcolm, 1842), pp. 21–22.

124 Quoted in Ashby and Anderson, "Studies in the Politics of Environmental Protection," p. 284.

125 Quoted in ibid.

126 Quoted in ibid., p. 286.

127 Quoted in ibid.

128 Ibid., p. 287.

129 *The Times,* 10 August 1853, p. 7, col. C.

130 Ibid.

131 Ibid.

132 Quoted in Ashby and Anderson, "Studies in the Politics of Environmental Protection," p. 288.

133 Quoted in ibid., pp. 288–89.

134 Quoted in ibid., p. 289.

135 Wohl, *Endangered Lives,* pp. 220–21, 223.

136 Ibid., p. 223.

2. Dickensian Gloom

1 The best of many modern biographies is Michael Slater, *Charles Dickens: A Life Defined by Writing* (New Haven, CT: Yale University Press, 2009).

2 George Gissing, "Dickens in Memory," in *Collected Works of George Gissing on Charles Dickens,* vol. 1, *Essays, Introductions and Reviews,* ed. Pierre Coustillas (Grayswood, UK: Grayswood, 2004), p. 50.

3 Arthur Compton-Rickett, *The London Life of Yesterday* (London: Constable, 1909), p. 18.

4 Henry Vollam Morton, *In Search of London* (London: Methuen, 1988), p. 384.

5 Charles Dickens, *Barnaby Rudge,* ed. Gordon Spence (1841; repr., London: Penguin, 1986), p. 308.

6 Charles Dickens, *The Life and Adventures of Martin Chuzzlewit,* ed. P. N. Furbank (1843–1844; repr., London: Penguin, 1987), p. 180.

7 Charles Dickens, *David Copperfield,* ed. Trevor Blount (1849–1850; repr., London: Penguin, 1988), p. 350.

8 Charles Dickens, *The Old Curiosity Shop,* ed. Angus Easson (1841; repr., London: Penguin, 1984), pp. 469–70.

9 Ibid., p. 562.

10 Ibid., p. 137.

11 Ibid., p. 139.

12 Ibid., p. 472 (my italics).

13 Ibid., p. 613.

14 Ibid.

15 Ibid.

16 Ibid., pp. 617, 618.

17 Ibid., p. 619; Exodus 10:22. See Chapter 1, in which newspapers referred to the darkness created by London fog as an Egyptian darkness.

18 Dickens, *Old Curiosity Shop,* pp. 617, 619.

19 Ibid., p. 619.

20 Ibid., p. 620.

21 Ibid.

22 Ibid.

23 Ibid.

24 Ibid.

25 Ibid., p. 416.

26 Ibid., p. 620 for Quilp's death and p. 654 for Nell's death.

27 *The Times,* 11 February 1834, p. 1, col. E.

28 Ibid.

29 *The Times,* 18 December 1835, p. 3, col. A.

30 Dickens, *Old Curiosity Shop,* pp. 618.

31 *The Times,* 11 February 1834, p. 1, col. E.

32 Dickens, *The Old Curiosity Shop,* p. 620. For a fuller analysis of Quilp's death, see Christine L. Corton, "Drowning in the Fog: The Significance of Quilp's Death in *The Old Curiosity Shop,*" *Dickens Studies Annual: Essays on Victorian Fiction* 44 (2013): pp. 111–26.

33 Dickens, *Chuzzlewit,* p. 157. Whittington refers to Dick Whittington who sets off to London to find his fortune.

34 Ibid., p. 180.

35 Ibid.

36 Ibid.

37 Ibid.

38 *The Times,* 30 November 1840, p. 7, col. B.

39 Charles Dickens, *A Christmas Carol* (1843), in *The Christmas Books,* ed. Michael Slater, vol. 1 (London: Penguin, 1985), p. 47.

40 Dickens, *Chuzzlewit,* p. 180.

41 *The Times,* 15 December 1829, p. 2, col. C.

42 Dickens, *Chuzzlewit,* p. 180.

43 Ibid., p. 296.

44 Ibid.

45 Ibid., p. 297.

46 Ibid., p. 298.

47 Ibid., p. 302.

48 Charles Dickens, *Bleak House,* ed. Norman Page (1853; repr., London: Penguin, 1974), p. 49.

49 Ibid.

50 Ibid. The Megalosaurus, a type of dinosaur first reconstructed in the 1820s, was presumably brought to Dickens's attention by the large model of it under construction in the grounds of the Crystal Palace in Sydenham in the early 1850s. Robert Chambers's book *Vestiges of the Natural History of Creation* (London: John Churchill, 1844) had already put forward the idea that life on earth should be measured in millions rather than thousands of years.

51 Dickens, *Bleak House,* p. 50.

52 Ibid.

53 Ibid.

54 F. S. Schwarzbach, "*Bleak House:* The Social Pathology of Urban Life," *Literature and Medicine* 9 (1990): p. 96.

55 Dickens, *Bleak House,* p. 50.

56 Ibid.

57 Ibid.

58 Ibid.

59 Ibid., pp. 50–51.

60 Ibid., p. 65.

61 Ibid., p. 278.

62 Ibid., p. 279.

63 There seems to be a general consensus that the disease contracted by Jo is smallpox, even though Dickens does not name it in the text. See Michael S. Gurney, "Disease as Device," *Literature and Medicine* 9 (1990): pp. 82–90. Also see Nancy Aycock Metz, "Narrative Gesturing in *Bleak House*," *Dickensian* 77 (Spring 1981): p. 19; and Schwarzbach, *"Bleak House,"* p. 97.

64 Dickens, *Bleak House*, p. 499.

65 Ibid., p. 500.

66 Ibid., p. 505.

67 Ibid., p. 131.

68 John Timbs, *Curiosities of London: Exhibiting the Most Rare and Remarkable Objects of Interest in the Metropolis with Nearly Fifty Years' Personal Recollections* (London: D. Bogue, 1855), p. 310.

69 Ibid.

70 Charles Dickens, "Speech to the Metropolitan Sanitary Association on 10 May 1851," in *The Speeches of Charles Dickens: A Complete Edition,* ed. K. J. Fielding (Brighton, UK: Harvester, 1988), p. 128.

71 *The Times,* 1 December 1840, p. 3, col. C.

72 Dickens, *Bleak House,* p. 683.

73 Ibid., p. 49.

74 Ibid., p. 99.

75 Ibid., p. 411.

76 Ibid., p. 497.

77 Ibid., p. 547.

78 Ibid., p, 547–48.

79 Ibid., p. 926.

80 Ibid., p. 927.

81 Ibid.

82 Ibid., p. 682.

83 Ibid., p. 691.

84 Ibid., p. 274.

85 Ibid., p. 325.

86 Ibid., p. 326.

87 Ibid.

88 Ibid., p. 705.

89 Ibid., p. 705.

90 Ibid., p. 858.

91 See Susan Shatto, *The Companion to Bleak House* (London: Unwin Hyman, 1988), p. 296, noting Dickens's interest in "the case of Laura Bridman, a blind, deaf, and dumb girl" in America in 1842 and his support of Harriet Martin-

eau's campaign to treat and train properly those children who are "deaf, dumb, blind, or mentally defective."

92 Charles Dickens to Miss Burdett-Coutts, 18 April 1852, in *The Letters of Charles Dickens*, vol. 6, *1850–1852*, ed. Graham Storey, Kathleen Tillotson, and Nina Burgis (Oxford, UK: Clarendon, 1990), p. 644.

93 Dickens, *Bleak House*, p. 49.

94 Ibid., p. 76.

95 Charles Dickens to Sir Edward Bulwer Lytton, 10 February 1851, in *Letters*, p. 287.

96 Charles Dickens, *Our Mutual Friend*, ed. Stephen Gill (1864-5; repr., London: Penguin, 1985), p. 479.

97 For further discussion of the significance of yellow, see Jeremy Tambling, *Lost in the American City: Dickens, James and Kafka* (New York: Palgrave, 2001), pp. 11–13.

98 Dickens, *Our Mutual Friend*, p. 479.

99 Robert Alter, *Imagined Cities: Urban Experience and the Language of the Novel* (New Haven, CT: Yale University Press, 2005), p. 77; Augustus Mayhew, *Paved with Gold*, vol. 3 (London: Chapman and Hall, 1858), p. 284: "There's no chance of 'nabbing any rust'" (an example of rust being a reference for money).

100 Dickens, *Our Mutual Friend*, p. 429.

101 Ibid., p. 479.

102 Ibid., p. 176. In reference to the Podsnaps' lack of visual depth, see J. Hillis Miller, *Victorian Subjects* (Hemel Hempstead, UK: Harvester Wheatsheaf, 1990), p. 72.

103 Dickens, *Our Mutual Friend*, p. 479.

104 For further discussion, see Roselee Robison, "Time, Death and the River in Dickens' Novels," *English Studies* 53 (1972): p. 449.

105 Dickens, *Our Mutual Friend*, p. 506.

106 Ibid., p. 874.

107 Ibid., p. 492.

108 Ibid., p. 479.

109 Nathaniel Hawthorne, *The Centenary Edition of the Works of Nathaniel Hawthorne, vol 22, The English Notebooks, 1856–1860*, ed. Thomas Woodson and Bill Ellis, (Columbus: Ohio State University Press, 1997), p. 446 (8 December 1857).

110 Dickens, *Old Curiosity Shop*, p. 173.

111 Alter, *Imagined Cities*, p. 55.

112 Dickens, *Our Mutual Friend*, p. 332.

113 Ibid., p. 334.

114 Ibid., p. 480.

115 Ibid., p. 492.

116 Ibid.

117 Alter, *Imagined Cities*, p. 79.

118 Dickens, *Our Mutual Friend*, p. 495.

119 Ibid., p. 502. Miss Abbey refers to the drowned body as "it."

120 Ibid., p. 501.

121 Ibid., p. 500.

122 Ibid., p. 501.

123 Ibid.

124 Ibid.

125 Alter, *Imagined Cities*, p. 50.

126 Ibid., p. 71.

127 Charles Dickens, *The Mystery of Edwin Drood*, ed. Arthur J Cox (1870; repr., London: Penguin, 1987), pp. 133–34.

128 Dickens, *Bleak House*, p. 76; *The Times*, 4 December 1837, p. 6, col. D.

129 Dickens, *Our Mutual Friend*, p. 479.

130 Ibid.

131 Ibid., pp. 479–80.

132 Ibid., p. 849.

133 Andrew Sanders, introduction to *Our Mutual Friend*, by Charles Dickens (London: Everyman's Library, 1994), p. xiv.

3. KING FOG

1 Jerry White, *London in the Nineteenth Century: "A Human Awful Wonder of God"* (London: Jonathan Cape, 2007), p. 189; Michael Ball and David Sunderland, *An Economic History of London, 1800–1914* (London: Routledge, 2001), pp. 289–90.

2 Rollo Russell, *London Fogs* (London: Edward Stanford, 1880), p. 22.

3 Georg Hartwig, *The Aerial World: A Popular Account of the Phenomena and Life of the Atmosphere* (London: Longmans, Green, 1874), p. 138.

4 Russell, *London Fogs*, p. 22.

5 *Daily News*, 10 December 1873, p. 2, col. A.

6 Hartwig, *Aerial World*, p. 139.

7 Mark Twain to Olivia L. Clemens, 11 December 1873, in *Mark Twain's Letters*, vol. 5, 1872–1873, ed. Lin Salamo and Harriet Elinor Smith (Berkeley: University of California Press, 1997), p. 508.

8 *Daily News*, 11 December 1873, col. D.

9 E. J. Powell, *History of the Smithfield Club, 1798 to 1900* (London: Smithfield Club, 1902), p. 54.

10 Hartwig, *Aerial World*, p. 138.

11 *Daily News*, 11 December 1873, p. 6, col. D.

12 Powell, *History of the Smithfield Club*, p. 15.

13 Russell, *London Fogs*, p. 22.

14 "Killed by the Fog," *Medical Times and Gazette: A Journal of Medical Science, Literature, Criticism and News*, 13 December 1873, p. 668, col. B.

15 Ibid.

16 Ibid.

17 Stephen Inwood, *City of Cities: The Birth of Modern London* (London: Macmillan, 2005), p. 7.

18 *British Medical Journal,* 20 December 1873, p. 731.

19 *The Times,* 29 December 1873, p. 4, col. C.

20 *The Times,* 2 January 1874, p. 11, col. E. "Phthisis" was the contemporary name for tuberculosis of the lungs.

21 For more detail on his life, see *Oxford Dictionary of National Biography,* ed. H. C. G. Matthew and Brian Harrison (Oxford: Oxford University Press, 2004) s.v. "Russell, (Francis Albert) Rollo."

22 Russell, *London Fogs,* p. 29.

23 Ibid., pp. 30–31.

24 J. Jackson Wray, *Will It Lift? The Story of a London Fog* (London: James Nisbet, 1888), p. 4.

25 Ibid., p. 34.

26 Ibid., p. 36.

27 Ibid., p. 1.

28 Ibid., pp. 1–2.

29 Ibid., p. 32.

30 Ibid., p. 9.

31 Ibid., p. 71.

32 Ibid., p. 126.

33 Ibid., p. 158.

34 Ibid., p. 170.

35 "Life and Talk in London: Political, Social, and Literary Affairs," *New York Times,* 16 February 1880. Quoted in David Stradling and Peter Thorsheim, "The Smoke of Great Cities: British and American Efforts to Control Air Pollution, 1860–1914," *Environmental History* 4, no. 1 (1999): p. 12.

36 Peter Brimblecombe, *The Big Smoke: A History of Air Pollution in London since Medieval Times* (London: Methuen, 1987), p. 111 (minimum estimates).

37 J. H. Brazell, *London Weather* (London: HMSO, Meteorological Office 783, 1968), p. 102.

38 Inwood, *City of Cities,* pp. 7–8.

39 Bill Luckin, " 'The Heart and Home of Horror': The Great London Fogs of the Late Nineteenth Century," *Social History* 28 (2003): p. 33.

40 Eric Ashby and Mary Anderson, "Studies in the Politics of Environmental Protection: The Historical Roots of the British Clean Air Act, 1956: II. The Appeal to Public Opinion over Domestic Smoke, 1880–1892," *Interdisciplinary Science Reviews* 2, no. 1 (1977): pp. 9–10.

41 Ball and Sunderland, *Economic History of London,* p. 42.

42 *Gardener's Magazine,* 10 January 1874, p. 13.

43 "Plant Life," *Smokeless Air* 85 (Spring 1953): p. 108.

44 Amy Levy, *A London Plane-Tree and Other Verse* (London: T. Fisher Unwin, 1889), p. 17.

45 See Hugh Johnson, *The Plane Forest: Does the City Have the Right Trees?* (lecture at Gresham College, 24 June 2013), http://www.gresham.ac.uk/professors-and-speakers/hugh-johnson-obe.

46 Russell, *London Fogs,* p. 30.

47 Ibid., p. 31.

48 *Illustrated London News,* 3 January 1880. Quoted in Stradling and Thorsheim, "Smoke of Great Cities," p. 10.

49 Daniel Pick, *Faces of Degeneration: A European Disorder, c. 1848–c. 1918* (Cambridge: Cambridge University Press, 1993), p. 174–75.

50 Laurence Binyon, "Deptford," in *London Visions* (London: Elkin Mathews, 1908), p. 30.

51 John Ruskin, "The Storm-Cloud of the Nineteenth Century," a lecture delivered on 4 February 1884 in *The Works of John Ruskin,* ed. E. T. Cook and Alexander Wedderburn, vol. 34 (London: George Allen, 1908), p. 39.

52 William Delisle Hay, *The Doom of the Great City; Being the Narrative of a Survivor, Written A.D. 1942* (1880), in *British Future Fiction: The End of the World,* ed. I. F. Clarke (London: Pickering and Chatto, 2001), p. 24.

53 William Delisle Hay, preface to *Brighter Britain! or, Settler and Maori in Northern New Zealand* (London: Richard Bentley and Son, 1882), pp. iii–iv.

54 Hay, *Doom of the Great City,* p. 23.

55 Ibid., p. 37.

56 Ibid., p. 38.

57 Ibid., p. 32.

58 Ibid., pp. 30–31.

59 Ibid., p. 39.

60 Ibid., p. 40.

61 Ibid., pp. 42–43.

62 Ibid., p. 43.

63 Ibid., p. 44.

64 Ibid., pp. 50–51.

65 Charles Dickens, *Our Mutual Friend,* ed. Stephen Gill (1864–5; repr., London: Penguin, 1985), p. 479.

66 Hay, *Doom of the Great City,* p. 36.

67 Ibid., p. 51.

68 Ibid., pp. 46, 51.

69 Ibid., p. 59.

70 Ibid.

71 Ibid., pp. 20, 25. For a discussion on an antiurban ideology that proposed a real or imagined pastoralization" of London, see Luckin, "Heart and Home of Horror," p. 33.

72 Hay, *Doom of the Great City*, p. 21.

73 Arthur Conan Doyle, *Memories and Adventures* (London: John Murray, 1930), p. 140.

74 Robert Barr, "The Doom of London," *Idler* 26 (March 1905): p. 540.

75 Robert Barr, "The Idlers' Club," *Idler* 26 (March 1905): p. 561.

76 Ibid. In the same editorial of 1905 Barr admits that Hay's device for killing the population of London was better than his, but then he proceeds to enumerate the flaws in Hay's writing. He cannot understand how the clerk manages to survive his walk through the fog: "He probably survived that he might confound me ten years later as a plagiarist. He also found gas still burning in a Strand theatre, which seems rather remarkable considering the state of the atmosphere" (p. 562).

77 Robert Barr, "The Doom of London," *Idler* 2 (January 1893): pp. 397–409.

78 Ibid., p. 398.

79 Ibid., p. 399.

80 Ibid.

81 Ibid., pp. 399–400.

82 *The Times*, 12 November 1880, p. 6, col. G.

83 Ibid.

84 J. E. H. Gordon, *Decorative Electricity* (London: S. Low, Marston, Searle and Rivington, 1891), p. 99.

85 George Gissing, *Isabel Clarendon*, vol. 2 (Brighton, UK: Harvester, 1969), p. 2.

86 'Fogs,' *The Lancet*, 23 October 1880, p. 666.

87 Barr, "Doom of London," p. 399.

88 Ibid., p. 404.

89 Barr, "The Idlers' Club," p. 561.

90 Adrian Desmond, *Huxley: From Devil's Disciple to Evolution's High Priest* (London: Penguin, 1998).

91 Barr, "The Idlers' Club," p. 561.

92 Barr, "Doom of London," p. 406.

93 Ibid.

94 Ibid., pp. 407–8.

95 Ibid., p. 409.

96 Ibid.

97 Ibid., p. 398.

98 For a discussion of scientific romance being "either catastrophic or millennial," see I. F. Clarke, "Science Fiction: Past and Present," *Quarterly Review* 295 (1957): p. 268.

99 Barr, "Doom of London," p. 398.

100 Judith R. Walkowitz, *City of Dreadful Delight: Narratives of Sexual Danger in Late-Victorian London* (London: Virago, 1992), pp. 24–26.

101 Shirley Nicholson, *A Victorian Household* (Stroud, UK: A. Sutton, 1994), p. 80.

102 Gareth Stedman Jones, *Outcast London: A Study in the Relationship between Classes in Victorian Society* (Oxford: Clarendon, 1971), pp. 284–303.

103 Henry James, "An English Easter," in *English Hours,* ed. Leon Edel (Oxford: Oxford University Press, 1981), p. 78 (first published in *Lippincott's Magazine,* July 1877).

104 J. P. Williams-Freeman, *The Effect of Town Life on the General Health with Especial Reference to London* (London: W. H. Allen, 1890), pp. 17–18. Williams-Freeman goes on to argue that a fourth-generation pure-bred Londoner cannot exist, which illustrates the extreme nature of the debate at this time.

105 George Gissing, *New Grub Street*, ed. John Goode (1891; repr., Oxford: Oxford University Press, 1993), p. 422.

106 "Degeneration amongst Londoners," *The Lancet,* 7 February 1885, p. 264.

107 Ibid., p. 265.

108 Israel Zangwill, *The Big Bow Mystery* (1891; repr., New York: Dybbuk, 2006), p. 1.

109 *Punch,* 13 November 1880, p. 220.

110 George Augustus Sala, *Living London: Being Echoes Re-echoed* (London: Kemington, 1883), p. 527.

111 *Punch,* 27 October 1888, p. 193.

112 Ibid., p. 194.

113 *Punch,* 21 January 1888, pp. 26–27.

114 Rollo Russell, *London Fog and Smoke* (lecture delivered at the Building Trades Exhibition, 28 April 1899), p. 15.

115 Peter Ackroyd, *London: The Biography* (London: Chatto and Windus, 2000), p. 435. Stevenson's story is properly called *Strange Case of Dr. Jekyll and Mr. Hyde,* but since the edition I am using employs the definite article, I follow this style.

116 Robert Louis Stevenson, *The Strange Case of Dr. Jekyll and Mr. Hyde,* in *The Strange Case of Dr. Jekyll and Mr. Hyde and Other Stories* (London: Penguin, 1979), p. 48.

117 Ibid.

118 Ibid., p. 59.

119 Ibid., p. 48.

120 Ibid.

121 Henry Mayhew, *London Labour and the London Poor,* vol. 2 (London: Frank Cass, 1967), p. 340.

122 For a picture of a pall, see John Wolffe, *Great Deaths: Grieving, Religion, and Nationhood in Victorian and Edwardian Britain* (Oxford: Oxford University Press, 2000), plate 7 (between pp. 214 and 215).

123 Shaw Desmond, *London Nights of Long Ago* (London: Duckworth, 1927), p. 31.

124 Also see echoes of *Bleak House* noted in Gordon Hirsch, "*Frankenstein*, Detective Fiction, and *Jekyll and Hyde*," in *Dr. Jekyll and Mr. Hyde: After One Hundred Years,* ed. William Veeder and Gordon Hirsch (Chicago: University of Chicago Press, 1988), p. 244n13. Stevenson, *Strange Case of Dr. Jekyll and Mr. Hyde*, p. 48.

125 Stevenson, *Strange Case of Dr. Jekyll and Mr. Hyde,* p. 48.

126 Ibid.

127 Ibid.

128 Ibid.

129 Jerry White, *London in the Nineteenth Century: "A Human Awful Wonder of God"* (London: Jonathan Cape, 2007), p. 143.

130 Stevenson, *Strange Case of Dr. Jekyll and Mr. Hyde,* p. 48.

131 Ibid., p. 30.

132 Ibid., p. 51.

133 Ibid., pp. 69–71.

134 Ibid., pp. 53–54.

135 Ibid., p. 54.

136 Ibid.

137 Ibid., p. 91.

138 Ibid.

139 Ibid., pp. 35–36.

140 Ibid., p. 38.

141 Robert Louis Stevenson, "A Chapter on Dreams," *Scribner's Magazine,* April 1888, p. 123.

142 See more on the psychological aspects of Stevenson's "brown fog" in William Veeder, "Children of the Night," in *Dr. Jekyll and Mr. Hyde: After One Hundred Years,* ed. William Veeder and Gordon Hirsch (Chicago: University of Chicago Press, 1988), pp. 107–60.

143 George Gissing, *The Private Papers of Henry Ryecroft* (London: Dent, 1964), p. 180.

144 Joseph Ashby-Sterry, "November," *The Lazy Minstrel* (London: T. Fisher Unwin, 1886), p. 141.

4. Women in Danger

1 *Daily Telegraph,* 12 October 1888, in *Jekyll and Hyde Dramatized: The 1887 Richard Mansfield Script and the Evolution of the Story on Stage,* ed. Martin A. Danahay and Alex Chisholm (Jefferson, NC: McFarland, 2005), "Appendix E: Jack the Ripper," p. 186.

2 *Philadelphia Inquirer,* 10 October 1888, p. 186.

3 Marie Belloc Lowndes, *The Lodger* (1911; repr., Oxford: Oxford University Press, 1996), p. 107.

4 Ibid., p. 30.

5 Ibid., p. 9.

6 Ibid., p. 3.

7 Ibid., pp. 30, 46.

8 Ibid., pp. 45, 38, 39, 90.

9 Ibid., pp. 94–97.

10 Ibid., p. 151.

11 Ibid., p. 102.

12 Ibid., p. 158.

13 Ibid., p. 98.

14 Ibid., p. 102.

15 Ibid., p. 109.

16 Ibid., p. 113.

17 Ibid., pp. 113, 100–101.

18 Ibid., p. 118.

19 Ibid., p. 202.

20 For links between the Ripper murders and the crisis of the social order in 1880s London, see Judith R. Walkowitz, *City of Dreadful Delight: Narratives of Sexual Danger in Late-Victorian London* (London: Virago, 1992), pp. 191–228; and Drew D. Gray, *London's Shadows: The Dark Side of the Victorian City* (London: Continuum Books, 2010).

21 William Hardinge, *Out of the Fog: A Tale* (London: Richard Bentley and Son, 1888), p. 23. The novel is dedicated to the author's sister, "in glad and sad remembrance of many fogs together."

22 Walkowitz, *City of Dreadful Delight*, p. 46.

23 Jerry White, *London in the Nineteenth Century* (London: Jonathan Cape, 2007), pp. 315–17.

24 Walkowitz, *City of Dreadful Delight*, pp. 15–40; see more generally Judith R. Walkowitz, *Prostitution and Victorian Society: Women, Class, and the State* (New York: Cambridge University Press, 1980).

25 Walkowitz, *City of Dreadful Delight*, pp. 41–120.

26 Henry James to Mrs. Henry James Sr., 24 December 1876, in *Henry James Letters*, vol. 2, *1875–1883*, ed. Leon Edel (London: Macmillan, 1975), pp. 85–86.

27 Henry James, "London," in *London Stories and Other Writings*, ed. David Kynaston (Padstow, UK: Tabb House, 1989), p. 241.

28 Ibid., p. 261.

29 George Gissing, *The Private Papers of Henry Ryecroft*, ed. Mark Storey (Oxford: Oxford University Press, 1987), p. 142.

30 George Gissing, *New Grub Street*, ed. John Goode (1891; repr., Oxford: Oxford University Press, 1993), p. 201.

31 Ibid.

32 Ibid.

33 Ibid., pp. 106–8.

34 Ibid., p. 107.

35 Henry James, "An English Easter," in *English Hours,* ed. Leon Edel (Oxford: Oxford University Press, 1981), p. 75 (first published in *Lippincott's Magazine,* July 1877).

36 James, "London," p. 247.

37 Henry James, "George Du Maurier," in *Partial Portraits* (Westport, CT: Greenwood, 1970), p. 339.

38 Ibid., p. 327.

39 Henry James, "Robert Louis Stevenson," in *Partial Portraits* (Westport, CT: Greenwood, 1970), p. 170.

40 Henry James, *The Portrait of a Lady,* ed. Geoffrey Moore (1881; repr., London: Penguin, 1986), p. 372.

41 Ibid, p. 373.

42 Ibid.

43 Ibid., p. 373.

44 Ibid., p. 214.

45 Ibid., p. 393.

46 Ibid., p. 606.

47 Ibid.

48 Ibid., p. 392; Ibid., p. 608.

49 Ibid.

50 Ibid.

51 Ibid.

52 Ibid., p. 635.

53 Ibid., p. 636.

54 James, "London," p. 261.

55 Henry James, *The Princess Casamassima* (1886; repr., London: David Campbell, 1991), p. 401.

56 James, "London," p. 247.

57 James, *Princess Casamassima,* p. 43.

58 James, *Portrait of a Lady,* p. 373.

59 James, *Princess Casamassima,* p. 57.

60 Ibid., p. 113.

61 Ibid., p. 57.

62 Ibid., p. 115.

63 Ibid., p. 236.

64 Ibid., p. 237.

65 Elizabeth Carolyn Miller, "The Inward Revolution: Sexual Terrorism in *The Princess Casamassima,*" *Henry James Review* 24, no. 2 (2003): pp. 146–67.

66 Herbert George Wells, *Love and Mr. Lewisham* (1900; repr., London: Penguin, 2005), p. 87.

67 Ibid., p. 94.

68 The story was published a year earlier in the United States in *McClure's Illustrated* with illustrations drawn by Oakley's sister, Violet (1874–1961), a well-known artist. The English edition was richly illustrated by Sir Amédée Forestier (1854–1930), a very well established *Illustrated London News* artist and later famed for his historical depictions.

69 Hester Caldwell Oakley, "Love in a Fog." *Illustrated London News* [London, England], 10 June 1899, p. 831. The quotation is from *The Rubaiyat of Omar Khayyam*.

70 Ibid., p. 831.

71 Ibid., pp. 831, 832.

72 Ibid., pp. 832, 833.

73 Ibid., p. 832.

74 Ibid., pp. 832, 833.

75 Maxwell Gray, *The Suspicions of Ermengarde* (London: John Long, 1908), p. 7.

76 Ibid., p. 11.

77 Ibid., p. 8.

78 Morley Roberts, "The Fog," *Strand Magazine: An Illustrated Monthly,* July to December 1908, vol. 36, p. 382.

79 Ibid., p. 383 (grammar as in original).

80 Ibid., p. 384.

81 Ibid., p. 385

82 Ibid., p. 387.

83 Ibid., p. 384.

84 Ibid., p. 385.

85 Ibid., p. 390.

86 Ibid.

87 Ibid., pp. 388, 390.

88 Ibid., p. 388.

5. The View from Abroad

1 Alex Butterworth, *The World That Never Was: A True Story of Dreamers, Schemers, Anarchists, and Secret Agents* (London: The Bodley Head, 2010), p. 162.

2 Alessandro Verri, quoted in Paul Langford, *Englishness Identified: Manners and Character, 1650–1850* (Oxford: Oxford University Press, 2000), p. 222.

3 Graham Robb, *Rimbaud* (London: Picador, 2000), p. 189.

4 Paul Verlaine, letter to Edmond Lepelletier, October 1872, *Correspondance de Paul Verlaine*, ed. A. van Bever, 3 vols., Geneva and Paris: Slatkine Reprints, 1983, vol. 1, p. 47. Translated in Joanna Richardson, *Verlaine* (London: Weidenfeld and Nicolson, 1971), p. 100.

5 Paul Verlaine, letter to Edmond Lepelletier, September 1872, *Correspondance de Paul Verlaine*, ed. A. van Bever, 3 vols., Geneva and Paris: Slatkine Reprints,

1983, vol.1, pp. 42–43. Translated in Robert Tombs and Isabelle Tombs, *That Sweet Enemy: The French and the British from the Sun King to the Present* (London: Heinemann, 2006), p. 388.

6 Arthur Rimbaud, "Childhood," in *Rimbaud Complete,* trans. Wyatt Mason (New York: Modern Library, 2002), p. 226.

7 Ibid.

8 Jules Vallès, *La Rue à Londres* in *Oeuvres,* ed. Lucien Scheler (Paris: Les Editeurs français réunis) 14 vols., 1950–1972, vol. 5, pp. 91, 250. Translated in Tombs and Tombs, *That Sweet Enemy,* p. 388.

9 Flora Tristan, *London Journal: A Survey of London Life in the 1830s,* trans. Dennis Palmer and Giselle Pincetl (London: George Prior, 1980), p. 2.

10 Ibid., p. 7.

11 Ibid., pp. 7–8.

12 Crispi to his father, 17 January 1855, quoted in Christopher Duggan, *Francesco Crispi, 1818–1901: From Nation to Nationalism* (Oxford: Oxford University Press, 2002), p. 121.

13 Max Schlesinger, *Saunterings in and about London (Wanderungen durch London),* trans. Otto Wenckstern (London: Nathaniel Cooke, 1853), pp. 82–83.

14 Ibid., pp. 84–85.

15 J. Bayard Taylor, *Views A-foot; or, Europe Seen with Knapsack and Staff,* vol. 1 (London: Wiley and Putnam, 1847), p. 37.

16 Ibid., p. 383.

17 Nathaniel Hawthorne, *The Centenary Edition of the Works of Nathaniel Hawthorne,* vol. 22, *The English Notebooks, 1856–1860,* ed. Thomas Woodson and Bill Ellis (Columbus: Ohio State University Press, 1997), p. 412.

18 Ibid., p. 413.

19 Ibid.

20 Ibid., p. 414.

21 Ibid., p. 433.

22 Ibid., pp. 443–44.

23 Ibid., pp. 447–48.

24 Mark Twain to Olivia L. Clemens, 9 December 1873, in *Mark Twain's Letters,* vol. 5, *1872–1873,* ed. Lin Salamo and Harriet Elinor Smith (Berkeley: University of California Press, 1997), p. 497.

25 Ibid.

26 *Punch,* 20 December 1873, p. 248.

27 Charles Warren Stoddard, *Exits and Entrances: A Book of Essays and Sketches* (Boston: Lothrop, 1903), p. 67.

28 Mark Twain to Shirley Brooks, 12 December 1873, in *Mark Twain's Letters,* vol. 5, p. 510.

29 Mark Twain to Olivia L. Clemens, 13 and 15 December 1873, in *Mark Twain's Letters,* vol. 5, pp. 512-13.

30 Mary H. Krout, *A Looker-On in London* (London: B. F. Stevens & Brown, 1899), p. 37. Note Krout's reference to Milton's "darkness visible," another repeated image in both fiction and newspapers. See p. 13.

31 *Life and Letters of H. Taine,* part 2, *1853–1870,* trans. Mrs. R. L. Devonshire (London: Archibald Constable, 1904), p. 157.

32 Hippolyte Taine to his mother, 25 June 1860, in ibid., p. 168.

33 Hippolyte Taine to Madame H. Taine, 20 May 1871, in *Life and Letters of H. Taine,* part 3, *1870–1892,* trans. E. Sparvel-Bayly (London: Archibald Constable, 1908), p. 44.

34 Hippolyte Taine, *Notes on England,* trans. Edward Hyams (London: Thames and Hudson, 1957), pp. 8–10.

35 Tombs and Tombs, *That Sweet Enemy,* pp. 410–11.

36 Eça de Queirós, *Eça's English Letters,* ed. Alison Aiken, trans. Alison Aiken and Ann Stevens (Manchester, UK: Carcanet, 2000), p. 2.

37 Ibid., pp. 132–33.

38 Ibid., p. 134.

39 Ibid., p. 50.

40 Ibid., p. 55.

41 Ibid., pp. 150–51.

42 For more on Kipling's life in London, see Andrew Lycett, *Rudyard Kipling* (London: Weidenfeld and Nicolson, 1999), particularly pp. 183-218.

43 John Evelyn, who wrote *Fumifugium,* also lived in Villiers Street.

44 Rudyard Kipling to Edmonia Hill, 11 November 1889, in *The Letters of Rudyard Kipling,* vol. 1, *1872–1889,* ed. Thomas Pinney (London: Macmillan, 1990), p. 361.

45 Ibid.

46 Ibid. All quotations from "In Partibus" are from *London: A History in Verse,* ed. Mark Ford (Cambridge, MA: Harvard University Press, 2012), pp. 468–70.

47 Rudyard Kipling to Margaret Mackail, 18 January, 1892, in *The Letters of Rudyard Kipling,* vol. 2, *1890–1899,* ed. Thomas Pinney (London: Macmillan, 1990), p. 46.

48 Rudyard Kipling to Edmonia Hill, 3-25 December 1889 in *Letters,* vol. 1, p. 369; Kipling to John Addington Symonds, 9 December 1899, in ibid., p. 380.

49 Rudyard Kipling, *Abaft the Funeral* (New York: B. W. Dodge, 1909), p. 252.

50 Ibid., p. 254.

51 Quoted in John W. Graham, *The Destruction of Daylight: A Study in the Smoke Problem* (London: George Allen, 1907), pp. 14–15.

52 David Roberts to Provost Dawson, 21 March 1862, in *The Life of David Roberts, R.A., Compiled from His Journals and Other Sources,* by James Ballantine (Edinburgh, UK: Adam and Charles Black, 1866), p. 216; see also Lynda Nead, *Victorian Babylon: People, Streets, and Images in Nineteenth-Century London* (New Haven, CT: Yale University Press, 2000), p. 56.

53 Samuel Luke Fildes to Henry Woods, 1 January 1880, in Caroline Dakers, *The Holland Park Circle: Artists and Victorian Society* (New Haven, CT: Yale University Press, 1999), p. 238.

54 Ibid.

55 David Roberts to Christine, 22 December 1838, in *Life of David Roberts*, p. 104.

56 Luke Howard, *The Climate of London Deduced from Meteorological Observations, Made in the Metropolis, and at Various Places around It*, vol. 3 (London: Harvey and Darton, 1833), p. 303.

57 Frederick Leighton, "An Artist's View of the Smoke Question," *Builder*, 25 March 1882, p. 367.

58 Brunet Debaines, "Trafalgar Square," *Art Journal* (May 1888): p. 149.

59 Benjamin Robert Haydon, *Life of Benjamin Robert Haydon, Historical Painter, from His Autobiography and Journals*, vol. 1, ed. Tom Taylor (London: Longman, Brown, Green, and Longmans, 1853), pp. 50–51. This autobiography, based on Haydon's diaries, was published after the painter's suicide in 1846.

60 See Canaletto's *London: The Thames and the City of Westminster from Lambeth*, probably 1746, Lobkowicz Collections, Nelahozeves Castle, Czech Republic.

61 M. A. Wyllie, *We Were One: A Life of W. L. Wyllie* (London: G. Bell & Sons, 1935), p. 45.

62 Ibid., pp. 45–46.

63 David Law, "Our Illustrations," *Art Journal* (July 1884): p. 200.

64 Eugène Delacroix to Messieurs Guillemardet and Pierret, 27 May 1825, "Letters from England or on English Art," trans. Edouard Roditi, *London Magazine*, February–March 1993, p. 49.

65 Giuseppe Pecchio, *Semi-serious Observations of an Italian Exile during His Residence in England* (London: E. Wilson, 1833), pp. 2–3. Note the reference again to Milton's famous phrase "darkness visible," a repeated trope.

66 Taine, *Notes on England*, p. 8.

67 Henry James, "London at Midsummer" in *Portraits of Places* (London: Duckworth, 2001), p. 191. Quoted in Nicholas Freeman, *Conceiving the City: London, Literature, and Art, 1870–1914* (Oxford: Oxford University Press, 2007), p. 92.

68 James Russell Lowell to Miss Sedgwick, 3 October 1888, in *Letters of James Russell Lowell*, vol. 3 (New York: AMS, 1966), p. 215.

69 Richard Dorment and Margaret F. MacDonald, *James McNeill Whistler* (London: Tate Gallery Publications, 1994), p. 108.

70 John House, "Visions of the Thames," in *Monet's London: Artists' Reflections on the Thames, 1859–1914* (St. Petersburg, FL: Museum of Fine Arts, 2005), p. 23.

71 *Standard*, 2 January 1884.

72 *Kensington News*, 29 May 1884.

73 John Ruskin, *Fors Clavigera*, ed. Dinah Birch (Edinburgh, UK: Edinburgh University Press, 2000), p. 265.

74 James McNeill Whistler, *Mr. Whistler's "Ten O'clock"* (London: Chatto and Windus, 1888), p. 15.

75 George Gissing, "On Battersea Bridge," *Pall Mall Gazette,* 30 November 1883, quoted in Jeremy Tambling, *Going Astray: Dickens and London* (Harlow, UK: Pearson, 2009), p. 266.

76 Claude Monet to Paul Durand-Ruel, 23 March 1903, quoted in *Monet and Modernism,* ed. Karin Sagner-Düchting (London: Prestel, 2001), p. 58.

77 Quoted in Daniel Wildenstein, *Monet, or, The Triumph of Impressionism* (Cologne, Germany: Taschen, 1999), p. 345.

78 Quoted in Nicholas Reed, *Monet and the Thames* (London: Lilburne, 1998), p. 34.

79 For the accuracy of Monet's pictures of London fogs, see John E. Thornes and Gemma Metherell, "Monet's 'London Series,'" in *Weather, Climate, Culture,* ed. Sarah Strauss and Ben Orlove (Oxford, UK: Berg, 2003), pp. 154–56.

80 René Gimpel, *Diary of an Art Dealer,* trans. John Rosenberg (London: Pimlico, 1992), p. 129.

81 Octave Mirbeau, *Correspondance avec Claude Monet,* ed. Pierre Michel and Jean-François Nivet (France:,Du Lérot,éditeur, 1990), p. 260.

82 Emma Bullet, "Macmonnies, the Sculptor, Working Hard as a Painter," *Eagle* (Brooklyn), 8 September 1901, p. 14.

83 Ruth B. Antosh, *Reality and Illusion in the Novels of J.-K. Huysmans* (Amsterdam: Rodopi, 1986), p. 7.

84 Ibid., p. 64.

85 Joris-Karl Huysmans, *Against Nature,* trans. Robert Baldick (1884; repr., London: Penguin Books, 2003), pp. 118, 119.

86 Ibid., p. 119.

87 Ibid., p. 120.

88 Ibid.

89 Ibid., p. 122.

90 Ibid., p. 123.

91 Ibid., p. 124.

92 Ibid., p. 129.

93 Ibid.

94 Oscar Wilde, "The Decay of Lying" (1891), in *De Profundis and Other Writings* (London: Penguin, 1984), pp. 78–79.

95 Arthur Symons, *London: A Book of Aspects* (London: privately printed, 1909), pp. 2–3.

96 Min-ch'ien T. Z. Tyau, *London through Chinese Eyes; or, My Seven and a Half Years in London* (London: Swarthmore, 1920), p. 29.

97 Ibid., p. 31.

98 Ibid.

99 Ibid., p. 30.

100 Yoshio Markino, *A Japanese Artist in London* (London: Chatto and Windus, 1919), p. 104.

101 Yoshio Markino, "An Essay by the Artist," in W. J. Loftie, *The Colour of London: Historic, Personal, & Local* (London: Chatto and Windus, 1914), pp. xxxvii–xxxviii.

102 Markino, *Japanese Artist in London,* p. 189.

103 Sammy I. Tsunematsu, introduction to *A Japanese Artist in London,* by Yoshio Markino (1919; repr., Brighton, UK: In Print, 1991), p. v.

104 Ibid., p. xix.

105 Marion Spielmann, introduction to Loftie, *Colour of London,* p. vii.

106 Markino, *Japanese Artist in London* (1919), p. 4.

107 Rose Barton, *Familiar London* (London: Adam and Charles Black, 1904), p. 5.

108 Ibid.

109 Quoted in *Rose Barton R.W.S.: Exhibition of Watercolours and Drawings* (1987: Crawford Municipal Art Gallery, Cork), p. 10.

110 Barton, *Familiar London,* pp. 195–96.

111 *Rose Barton R.W.S.: Exhibition of Watercolours and Drawings,* p. 26, plate 34.

112 In Barton, *Familiar London,* plate opposite p. 26.

113 Ibid., p. 196.

114 Rose Barton to Mildred Anne Butler, 23 January 1924, Department of History of Art, Trinity College, Dublin, quoted in *Rose Barton R.W.S.: Exhibition of Watercolours and Drawings,* p. 13.

115 Alvin Langdon Coburn, Introduction by Hilaire Belloc, *London* (London: Duckworth, 1909).

116 Ibid., p. 20.

117 Alvin Langdon Coburn, *Alvin Langdon Coburn, Photographer: An Autobiography,* ed. Helmut Gernsheim and Alison Gernsheim (1966; repr., New York: Dover, 1978), p. 74.

118 George Bernard Shaw, unpublished foreword for *London,* quoted in ibid.

119 Quoted in Coburn, *Alvin Langdon Coburn,* p. 77.

120 See Museum of London, Image number: 006856.

121 Belloc, essay, p. 18.

122 James McNeill Whistler, *The Gentle Art of Making Enemies* (1890; repr., London: Heinemann, 1994), p. 128.

6. London Apocalypse

1 Edward Maitland, *By and By: An Historical Romance of the Future,* vol. 1 (London: Richard Bentley and Son, 1873), p. 98.

2 Ibid.

3 Eric Ashby and Mary Anderson, "Studies in the Politics of Environmental Protection: The Historical Roots of the British Clean Air Act, 1956: II. The

Appeal to Public Opinion over Domestic Smoke, 1880–1892," *Interdisciplinary Science Reviews* 2, no. 1 (1977): pp. 9–13.

4 David Stradling and Peter Thorsheim, "The Smoke of Great Cities: British and American Efforts to Control Air Pollution, 1860–1914," *Environmental History* 4, no. 1 (1999): p. 15.

5 Peter Brimblecombe, *The Big Smoke: A History of Air Pollution in London since Medieval Times* (London: Methuen, 1987), pp. 136–60.

6 *The Times*, 10 January 1881, p. 4, col. F.

7 Ibid., p. 116; and Stradling and Thorsheim, "Smoke of Great Cities," p. 11.

8 Stradling and Thorsheim, "Smoke of Great Cities," p. 11.

9 HL Deb 26 May 1884 vol 288 cc1265–73 (1267).

10 Brimblecombe, *Big Smoke*, p. 116.

11 Ibid., p. 163.

12 Eric Ashby and Mary Anderson, "Studies in the Politics of Environmental Protection: The Historical Roots of the British Clean Air Act, 1956: III. The Ripening of Public Opinion, 1898–1952," *Interdisciplinary Science Reviews* 2, no. 3 (1977): pp. 194–95.

13 Ian O'Neill, email to the author, 28 January 2015.

14 Sir William Richmond, letter to *The Times*, 19 November 1898, p. 11, col. D. See also *The Times*, 21 November 1898, p. 12, col. F.

15 *The Times*, 18 November 1898, p. 8, col. D.

16 Quoted in Ashby and Anderson, "Studies: III," p. 192.

17 Ibid., pp. 192–93.

18 Henry T. Bernstein, "The Mysterious Disappearance of Edwardian London Fog," *London Journal* 11, no. 2 (1975): p. 202.

19 Stephen Inwood, *City of Cities: The Birth of Modern London* (London: Macmillan, 2005), p. 8.

20 Ashby and Anderson, "Studies: III," p. 194.

21 Ibid., p. 192.

22 John Burnett, *A Social History of Housing, 1815–1985*, 2nd ed. (London: Routledge, 1986), pp. 215–16.

23 Quoted in Inwood, *City of Cities*, p. 8.

24 Roy Porter, *London: A Social History* (Cambridge, MA: Harvard University Press, 1994), pp. 330–31.

25 Bernstein, "Mysterious Disappearance," pp. 201–6.

26 "An Encouraging Feature of the Recent Fog," *The Lancet* 11 (October 1899): p. 1183.

27 Sir C. A. Cookson, "A Smokeless London," *Journal of State Medicine* 9 (November 1901): p. 692.

28 Arnold Marsh, "R. Morton Rowe: An Interview," *Journal of the National Smoke Abatement Society* 2 (1931): p. 5.

29 Fred. M. White, "The Four Days' Night," *Pearson's Magazine* 15 (1903): pp. 166–78.

30 Ibid., p. 167.

31 Ibid., p. 171.

32 Ibid., p. 170.

33 Ibid., p. 173.

34 Ibid., p. 174.

35 Ibid.

36 For earliest reference to a "Fog Dispersing Machine" invented by Demitrio Maggiora see *Washington Post*, 1 December 1907, p. 4.

37 White, "The Four Days' Night," p. 174 (my italics).

38 Ibid., p. 178.

39 G. R. Searle, *A New England? Peace and War, 1886–1918* (Oxford, UK: Clarendon, 2004), p. 201.

40 Ibid., p. 195–96.

41 I. F. Clarke's *Voices Prophesying War* (London: Panther, 1970) gives a good overview of this literature and the alarmism that underlay it.

42 Hugh Owen, "The Poison Cloud," *Pearson's Magazine* 26 (1908): pp. 657–89.

43 Ibid., pp. 659, 660.

44 Ibid., p. 664.

45 Roy Church, *The History of the British Coal Industry, 1830–1913: Victorian Preeminence* (Oxford, UK: Clarendon, 1986), p. 37.

46 For more on this topic, see Anne Kershen, "The 1905 Aliens Act," *History Today* 55 (2005): pp. 13–19.

47 Owen, "Poison Cloud," p. 660.

48 Ibid., p. 666.

49 Ibid.

50 Ibid. p. 661.

51 Ibid., p. 665.

52 Ibid., p. 679.

53 It is surprising that Owen should have chosen smallpox to describe one of the possible effects of this situation since smallpox had been one of the success stories of the nineteenth century. A compulsory vaccination campaign had led to a decline in deaths from smallpox after Edward Jenner's discovery of the effectiveness of the cowpox vaccine in 1798; indeed, according to Anthony Wohl, this had "accounted for 20 percent of the total reduction in mortality from disease in Victoria's reign." See Anthony S. Wohl, *Endangered Lives: Public Health in Victorian Britain* (London: J. M. Dent and Sons, 1983), p. 132. It was more likely that the danger would have been from cholera, typhoid, or some other waterborne disease, especially if the water supply had been infected by the dead bodies of people and animals.

54 Owen, "Poison Cloud," p. 671.

55 Ibid., p. 688.

56 Ibid., p. 677.

57 Ibid., p. 684.

58 For more, see Searle, *A New England?*, pp. 312–14.

59 Gareth Stedman Jones, *Outcast London: A Study in the Relationship between Classes in Victorian Society* (Oxford: Clarendon, 1984), p. 325.

60 Quoted in Alan Palmer, *The East End: Four Centuries of London Life* (London: John Murray, 1989), p. 106.

61 "Tariff Reform and Unemployment," 15 December 1904, in *Mr. Chamberlain's Speeches,* vol. 2, ed. Charles W. Boyd (London: Constable, 1914), p. 262.

62 Owen, "Poison Cloud," p. 688.

63 Ibid., p. 667.

64 Arthur Conan Doyle, *The Poison Belt* (London: Hodder and Stoughton, 1913).

65 Edward Garnett, "The Novel of the Week," *Nation,* 23 September 1907, quoted in "Contemporary Reviews," *Conrad: The Secret Agent: A Casebook,* ed. Ian Watt (London: Macmillan, 1973), p. 43.

66 Joseph Conrad, *The Secret Agent* (1907; repr., London: Penguin, 1963), p. 65.

67 Ibid., p. 87.

68 Ibid., p. 77.

69 Ibid., p. 19.

70 Ibid., p. 31.

71 Ibid., p. 218.

72 Ibid., pp. 249, 88.

73 Ibid., p. 88.

74 Ibid.

75 Ibid., p. 124.

76 Ibid.

77 Joseph Conrad, *A Personal Record* (London: Penguin Books, 1998), p. 116. Conrad refers to Dickens as "the master for which I have such an admiration, or rather such an intense and unreasoning affection, dating from the days of my childhood."

78 Charles Dickens, *Bleak House*, ed. Norman Page (1853; repr., London: Penguin, 1974), p. 49.

79 Conrad, *The Secret Agent,* p. 218.

80 Ibid., p. 241.

81 Ibid., p. 233.

82 Ibid., p. 196.

83 Ibid.

84 Arthur Machen, *The Great God Pan* and *The Hill of Dreams* (1916 and 1907; repr., New York: Dover Publications, 2006), pp. 190–91. Quoted in Nicholas Freeman, *Conceiving the City: London, Literature, and Art, 1870–1914* (Oxford: Oxford University Press, 2007), pp. 158–59.

85 Richard Harding Davis to Mother, 29 December 1897, in *Adventures and Letters of Richard Harding Davis,* ed. Charles Belmont Davis (New York: Charles Scribner's Sons, 1917), p. 220.

86 Ibid., pp. 220–21.

87 Ibid., pp. 222–23.

88 Richard Harding Davis, *In the Fog* (London: Heinemann, 1902), pp. 28–29.

89 Ibid., p. 31.

90 Ibid., p. 33.

91 Ibid.

92 Sir Arthur Conan Doyle, "The Adventure of the Bruce-Partington Plans," in *His Last Bow: Some Reminiscences of Sherlock Holmes* (London: Penguin, 1997), pp. 83–84. First published in the *Strand Magazine* in December 1908 and in *Collier's Weekly* on 12 December 1908.

93 Sir Arthur Conan Doyle, *The Sign of Four* (1890; repr., London: Penguin, 2001), p. 21.

94 Ibid., p. 12.

95 Ibid.

96 Ibid., p. 21.

97 Ibid., p. 24, p. 21.

98 Ibid.

99 Ibid.

100 Ibid., p. 34.

101 Sir Arthur Conan Doyle, "The Adventure of the Copper Beeches" (1892), in *The Adventures and Memoirs of Sherlock Holmes* (London: Vintage, 2009), p. 230.

102 Ibid.

103 Ibid.

104 Conan Doyle, "Adventure of the Bruce-Partington Plans," p. 83.

105 Ibid., p. 95.

106 Ibid., p. 112.

107 Ibid., p. 91.

108 Ibid., p. 103.

109 Ibid., p. 105.

110 Sir Arthur Conan Doyle, "The Red Circle" (1911), in *The New Annotated Sherlock Holmes,* vol. 2 (New York: W. W. Norton & Company, 2005), p. 1280. Published in the *Strand Magazine* in March and April 1911.

111 Sir Arthur Conan Doyle, "The Dying Detective" (1913), in ibid., p. 1342. First published in the *Strand Magazine* in December 1913.

112 Conan Doyle, *Sign of Four,* p. 34.

113 Daniel Stashower, *Teller of Tales: The Life of Arthur Conan Doyle* (London: Allen Lane, 2000), p. 242.

114 David Stephenson, *With Our Backs to the Wall: Victory and Defeat in 1918* (London: Penguin, 2011), pp. 200–205.

7. LAND OF THE LIVING DEAD

1 Min-Ch'ien T. Z. Tyau, *London through Chinese Eyes; or, My Seven and a Half Years in London* (London: Swarthmore, 1920), p. 29.

2 Eric Ashby and Mary Anderson, "Studies in the Politics of Environmental Protection: The Historical Roots of the British Clean Air Act, 1956: III. The Ripening of Public Opinion, 1898–1952," *Interdisciplinary Science Reviews* 2, no. 3 (1977): p. 194.

3 *The Times,* 29 November 1921, p. 7, col. A.

4 Ibid.

5 *Pall Mall and Globe,* 28 November 1921, p. 1. cols. A and B.

6 *The Times,* 29 November 1921, p. 7. col. A.

7 *Pall Mall and Globe,* 28 November 1921, p. 2, col. E.

8 Ibid.

9 *The Times,* 29 November 1921, p. 13, col. E.

10 *Pall Mall and Globe,* 23 January 1922, p. 8. col. C.

11 Ibid.

12 *The Times,* 23 January 1922, p. 6, col. E.

13 *Pall Mall Gazette,* 16 November 1922, p. 9, col. A.

14 *The Times,* 17 November 1922, p. 9, col. A.

15 *The Times,* 22 November 1922, p. 14, col. A.

16 *Pall Mall Gazette,* 14 November 1922, p. 9, col. C. See also *The Times,* 15 November 1922, p. 16, col. A, on Sir Cyril Cobb, Unionist Party candidate, canvassing in fog.

17 *Pall Mall Gazette,* 15 November 1922, p. 1, col. B.

18 Carmel Haden Guest, *Children of the Fog: A Novel of Southwark* (London: George G. Harrap, 1927), p. 7.

19 Ibid.

20 Ibid., p. 303.

21 Ibid., p. 152.

22 Ibid., p. 217.

23 Ibid., pp. 210–11.

24 Ibid., p. 211.

25 T. S. Eliot, *The Waste Land,* in *The Waste Land and Other Writings* (New York: Random House, 2001), p. 40, lines 60–61.

26 *The Times,* 5 April 1922, p. 13, col. G. Also see *The Times,* 23 August 1921, p. 9, col. G.

27 *The Times,* 29 November 1921, p. 7, col. A.

28 *Pall Mall and Globe,* 28 November 1921, cols. A and B.

29 Ibid.

30 *The Times,* 29 November 1921, p. 7, col. A.

31 John S. Owens and Napier Shaw, *The Smoke Problem of Great Cities* (London: Constable, 1925).

32 *The Times,* 3 December 1924, p. 18, col. A.

33 Ibid., p. 14, col. B.

34 *The Times,* 11 December 1924, p. 14, col. D.

35 Ibid., p. 18, col. A. For a list of burglaries under cover of fog, see also ibid., p. 16, col. A.

36 *The Times,* 12 December 1924, p. 14, col. E.

37 *Illustrated London News,* 20 December, 1924, p. 1207.

38 *The Times,* 12 January 1925, p. 12, col. F.

39 Ibid.

40 Ibid., p. 13, col. E.

41 *Evening Standard,* 1 October 1925, p. 9, col. A.

42 *Evening Standard,* 4 December 1925, p. 1, cols. B and C.

43 Ibid.

44 Henry Vollam Morton, *The Heart of London* (London: Methuen, 1926), pp. 74–75.

45 *Evening Standard,* 5 December 1925, p. 7, cols. A and B.

46 For further details, see Michael Bartholomew, *In Search of H. V. Morton* (London: Methuen, 2004), pp. 83–86.

47 Morton, *Heart of London,* p. 34.

48 Ibid.

49 Ibid., p. 35.

50 Ibid., p. 34.

51 Henry Vollam Morton, *A London Year* (London: Methuen, 1926), p. 195.

52 Ibid., p. 196.

53 Ibid.

54 *Punch, or The London Charivari,* 21 March 1923, p. 275.

55 *The Times,* 11 December 1924, p. 15, col. E.

56 *Evening Standard,* 4 December 1925, p. 7, cols. A and B.

57 Ibid.

58 Ibid. The tide of opinion was not always in favour of the coal fire. For support of gas and electricity, see *The Times,* 23 January 1931, p. 15, col. E.

59 Edward Garnett to John Galsworthy, 27 May 1905, in *Letters from John Galsworthy, 1900–1932,* ed. Edward Garnett (London: Jonathan Cape, 1934), p. 68. In fact *The Forsyte Saga* was dedicated to Garnett. Interestingly Garnett is the same person who commented on the fog in Conrad's *The Secret Agent* (see above, p. 218).

60 Garnett to Galsworthy, 27 May 1905, in ibid., pp. 69–70.

61 Galsworthy to Garnett, 2 June 1905, in ibid., p. 77.

62 John Galsworthy, *The Forsyte Saga* (Oxford: Oxford University Press, 1999) p. 250.

63 Ibid., p. 252.

64 Ibid., p. 253.

65 Ibid., p. 252.

66 Ibid., p. 254.

67 Ibid., pp. 255–56.

68 Ibid., p. 256.

69 Ibid., pp. 256–59.

70 Ibid., p. 291.

71 See Chapter 5, especially the thoughts of Flora Tristan and Hippolyte Taine.

72 John Galsworthy, *A Modern Comedy* (London: Penguin Books, 1980), p. 426.

73 Ibid., pp. 428–30.

74 Ibid., p. 430.

75 The scene is set in December 1924, as Soames receives a letter dated January 6, 1925, a few pages later, and they have celebrated Christmas since this foggy day. Ibid., p. 438.

76 *The Times,* 17 December 1926, p. 10, col. F.

77 *The Times,* 25 November 1929, p. 12, col. E.

78 *The Times,* 2 December 1921, p. 6, col. A.

79 *The Times,* 30 March 1921, p. 4, col. C.

80 HL Deb 24 March 1914 vol 15 cc661–72 (662).

81 Ibid.

82 For more on these attempts to introduce a Bill at this time, see Ashby and Anderson, "Studies," p. 196.

83 Ministry of Health, *Committee on Smoke and Noxious Vapours Abatement, Final Report* (London: HMSO, 1921).

84 HC Deb 29 November 1922 vol 159 c695.

85 The pressure for Smoke Abatement was continued by others supporting Newton; see HL Deb 25 April 1923 vol 53 cc873–914.

86 *The Times,* 24 July 1953, p. 12, col. A.

87 HL Deb 29 November 1920 vol 42 cc696–703 (696).

88 Ibid., (698).

89 For debates, see HC Deb 16 December 1921 vol 149 cc300–1W; HL Deb 10 May 1922 vol 50 cc371–4.

90 HL Deb 10 July 1922 vol 51 cc317–21 (320).

91 Ashby and Anderson, "Studies," pp. 198–99.

92 HL Deb 24 July 1922 vol 51 cc685–96.

93 HC Deb 06 March 1919 vol 113 cc611–2 (612). For Mond's reply, see HC Deb 28 October 1920 vol 133 cc1996–8W. For continuing debate, see HL Deb 24 July 1922 vol 51 cc685–96.

94 HC Deb 30 November 1926 vol 200 cc1020–1W.

95 HL Deb 29 May 1923 vol 54 cc267–72 (269).

96 HL Deb 26 July 1923 vol 54 cc1414–22.

97 For further debates, see HL Deb 27 May 1924 vol 57 cc688–9; and HC Deb 28 May 1924 vol 174 c440W.

98 For discussion of the second reading, see HL Deb 16 July 1924 vol 58 cc652–9; and Newton's reactions to further delays: HL Deb 28 July 1924 vol 58 c1110.

99 HL Deb 01 August 1924 vol 59 cc203–21 (207).

100 Ibid., (216).

101 Ibid., (220).

102 *The Times*, 22 October 1925, p. 14, col. D.

103 HC Deb 10 December 1925 vol 189 c717W.

104 For further details of the debate, see HL Deb 23 March 1926 vol 63 cc714–26; and HC Deb 25 March 1926 vol 193 cc1370–1; for the Bill's progress through the legislature, see Ashby and Anderson, "Studies," pp. 196–200.

105 HL Deb 22 April 1926 vol 63 cc898–932.

106 HC Deb 22 June 1926 vol 197 cc264–318 (266).

107 Ashby and Anderson, "Studies," p. 201.

108 HC Deb 22 June 1926 vol 197 cc264–318 (276).

109 Ibid., (278).

110 Ibid., (279).

111 Ibid., (284).

112 Ibid., (287–88).

113 Ibid., (302).

114 *The Times*, 26 November 1926, p. 18, col. D.

115 *The Times*, 30 November 1926, p. 10, col. C.

116 Quoted in Ashby and Anderson, "Studies," p. 201.

117 Ibid., p. 202.

118 *The Times*, 5 April 1922, p. 13, col. G; Ashby and Anderson, "Studies," p. 202.

119 HC Deb 01 June 1921 vol 142 cc1048–9.

120 *The Times*, 24 November 1927, p. 15, col. E.

121 Ibid., p. 14, col. F.

122 *The Times*, 30 November 1927, p. 14, col. C.

123 *The Times*, 29 November 1927, p. 12, col. E.

124 *The Times*, 7 November 1928, p. 12, col. E.

125 Rose Macaulay, introduction to *Fumifugium*, by John Evelyn (London: National Smoke Abatement Society, 1933), p. 4.

126 Sarah LeFanu, *Rose Macaulay* (London: Virago, 2003), p. 198.

127 *The Times*, 2 March 1934, p. 15, col. E.

128 Ashby and Anderson, "Studies," p. 202.

129 Ibid., p. 194.

130 *The Times*, 22 January 1930, p. 18, col. A.

131 *The Times,* 28 November 1930, p. 20, col. A; and *The Times,* 6 December 1930, p. 16, col. A.

132 *The Times,* 18 December 1930, p. 18, col. A; and *The Times,* 23 December 1930, p. 14, col A.

133 Ben Travers, *A-Sitting on a Gate: Autobiography* (London: W. H. Allen, 1978), p. 110. *A Night Like This* was first produced on February 18, 1930, at the Aldwych and enjoyed 268 performances. A "growler" is actually a secondhand "clarence," which was a closed, four-wheeled, horse-drawn carriage in which the passengers would sit inside and the driver would sit outside. "Growlers" earned their name because of the sound they made on the cobbled streets of London.

134 *The Times,* 28 October 1931, p. 16, col. A; and *The Times,* 1 December 1931, p. 18, col. A.

135 Eric Hobsbawm, "Tagebuch," 18–23 November 1934 (manuscript in private possession). Trans. Richard J. Evans.

136 See https://www.youtube.com/watch?v=NnB81GsBN8o.

137 George Gershwin and Ira Gershwin, "A Foggy Day in London Town."

138 *The Times,* 14 January 1933, p. 14. col. A; *The Times,* 23 January 1934, p. 16, col. A; *The Times,* 24 December 1935, p. 7, col. C; *The Times,* 25 February 1936, p. 18, col. A; *The Times,* 23 September 1936, p. 7, col. B; *The Times,* 26 October 1938, p. 18, col. A; *The Times,* 7 January 1939, p. 9, col. B.

139 *The Times,* 26 November 1934, p. 13, col. D.

140 *The Times,* 7 June 1935, p. 17, col. E.

141 Chiang Yee, *The Silent Traveller: A Chinese Artist in Lakeland* (London: Country Life, 1937), p. 4.

142 Ibid., p. 5.

143 Chiang Yee, *The Silent Traveller in London* (1938; repr., Oxford, UK: Signal Books, 2002), p. 59.

144 Ibid., p. 60.

145 Ibid., pp. 60–61.

146 Ibid., p. 60.

147 Ibid., p. 64.

148 Ibid., p. 61.

149 *The Times,* 2 January 1934, p. 10, col. D.

150 Chiang, *Silent Traveller in London,* p. 61.

151 Ibid., p. 63.

152 Yuki Yoshida, *Whispering Leaves in Grosvenor Square, 1936–37* (1938; repr., Kent, UK: Global Oriental, 1997), p. 72.

153 Ibid., pp. 69–70.

154 *The Times,* 13 December 1930, p. 10, col. A. William Arbuthnot-Lane was part of the deputation that visited Sir Alfred Mond, the then Minister of Health, in March 1922.

155 *The Times,* 1 December 1934, p. 10, col. A.

156 George Barker, "Battersea Park" (1940), in *Thames: An Anthology of River Poems,* ed. Anna Adams (London: Enitharmon, 1999), p. 45, lines 2–4.

157 Ibid., lines 4–6.

158 Ibid., lines 19–21.

159 John Updike, introduction to *Loving, Living, Party Going,* by Henry Green (London: Penguin, 1978), p. 13.

160 Jeremy Treglown, "Introduction" to Henry Green, *Party Going* (London: Harvill, 1996), p. vii.

161 Henry Green, *Party Going* (London: Harvill, 1996), p. 1.

162 Ibid.

163 Ibid., p. 7.

164 Ibid.

165 Ibid., pp. 8–9.

166 Ibid., p. 9.

167 Ibid., pp. 27–28.

168 Ibid., p. 15.

169 Ibid., p. 25.

170 Ibid., p. 27.

171 Ibid.

172 Ibid., p. 129.

173 Frank Kermode, *The Genesis of Secrecy: On the Interpretation of Narrative* (Cambridge, MA: Harvard University Press, 1979), p. 11. See Kermode's interpretation of the novel on pp. 5–17.

174 Ibid., p. 14.

175 Ibid.

8. The Last Gasp

1 Evelyn Waugh, *Put Out More Flags* (1941; repr., London: Penguin, 2000), pp. 174–75.

2 Frank Markham later became Major Sir Frank Markham. He represented Nottingham South at this time as a National Labour MP; in 1950 he was elected by Buckingham as a Conservative representative.

3 HC Deb 29 February 1944 vol 397 cc1251–321 (1313).

4 HC Deb 14 March 1944 vol 398 c5. For other occasions smoke abatement was raised in the House of Commons debates, see HC Deb 28 March 1944 vol 398 cc1233–4 (1234); HC Deb 05 April 1944 vol 398 c2019W; HC Deb 20 June 1944 vol 401 cc29–153 (116); HC Deb 26 October 1944 vol 404 cc340–1; HC Deb 19 December 1944 vol 406 c1641. W. Keeling had been awarded the Military Cross in 1918. He was director of a coal company, became Mayor of Westminster in 1945, and was knighted in 1952.

5   *Evening Standard,* 19 January 1946, p. 2, col. A.

6   HC Deb 16 March 1945 vol 409 cc536–57 (547).

7   See *Evening Standard,* 21 January 1945, p. 1, col. F; and *Evening Standard,* 22 January 1945, p. 1, col. A.

8   *Time,* 14 January 1946.

9   Ibid.

10 *The Times,* 25 November 1948, p. 5, col. D.

11 Ibid.

12 *Evening Standard,* 30 November 1948, p. 1, col. F.

13 *Evening Standard,* 29 November 1948, p. 1, cols. A and B.

14 *Evening Standard,* 1 December 1948, p. 8, col. C

15 *Evening Standard,* 30 November 1948, p. 1, col. F.

16 *The Times,* 4 December 1948, p. 5, col. D.

17 *Evening Standard,* 29 November 1948, p. 2, col. C.

18 *Evening Standard,* 1 December 1948, p. 6, col. E.

19 See *Evening Standard,* 1 December 1948, p. 8, col. C, and p. 3, col. F.

20 *Evening Standard,* 29 November 1948, p. 2, col. A.

21 Ibid.

22 *The Times,* 10 December 1948, p. 2, col. F.

23 HC Deb 05 February 1948 vol 446 cc312–3W.

24 HC Deb 09 December 1948 vol 459 cc557–8 (557).

25 Ibid.

26 HC Deb 02 June 1949 vol 465 c2297.

27 HC Deb 19 July 1949 vol 467 c59W.

28 HC Deb 14 April 1949 vol 463 cc255–6W.

29 HC Deb 19 September 1950 vol 478 cc1841–50 (1843).

30 Ibid., 1849.

31 *Evening Standard,* 8 December 1945, p. 6.

32 Henry Vollam Morton, *In Search of London* (1951; repr., London: Methuen, 1988), p. 144.

33 Ibid., p. 145.

34 Ibid., p. 144.

35 Doreen Fischer, quoted in Greg Neale, ed., "Witness: The Great London Smog, December 1952," *BBC History Magazine* 3, no. 12 (December 2002): p. 48.

36 Stephen F. Kelly, *You've Never Had It So Good! Recollections of Life in the 1950s* (Stroud, UK: History Press, 2012), p. 39.

37 *The Times,* 8 December 1952, p. 8, col. A.

38 *The Times,* 9 December, 1952, p. 8, col. D.

39 Ibid.; see also Peter Brimblecombe, *The Big Smoke: A History of Air Pollution in London since Medieval Times* (London: Methuen, 1987), pp. 165–69.

40 *The Times,* 8 December 1952, p. 3, col. E.

41 Ibid., p. 8, col. A.

42 HC Deb 08 December 1952 vol 509 cc106–201 (165); and see David Renton (Huntingdon), HC Deb 05 December 1952 vol 508 cc1989–2009 (1999).

43 Mary Sutherland, quoted in Neale, "Witness," p. 48.

44 *The Times*, 8 December 1952, p. 8, col. A.

45 London Airport's name was changed to Heathrow in 1966.

46 *The Times*, 1 November 1950, p. 4, col. E.

47 *The Times*, 8 December 1952, p. 8, col. A.

48 Ibid.

49 *The Times*, 9 December 1952, p. 8, col. D.

50 *The Times*, 8 December 1952, p. 8, col. A.

51 Ibid., p. 8, col. B.

52 Ibid.

53 Carol Handley, email to the author, May 2012.

54 *The Times*, 8 December 1952, p. 8, col. A.

55 "The London Fog: A First Survey of the December Disaster," *Smokeless Air: The Smoke Abatement Journal* 85 (Spring 1953): p. 107.

56 "The Anti-Smog Bottle," *Smokeless Air: The Smoke Abatement Journal* 96 (Winter 1955): p. 106.

57 "Smoke and the Zoo: How the Animals Are Affected," *Journal of the National Smoke Abatement Society* 25, vol. vii, (February 1936), p. 9. *The Journal of the National Smoke Abatement Society* changed its name to *Smokeless Air* in 1939.

58 Devra Davis, quoted in Neale, "Witness," p. 49.

59 *The Times*, 20 December 1952, p. 3, col. C. See also HC Deb 18 December 1952 vol 509 c237W.

60 Michelle L. Bell, Devra L. Davis, and Tony Fletcher, "A Retrospective Assessment of Mortality from the London Smog Episode of 1952: The Role of Influenza and Pollution," *Environmental Health Perspectives* 112, no. 1 (2004): p. 8.

61 *The Times*, 20 December 1952, p. 3, col. C.

62 Bell, Davis, and Fletcher, "Retrospective Assessment," p. 8.

63 Ibid.

64 *Daily Express*, 18 March 1953, p. 5.

65 "A Personal Experience," Letter from Donald V. H. Smith, *Smokeless Air: The Smoke Abatement Journal* 86 (Summer 1953): p. 151.

66 Ibid.

67 "The Economic Costs," *Smokeless Air* 85 (Spring 1953): p. 110.

68 Lynne Reid Banks, *The L-Shaped Room* (1960; repr., London: Vintage, 2004), p. 115.

69 Ibid., p. 143–44.

70 "The Bournemouth Conference," *Smokeless Air* 96 (Winter 1955): p. 85.

71 Sam Selvon, *The Lonely Londoners* (1956; repr., London: Penguin, 2006), p. 1.

72 Ibid., p. 4.

73 Ibid., p. 5.

74 Ibid., p. 12. "Test" is a person and "Watchekong" are shoes.

75 Ibid., p. 23.

76 Ibid., p. 57.

77 Ibid., p. 134.

78 Ibid., p. 1.

79 Susheila Nasta, introduction to ibid., p. viii.

80 P. D. James, introduction to *London Particular* (1952), by Christianna Brand (London: Pandora, 1988), p. vii.

81 Ibid.

82 Brand, *London Particular,* p. 1.

83 Ibid.

84 Ibid., p. 3.

85 J. J. Marric, *Gideon's Fog* (New York: Harper, 1974), p. 3.

86 Ibid., p. 4.

87 Ibid., p. 21.

88 Ibid.

89 Ibid., p. 101.

90 Frankie Howerd, *On the Way I Lost It* (London: W. H. Allen, 1976), p. 106.

91 Andy Merriman, *Margaret Rutherford: Dreadnought With Good Manners* (London: Aurum Press Ltd, 2009), pp. 133–34.

92 HC Deb 17 December 1952 vol 509 c221W.

93 HC Deb 22 January 1953 vol 510 cc382–3.

94 Ibid.

95 Ibid. See HC Deb 15 December 1953 vol 522 cc188–9, where both Norman Dodds and Hugh Gaitskell requested financial help to be given to the Smoke Abatement Society. Their requests were turned down by Harold Macmillan.

96 *The Times,* 20 December 1952, p. 3, col. C.

97 *Daily Express,* 4 September 1953, p. 4.

98 *Picture Post,* 31 October 1953, pp. 16, 18; and *Picture Post,* 14 November 1953, pp. 42, 43.

99 Quoted in *The Times,* 20 December 1952, p. 3, col. C.

100 HC Deb 27 January 1953 vol 510 cc828–31 (828). Dodds had already asked about legislation; see HC Deb 18 December 1952 vol 509 c265W.

101 Ibid., (830).

102 Ibid., (831).

103 "London Enshrouded," *Smokeless Air* 85 (Spring 1953): pp. 97–98.

104 Confidential Cabinet Memorandum, 18 November 1953, C. (53) 322, Cat, Ref. CAB / 129 / 64 in The National Archives, Kew, http://discovery.national archives.gov.uk/details/r/D7657235.

105 Ibid.

106 *The Times,* 14 November, 1953, p. 3, col. A.

107 Kelly, *You've Never Had It So Good!,* p. 38.

108 *Illustrated London News,* 7 November 1953, p. 751.

109 See Devra Davis, *When Smoke Ran Like Water: Tales of Environmental Deception and the Battle against Pollution* (Oxford, UK: Perseus, 2002), p. 46.

110 *Punch,* 25 November 1953, p. 620. It is headed "Announcement by the Minister of Health."

111 Obituary of Denisa Lady Newborough, 28 March 1987 in *The "Daily Telegraph" Book of Obituaries: A Celebration of Eccentric Lives,* ed. Hugh Massingberd (London: Macmillan, 1995), p. 23.

112 Confidential Cabinet Memorandum, 18 November 1953.

113 *The Times,* 14 November 1953, p. 3, col. A.

114 HC Deb 08 May 1953 vol 515 cc841–52 (841).

115 Ibid (843).

116 Ibid.

117 Ibid (850).

118 Ibid (850–1).

119 Confidential Cabinet Memorandum, 18 November 1953.

120 HC Deb 21 July 1953 vol 518 cc201–3 (201).

121 For more on the composition of the committee, see HC Deb 21 July 1953 vol 518 cc201–3; and J. B. Sanderson, "The National Smoke Abatement Society and the Clean Air Act (1956)," in *Campaigning for the Environment,* ed. Richard Kimber and J. J. Richardson (London: Routledge, 1974), pp. 36–37.

122 "Committee of Inquiry," *Smokeless Air* 86 (Summer 1953): p. 145.

123 Confidential Cabinet Memorandum, 18 November 1953.

124 Confidential Cabinet Minutes, 19 November 1953, C.C. (53), Cat. Ref. CAB/128/26, p. 104.

125 Confidential Cabinet Memorandum, 18 November 1953.

126 Confidential Cabinet Memorandum, 27 November 1953, C (53) 333, Cat. Ref. CAB/129/64.

127 HL Deb 18 November 1953 vol 184 cc364–93 (364–74).

128 Ibid (366).

129 Ibid (375).

130 HC Deb 27 January 1953 vol 510 cc828–31 (829).

131 HC Deb 02 December 1953 vol 521 cc1160–2 (1161).

132 Ibid.

133 Ibid (1162).

134 HC Deb 09 November 1954 vol 532 c117W.

135 HC Deb 16 November 1954 vol 533 c21W.

136 HC Deb 24 November 1954 vol 533 cc159–60W (159).

137 Brimblecombe, *Big Smoke,* p. 169.

138 HL Deb 01 December 1954 vol 190 cc35–106 (49).

139 HC Deb 07 December 1954 vol 535 cc770–1 (771).

140 *Picture Post,* 28 November 1953, p. 11.

141 "News," *Smokeless Air* 97 (Spring 1956): p. 153.

142 "Quick March!," *Smokeless Air* 93 (Spring 1955): pp. 132–3.

143 Ibid., p. 133.

144 "That Darkness at Noon," ibid., p. 138.

145 *Evening Standard,* 17 January 1955, p. 4, col. A.

146 *Evening Standard,* 19 January 1955, p. 1, col. E.

147 Brimblecombe, *Big Smoke,* p. 122.

148 W. P. D. Logan, "Mortality from Fog in London, January, 1956," *British Medical Journal,* 31 March 1956, p. 723 (pp. 722–25).

149 "Fog Cuttings," *Smokeless Air* 86 (Summer 1953): p. 151.

150 Brimblecombe, *Big Smoke,* pp. 169–72.

151 "Smokeless Zone News," *Smokeless Air: The Smoke Abatement Journal* 90 (Summer 1954): p. 191.

152 "A Smokeless Zone Advisory Centre: City of London Publicity," *Smokeless Air: The Smoke Abatement Journal* 95 (Autumn 1955): p. 33.

153 "Railway Smoke Summonses Dismissed," *Smokeless Air: The Smoke Abatement Journal* 96 (Winter 1955): p. 107.

154 "Chalk Farm Anti-Smog Week," *Smokeless Air* 99 (Autumn 1956): p. 54.

155 Metropolitan Borough of Holborn Report, 1962, p. 32.

156 *Shadows of Progress: Documentary Film in Post-War Britain*, ed. Patrick Russell and James Piers Taylor, (London: Palgrave Macmillan, 2010), p. 68.

157 See for instance "Guilty Chimneys," *Smokeless Air* 90 (Summer 1954): pp. 196–97.

158 Russell and Taylor, *Shadows of Progress,* p. 148.

159 Ibid., p. 112.

160 Bob Hope, *I Owe Russia $1200* (London: Robert Hale, 1963), p. 31.

CONCLUSION

1 *The Times,* 21 April 1956, p. 6, col. A.

2 *Evening Standard,* 4 December 1962, p. 17, cols. A, B, and C.

3 *The Times,* 7 December 1962, p. 12, col. G.

4 *The Times,* 5 December 1962, p. 3, col. G. For more on Fragoso see ibid., 11 December 1962, p. 4, col. F.

5 *The Times,* 4 December 1962, p. 6, col. C.

6 *The Times,* 14 December 1962, p. 1, col. C. Also *The Times,* 7 December 1962, p. 18, col. A.

7 *The Times,* 7 December 1962, p. 12, col. G.

8 *The Times,* 5 December 1962, p. 12, col. C.

9 *The Times,* 6 December 1962, p. 4, col. F.

10 *The Times,* 7 December 1962, p. 12, col. F.

11 Ibid., p. 15, cols. A, B, and C.

12 *The Times,* 6 December 1962, p. 12, col. C. See also *Evening Standard,* 5 December 1962, p. 16, col. D.

13 *The Times,* 7 December 1962, p. 12, col. G. Also see "How Fared Birds in the Fog?," *The Times,* 8 December 1962, p. 10, col. E.

14 *Evening Standard,* 5 December 1962, p. 12, col. B.

15 Ibid., p. 16, col. D.

16 *Evening Standard,* 6 December 1962, p. 15, col. C.

17 Ibid., p. 17, cols. C, D, and E.

18 *Evening Standard,* 7 December 1962, p. 16, cols. D and E.

19 *Evening Standard,* 5 December 1962, p. 6, col. B.

20 Ibid., and see also p. 16, col. D; and *Evening Standard,* 6 December 1962, p. 3, col. D.

21 *Evening Standard,* 7 December 1962, p. 16, col. C.

22 *Evening Standard,* 6 December 1962, p. 16, col. E.

23 Michael Darlow, *Terence Rattigan: The Man and His Work* (1979; repr., London: Quartet Books, 2000), p. 374.

24 Ibid.

25 Alexander Walker, *Vivien: The Life of Vivien Leigh* (London: Orion Books, 2001), p. 304.

26 Ibid.

27 *The Times,* 6 December 1962, p. 12, col. C.

28 *The Times,* 7 December 1962, p. 12, col. F.

29 *The Times,* 8 December 1962, p. 8, col. G; HC Deb 02 February 1968 vol 757 cc1801-8 (1803).

30 "The December Smog: A First Survey," *Smokeless Air: The Smoke Abatement Journal* 125 (Spring 1963): pp. 186–87.

31 Ibid.

32 *The Times,* 6 December 1962, p. 12, col. C.

33 *The Times,* 7 December 1962, p. 13, col. E.

34 Ibid.

35 D. Davies, "Power Stations and Pollution," *British Journal of Diseases of the Chest* 56 (October 1962): p. 172. See also *The Times,* 8 December 1962, p. 8, col. G.

36 *The Times,* 8 December 1962, p. 8, col. G.

37 *The Times,* 20 December 1962, p. 4, col. C.

38 *Evening Standard,* 5 December 1962, p. 1, col. A.

39 *The Times,* 8 December 1962, p. 9, col. B.

40 *The Times,* 20 December 1962, p. 4, col. C. Also "The Winter Supplement," *Smokeless Air* 125 (Spring 1963): p. 200.

41 *The Times,* 20 December 1962, p. 4, col. C.

42 *The Times,* 15 January 1963, p. 4, col. F.

43 HC Deb 02 February 1968 vol 757 cc1801–8.

44 David Watkins, *Seventeen Years in Obscurity: Memoirs from the Back Benches* (London: Book Guild, 1996).

45 HC Deb 03 February 1970 vol 795 cc291–350 (319).

46 *The Times,* 8 August 2003, p. 3, col. B.

47 Ibid.

48 *Guardian,* 25 January 2014, p. 21, col. D.

49 *Guardian,* 3 March 2015, p. 17.

50 *Guardian,* 9 July 2014, p. 30, cols. A–D.

51 Ibid.

52 *Guardian (G2),* 20 March 2013, p. 9.

53 Ibid., p. 8.

54 From website of ClientEarth, http://www.clientearth.org.

55 *The Times,* 20 December 1972, p. 12, col. A.

56 *The Times,* 30 October 1972, p. 4, col. D.

57 *The Times,* 9 August 1973, p. 4, cols. A and B.

58 *The Times,* 11 March 1982, p. 11, cols. A and B.

59 *New York Times,* 13 March 1954, quoted in "London Fog Industries, Inc. History," Funding Universe, http://www.fundinguniverse.com/company-histories /london-fog-industries-inc-history/.

60 C. J. Sansom, *Dominion* (London: Mantle, 2012).

61 See Richard J. Evans, *Altered Pasts: Counterfactuals in History* (Waltham, MA, 2013, Brandeis University Press), p. 109.

62 *Guardian,* 12 December 2013, p. 9, cols A–E.

63 *Penny Dreadful,* written by John Logan (Showtime Network, 2014).

64 Gavin Brend, *My Dear Holmes: A Study in Sherlock* (London: Allen and Unwin, 1951), p. 136.

65 Pierre Nordon, *Conan Doyle: A Biography,* trans. Francis Partridge (London: John Murray, 1966), p. 264.

66 Gary Coville and Patrick Lucanio, *Jack the Ripper: His Life and Crime in Popular Entertainment* (Jefferson, NC: McFarland, 1999), p. 113. *A Study in Terror,* dir. James Hill (Compton-Cameo-Tekli/Sir Nigel, 1965).

67 *The Times,* 2 January 1974, p. 4, col. C.

68 Quoted in Richard Lancelyn Green, introduction to *The Further Adventures of Sherlock Holmes: After Sir Arthur Conan Doyle,* ed. Green (London: Penguin, 1985), pp. 20–21.

69 Christopher Frayling, *Nightmare: The Birth of Horror* (London: British Broadcasting Corporation, 1996), p. 164.

70 *Radio Times,* 18–31 December 2004, p. 26. The Sherlock Holmes story was *Sherlock Homes and the Case of the Silk Stocking,* with Rupert Everett as Holmes.

71 J. K. Van Dover, *We Must Have Certainty: Four Essays on the Detective Story* (Selinsgrove, PA: Susquehanna University Press, 2005), p. 71.

72 Peter Ackroyd, introduction to *The Sign of Four*, by Arthur Conan Doyle (London: Penguin, 2001), p. viii.

73 Arthur Conan Doyle, *The New Annotated Sherlock Holmes*, vol. 2, ed. Leslie S. Klinger (New York: Norton, 2005), p. 1158. "The Abbey Grange" was first published in the *Strand Magazine* in September 1904 and in *Colliers Weekly* on 31 December 1904.

74 Jean Dorsenne, *Jack L'Éventreur: Scenes from Life*, trans. Molly Whittington-Egan (Malvern, UK: Cappella Archive, 2003), p. 1.

75 *The Avengers*, ABC, first aired 12 March 1969 in UK and 17 February 1969 in USA.

76 "Wolf in the Fold," *Star Trek*, NBC, first aired 22 December 1967; cited in Coville and Lucanio, *Jack the Ripper*, p. 71.

77 John Douglas and Mark Olshaker, *The Cases That Haunt Us* (London: Simon and Schuster, 2002), p. 19.

78 Coville and Lucanio, *Jack the Ripper*, p. 107.

79 *Frenzy*, dir. Alfred Hitchcock (Universal, 1972).

80 Douglas and Olshaker, *Cases That Haunt Us*, pp. 19–20.

Acknowledgements

This book has taken me many years to complete, and many people have supported me and given me help and advice along the way. I am grateful to them all. The idea was initially based on writing about Charles Dickens and London fog and gradually grew from there to its present, more comprehensive form. I was partly inspired by Peter Brimblecombe's book *The Big Smoke: A History of Air Pollution since Medieval Times* (London: Methuen, 1987) and he generously sent me some information from his own lectures in the early stages of my research. Some of the ideas in the earlier chapters of this book were initially formulated during my student days. My advisor, Malcolm Andrews, emeritus professor of English at the University of Kent, gave me the confidence to pursue and develop those concepts when I feared it might be beyond my capabilities. For the present work I have cut down the academic detail and added a large quantity of new material to include coverage of the politics of air pollution and extend the scope of the book from 1914 to the 1960s. I am also indebted to Michael Slater, emeritus professor of English at Birkbeck, University of London, a great teacher during my time studying at Birkbeck and a very helpful reader of my chapter on Dickens. Professor Ian Gordon and Dr. Felicia Gordon read various portions of the book manuscript. Their support together with that of the "tea-room group" at the Cambridge University Library, Dr. Jennifer Fellows, Dr. Robert Inglesfield, and especially Dr. Martin Garrett, who also aided me in tracking down references in French, all put up with my never-ending stories of London fog. I would also like to thank Stewart Sinclair for his help with the map of the Thames Basin.

Other friends have also put up cheerfully with my monologues on London fog. I remember with great warmth and affection my friends Jean Rhodes and Allison Paech-Ujejski rushing over, as I desperately tried to print out chapters, both sitting on the floor sorting out the pages in the correct order as I attempted to make a postal deadline. Vic Gatrell, emeritus professor of history at the University of Essex, gave me invaluable advice on illustration permissions and generously steered me on the right course. Dr. Astrid Swenson of Brunel University also gave me some helpful advice on illustration permissions and saved me lots of time. Dr. Bianca Gaudenzi and Dr. Anna Bagnoli of Wolfson College, Cambridge, helped me out on De Nittis and other items that could be retrieved only via the Italian language. Dr. Ruth Scurr, at Cambridge University, also gave me much encouragement and sage advice. The University Library here in Cambridge was an unfailing resource, and the staff, especially Paul and Neil Hudson, put up with my constant questions and answered them with enthusiasm and expertise. The editors of the *Dickens Studies Annual* (vol. 44) kindly granted me permission to incorporate brief portions of my article "Drowning in the Fog: The Significance of Quilp's Death in *The Old Curiosity Shop*," copyright © AMS Press, Inc. (2013), in the opening section of Chapter 2.

Our family life has ended up at Wolfson College, Cambridge, a very modern institution celebrating its fiftieth anniversary in the year of the publication of this book. It is a largely international college for mature undergraduates and postgraduates. I have found the environment stimulating and welcoming. I am not an Oxbridge graduate, but Wolfson has found a place for me and allowed me to grow intellectually. I have appreciated the warmth of its staff and students. The English literature undergraduates have always allowed me to ask about their work and have listened to me talking about my own with great patience. Dr. Michael Hrebeniak, director of studies in English at Wolfson, is an inspiration for his energy, passion, and inclusivity. Dr. Meredith Hale, art historian and friend, has shared stories of the hazards of trying to write and more importantly trying to finish a book. Sheila Betts, college secretary at Wolfson, guided me through the mysteries of Photoshop and scanning images, especially those from *Punch*. She was never too busy to help and advise. I should also make a special thanks to the Lee Library at Wolfson and its staff, who allowed me down into the stacks to riffle through their old copies of *Punch*. The IT department always ensured that disaster did not strike. Michelle Searle and Kim Allen also offered their support when required. Trudy Reid and Dawn Robinson aided me with a morning cup of coffee as I sat hunched over my laptop and have unfailingly made my life so much easier. It is a privilege to be part of the community at Wolfson.

In Cambridge, with the help of Professor Ian Gordon and Dr. Rick Allen, I established the Dickens Fellowship (Cambridge Branch). I would very much like to thank the members for their intellectual conversation and their support. The Cambridge Branch has been a great success, and I do hope it continues to flourish in the future.

When this book started to go through the production process, I had the good fortune to travel to the United States of America and made time to go to Boston to meet the staff at Harvard University Press. The press has been unfailingly helpful and supportive. Lisa LaPoint and Joy Deng have been especially creative and helpful. Edward Wade did a great job managing the production process, and Andrew Katz provided excellent copyediting. Maria Ascher kept me going towards the end of the publishing process with her calm and professional help. I would also like to thank Ian Malcolm, who commissioned this book and who supplied acute and helpful comments in the early stages. Also the anonymous Readers who were so enthusiastic about the project. Harvard University Press has produced a book that I am proud to call my own. For all the people who have commented and helped, I would like to thank them for their generosity but also acknowledge that any mistakes will be my own. The publisher and I have made every effort to track down copyright holders and obtain permission to reproduce the illustrations in this book and would be glad to hear from anyone whose rights have inadvertently been left unacknowledged.

My friend Catharine Walston stepped in at the last moment and did a wonderful job of proofreading, and David Atkinson has constructed a most useful index. Miranda Harvey died just before the page proofs arrived. She was a good friend and a great editor. I know that she would have gladly given up her time to read the proofs expertly and precisely. We discussed this project often, and I greatly miss her encouraging presence.

My father would have been so proud to have seen my name on the title page. His life also ended far too early. My mother, Marjorie Rose, can enjoy seeing this book in print, as will my brother, Steven, and my sister, Sharon.

Last, but not least, I give special thanks to my husband, Richard J. Evans, who never gave up faith in me and never doubted that I would complete the thesis and get the book published. He has always read my work and commented on it, and without him there is no doubt in my mind that the book would not have been written. Our two sons have grown up with this project. I am not entirely sure they have always found the subject as stimulating as I have done, but their humour and down-to-earth perspective have kept me working at it. Tuppence, our chocolate brown Labrador, kept me from thinking too much about the book as we went on long walks, and her sympathetic brown eyes were always a source of moral support. This book is dedicated to them all.

Index

Note: Figures are indexed in italic.